Foundation 1

for **AQA, Edexcel** and **OCR two-tier GCSE mathematics**

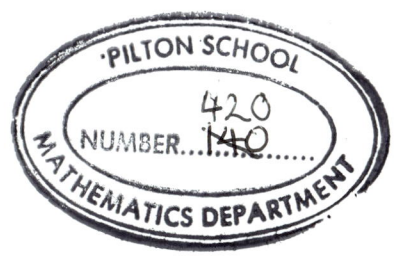

The School Mathematics Project

Writing and editing for this edition John Ling, Paul Scruton, Susan Shilton, Heather West
SMP design and administration Melanie Bull, Pam Keetch, Nicky Lake, Cathy Syred, Ann White

The following people contributed to the original edition of SMP Interact for GCSE.

Benjamin Alldred	David Cassell	Spencer Instone	Susan Shilton
Juliette Baldwin	Ian Edney	Pamela Leon	Caroline Starkey
Simon Baxter	Stephen Feller	John Ling	Liz Stewart
Gill Beeney	Rosemary Flower	Carole Martin	Biff Vernon
Roger Beeney	John Gardiner	Lorna Mulhern	Jo Waddingham
Roger Bentote	Colin Goldsmith	Mary Pardoe	Nigel Webb
Sue Briggs	Bob Hartman	Paul Scruton	Heather West

CAMBRIDGE UNIVERSITY PRESS
Cambridge, New York, Melbourne, Madrid, Cape Town, Singapore, São Paulo

Cambridge University Press
The Edinburgh Building, Cambridge CB2 2RU, UK

www.cambridge.org
Information on this title: www.cambridge.org/9780521694315

© The School Mathematics Project 2006

First published 2006

Printed in the United Kingdom at the University Press, Cambridge

A catalogue record for this publication is available from the British Library

ISBN-13   978-0-521-69431-5 paperback
ISBN-10   0-521-69431-0 paperback

Typesetting and technical illustrations by The School Mathematics Project
Other illustrations by Robert Calow and Steve Lach at Eikon Illustration
Cover design by Angela Ashton
Cover image by Jim Wehtje/Photodisc Green/Getty Images

The authors and publisher thank the following for supplying photographs: pages 92 and 179 David Cassell; page 164 Sheila Terry/Science Photo Library; page 219 John White; all other photographs by Graham Portlock

The authors and publisher are grateful to the following examination boards for permission to reproduce questions from past examination papers, identified in the text as follows.
AQA   Assessment and Qualifications Alliance
Edexcel   Edexcel Limited
OCR   Oxford, Cambridge and RSA Examinations
WJEC   Welsh Joint Education Committee

The map on page 212 is based on Ordnance Survey mapping and the map on page 217 consists of Ordnance Survey mapping with the permission of the Controller of Her Majesty's Stationery Office © Crown copyright. All rights reserved. Licence number 100001679

NOTICE TO TEACHERS
It is illegal to reproduce any part of this work in material form (including photocopying and electronic storage) except under the following circumstances:
(i) where you are abiding by a licence granted to your school or institution by the Copyright Licensing Agency;
(ii) where no such licence exists, or where you wish to exceed the terms of a licence, and you have gained the written permission of Cambridge University Press;
(iii) where you are allowed to reproduce without permission under the provisions of Chapter 3 of the Copyright, Designs and Patents Act 1988, which covers, for example, the reproduction of short passages within certain types of educational anthology and reproduction for the purposes of setting examination questions.

Using this book

This book, *Foundation 1*, is the first of two main books for Foundation tier GCSE. It prepares up to GCSE grades D/E and is suitable as a year 10 text for students who have followed any 'core' course in key stage 3. It is also designed to follow on from *Foundation transition*, a preparatory key stage 4 text for those who have followed a 'support' course in key stage 3.

To help users identify material that can be omitted by some students – or just dipped into for revision or to check competence – chapter sections estimated to be at national curriculum level 4 are marked as such. These levels are also given in the detailed contents list on the next few pages.

At the end of the contents list is a precedence diagram to help those who want to use chapters selectively or in a different order from that of the book.

Each chapter begins with a summary of what it covers and ends with a self-assessment section ('Test yourself').

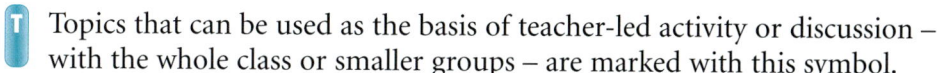
Topics that can be used as the basis of teacher-led activity or discussion – with the whole class or smaller groups – are marked with this symbol.

There are clear worked examples – and past exam questions, labelled by board, to give the student an idea of the style and standard that may be expected, and to build confidence.

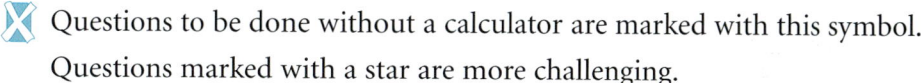
Questions to be done without a calculator are marked with this symbol.

Questions marked with a star are more challenging.

Suggestions for work on a spreadsheet and for web searches are marked like this.

After every few chapters there is a review section containing a mixture of questions on previous work.

The resource sheets linked to this book can be downloaded in PDF format from www.smpmaths.org.uk and may be printed out for use within the institution purchasing this book.

Practice booklets

There is a practice booklet for each students' book. The practice booklet follows the structure of the students' book, making it easy to organise extra practice, homework and revision. The practice booklets do not contain answers; these can be downloaded in PDF format from www.smpmaths.org.uk

Contents

1 **Reflection and rotation symmetry** 10
   A Reflection symmetry level 4 10
   B Rotation symmetry 11
   C Both types of symmetry 12
   D Special triangles and quadrilaterals 13
   E Symmetrical and regular polygons 14
   F Using coordinates 16

2 **Fractions** 18
   A Fraction of a number 18
   B Equivalent fractions 18
   C Simplifying a fraction 19
   D Mixed numbers 20
   E Writing one number as a fraction of another 21
   F Adding and subtracting fractions 22
   G Multiplying a fraction by a whole number 23

3 **Reading scales** 25
   A Whole numbers level 4 25
   B Decimals level 4 26

4 **Arrow diagrams and equations** 29
   A Mathematical whispers level 4 29
       (arrow diagram for a set of operations)
   B Using letters 31
   C Solving equations 32
   D Number puzzles 34

5 **Decimals** 36
   A One and two decimal places level 4 36
   B More than two decimal places 37
   C Rounding to the nearest whole number 38
   D Rounding to one decimal place 39
   E Rounding to more than one decimal place 40
   F Multiplying and dividing by powers of ten 41

6 **Angles, triangles and quadrilaterals** 42
   A Review: angles round a point, on a line, in a triangle 42
   B Angles in an isosceles triangle 45
   C Properties of special quadrilaterals 47

7 **Experiments** 49
   A Specifying the problem and planning 49
   B Processing and representing 50
   C Interpreting and discussing 52

8 **Multiples, factors and primes** 53
   A Multiples level 4 53
   B Factors level 4 54
   C Multiples and factors level 4 55
   D Common multiples and factors 56
   E Prime numbers 58
   F Products of prime factors 59

Review 1 61

9 **Working with formulas 1** 63
   A Review: expressions 63
   B Arranging tables and chairs 64
       (formulas from spatial arrangements)
   C Designing pendants 67
       (formulas from spatial arrangements)
   D Equations and arrow diagrams 70

10 **Representing 3-D objects** 73
   A The Soma cube 73
       (idea of volume, drawing on triangular dotty paper)
   B Plan and elevations 74
   C Nets 77
   D Prisms 78
   E Reflection symmetry 79

11 Written calculation 1 82
   A Adding and subtracting whole numbers and decimals level 4 82
   B Multiplying whole numbers level 4 83
   C Multiplying decimals 84
   D Dividing whole numbers level 4 85
   E Dividing decimals 86
   F Mixed questions 87

12 Frequency 89
   A Stem-and-leaf tables 89
   B Median and range 91
   C Comparisons 92
   D Grouping 94
   E Mean 97

13 Fractions, decimals and percentages 100
   A Fractions and percentages 100
   B Decimals and percentages 101
   C Fractions and decimals 102
   D Thirds 102
   E Converting between fractions, decimals and percentages 103

14 Area of a parallelogram 105
   A Changing a parallelogram into a rectangle 105
   B Using the formula 106

15 Negative numbers 109
   A Temperature changes 109
   B Adding negative numbers 110
   C Subtracting a negative number 111
   D Multiplying a negative by a positive number 112

16 Metric units 114
   A Using metric units 114
   B Converting between metric units 116

17 Working with expressions 1 119
   A Simplifying expressions such as $4 + 2n - 3 + n$ 119
   B Substituting into expressions such as $7 - 2n$ 121
   C Simplifying expressions such as $4 + 2n - 3 - 5n$ 122

Review 2 124

18 Graphs of changes over time 126
   A Noise level 126
   B Pulse rate 128
   C Temperature 129

19 Chance 132
   A Probability as a fraction 132
   B Listing outcomes 134
   C Using a grid 136

20 Area of a triangle and of composite shapes 140
   A Area of a triangle 140
   B Area of composite shapes 142

21 Working with percentages 145
   A Review: fractions, decimals and percentages 145 (converting from one to another)
   B Finding a percentage of an amount (mentally) 146
   C Finding a percentage of an amount (with a calculator) 148
   D Expressing one number as a percentage of another 149
   E Expressing one number as a percentage of another (with a calculator) 150
   F Mixed questions 151

22 Representing data 153
   A Two-way tables 153
   B Two-way tables with grouped data 155
   C Pictograms and bar charts 156
   D Dual bar charts 158
   E Line graphs for time series 159
   F Index numbers 161

continues >

23 Ratio and proportion 164
- A Recipes 164
  (scaling up and down)
- B Comparing prices 166
  (where one item is a multiple of the other)
- C Unitary method 167
- D Unit cost 168
- E Mixtures and ratio 170
- F Writing a ratio in its simplest form 173

24 Cuboids 175
- A Volume of a cuboid 175
- B Cubic metres 179
- C Surface area 180
- D Volume of a solid made from cuboids 181

Review 3 184

25 Scatter diagrams and correlation 186
- A Scatter diagrams 186
- B Correlation 189
- C Line of best fit 191

26 Square and cube numbers 195
- A Squares and square roots 195
- B Cubes and cube roots 197
- C Squares, cubes and higher powers 198

27 Surveys 200
- A Starting a project 200
- B Designing a questionnaire 201
- C Choosing a sample 203
- D Summarising results 204
- E Writing a report 205

28 Imperial measures 206
- A Length 206
- B Weight 208
- C Liquid measure 209
- D Mixed questions 210

29 Navigation 212
- A Four-figure grid references and points of the compass 212
- B Scales and points of the compass 214
- C Review: angles level 4 216
- D Bearings 218

30 Rounding with significant figures 221
- A Rounding a whole number to one significant figure 221
- B Rounding a decimal to one significant figure 222
- C Multiplying decimals 223
- D Rough estimates with decimals 225
- E Rounding answers 226

31 Solving equations 228
- A Balance puzzles 228
- B Seeing a balance puzzle as an equation 230
- C Solving an equation using balancing 231
- D Finding unknown lengths on strips 232
- E Undoing a subtraction in an equation 233
- F Decimal, negative and fractional solutions 234
- G Problem solving 234

32 Written calculation 2 236
- A Multiplying by a two-digit number 236
- B Dividing by a two-digit number 237
- C Mixed questions 238

Review 4 240

33 Sequences 242
- A Continuing a sequence 242
- B Describing numbers in some sequences 244
- C Sequences from patterns 245

34 Problem solving with a calculator 248
- A Which calculation? 248
- B Showing working 250
- C Changing money to a different currency 251

35 Working with expressions 2 253
  A Substituting into expressions such as $2a - b$ 253
  B Simplifying expressions such as $3a + 2b + a + 5b$ 254
  C Simplifying expressions such as $3a + 2b + a - 5b$ 255

36 Calculating with negative numbers 256
  A Adding and subtracting 256
  B Multiplying 257
  C Dividing 259
  D Negative square roots and cube roots 261
  E Mixed questions 262

37 Brackets 264
  A Dividing an expression by a number 264
  B Expressions with brackets 265
  C Factorising an expression 266
  D Factorising more complex expressions 267
  E Adding an expression containing brackets 268
  F Subtracting an expression containing brackets 268

38 Pie charts 270
  A Review: fractions, percentages and angles 270
  B Reading a pie chart: simple fractions and percentages 271
  C Reading a pie chart: the unitary method 272
  D Drawing a pie chart: angles 274
  E Drawing a pie chart: percentages 276
  F Handling real data 278

39 Working with expressions 3 280
  A Substituting into linear expressions 280
  B Squares and cubes 281
  C Using more than one letter 283
  D Area and simplifying 284

40 Multiplying and dividing fractions 287
  A Finding a fraction of a quantity: fractional results 1 287
  B Finding a fraction of a quantity: fractional results 2 288
  C Dividing a unit fraction by a whole number 289
  D Dividing a fraction by a whole number 290
  E Multiplying fractions 291

41 Working with formulas 2 293
  A Formulas and graphs 293
  B Forming and using formulas 296
  C Forming and using expressions and formulas 298

Review 5 302

42 Travel 304
  A Calculating speed 304
  B Distance–time graphs 306
  C Calculating distance and time 309

43 Graphs from rules 312
  A Patterns in coordinates 312
  B Drawing a straight-line graph 313
  C Including negative coordinates 315
  D Equations of horizontal and vertical lines 316
  E Implicit equations 317

44 Working with coordinates 320
  A Shapes on a grid 320
  B Mid-points 322
  C Reflection 323
  D Rotation 324

45 Trial and improvement 328
  A Searching for whole numbers 328
  B Searching for decimals 329
  C Searching for approximate values 330

continues >

46 Constructions 332

   A Drawing a triangle using lengths 332

   B Drawing a triangle using angles 334

   C Drawing a triangle using two sides and an angle 335

   D Scale drawings 336

Review 6 337

Index 339

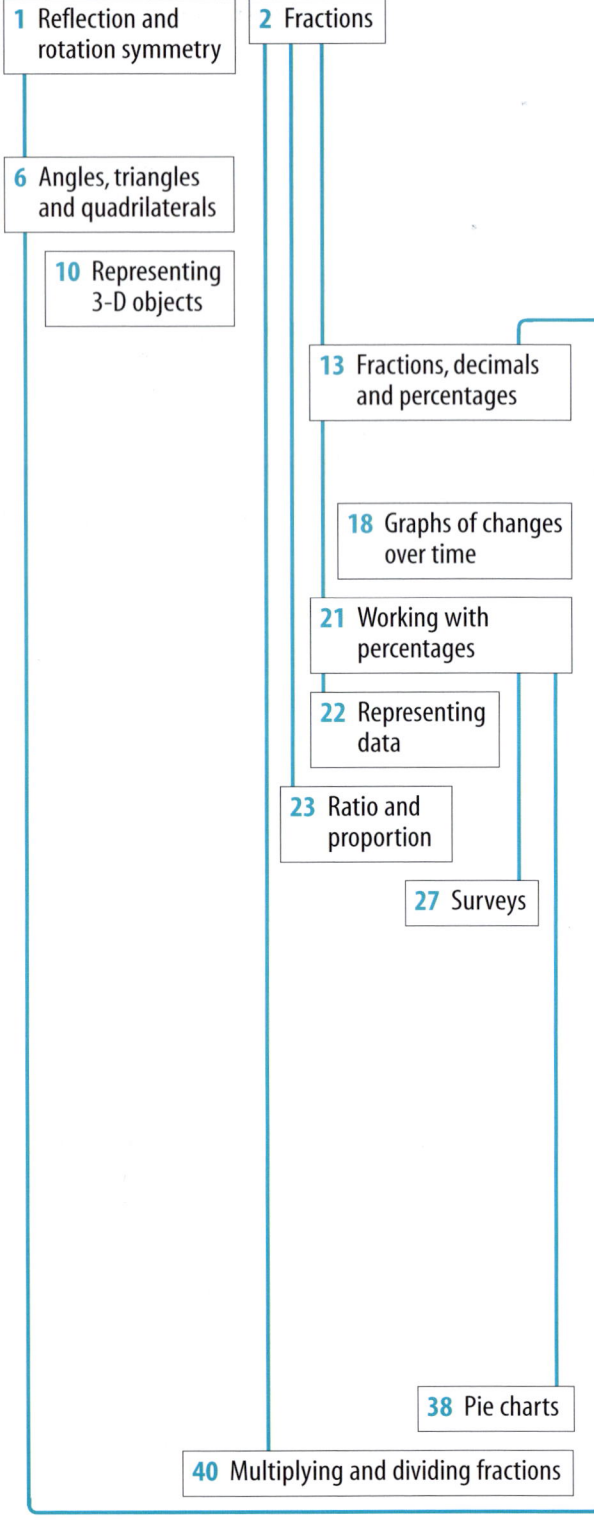

This precedence diagram is designed to help with planning, especially where the teacher wishes to select from the material to meet the needs of particular students or to use chapters in a different order from that of the book. A blue line connecting two chapters indicates that, to a significant extent, working on the later chapter requires competence with topics dealt with in the earlier one.

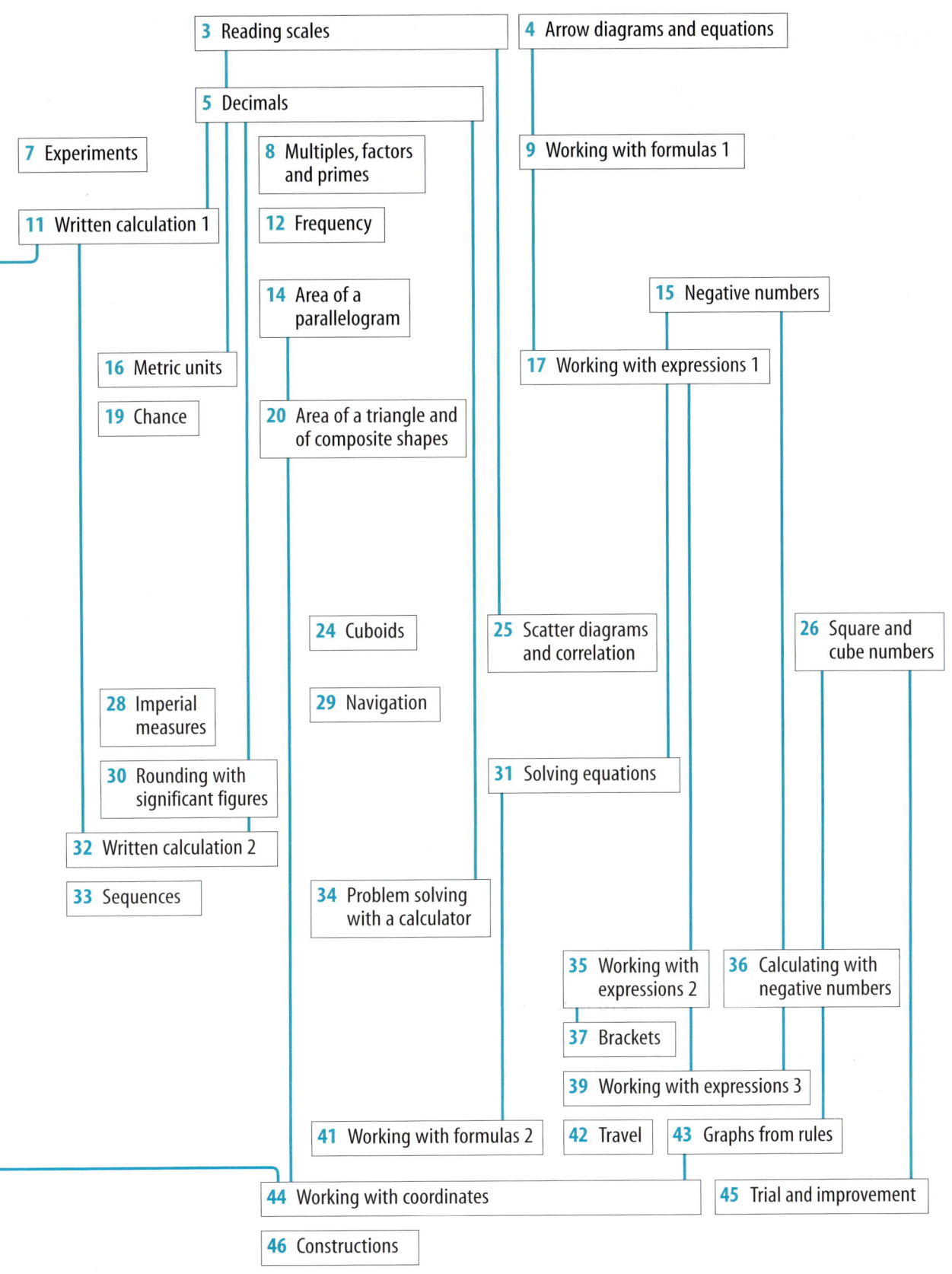

1 Reflection and rotation symmetry

This work will help you
- recognise reflection symmetry and rotation symmetry in a shape
- complete a shape with given reflection or rotation symmetry
- name types of triangle and quadrilateral, and recognise symmetrical and regular polygons

You need sheets F1–1, F1–2, F1–3 and F1–4.

A Reflection symmetry   level 4

A shape with **reflection symmetry** has one or more mirror lines that reflect one half of the shape exactly on to the other half.

These mirror lines are called **lines of symmetry**.

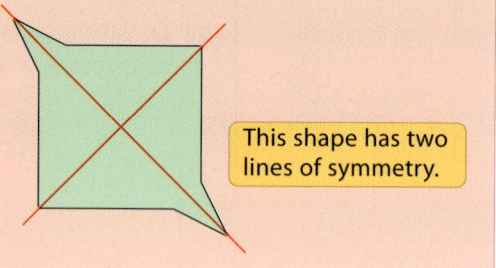

This shape has two lines of symmetry.

A1 How many lines of symmetry has each of these shapes?

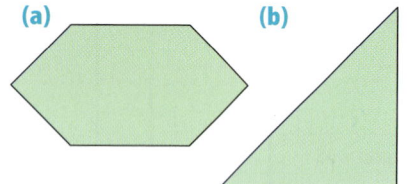 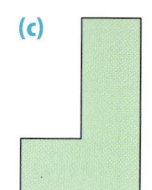 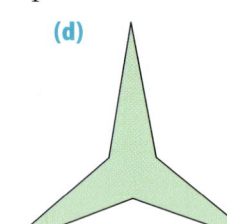 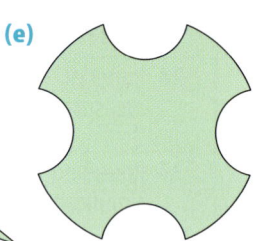

(a)   (b)   (c)   (d)   (e)

A2 This question is on sheet F1–1.

A3 This question is on sheet F1–2.

A4 Copy each diagram and follow the instruction below it.

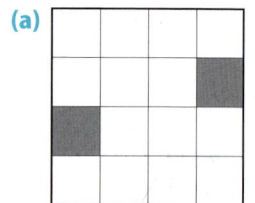

(a) Shade two more squares to make a pattern with 2 lines of symmetry.

(b) Shade two more squares to make a pattern with 1 line of symmetry.

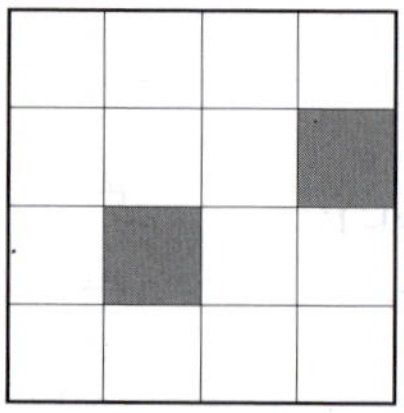

(c) Shade three more squares to make a pattern with 4 lines of symmetry.

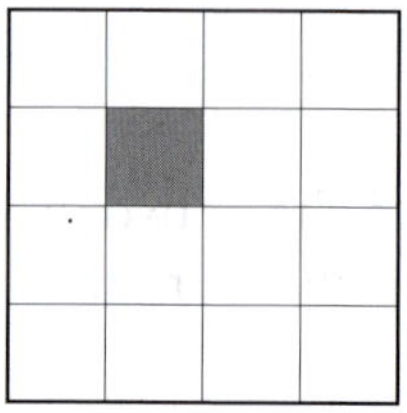

(d) Shade two more squares to make a pattern with 1 line of symmetry.

B Rotation symmetry

A shape with **rotation** (or rotational) **symmetry** can be rotated round its centre so that it fits on top of itself more than one way. The **order** of rotation symmetry is the number of different positions a shape fits on top of itself.

This shape has rotation symmetry of order 2.

We say that a shape with **no rotation symmetry** has **order 1** as it fits on top of itself in only one way.

B1 What is the order of rotation symmetry of each of these?

(a) 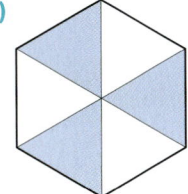   (b) 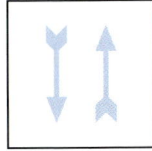   (c) 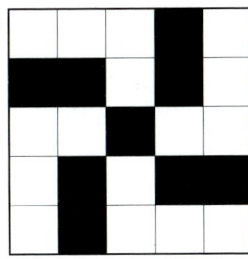   (d)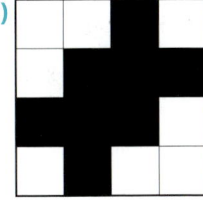

B2 This question is on sheet F1–3.

B3 Copy each diagram and complete it as stated.

(a) 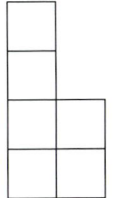   (b) 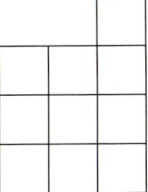   (c)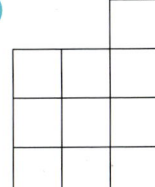

Add two more squares so that the final shape has rotation symmetry of order 2.

Add three more squares so that the final shape has rotation symmetry of order 4.

Add three more squares so that the final shape has no rotation symmetry.

B4 Copy this diagram and shade two more squares so that it has rotation symmetry of order 4.

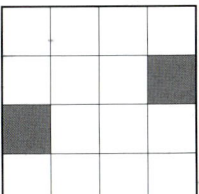

1 Reflection and rotation symmetry   11

C Both types of symmetry

A shape can have reflection symmetry and rotation symmetry

This shape has reflection symmetry but no rotation symmetry.	This shape has rotation symmetry but no reflection symmetry.	This shape has **both** reflection and rotation symmetry.
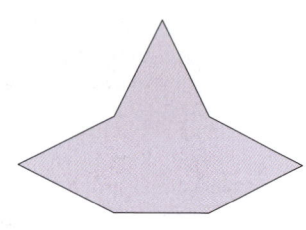		
• How many lines of symmetry does it have?	• What is its order of rotation symmetry?	• Describe the symmetry of this shape.

C1 For each design below

(i) write down how many lines of symmetry it has

(ii) write down the order of rotation symmetry

(a) (b) (c) (d)

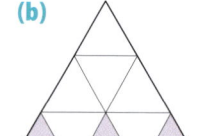

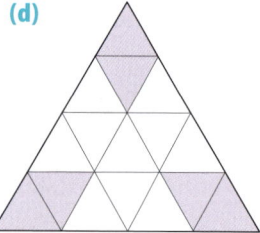

(e) (f) (g) (h)

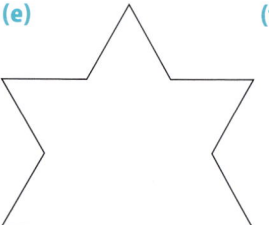
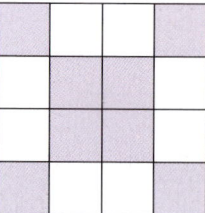
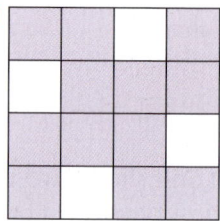
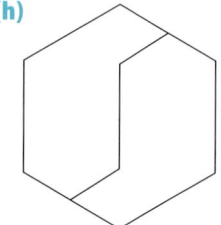

C2 This question is on sheet F1–4.

12 1 Reflection and rotation symmetry

D Special triangles and quadrilaterals

A mosaic pattern is made by joining the centres of regular hexagons. This is part of the pattern with some shapes shaded.

- What kind of triangle is shape A?
- Name each of the shaded quadrilaterals.
- How many lines of symmetry has each shape?
- What is the order of rotation symmetry of each shape?

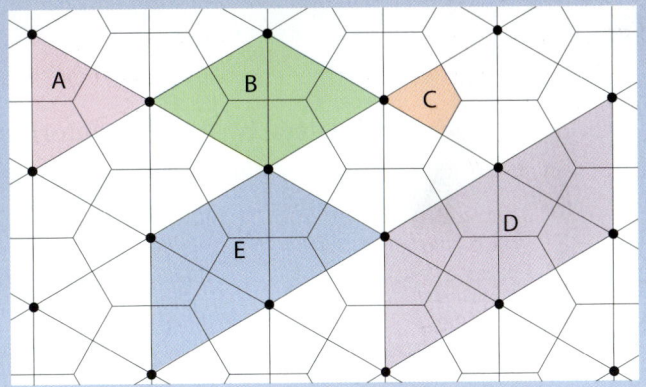

D1 This diagram shows a regular hexagon split into four triangles. How many of these triangles are isosceles?

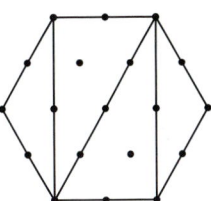

D2 Here is another way to split up a regular hexagon.
What is the name of the quadrilateral in this hexagon?

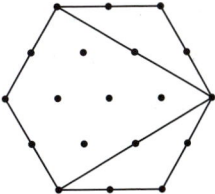

D3 Show how to split up a regular hexagon into
  (a) a rectangle and two isosceles triangles
  (b) two trapeziums
  (c) three rhombuses
  (d) an equilateral triangle and three isosceles triangles

D4 Draw an isosceles triangle.
Show clearly any lines of symmetry.

D5 (a) Draw a rectangle and show any lines of symmetry it has.
  (b) What order of rotation symmetry does a rectangle have?

D6 Describe the symmetry of a square.

D7 Draw a trapezium that has no reflection symmetry.

Lines that join corners across a shape are called its **diagonals**.

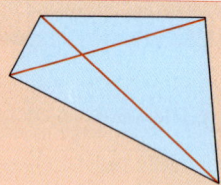

The diagonals of this quadrilateral are not the same length and do not cross at right angles.

D8 Identify each quadrilateral by the given information.

(a) I have rotation symmetry of order 2. My diagonals cross at right angles.

(b) My diagonals are the same length. I have rotation symmetry of order 4.

(c) I have reflection symmetry but no rotation symmetry. My diagonals cross at right angles.

(d) My diagonals are the same length. I have rotation symmetry of order 2.

(e) I have no reflection symmetry. I have two pairs of parallel sides.

E Symmetrical and regular polygons

A **polygon** is a shape with straight edges. Some polygons that have special names are shown in this table.

Number of sides	Name of polygon
3	triangle
4	quadrilateral
5	pentagon
6	hexagon
8	octagon
10	decagon

E1 All these shapes are hexagons.

Which hexagon has

(a) only one line of symmetry

(b) rotation symmetry but no reflection symmetry

(c) rotation symmetry of order 3 and 3 lines of symmetry

(d) no reflection or rotation symmetry

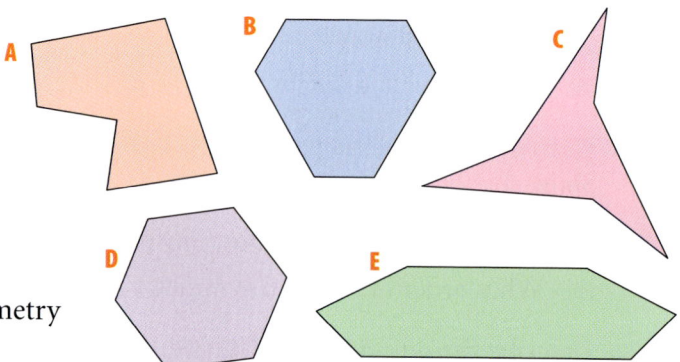

14   1 Reflection and rotation symmetry

E2 Here are some polygons.

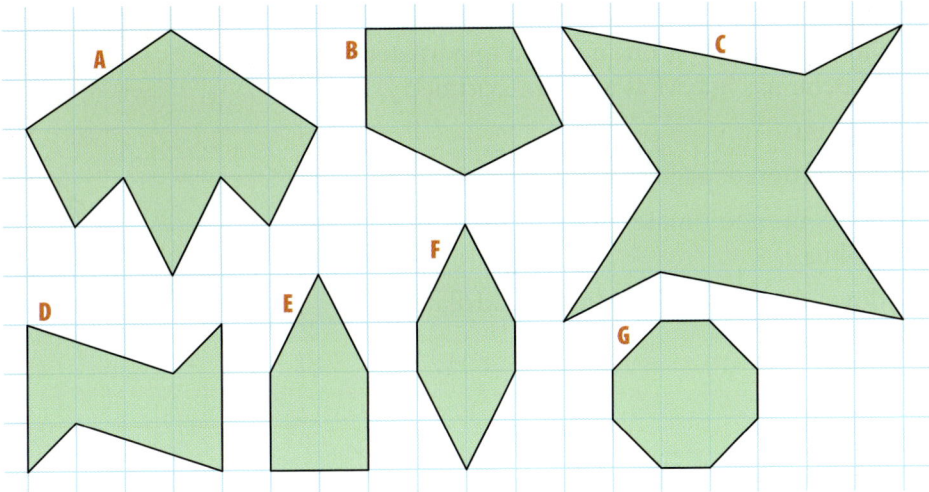

Which of these polygons is

(a) a pentagon with reflection symmetry

(b) an octagon with reflection symmetry but no rotation symmetry

(c) a hexagon with rotation symmetry but no reflection symmetry

(d) an octagon with rotation symmetry but no reflection symmetry

E3 Draw a decagon with only one line of symmetry.

A polygon that has all its edges equal and all its angles equal is called a **regular polygon**.

E4 Here are some regular polygons.

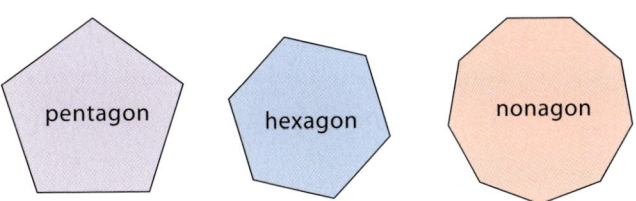

(a) Copy and complete this table.

Polygon	Number of sides	Lines of symmetry	Order of rotation symmetry
Equilateral triangle	3	3	3
Square	4		
Regular pentagon	5		
Regular hexagon			
Regular nonagon			

(b) An icosagon is a polygon with 20 sides.
What symmetry does a regular icosagon have?

1 Reflection and rotation symmetry 15

F Using coordinates

F1 Each shape in this diagram is one half of a quadrilateral. Each quadrilateral has line M as a line of symmetry.

Copy the diagram.

(a) Draw a reflection of each shape in line M.

(b) Write down the coordinates of each corner of the rhombus.

(c) Write down the name of the other quadrilateral.

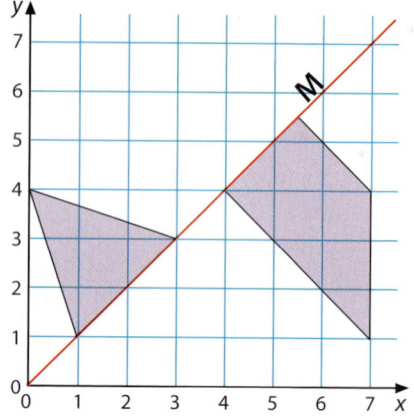

F2 The shape in this diagram is part of a hexagon. The x-axis is a line of symmetry of the hexagon.

(a) Copy the diagram and complete the hexagon.

(b) Write down the coordinates of each corner of the hexagon.

(c) How many lines of symmetry does the hexagon have?

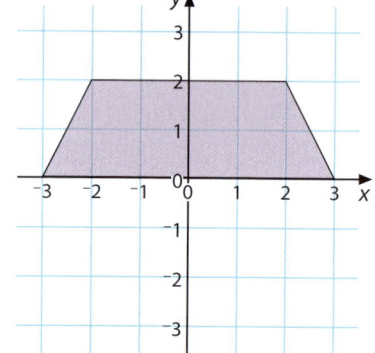

F3 This diagram shows half a quadrilateral. The quadrilateral has rotation symmetry of order 2.

(a) (i) Copy the diagram and complete the quadrilateral.

(ii) What are the coordinates of the fourth corner of the quadrilateral?

(b) What is the name of this quadrilateral?

(c) How many lines of symmetry does the quadrilateral have?

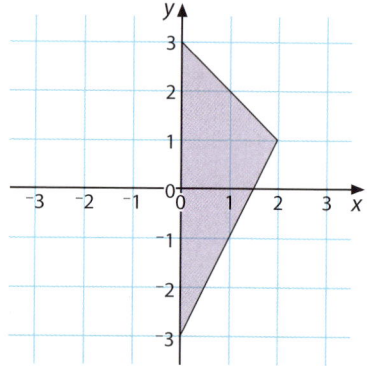

F4 Draw a grid going from ⁻4 to 4 on both axes.

(a) Draw a straight line from (2, 0) to (2, 3).
Then draw a straight line from (2, 3) to (⁻2, 0).

(b) (i) Add another point to make a quadrilateral with rotation symmetry of order 2.

(ii) What are the coordinates of this point?

Test yourself

T1 Here are four road signs.

A   B   C   D

Two of these road signs have one line of symmetry.

(a) Write down the letters of each of these two road signs.

Only one of these four road signs has rotational symmetry.

(b) (i) Write down the letter of this road sign.

(ii) Write down its order of rotational symmetry.

Edexcel

T2 Judith has lots of tiles, all like this one.

(a) Judith makes these patterns.

For each pattern, write down the number of lines of symmetry it has.
If the pattern does not have reflection symmetry, write 0.

(i)    (ii)    (iii)    (iv)    (v)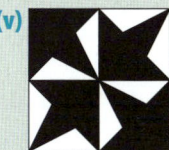

(b) Copy and complete this tiling pattern so that it has rotation symmetry of order 4.

OCR

T3 This design is made from a regular hexagon and four equilateral triangles.

(a) What is its order of rotation symmetry?

(b) Write down the number of lines of symmetry it has.

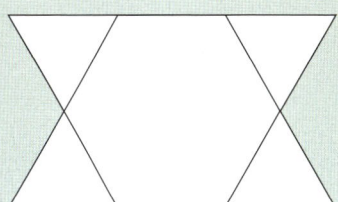

1 Reflection and rotation symmetry   17

2 Fractions

You should know how to
- identify fractions of a shape
- find a fraction of a number

This work will help you
- use equivalent fractions and mixed numbers
- write one number as a fraction of another
- add and subtract simple fractions
- multiply a fraction by an integer

You need sheet F1–5.

A Fraction of a number

A1 Work these out.

(a) $\frac{1}{2}$ of 8   (b) $\frac{1}{4}$ of 12   (c) $\frac{1}{3}$ of 9   (d) $\frac{1}{5}$ of 50   (e) $\frac{1}{10}$ of 120

A2 Jane eats half a bar of chocolate that weighs 60 grams. What weight of chocolate has she eaten?

A3 Work these out.

(a) $\frac{3}{4}$ of 8   (b) $\frac{2}{3}$ of 9   (c) $\frac{4}{5}$ of 15   (d) $\frac{5}{8}$ of 16   (e) $\frac{7}{10}$ of 90

A4 Out of a class of 28 students, $\frac{3}{4}$ of them bring a packed lunch to school. How many of the students have a packed lunch?

B Equivalent fractions

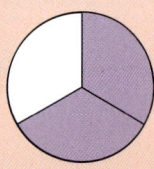

$$\frac{2}{3} \overset{\times 4}{\underset{\times 4}{=}} \frac{8}{12}$$

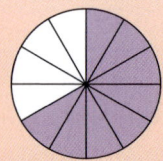

This circle is split into 3 equal parts.
2 parts are shaded.
So $\frac{2}{3}$ of the circle is shaded.

There are 4 times as many parts in this circle.
4 times as many parts are shaded.

The two fractions are the same. We say that $\frac{2}{3}$ is **equivalent** to $\frac{8}{12}$.

B1 Each pair of diagrams shows two fractions that are equivalent.
Write down the two fractions for each pair.

(a) 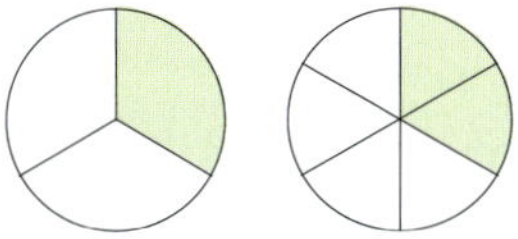 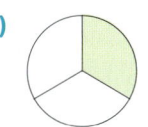 (b) 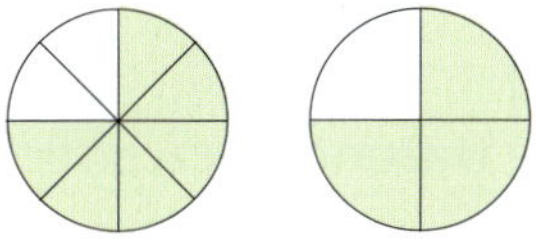 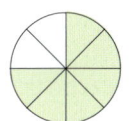 (c)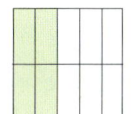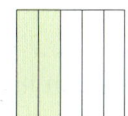

B2 (a) What number does '?' stand for here?

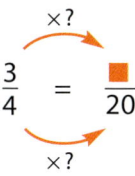

(b) Copy and complete the second fraction.

B3 Copy these and find the missing numbers.

(a) $\frac{2}{3} = \frac{\blacksquare}{15}$ (b) $\frac{5}{6} = \frac{\blacksquare}{24}$ (c) $\frac{3}{4} = \frac{\blacksquare}{12}$ (d) $\frac{2}{5} = \frac{\blacksquare}{30}$ (e) $\frac{3}{7} = \frac{9}{\blacksquare}$

B4 Copy these and find the missing numbers.

(a) $\frac{3}{8} = \frac{\blacksquare}{32}$ (b) $\frac{5}{7} = \frac{\blacksquare}{35}$ (c) $\frac{4}{9} = \frac{\blacksquare}{18}$ (d) $\frac{5}{8} = \frac{\blacksquare}{24}$ (e) $\frac{3}{10} = \frac{18}{\blacksquare}$

C Simplifying a fraction

The top number in a fraction is called the **numerator**. → $\frac{3}{5}$
The bottom number is called the **denominator**. →

You can often **simplify** a fraction by dividing the numerator and denominator by the same number.

For example, start with $\frac{6}{15}$.

Divide the numerator and denominator by 3. $\frac{6}{15} = \frac{2}{5}$ (÷ 3)

You can simplify $\frac{4}{12}$ to $\frac{2}{6}$. $\frac{4}{12} = \frac{2}{6}$ (÷ 2)

But $\frac{2}{6}$ can be simplified further, to $\frac{1}{3}$.

$\frac{1}{3}$ is the **simplest form** of $\frac{4}{12}$.

$\frac{2}{6} = \frac{1}{3}$ (÷ 2)

C1 Write each of these fractions in its simplest form.

(a) $\frac{8}{10}$ (b) $\frac{4}{8}$ (c) $\frac{9}{12}$ (d) $\frac{15}{20}$ (e) $\frac{6}{16}$

2 Fractions 19

C2 Write each of these fractions in its simplest form.
(One of them is in its simplest form already.)

(a) $\frac{6}{20}$ (b) $\frac{5}{10}$ (c) $\frac{3}{15}$ (d) $\frac{4}{5}$ (e) $\frac{12}{16}$

C3 Write, in its simplest form, the fraction of each rectangle that is shaded.

(a)  (b)   (c) 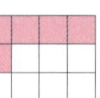 (d) 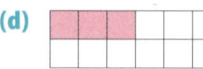 (e)

(f)   (g)  (h) 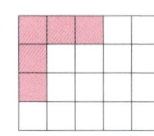 (i)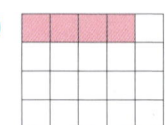

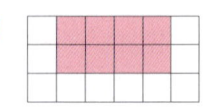

C4 Look at the fractions in the box.

(a) Which of the fractions are equivalent to $\frac{3}{4}$?

(b) Which are equivalent to $\frac{2}{3}$?

(c) One fraction is left over. What is the simplest form of this fraction?

$\frac{6}{8}$ $\frac{10}{15}$ $\frac{16}{24}$ $\frac{6}{16}$ $\frac{15}{20}$ $\frac{30}{40}$ $\frac{40}{60}$ $\frac{12}{18}$ $\frac{18}{24}$

D Mixed numbers

- $\frac{3}{4}$ is a **proper** fraction (the numerator is smaller than the denominator).
- $\frac{4}{3}$ is an **improper** fraction (the numerator is larger than the denominator).
- $3\frac{1}{4}$ is a **mixed number** (it has a whole-number part and a fraction part).

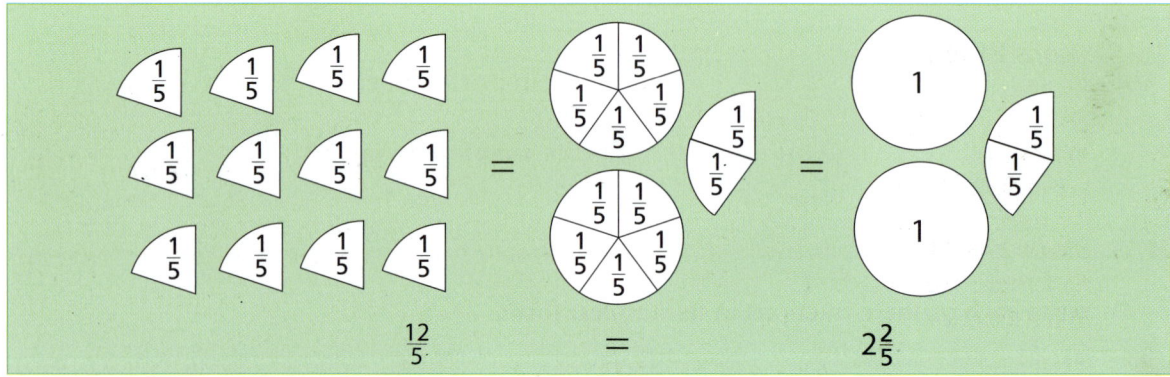

20 2 Fractions

D1 Change these mixed numbers into improper fractions.
(a) $2\frac{1}{2}$ (b) $1\frac{1}{4}$ (c) $1\frac{1}{5}$ (d) $1\frac{1}{3}$ (e) $2\frac{1}{4}$
(f) $1\frac{2}{3}$ (g) $1\frac{3}{10}$ (h) $3\frac{1}{2}$ (i) $2\frac{3}{5}$ (j) $4\frac{2}{5}$

D2 Change these improper fractions into mixed (or whole) numbers.
(a) $\frac{7}{5}$ (b) $\frac{7}{4}$ (c) $\frac{11}{10}$ (d) $\frac{7}{6}$ (e) $\frac{9}{2}$
(f) $\frac{11}{4}$ (g) $\frac{11}{5}$ (h) $\frac{20}{10}$ (i) $\frac{13}{4}$ (j) $\frac{7}{3}$

D3 Which of these fractions is the largest? $\frac{9}{2}$ $\frac{13}{10}$ $\frac{17}{4}$ $\frac{18}{5}$

D4 Arrange these fractions in order of size, smallest first.
$\frac{11}{4}$ $\frac{15}{5}$ $\frac{17}{10}$ $\frac{10}{3}$ $\frac{8}{7}$

D5 Jane is a teacher and has $9\frac{1}{2}$ bars of chocolate.
She gives $\frac{1}{2}$ of a bar to each of her students and has no chocolate left for herself.
How many students are there in her class?

D6 (a) Copy and complete: $\frac{8}{6} = 1\frac{2}{6} = 1\frac{\blacksquare}{3}$
(b) Write each improper fraction as a mixed number in its simplest form.
(i) $\frac{10}{4}$ (ii) $\frac{15}{10}$ (iii) $\frac{22}{8}$ (iv) $\frac{50}{15}$

E Writing one number as a fraction of another

Karishma has a set of 12 mugs.
4 of the mugs have broken handles.

$\frac{4}{12}$ of the set have broken handles.
This fraction can be simplified to $\frac{1}{3}$.

In questions E1 to E8, write fractions in their simplest form.

E1 In a set of 8 plates, 2 are cracked.
What fraction of the plates are cracked?

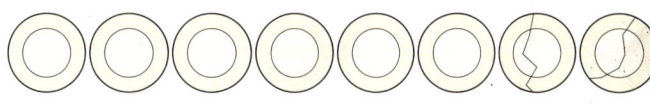

E2 Jacqui has 9 CDs.
6 of them are scratched.
What fraction are scratched?

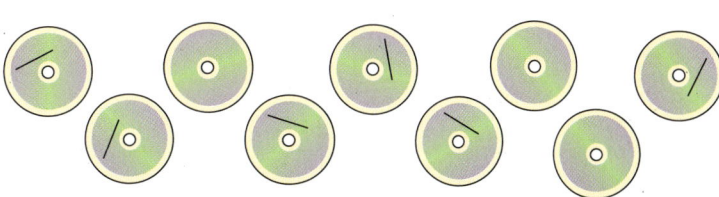

E3 There are 15 children in a choir.
5 of the children have flu.
What fraction of the choir have flu?

E4 There are 30 children in a class. 12 of them are girls.
What fraction of the class are girls?

E5 Pat has 10 unbroken bottles and 5 broken bottles.
(a) How many bottles has Pat got altogether?
(b) What fraction of Pat's bottles are broken?
(c) What fraction are unbroken?

E6 Sita has 4 brown rabbits and 12 white rabbits.
What fraction of her rabbits are
(a) brown
(b) white

E7 What fraction of CELEBRATIONS is RAT?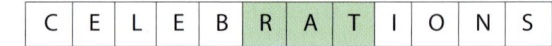

E8 What fraction of
(a) SATURDAY is SAT
(b) CORRESPONDENCE is POND
(c) DIPLODOCUS is PLOD
(d) PERSONIFICATION is PERSON
(e) ANTIDISESTABLISHMENTARIANISM is STAB

F Adding and subtracting fractions

Adding and subtracting are straightforward when the fractions have the same denominators.

$$\frac{4}{7} + \frac{5}{7} = \frac{9}{7} = 1\frac{2}{7}$$

$$\frac{5}{8} - \frac{1}{8} = \frac{4}{8} = \frac{1}{2}$$

Always give the answer in its simplest form.

F1 Simon and Alison buy a cake.
Simon eats $\frac{1}{5}$ of the cake and Alison eats $\frac{2}{5}$ of the cake.
What fraction of the cake have they eaten altogether?

F2 Work these out.
(a) $\frac{1}{3} + \frac{1}{3}$
(b) $\frac{1}{5} + \frac{3}{5}$
(c) $\frac{4}{7} + \frac{1}{7}$
(d) $\frac{2}{5} + \frac{2}{5}$
(e) $\frac{3}{10} + \frac{4}{10}$
(f) $\frac{3}{7} - \frac{1}{7}$
(g) $\frac{4}{5} - \frac{3}{5}$
(h) $\frac{7}{8} - \frac{2}{8}$
(i) $\frac{7}{9} - \frac{5}{9}$
(j) $\frac{5}{6} - \frac{4}{6}$

F3 Steve drinks $\frac{3}{4}$ of a can of lemonade.
What fraction of the drink is left?

F4 Work these out. Give your answers as mixed (or whole) numbers.
(a) $\frac{3}{5} + \frac{4}{5}$
(b) $\frac{2}{3} + \frac{2}{3}$
(c) $\frac{3}{4} + \frac{1}{4}$
(d) $\frac{3}{7} + \frac{5}{7}$
(e) $\frac{5}{9} + \frac{8}{9}$

F5 Match each calculation with its result.

A $\frac{3}{4} - \frac{1}{4}$ B $\frac{2}{9} + \frac{1}{9}$ C $\frac{3}{4} + \frac{3}{4}$ P $\frac{1}{3}$ Q $\frac{2}{5}$ R $\frac{1}{2}$

D $\frac{3}{10} + \frac{1}{10}$ E $\frac{7}{8} - \frac{1}{8}$ F $\frac{5}{6} - \frac{1}{6}$ S $1\frac{1}{2}$ T $\frac{2}{3}$ U $\frac{3}{4}$

F6 Work these out. Simplify each answer.
(a) $\frac{1}{4} + \frac{1}{4}$
(b) $\frac{3}{8} + \frac{1}{8}$
(c) $\frac{5}{9} + \frac{1}{9}$
(d) $\frac{7}{8} - \frac{5}{8}$
(e) $\frac{7}{10} - \frac{1}{10}$

F7 Solve the cover-up puzzle on sheet F1–5.

G Multiplying a fraction by a whole number

Examples

$\frac{1}{2} \times 5 = \frac{1}{2} + \frac{1}{2} + \frac{1}{2} + \frac{1}{2} + \frac{1}{2}$
$= \frac{5}{2}$
$= 2\frac{1}{2}$

$\frac{1}{4} \times 6 = \frac{1}{4} + \frac{1}{4} + \frac{1}{4} + \frac{1}{4} + \frac{1}{4} + \frac{1}{4}$
$= \frac{6}{4}$
$= 1\frac{2}{4}$
$= 1\frac{1}{2}$

$\frac{2}{5} \times 3 = \frac{2}{5} + \frac{2}{5} + \frac{2}{5}$
$= \frac{6}{5}$
$= 1\frac{1}{5}$

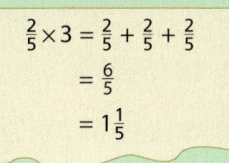

G1 Snowy the cat eats $\frac{1}{2}$ a tin of cat food each day.
(a) How many tins of cat food does Snowy eat in a week?
(b) How many days will 5 tins of cat food last Snowy?

G2 Morag uses $\frac{1}{4}$ of a pint of milk each day to make her porridge.
How much milk will she need for her porridge for a 12-day holiday?

G3 Work these out. Give your answers as mixed (or whole) numbers.

(a) $\frac{1}{2} \times 3$ (b) $\frac{1}{4} \times 5$ (c) $\frac{1}{2} \times 4$ (d) $\frac{1}{3} \times 5$ (e) $\frac{1}{3} \times 7$

(f) $\frac{3}{4} \times 3$ (g) $\frac{2}{5} \times 4$ (h) $\frac{1}{6} \times 8$ (i) $\frac{3}{8} \times 4$ (j) $\frac{2}{9} \times 6$

G4 Pluto eats $\frac{2}{3}$ of a tin of dog food each day.
How many tins of dog food will Pluto eat in 12 days?

Test yourself

T1 (a) Write down the fraction of this shape that is shaded.
Write your fraction in its simplest form.

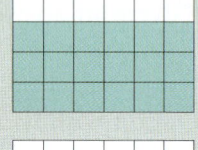

(b) Copy this shape.
Shade $\frac{2}{3}$ of the shape.

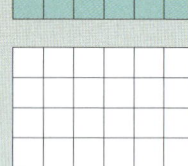

Edexcel

T2 Work these out.
Give each answer in its simplest form.

(a) $\frac{1}{10} + \frac{7}{10}$ (b) $\frac{4}{5} - \frac{1}{5}$ (c) $\frac{5}{6} + \frac{4}{6}$ (d) $\frac{3}{4} - \frac{1}{4}$

T3 (a) Margaret has 375 g of butter.
She uses $\frac{4}{5}$ of it.
How much butter does she use?

(b) A bag contains 1 kg of flour.
Margaret uses 200 g of flour.
What fraction of the flour is this?
Give your answer in its simplest form.

OCR

T4 Write $\frac{17}{5}$ as a mixed number.

T5 Jake has 28 DVDs. 7 of them are music DVDs.

(a) What fraction of his DVDs are music? Write the fraction in its simplest form.

(b) What fraction are not music?

T6 Work these out.
Give each answer in its simplest form.

(a) $\frac{1}{3} \times 8$ (b) $\frac{1}{4} \times 10$ (c) $\frac{3}{5} \times 4$ (d) $\frac{2}{7} \times 5$

3 Reading scales

This work will help you interpret a variety of scales.

You need sheets F1–6 and F1–7.

A Whole numbers   level 4

- What number does each arrow point to?

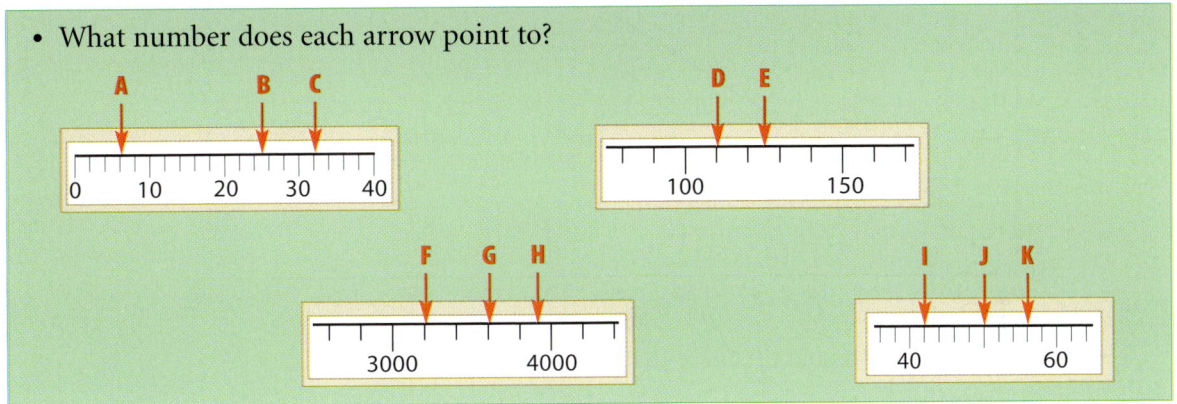

A1 What number does each arrow point to?

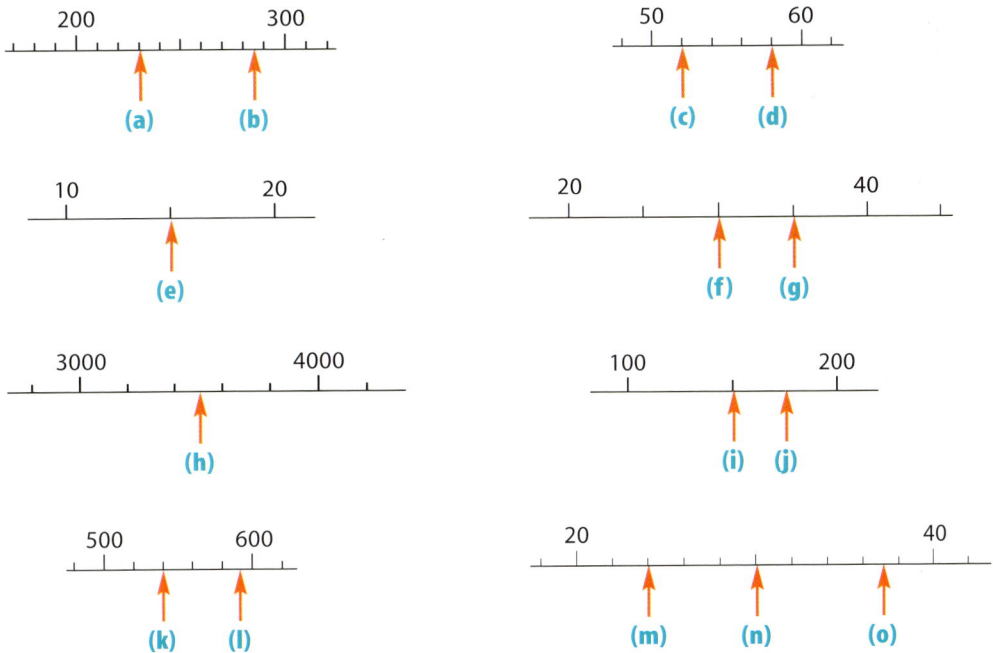

A2 This question is on sheet F1–6.

A3 This graph can be used to convert between miles and kilometres.

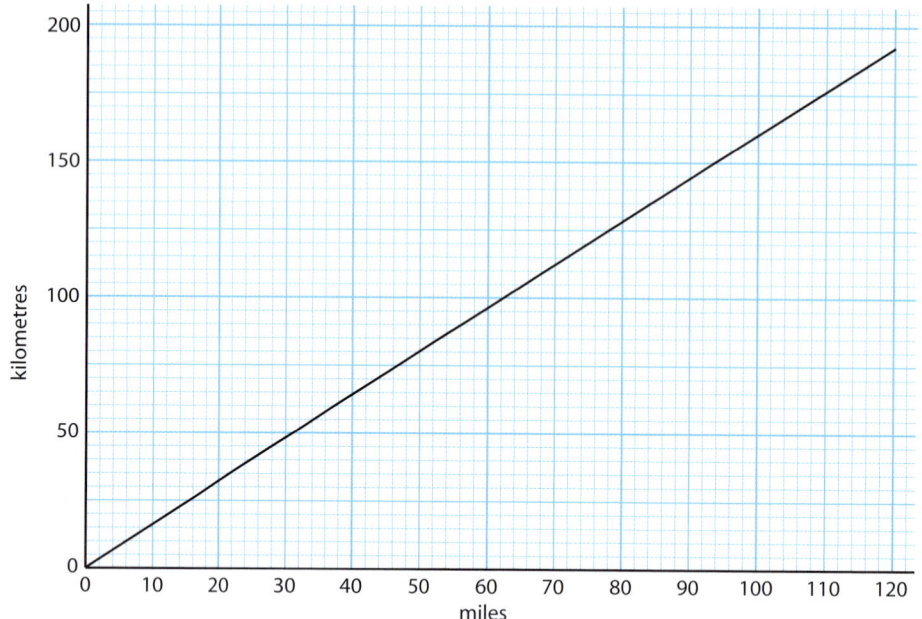

(a) Use the graph to convert these distances to kilometres.

(i) 50 miles (ii) 22 miles (iii) 85 miles

(b) Helen drives from Edinburgh to Newcastle, a distance of 110 miles. About how many kilometres did she travel?

(c) Use the graph to convert these distances to miles.

(i) 160 km (ii) 125 km (iii) 40 km

(d) The distance from Dundee to Edinburgh in 90 kilometres. How far is this in miles?

B Decimals

level 4

- What number does each arrow point to?

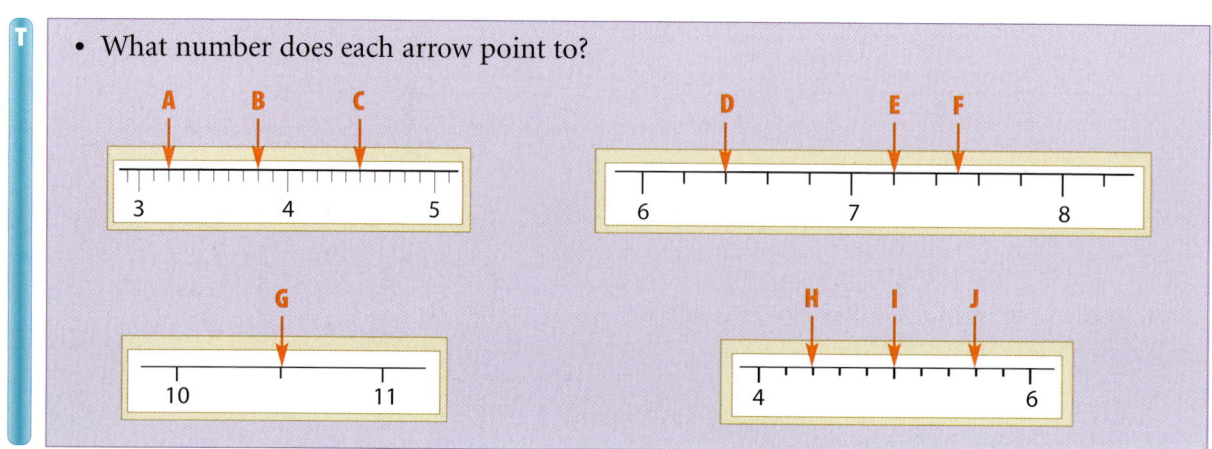

B1 What number does each arrow point to?

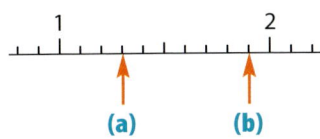 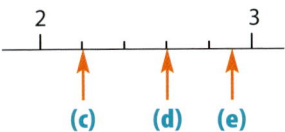

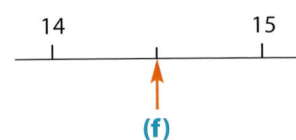 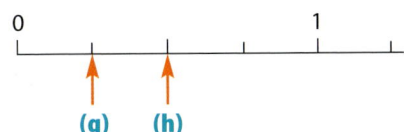

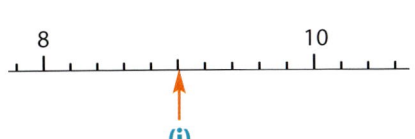 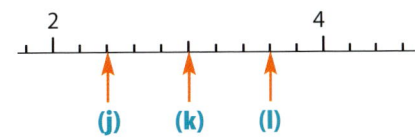

B2 This question is on sheet F1–7.

B3 This graph can be used to convert between pints and litres.

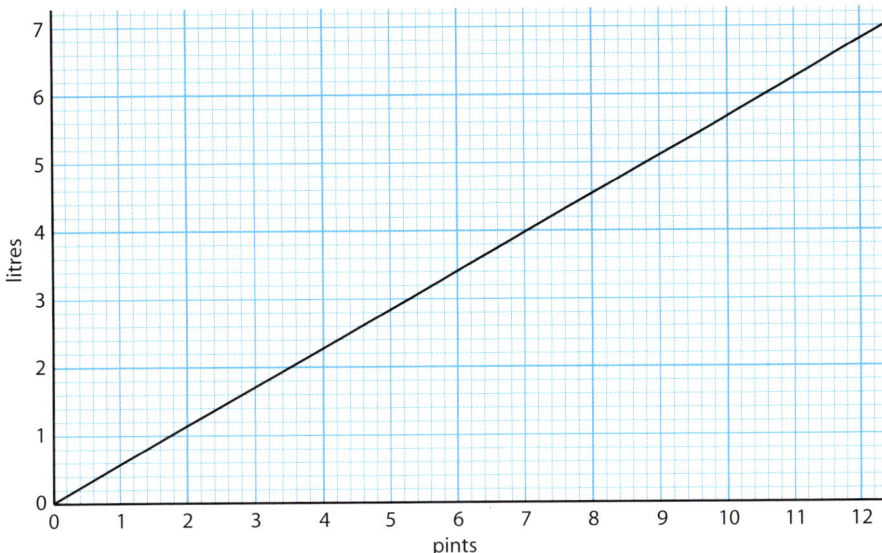

Use the graph to convert
(a) 6 pints to litres
(b) 10.2 pints to litres
(c) 3.5 pints to litres
(d) 5 litres to pints
(e) 6.6 litres to pints
(f) 2.5 litres to pints

B4 What number does each arrow point to?

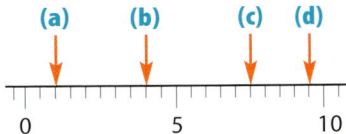

3 Reading scales 27

B5 This graph is for conversion between pounds (£) and US dollars ($).

Use the graph to change

(a) £3 to US dollars ($)

(b) $2 to pounds (£)

(c) £1.70 to US dollars ($)

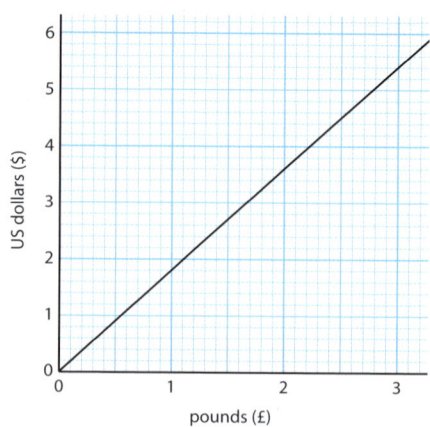

Test yourself

T1 What number does each arrow point to?

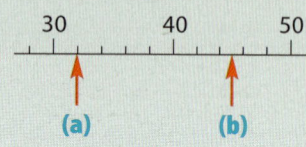 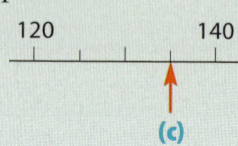 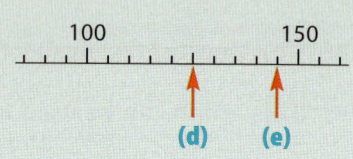

T2 The graph shows the number of bottle bank sites between 1977 and 1996.

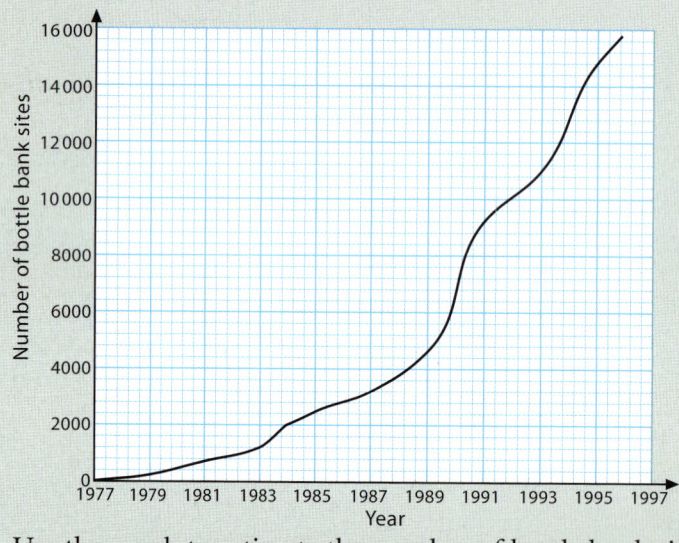

(a) Use the graph to estimate the number of bottle bank sites in 1993.

(b) Use the graph to estimate in which year the number of bottle bank sites was 2000.

AQA

T3 What number does each arrow point to?

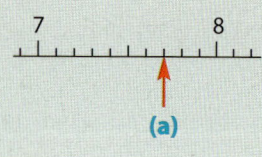 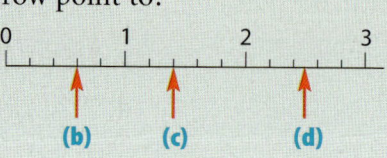 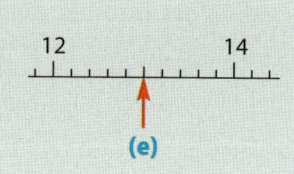

4 Arrow diagrams and equations

You should know that

- $\frac{a}{5}$ means $a \div 5$ and $5a$ means $5 \times a$
- $2n - 5$ means 'multiply n by 2 and then take off 5'

This work will help you

- solve an arrow diagram puzzle by reversing the diagram
- turn an arrow diagram into an equation
- solve an equation using arrow diagrams
- write and solve an equation for a number puzzle

A Mathematical whispers   level 4

Pete — Ceri: "I think of a number and whisper it to Ceri."

Ceri — Irvine: "I multiply it by 4 and whisper the answer to Irvine."

Irvine — Alli: "I subtract 12 and whisper the answer to Alli."

- Pete thinks of the number 5 and sends it along this 'whisper chain'. What number does Irvine whisper to Alli?
- Pete starts another chain that ends with Irvine whispering the number 28 to Alli.

  We can show this chain as an arrow diagram. What number did Pete think of this time?

  ○ —×4→ ○ —−12→ 28

- Try some 'mathematical whispering' for yourself.

A1 Copy and complete each of these arrow diagrams.

(a) 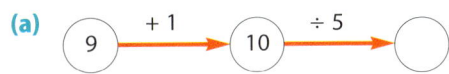   (b)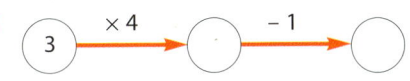

(c)    (d)

A2 Dave starts a mathematical whisper.

He thinks of a number and whispers it to Jo.	Jo takes Dave's number and multiplies by 3.	Raj adds 10 to Jo's answer. Raj ends up with 40.

(a) Copy and complete this arrow diagram for the whisper.

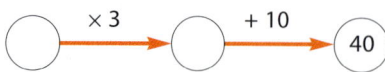

(b) What number did Dave think of?

A3 Copy and complete each of these arrow diagrams.

(a) 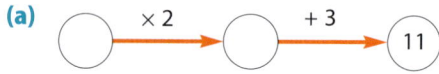   (b)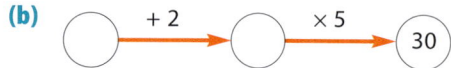

(c) 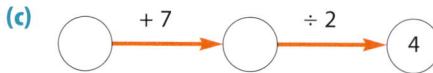   (d)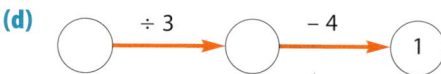

A4 Copy and complete each of these arrow diagrams.

(a)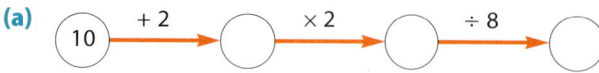

(b)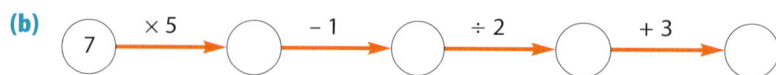

A5 Draw an arrow diagram for this whisper.
Work out what number Dave started with.

Dave thinks of a number and subtracts 9.	Jo takes Dave's answer and divides by 5.	Raj adds 10 to Jo's answer. Raj ends up with 13.

A6 Copy and complete this arrow diagram.

30 4 Arrow diagrams and equations

B Using letters

For this puzzle …

… we can use a letter to stand for the number that goes into the puzzle.

In each box we can show what happens to the letter.

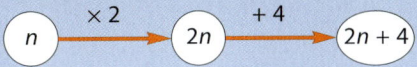

So the puzzle can be written as

$$2n + 4 = 10$$

We call this an **equation**.

B1 Suppose the letter n goes into each of these puzzles.
Match each puzzle with its equation.

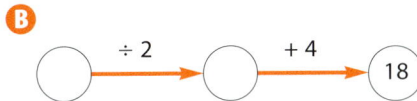

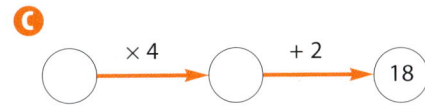

P $4n + 2 = 18$

Q $\dfrac{n}{2} + 4 = 18$

R $2n + 4 = 18$

B2 Which of the equations below matches this puzzle?

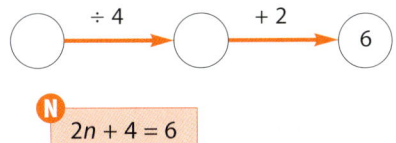

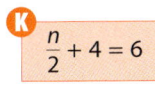 $\dfrac{n}{2} + 4 = 6$

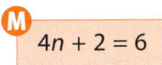 $\dfrac{n}{4} + 2 = 6$

M $4n + 2 = 6$

N $2n + 4 = 6$

B3 Which of the puzzles below matches the equation $3x - 2 = 16$?

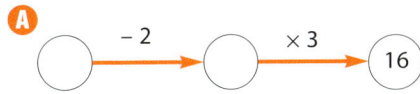

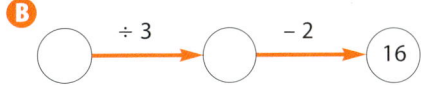

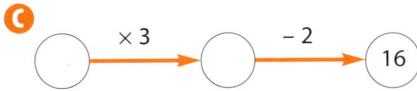

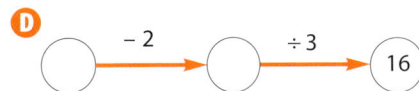

4 Arrow diagrams and equations

B4 Draw a puzzle for each of these equations.

(a) $3n - 4 = 8$ (b) $\frac{a}{5} + 7 = 9$

B5 Write an equation for each of these puzzles.
Choose your own letters to stand for the numbers that go into the puzzles.

(a)

(b)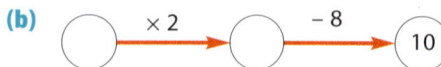

(c)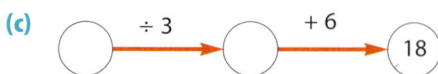

(d)

C Solving equations

Solving the equation $3y + 9 = 45$ means finding the number that y stands for. We are finding what number fits the equation.

We can do this by first writing the equation as an arrow diagram. Then we just reverse the flow of the arrow diagram.

Draw an arrow diagram for the equation.

$3y + 9 = 45$

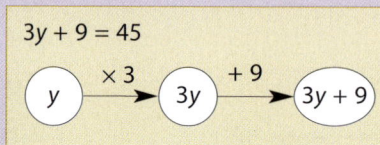

Reverse the arrow diagram to find the value of y.

$y = 12$

Check that the value of y works in the original equation.

Check
When $y = 12$,
$3y + 9 = 3 \times 12 + 9$
$= 36 + 9$
$= 45$, which is correct.

- Use this method to solve these equations.

P $2n + 11 = 31$

Q $5x - 2 = 33$

R $\frac{a}{2} + 3 = 8$

S $\frac{b}{3} - 1 = 3$

C1 (a) Copy and complete this working to solve the equation $9k - 3 = 15$.

(b) Check that your answer works in the original equation.

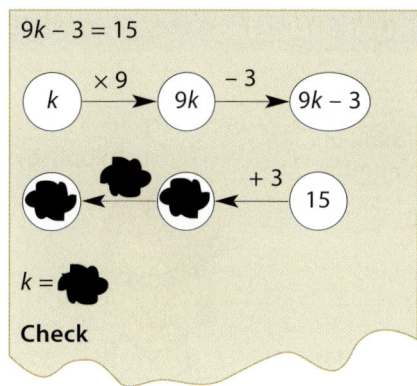

C2 Draw an arrow diagram for each of these equations. Then reverse the diagram and solve the equation.

Check each of your solutions.

(a) $2n + 9 = 15$ (b) $3x - 2 = 19$ (c) $7a - 5 = 23$
(d) $5b + 3 = 38$ (e) $8p - 4 = 20$ (f) $4y + 12 = 60$

C3

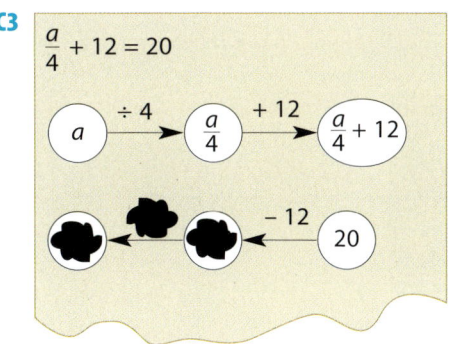

(a) Copy and complete this working to solve the equation $\frac{a}{4} + 12 = 20$.

(b) Check that your answer works in the original equation.

C4 Draw an arrow diagram and reverse it to solve each of these equations. Check each of your solutions.

(a) $\frac{w}{4} - 16 = 4$ (b) $\frac{m}{2} + 6 = 10$ (c) $\frac{x}{5} - 2 = 3$

C5 Solve each of these equations.

(a) $3a - 5 = 3.4$ (b) $2n + 1.5 = 13.9$
(c) $2.5y - 3 = 62$ (d) $\frac{k}{4} - 1.8 = 2.7$

D Number puzzles

Suppose *n* stands for the number that Mary first thinks of.
Then we can write the number puzzle as an equation. $2n + 3 = 31$

We can also show the puzzle as an arrow diagram.

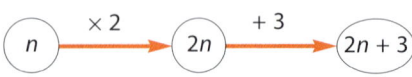

Now we can reverse the arrow diagram
to solve the equation and find Mary's number.

D1 Here is a number puzzle.

> I think of a number.
> I multiply by 4.
> I take off 6.
> My answer is 22.
> What was my number?

(a) Copy and complete this equation for the number puzzle.

■n − ■ = 22

(b) Draw an arrow diagram for the equation.

(c) Draw a reverse arrow diagram.

(d) Use the reverse arrow diagram to solve the number puzzle.

D2 Write an equation for each of these number puzzles.
Then solve your equation using arrow diagrams.

(a)
> I think of a number.
> I multiply by 5.
> I subtract 8.
> My answer is 97.
> What was my number?

(b)
> I think of a number.
> I divide by 7.
> I add 2.
> My answer is 10.
> What was my number?

(c)
> I think of a number.
> I divide by 4.
> subtract 5.
> My answer is 47.
> What was my number?

D3 Write a number puzzle of your own.
Make sure you can find the answer!

Now give someone else your puzzle to solve.

D4 (a) Write a number puzzle for the equation $3n - 4 = 20$.

(b) Solve the equation using an arrow diagram.

D5 Use arrow diagrams to solve these equations.

(a) $4x + 3.5 = 9.9$ (b) $3n + 2.2 = 12.7$ (c) $1.5k + 4 = 10$

Test yourself

T1 Copy and complete these arrow diagrams.

(a)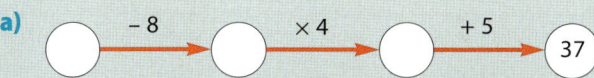

(b)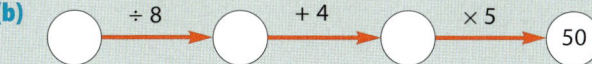

T2 Draw an arrow diagram for each of these equations.
Then reverse the arrow diagram and solve the equation.

(a) $3m - 6 = 18$ (b) $4s + 2 = 30$

(c) $\frac{w}{2} - 4 = 10$ (d) $\frac{v}{5} - 4 = 6$

T3 Write an equation for each of these number puzzles.
Then solve your equation using arrow diagrams.

(a)
I think of a number.
I multiply by 4.
I subtract 2.
My answer is 30.
What was my number?

(b)
I think of a number.
I divide by 2.
I subtract 10.
My answer is 17.
What was my number?

4 Arrow diagrams and equations

5 Decimals

This work will help you

- compare and order decimals with up to three decimal places
- round to the nearest whole number and to one, two and three decimal places
- multiply and divide by 10, 100 and 1000

A One and two decimal places   level 4

A1 What number does each arrow point to?

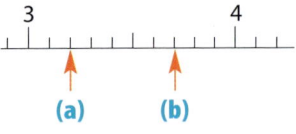 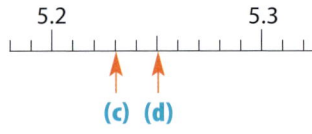 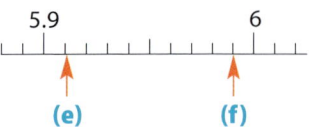

A2 Decide whether each of these is true or false.

(a) 4.6 is between 4 and 5.   (b) 3.26 is between 3.6 and 3.7.

A3 What number does each arrow point to?

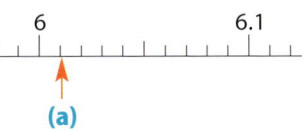 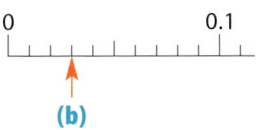

A4 This table shows the weights of some newborn baby boys.
The mean birth weight of a baby boy in the UK is about 3.4 kg.
Which of these baby boys weighed more than this?

Name	Weight (kg)
Daniel	3.81
Andrew	4.22
Ben	3.26
Jake	3.08

A5 Put each list of numbers in order, smallest first.

(a) 2.4, 4, 3.8, 2.45, 2.5   (b) 8.1, 8.92, 9, 8.4, 8.27

(c) 3.07, 2.9, 3.1, 3.7, 3.61   (d) 0.5, 0.26, 0.03, 0.49, 0.7

A6 Joel says this arrow points to 3.62 but Josie says it points to 3.64.
Who is right?

A7 What number does each arrow point to?

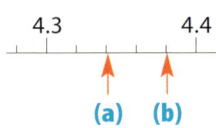

A8 What number is halfway between

(a) 8 and 9   (b) 5.1 and 5.2   (c) 7 and 7.1

36   5 Decimals

B More than two decimal places

[Scale from 7.3 to 7.4 in kilograms, with pointers A (near 7.335), B (near 7.352), and C (near 7.378)]

- What weight is shown by each pointer?
- Which is heavier, 7.36 kg or 7.352 kg?
- Give a weight between 7.38 kg and 7.39 kg.
- Put these weights in order, lightest first.

  7.38 kg   7.309 kg   7.4 kg   7.364 kg   7.356 kg   7.32 kg

B1 Decide whether each of these is true or false.
The scale above may help you decide.
  (a) 7.351 is between 7.3 and 7.4.   (b) 7.386 is between 7.384 and 7.388.
  (c) 7.376 is between 7.37 and 7.38.   (d) 7.385 is between 7.35 and 7.36.

B2 What number does each arrow point to?

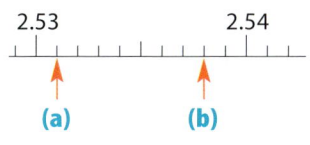

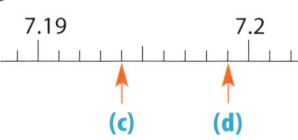

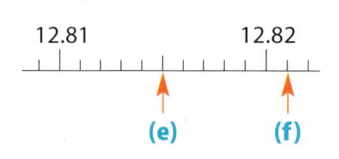

[Three number lines: 2.53 to 2.54 with arrows (a) and (b); 7.19 to 7.2 with arrows (c) and (d); 12.81 to 12.82 with arrows (e) and (f)]

B3 Put each set of lengths in order, shortest first.
  (a) 1.273 m, 1.109 m, 1.891 m   (b) 7.6 m, 7.319 m, 7.32 m
  (c) 2.537 km, 2.54 km, 2.5 km   (d) 1.006 km, 1.4 km, 1.25 km

B4 What number is halfway between 2.97 and 2.98?

> The process of dividing again and again into ten equal divisions can go on for ever.

B5 What number does each arrow point to?

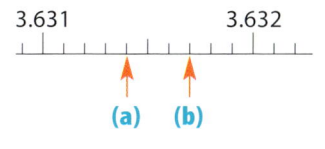

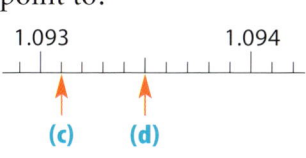

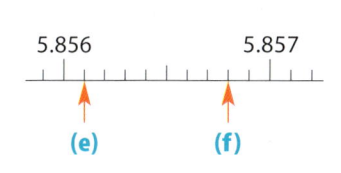

[Three number lines: 3.631 to 3.632 with arrows (a) and (b); 1.093 to 1.094 with arrows (c) and (d); 5.856 to 5.857 with arrows (e) and (f)]

B6 What number is halfway between 4.862 and 4.863?

5 Decimals 37

C Rounding to the nearest whole number

On a motorway there is a phone every kilometre.
There are distance posts every 100 metres.

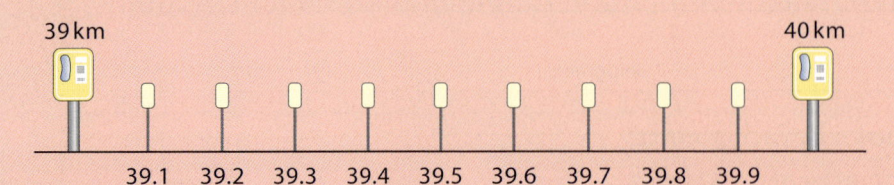

39 km ... 40 km

39.1 39.2 39.3 39.4 39.5 39.6 39.7 39.8 39.9

If you break down, you want to walk to the nearest phone.
- Which phone would you walk to if you broke down next to the post at 39.8?
- Which phone is nearest to 39.37 km?

Finding the closest whole number to a decimal is called **rounding to the nearest whole number**.

C1 Which whole number is nearest to each of these?
(a) 3.9   (b) 4.1   (c) 18.7   (d) 13.9   (e) 27.4

C2 Round these to the nearest metre.
(a) 4.6 m   (b) 17.2 m   (c) 20.3 m   (d) 5.8 m   (e) 47.9 m

C3 Round these to the nearest kilometre.
(a) 134.2 km   (b) 12.7 km   (c) 981.3 km   (d) 26.8 km   (e) 89.6 km

C4 Which whole number is nearest to each of these?
(a) 4.83   (b) 2.34   (c) 7.88   (d) 5.36   (e) 16.75

C5 Round these to the nearest kilogram.
(a) 5.73 kg   (b) 1.09 kg   (c) 14.64 kg   (d) 10.59 kg   (e) 18.29 kg

C6 Round these to the nearest litre.
(a) 17.77 litres   (b) 53.91 litres   (c) 37.02 litres   (d) 0.92 litre   (e) 15.08 litres

C7 Round these to the nearest whole number.
(a) 6.7   (b) 31.17   (c) 53.47   (d) 19.59   (e) 0.89

C8 Round these to the nearest kilogram.
(a) 6.891 kg   (b) 5.479 kg   (c) 1.901 kg   (d) 3.573 kg   (e) 10.032 kg

C9 Round 29.641 kg to the nearest kilogram.

D Rounding to one decimal place

Examples

Round 1.72 to one decimal place.

> 1.72 is between 1.7 and 1.8.
> It is closer to 1.7 (the '2' tells you this) so 1.72 rounds to 1.7.

Round 3.256 71 to one decimal place.

> 3.256 71 is between 3.2 and 3.3.
> It is closer to 3.3 (the '5' tells you this) so 3.256 71 rounds to 3.3.

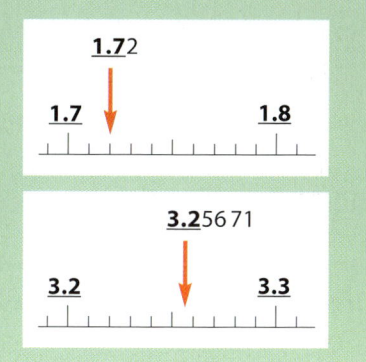

This is a simple rule for rounding to one decimal place.

> If the digit in the second decimal place is
> • 5 or above, round up
> • 4 or below, round down

D1 The numbers in the rectangles are written to one decimal place in the circles. Find five matching pairs.

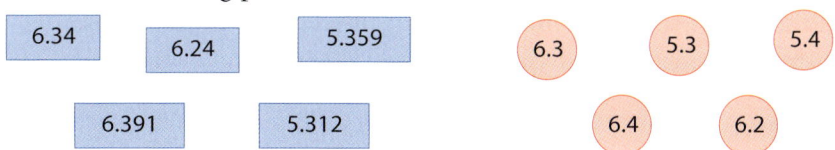

6.34   6.24   5.359   6.391   5.312

6.3   5.3   5.4   6.4   6.2

D2 Round these numbers to one decimal place.
- (a) 1.21
- (b) 5.67
- (c) 0.18
- (d) 12.39
- (e) 14.34
- (f) 4.578
- (g) 9.345
- (h) 12.417
- (i) 0.380
- (j) 1.308

D3 Round these numbers to one decimal place.
- (a) 6.783 24
- (b) 1.539 2435
- (c) 7.108 4623
- (d) 2.063 2193

D4

A	B	E	H	I	G	L	N	P	R	T	W
2.0	2.1	2.2	2.3	2.4	2.5	2.6	2.7	2.8	2.9	3.0	3.1

Round each decimal below to one decimal place and find a letter for each one. Rearrange each set of letters to spell an animal.
- (a) 2.8604, 2.24, 2.138, 2.034
- (b) 2.609, 2.2561, 2.1901, 1.964, 3.101 31
- (c) 2.51, 2.908, 2.412, 2.98, 2.1984
- (d) 2.764 123, 2.2461, 2.5543, 2.344 52, 1.983 61, 3.0499, 2.221 09, 2.706 71

E Rounding to more than one decimal place

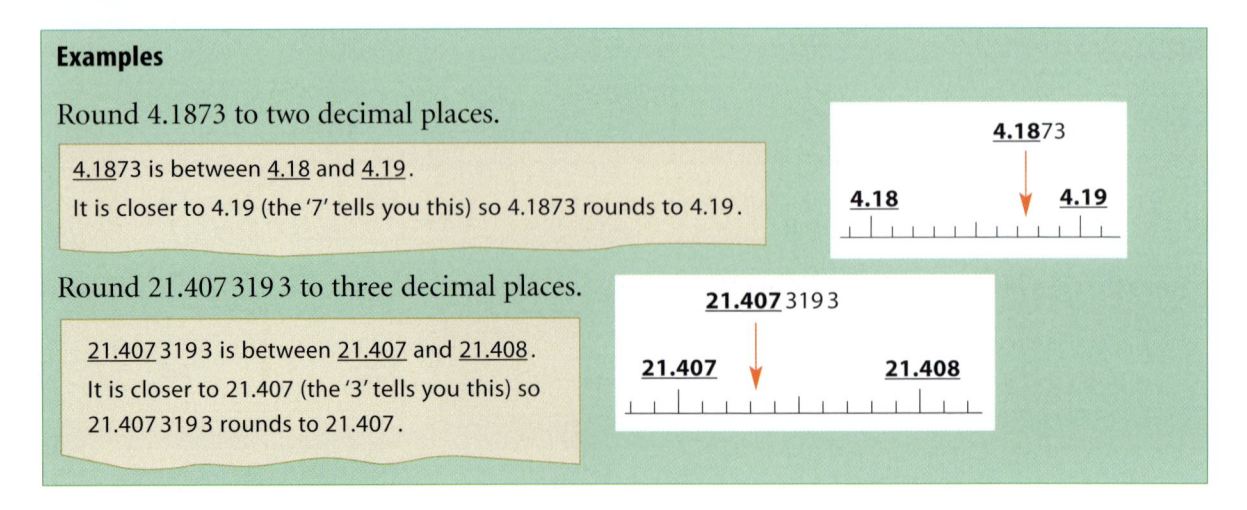

Examples

Round 4.1873 to two decimal places.

4.1873 is between 4.18 and 4.19.
It is closer to 4.19 (the '7' tells you this) so 4.1873 rounds to 4.19.

Round 21.407 319 3 to three decimal places.

21.407 319 3 is between 21.407 and 21.408.
It is closer to 21.407 (the '3' tells you this) so 21.407 319 3 rounds to 21.407.

This is a rule for rounding decimals.

Find the last column you are interested in (1st, 2nd, 3rd, … decimal place).
If the next digit on the right is
- 5 or above, round up
- 4 or below, round down

E1 The numbers in the rectangles are written to two decimal places in the loops. Find five matching pairs.

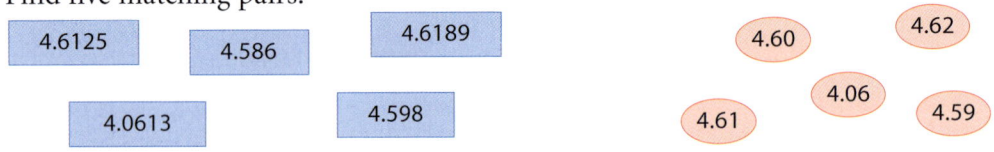

4.6125   4.586   4.6189   4.60   4.62
4.0613   4.598   4.06   4.61   4.59

E2 Round these numbers to two decimal places.

(a) 5.631   (b) 16.126   (c) 6.401   (d) 23.089   (e) 1.325

E3 Round these to the nearest penny.

(a) £1.681 23   (b) £14.926 04   (c) £5.235 631   (d) £26.501 396 4

E4 The numbers in the rectangles are written to **three** decimal places in the loops. Find five matching pairs.

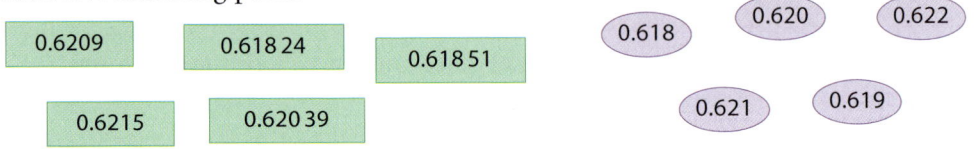

0.6209   0.618 24   0.618 51   0.618   0.620   0.622
0.6215   0.620 39   0.621   0.619

E5 Round these numbers to three decimal places.

(a) 1.4936   (b) 1.9284   (c) 3.581 29   (d) 13.245 61
(e) 1.590 01   (f) 1.239 91   (g) 15.479 12   (h) 0.879 78

F Multiplying and dividing by powers of ten

Examples

$2.564 \times 100 = 256.4$

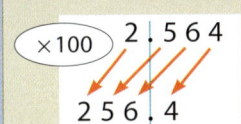

Multiplying by 100 moves figures two places to the left.

$45.3 \times 1000 = 45\,300$

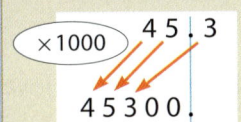

Multiplying by 1000 moves figures three places to the left.

$349 \div 10 = 34.9$

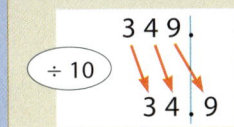

Dividing by 10 moves figures one place to the right.

$19.3 \div 1000 = 0.0193$

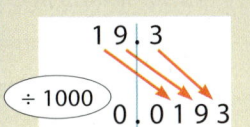

Dividing by 1000 moves figures three places to the right.

F1 Calculate each of these.
- (a) 2.89×10
- (b) 4.91×100
- (c) 59.436×100
- (d) 0.904×1000
- (e) 9.5×100
- (f) 0.549×1000
- (g) 13.2×100
- (h) 2.31×1000

F2 Calculate each of these.
- (a) $46.1 \div 10$
- (b) $4290.6 \div 100$
- (c) $5932 \div 1000$
- (d) $53.2 \div 100$
- (e) $9.3 \div 100$
- (f) $0.5 \div 10$
- (g) $13 \div 1000$
- (h) $0.12 \div 1000$

F3 Calculate each of these.
- (a) 3.09×10
- (b) $4.2 \div 10$
- (c) 23.41×100
- (d) 0.21×1000
- (e) $54 \div 100$
- (f) $2.34 \div 100$
- (g) 1.2×1000
- (h) $0.34 \div 100$

F4 Find the missing number in each calculation.
- (a) ■ $\times 10 = 67.3$
- (b) $678 \div$ ■ $= 6.78$
- (c) $3.01 \times$ ■ $= 3010$

Test yourself

T1 (a) The average weight for the men in a local football team is 74.85 kg. What is this to the nearest kilogram?

(b) Round 2.367 89 to one decimal place.

T2 Put each set of numbers in order, smallest first.
- (a) 0.45, 0.8, 0.71, 0.9
- (b) 0.67, 0.078, 0.7, 0.76, 0.706

T3 Round these numbers to two decimal places.
- (a) 2.436
- (b) 1.091
- (c) 3.9871
- (d) 6.7152

T4 Calculate each of these.
- (a) 7.92×10
- (b) $4.8 \div 10$
- (c) 1.267×100
- (d) 0.73×1000

5 Decimals

6 Angles, triangles and quadrilaterals

You will revise using the sum of the angles round a point, on a straight line and in a triangle.

This work will help you
- work with angles in an isosceles triangle
- use properties of the square, rectangle, rhombus, parallelogram, trapezium and kite

A Review: angles round a point, on a line, in a triangle

A full turn is 360°.

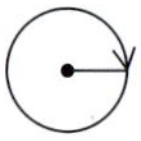

A1 Use this fact to find the missing angle in each of these sketches. ('Sketch' means the diagram is not drawn accurately – so you have to work angles out, not measure them.)

(a) 200°, ?

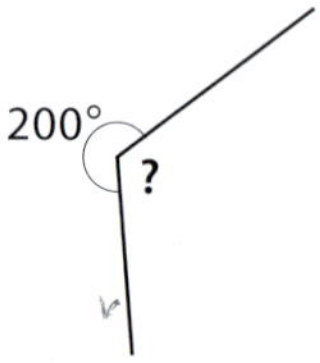

(b) 130°, 80°, ?

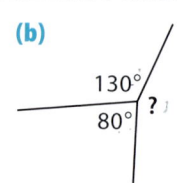

(c) 120°, ?, 100°, 60°

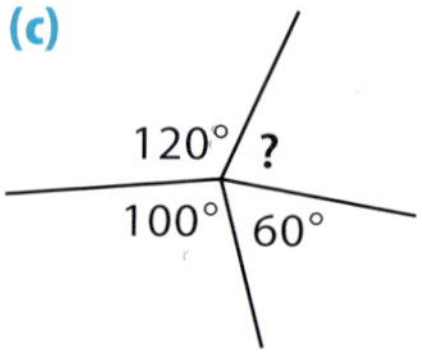

(d) 135°, ?, 55°, 75°

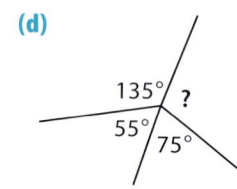

A2 One of these sketches has something wrong with it. Which is wrong and what is the problem?

P: 240°, 120°

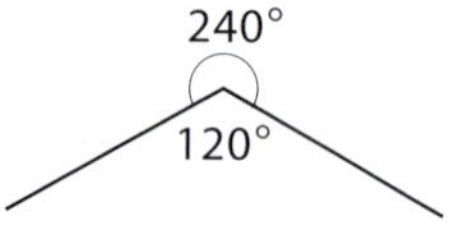

Q: 130°, 110°, 130°

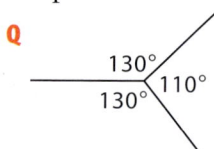

R: 90°, 108°, 34°, 128°

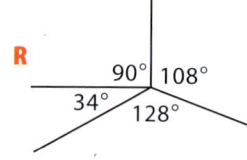

A half turn is 180°.

A3 Use this fact to find the missing angle in each of these sketches.

(a) 110°, ?

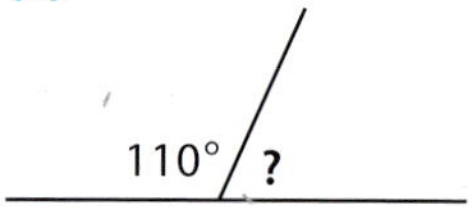

(b) 90°, ?, 60°

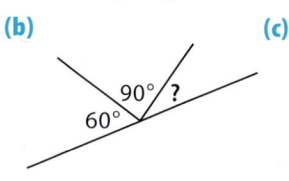

(c) 35°, ?, 45°

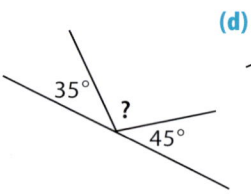

(d) 20°, 65°, 45°, ?

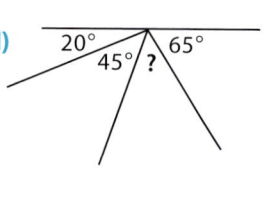

A4 One of these sketches has something wrong with it. Which is wrong and what is the problem?

S: 72°, 108°

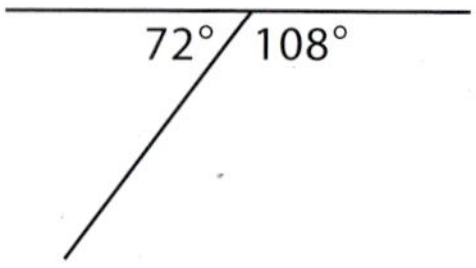

T: 95°, 30°, 55°

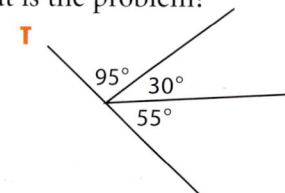

U: 35°, 28°, 51°, 67°

42 6 Angles, triangles and quadrilaterals

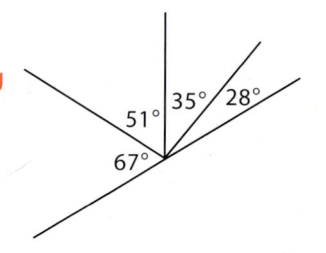

If you have any triangle 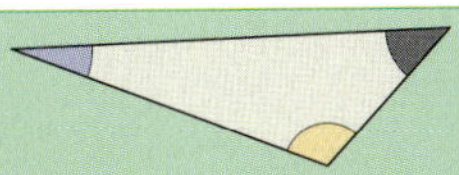 you can put exact copies of it together to make a tessellation.

If you look in the tessellation for a set of angles on a straight line, you always find blue + yellow + grey (not necessarily in that order), so blue + yellow + grey = 180°.

But the angles of the triangle you started with are blue, yellow and grey So the angles of that triangle add up to 180°.
This is true for any triangle.

A5 Use the fact that the angles of a triangle add up to 180° to find the missing angles here.

(a) 80°, 40°, ?

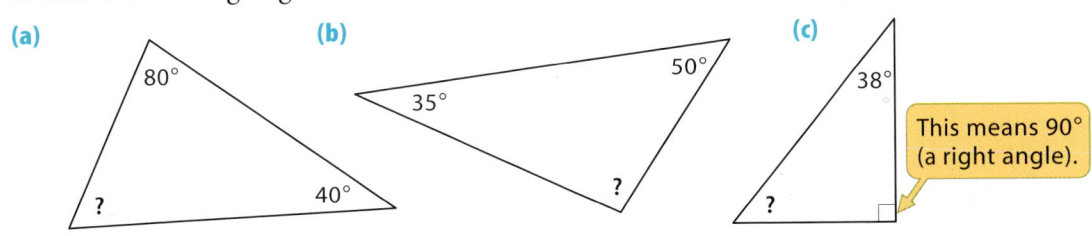

(b) 50°, 35°, ?

(c) 38°, ?, (This means 90° (a right angle).)

Where two straight lines cross, two angles that point towards one another are equal, like this 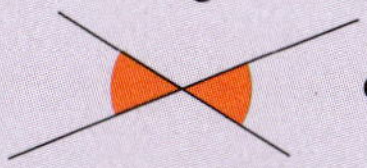 or like this.

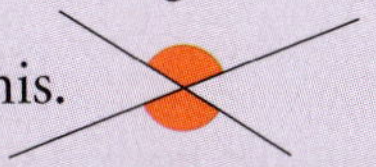

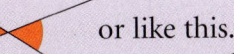

We call these **vertically opposite angles** (or opposite angles at a vertex).
(You can see plenty of vertically opposite angles in the tessellation above.)

A6 Write down the angles marked with letters in these sketches.

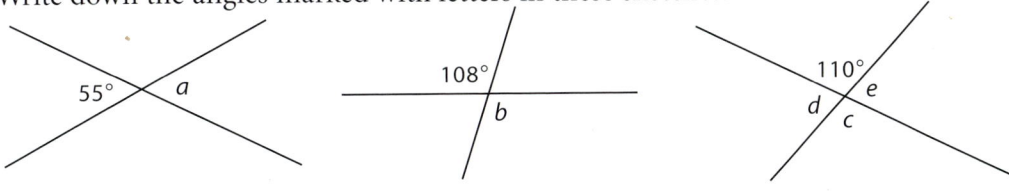

55°, a

108°, b

110°, e, d, c

A7 (a) Find the value of angle p.
  (b) What fact about angles have you used to find p?
  (c) Find the value of angle q.
  (d) What fact about angles have you used to find q?

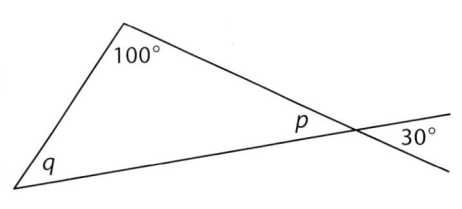

100°, p, 30°, q

6 Angles, triangles and quadrilaterals   43

Summary

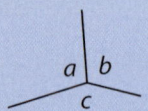

Angles around a point add up to 360°:
$a + b + c = 360°$

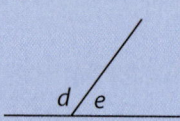

Angles on a line add up to 180°:
$d + e = 180°$

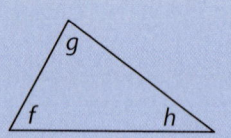

Angles in a triangle add up to 180°:
$f + g + h = 180°$

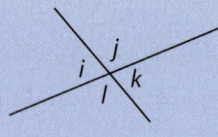

Vertically opposite angles are equal:
$i = k$ and $j = l$

A8 (a) Find the value of angle x.
(b) What fact about angles have you used to find x?
(c) Find the value of angle y.
(d) What fact about angles have you used to find y?

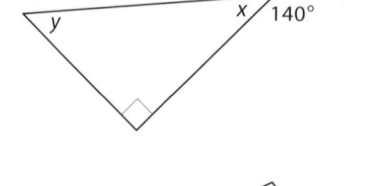

A9 (a) Find the value of angle a.
(b) What fact about angles have you used to find a?
(c) Find the value of angle b.
(d) What fact about angles have you used to find b?

A10 (a) Find the value of angle e, giving reasons for your answer.
(b) Find the value of angle f, giving reasons for your answer.

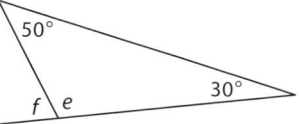

A11 (a) Find the value of angle r, giving reasons for your answer.
(b) Find the value of angle s, giving reasons for your answer.

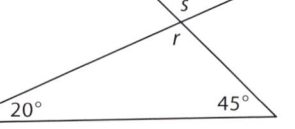

A12 (a) Find the value of angle c, giving reasons for your answer.
(b) Find the value of angle d, giving reasons for your answer.

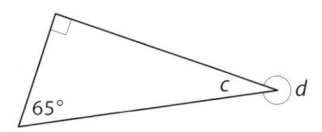

A13 Find the angles marked with letters, giving your reasons.

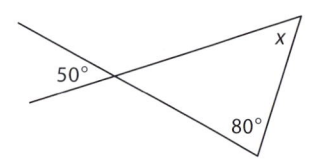

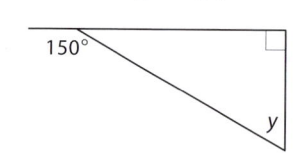

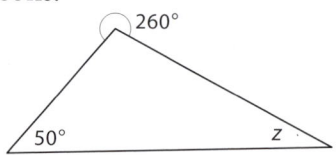

A14 Work out the value of a.

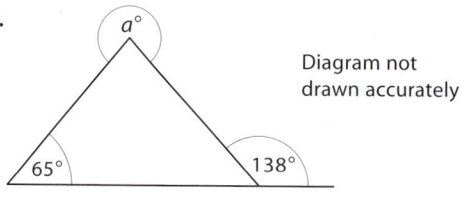

Diagram not drawn accurately

Edexcel

44 6 Angles, triangles and quadrilaterals

B Angles in an isosceles triangle

A triangle that has two sides the same length is called an **isosceles** triangle.

An isosceles triangle has reflection symmetry, so these two angles are equal.

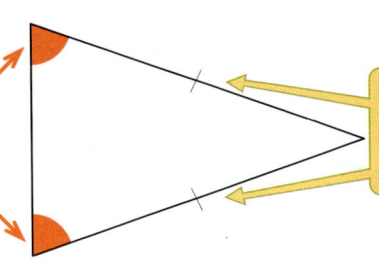

Marks like these show sides that are the same length as one another.

B1 One of these sketches has something wrong with it. Which sketch is wrong and what is wrong with it?

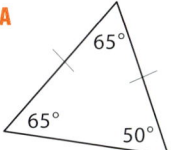

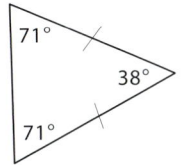

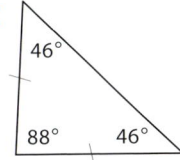

A: 65°, 65°, 50°
B: 71°, 38°, 71°
C: 46°, 88°, 46°

B2 (a) State the value of angle *p*.
(b) Use the sum of the angles of a triangle to find angle *q*.

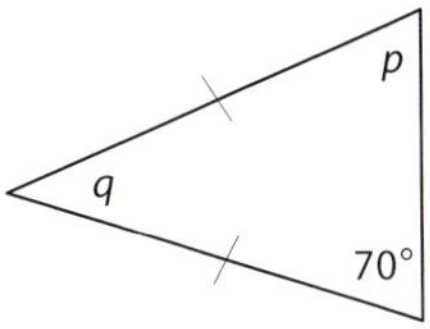

(triangle with *p*, *q*, 70°)

B3 Find the lettered angle in each of these.

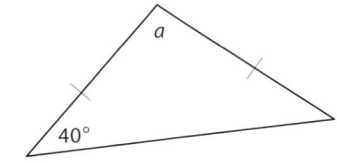

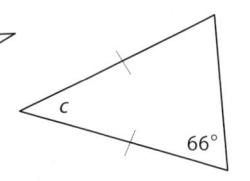

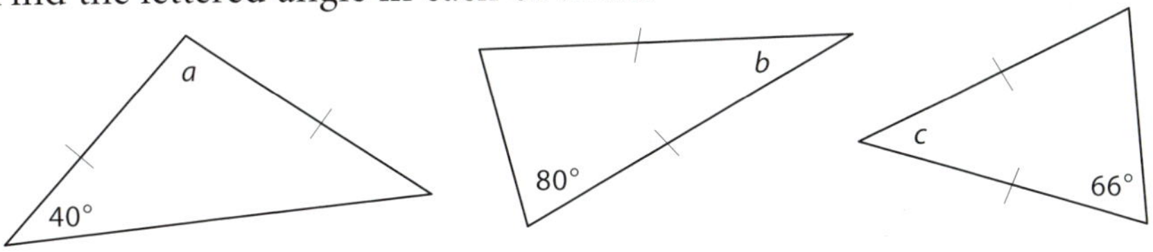

(triangle with *a*, 40°)
(triangle with *b*, 80°)
(triangle with *c*, 66°)

Example

Find the missing angles in this isosceles triangle.

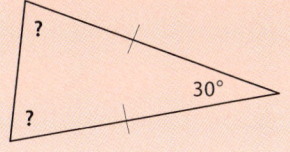

(triangle with ?, ?, 30°)

We know one angle is 30°.
We know the angles of a triangle add up to 180°.
So we take 30° from 180° to get 150°, the total of the two missing angles.
But the two missing angles are equal (because of where they are in the isosceles triangle).
So each missing angle is 75° (150° ÷ 2).

B4 Find the lettered angles in each of these triangles.

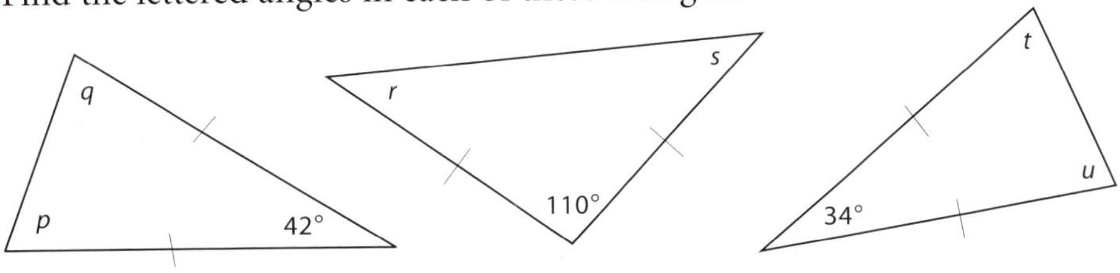

(triangle with *p*, *q*, 42°)
(triangle with *r*, *s*, 110°)
(triangle with *t*, *u*, 34°)

B5 Find the lettered angle in each of these isosceles triangles.

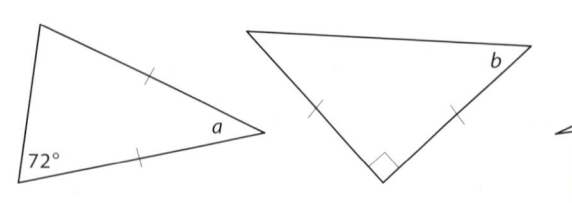

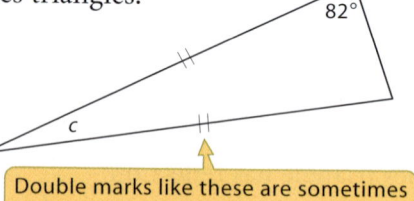

Double marks like these are sometimes used to show equal sides.

B6 Find the missing angle in each of these.
Each one involves angles in an isosceles triangle.
It may help to sketch each diagram then fill in each angle as you find it.

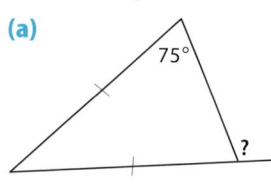

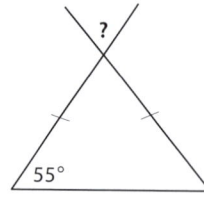

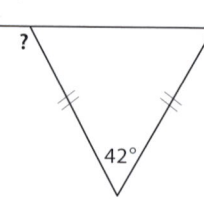

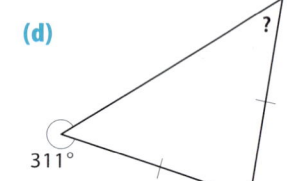

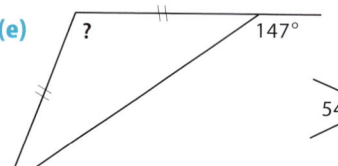

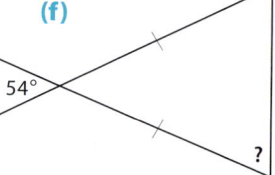

(a)   (b)   (c)

(d)   (e)   (f)

A triangle that has three sides the same length is called an **equilateral** triangle. Its three angles are the same size.

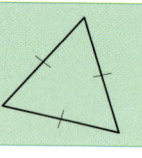

B7 What is the size of one angle of an equilateral triangle?

B8 This pattern is made from equilateral triangles.
Find the lettered angles.

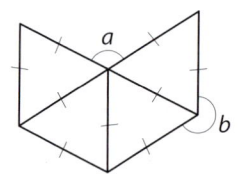

B9 In this sketch PMQ is a straight line.
  (a) Work out angle a.
      Give a reason for your answer.
  (b) Work out angle b.
      Give reasons for your answer.
  (c) Explain how you can tell that the line PR is at right angles to the line RQ.

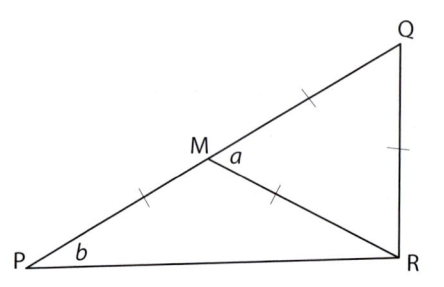

46 6 Angles, triangles and quadrilaterals

C Properties of special quadrilaterals

These are examples of special types of quadrilateral.

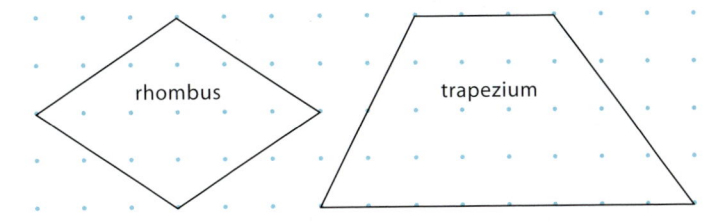

rhombus   trapezium

C1 Copy this rhombus and trapezium on to squared paper or square dotty paper. On the same paper draw an example of each of the following quadrilaterals.

square   rectangle   parallelogram   kite

Label each quadrilateral with its name.
Use your diagrams to help you with the following work.

C2 For each of the following descriptions, give the names of as many special quadrilaterals as you can that match it.

(a) All four angles are right angles.

(b) All four sides are the same length.

(c) Two angles opposite one another are equal and the other two angles are equal to one another.

(d) Two angles opposite one another are equal in size (but the other two angles are not equal to one another).

(e) Two sides opposite one another are parallel and the other two sides are parallel to one another.

C3 On squared paper, draw a quadrilateral that has only two right angles and only two parallel sides. What type of quadrilateral is it an example of?

Draw the two diagonals on each of the quadrilaterals you have drawn.
Each diagonal is divided into two parts by the other diagonal crossing it.

C4 (a) Name the quadrilaterals where both diagonals are divided exactly in half.

(b) Name the quadrilaterals where all four halves of the diagonals have the same length.

Lines *l* and *m* are at right angles to one another.
We say 'Line *l* is **perpendicular** to line *m*' or
'Lines *l* and *m* are perpendicular'.

C5 (a) Name the quadrilaterals where the diagonals are perpendicular.

(b) Name the quadrilaterals where there are perpendicular sides.

C6 (a) Which of the quadrilaterals you drew have rotation symmetry of order 2?

(b) Which one of them has rotation symmetry of order 4?

Test yourself

T1 (a) The diagram shows three angles on a straight line AB.
Work out the value of x.

Not drawn accurately

(b) The diagram shows three angles meeting at a point.
Work out the value of y.

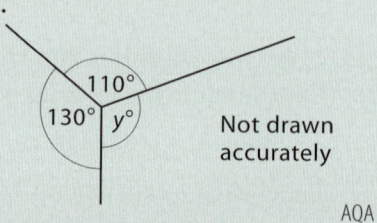

Not drawn accurately

AQA

T2 This triangle has two equal sides.
(a) What name is given to this type of triangle?
(b) Find the values of a and b.

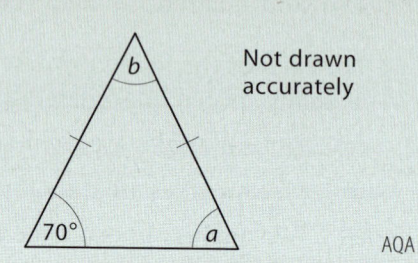

Not drawn accurately

AQA

T3 PQ is a straight line.
(a) Work out the size of the angle marked $x°$.
(b) (i) Work out the size of the angle marked $y°$.
(ii) Give reasons for your answer.

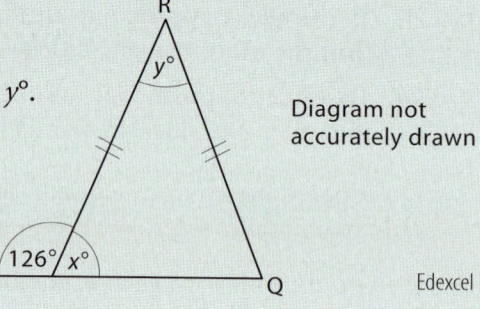

Diagram not accurately drawn

Edexcel

T4 ABC and EBD are straight lines.
BD = BC
Angle CBD = 42°.
(a) Write down the size of the angle marked $e°$.
(b) Work out the size of the angle marked $f°$.

Diagram not accurately drawn

Edexcel

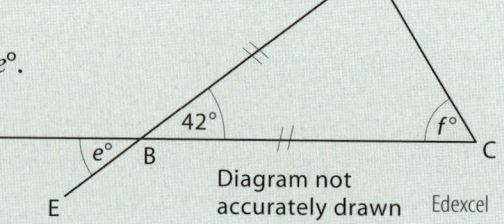

T5 The diagonals of a certain quadrilateral are perpendicular.
They are not equal in length.
Each diagonal is cut exactly in half by the other diagonal.
What kind of quadrilateral is this?

7 Experiments

This work will help you design an experiment to answer a question and write a report on it.

You will learn to use means, medians, modes, ranges, frequency tables and charts to help you write your report.

You may need sheet F1–8.

A Specifying the problem and planning

Look at the sets of words, pictures and numbers below.

- Which set do you think people would find it easiest to remember?

Words		Pictures	Numbers	
heather	school		16	23
lamp	sky		37	142
hate	spoon		53	97
necklace	birthday		86	21
hair	leaf		50	13

Here are some descriptions of how some students carried out a memory experiment.

> We used 10 words to test the memory of our class.
> We asked the class next door to do a memory test using 10 pictures and another class to use 10 numbers.
> We then compared the results from the three classes.

> We have roughly the same number of boys as girls in our class, so we got the boys to remember words and the girls pictures.
> The boys had 10 words to remember.
> The girls had 15 pictures as we thought pictures were easier.
> We showed them for 30 seconds and we had 1 minute to write down as many as we could remember from our lists.

- Do you think they are good methods? Give your reasons.

7 Experiments 49

Plan your own experiment to decide whether people are better at remembering words, pictures or numbers.

- How many words, pictures and numbers will you use?
- Which words, pictures and numbers will you use?
  You could use the pictures on sheet F1–8.
- Who will you ask? How many people will you ask?
- What equipment will you need?
- How will you collect the results?
- How long will you give people to memorise the objects? How long to answer?

Carry out your memory experiment and collect your results.

B Processing and representing

Twenty-five students in a class took part in a memory experiment.
Here are the results of the number of words they remembered out of 10.

Number of words remembered: 8, 5, 5, 7, 8, 10, 9, 10, 9, 8, 9, 10, 9, 7, 8, 10, 7, 7, 8, 9, 10, 9, 9, 7, 8

Here are some clearer ways to show the results.

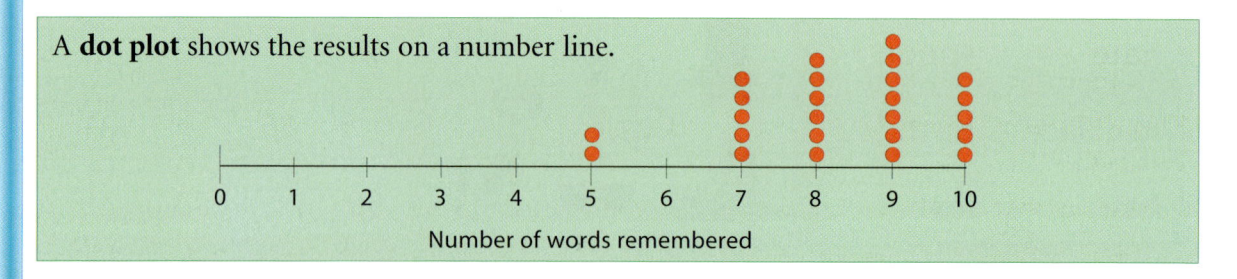

A **dot plot** shows the results on a number line.

A **frequency table** is useful for storing the results.

Words	Tally	Frequency
5	II	2
6		0
7	IIII	5
8	IIII I	6
9	IIII II	7
10	IIII	5
	Total	25

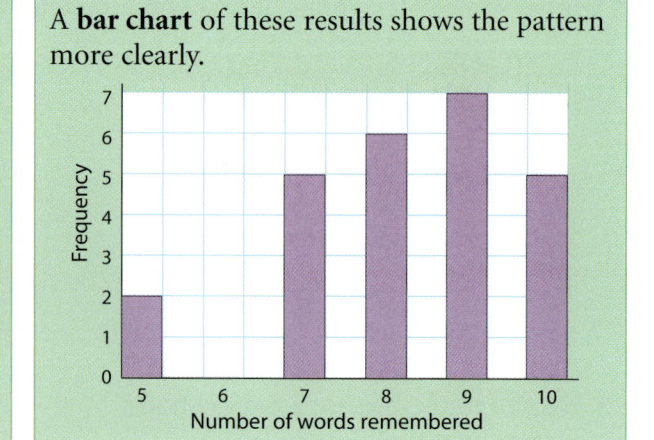

A **bar chart** of these results shows the pattern more clearly.

50 7 Experiments

Use the charts on the previous page to answer these questions.
- How many students remembered all 10 words correctly?
- What was the least number of words remembered?
- How many students remembered more than half of the words?
- Which way do you think shows the results for this experiment most clearly?

Display the results for your memory experiment.
Show the results for words, pictures and numbers.
- What do your charts show?

> The **mode** or **modal** value is the one with the highest frequency.
> The modal number of words remembered in the class is 9.

> The **median** is the middle number when they are put in order.
> The **range** is the difference between the largest number and the smallest number.
> Here are the numbers of words remembered by the class in order.
> Words: 5, 5, 7, 7, 7, 7, 7, 8, 8, 8, 8, 8, ⑧, 9, 9, 9, 9, 9, 9, 9, 10, 10, 10, 10, 10
> The median is 8 words.
> The range is 10 − 5 = 5 words.

> Sometimes the **mean** is used instead of the median.
> This is found by adding up all the results and dividing by the number of results there are.
> For the number of words remembered by the class:
> Total = 5+5+7+7+7+7+7+8+8+8+8+8+8+9+9+9+9+9+9+9+10+10+10+10+10 = 206
> Mean = 206 ÷ 25 = 8.24 words

- Work out the mode, median, mean and range for each of your sets of results.
- Use these values to help you write a few sentences comparing people's ability to remember words, pictures and numbers.

C Interpreting and discussing

T Write a short report on your memory experiment.
Make sure you include your comments on what you can tell from the modes, medians, ranges and means.

Use the tips below to help you.

- State clearly the question you wanted to answer.

> **Remembering words, pictures and numbers**
> We wanted to see whether there was any difference between how good young people are at remembering words, pictures and numbers.

- Describe carefully how you carried out your investigation and what you did to make sure it was done fairly.

> We chose one class at random from each year from year 7 to year 13 to take part.
> We made three charts which showed
> - 10 words that had no connection with each other
> - 10 pictures of simple objects
> - 10 numbers between 10 and 99
>
> We showed each class the 10 words for 30 seconds and then gave them 1 minute to write down as many as they could remember. The order didn't matter.
> We then did the same with the pictures and the numbers.
> We asked them to swap papers to mark them and everyone wrote their three scores on a slip of paper.

- When drawing diagrams and calculating values such as the mean, only use those that actually help you to answer your question.
- When writing about what you find, only make statements which your results clearly show are true.

> The mean and the median are highest for remembering pictures so we think that pictures are the easiest to remember. Pictures also had the highest range, which shows that the results were more spread out.

- Make some suggestions as to how you could improve your experiment or carry out more research.

> We would like to try this experiment again using 20 words, pictures and numbers as quite a few people got them all right with just 10.

8 Multiples, factors and primes

This work will help you
- work with factors, multiples and prime numbers
- find the lowest common multiple and highest common factor of two numbers
- use a factor tree to write a number as a product of primes

A Multiples   level 4

Multiples of 7 are numbers that are in the 7 times table: 7, 14, 21, 28, 35, …
Multiples of 7 can be divided exactly by 7.
For example, 42 ÷ 7 = 6 so 42 is a multiple of 7.

Lock up

A prison has 25 prisoners (one in each cell) and 25 jailers.
The cells are numbered 1 to 25.

The jailers all go to a party one night and return very merry!
- The first jailer unlocks every cell.
- The second jailer locks every cell whose number is a multiple of 2.
- The third jailer turns his key in the lock for cells whose numbers are multiples of 3. (He locks or unlocks these cells.)
- The fourth jailer turns his key in the lock for cells whose numbers are multiples of 4 … and so on till the twenty-fifth jailer.

All the jailers then fall asleep and the prison is silent.
- The prisoners all try their doors. Which ones escape?

A1 Which numbers in this list are multiples of 6?

36, 6, 3, 16, 12, 60, 600, 80

A2 Write down six different multiples of 4.

A3 Which numbers in the loop are multiples of
- (a) 5
- (b) 2
- (c) 3
- (d) 9
- (e) 2 **and** 5

(loop contains: 21, 27, 30, 6, 9, 45, 42, 15, 20, 90)

A4 List all the numbers in the loop that are odd multiples of 9.

A5 Which number in the loop is an even multiple of 7?

8 Multiples, factors and primes 53

B Factors

level 4

12 can be divided exactly by 2 ($12 \div 2 = 6$) so 2 is a **factor** of 12.

Factors can be found in pairs.

$1 \times 12 = 12$
$2 \times 6 = 12$
$3 \times 4 = 12$
So the factors of 12 are 1, 2, 3, 4, 6, 12

Factor pairs for 12

1 2 3 4 6 12

B1 One number in this list is not a factor of 8. Which is it?

1, 2, 4, 6, 8

B2 One factor of 32 is missing from this list. What is it?

16, 4, 2, 1, 32

B3 Which of these numbers are factors of 36?

5, 8, 2, 3, 4, 10, 9, 12, 36

B4 List all the factors of these numbers.

(a) 6 (b) 15 (c) 9 (d) 48 (e) 17

B5 Which numbers in the loop are

(a) factors of 8 **and** 10
(b) factors of 12 **and** 30
(c) factors of 24 **and** 36

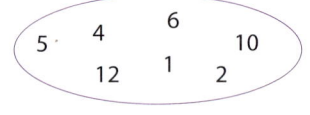

(5, 4, 6, 10, 12, 1, 2)

B6 This is a 'factor grid'.

Jim is trying to fit these numbers into the grid.

1 2 3 4

	is a factor of 8	is a factor of 18
is a factor of 12	4	
is a factor of 15		

He can put the 4 here as it is a factor of 12 **and** a factor of 8.

Copy and complete the factor grid. You can only have one number in each box.

B7 Show how you can fit these numbers into this grid, one number in each box.

3 4 5 6

	is a factor of 15	is a factor of 12
is a factor of 6		
is a factor of 20		

54 8 Multiples, factors and primes

Grid factor a game for three or more players

What you need

- Each player needs to make a copy of the grid shown on the right.
- One person is the 'caller' and needs a dice.

On each turn

- The caller rolls a dice and calls out the number on the dice.
- Each player writes the number in one of their boxes (if it fits).

	is a factor of 15	is a factor of 12
is a factor of 20		
is a factor of 24		

You can only have **one** number in each box.

The points

- After four numbers have been called, each number in the grid is worth a point.
- Start another round on a new grid.

The winner

- The winner is the player with most points at the end of the game. (A game can have as many rounds as you like.)

C Multiples and factors   level 4

C1 Decide whether each statement is true or false.

(a) 5 is a factor of 10.   (b) 6 is a multiple of 12.   (c) 14 is a multiple of 7.

(d) 8 is a factor of 4.   (e) 28 is a multiple of 4.   (f) 4 is a factor of 28.

C2 (a) Write down three different factors of 10.

(b) List three different multiples of 10.

C3 Which word, either 'factor' or 'multiple', should go in each statement?

(a) 6 is a ……… of 30.   (b) 30 is a ……… of 6.

(c) 20 is a ……… of 5.   (d) 20 is a ……… of 40.

C4 Write down a number from the loop to complete each statement.

(a) ■ is a factor of 16.   (b) ■ is a multiple of 9.

(c) 7 is a factor of ■.   (d) ■ is a multiple of 32.

(e) 15 is a factor of ■.   (f) 26 is a multiple of ■.

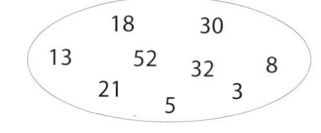

(18   30   13   52   32   8   21   5   3)

C5 (a) Write down a number that is a multiple of 5 **and** a factor of 30.

(b) Write down a number that is a factor of 24 **and** a multiple of 4.

D Common multiples and factors

Common multiples of two numbers are numbers that are multiples of **both** numbers.
For example
- multiples of 6 are   6, 12, **18**, 24, 30, **36**, 42, 48, **54**, 60, 66, **72**, ...
- multiples of 9 are   9, **18**, 27, **36**, 45, **54**, 63, **72**, 81, **90**, 99, ...

Common multiples appear in **both** lists.
So common multiples of 6 and 9 are 18, 36, 54, ...

The lowest number in this list is 18.
So 18 is the **lowest common multiple** of 6 and 9.   The lowest common multiple is sometimes shortened to LCM.

D1 Emma is finding common multiples of 3 and 5.

| Multiples of 3 | 3 | 6 | 9 |
| Multiples of 5 | 5 | 10 | |

(a) Copy and complete the lists to show the first ten multiples of each number.
(b) Find two common multiples of 3 and 5.
(c) What is the lowest common multiple of 3 and 5?

D2 (a) List the first ten multiples of 4.
(b) List the first ten multiples of 6.
(c) What are three common multiples of 4 and 6?
(d) What is the lowest common multiple of 4 and 6?

D3 (a) List four common multiples of 2 and 3.
(b) What is the lowest common multiple of 2 and 3?

D4 What is the lowest common multiple of
(a) 2 and 5   (b) 6 and 8   (c) 4 and 8

Common factors of two numbers are numbers that are factors of **both** numbers.
For example
- the factors of 8 are   **1**, **2**, **4**, 8
- the factors of 12 are   **1**, **2**, 3, **4**, 6, 12

Common factors appear in **both** lists.
So the common factors of 8 and 12 are 1, 2 and 4.

The highest number in this list is 4.
So 4 is the **highest common factor** of 8 and 12.   The highest common factor is sometimes shortened to HCF.

D5 (a) List the factors of 15.

(b) List the factors of 10.

(c) What are the common factors of 15 and 10?

(d) What is the highest common factor of 15 and 10?

D6 (a) Find the common factors of 12 and 20.

(b) What is the highest common factor of 12 and 20?

D7 What is the highest common factor of 10 and 14?

D8 What is the highest common factor of

(a) 9 and 12   (b) 24 and 40   (c) 8 and 21

D9 (a) Find the lowest common multiple of 6 and 15.

(b) Find the highest common factor of 6 and 15.

D10 (a) Find the lowest common multiple of 5 and 8.

(b) Find the highest common factor of 5 and 8.

D11 Two bell-ringers ring their bells like this:

   Petra – every 6 seconds
   Hera – every 5 seconds

If they both start at the same time, how long will it be before both bells ring at the same time?

D12 Two lighthouses flash like this.

   Treble rock – flashes every 8 seconds
   Start point – flashes every 10 seconds

They both flash together at midnight.
How long will it be before they next flash together?

*D13 Harry has 20p.
Amit has 36p.
Both boys buy some fruit chews.
They both spend all their money.

What is the maximum possible cost of a fruit chew?

*D14 Jane and Sue each have a bag of sweets.
The bags contain the same number of sweets.

Jane shares her bag between 5 people.
Sue shares her bag between 7 people.
There are no left-over sweets.

What is the smallest number of sweets that could be in each bag?

8 Multiples, factors and primes

E Prime numbers

A **prime number** has only two factors, 1 and the number itself.

For example,
- 7 has **two** factors (1 and 7) so 7 **is** a prime number.
- 4 has **three** factors (1, 2 and 4) so 4 **is not** a prime number.

Prime line a game for two players

What you need
- 10 counters or tiles each (one colour for each player)

How to play the game
- The first player puts down 2, 3 or 5 counters in a straight line.
- Then players take turns to add 1, 2, 3, 4 or 5 counters to the line.
- The number of counters in the line must always be a **prime number**.
  (If you cannot play, you miss your turn.
  If you make a mistake, the other player wins.)
- Carry on like this until one player has run out of counters.

The winner
- The winner is the player who gets rid of their counters first.

E1 List all the prime numbers between 1 and 20.

E2 Four of the numbers in the loop are not prime. Which ones are they?

32, 61, 97, 235, 311, 461, 140, 438

E3 Which of the numbers below are prime?

23, 25, 41, 47, 49

E4 List all the prime numbers between 30 and 40.

E5 Explain why 1 is not a prime number.

E6 Write down a number less than 10 that is
  (a) an even prime number
  (b) a prime number and a factor of 9
  (c) a prime number and a common factor of 10 and 25

F Products of prime factors

$3 \times 5 = 15$ so we can say that 15 is the **product** of 3 and 5.

Every whole number can be written as the product of a set of prime numbers.

One way to find this product is to start with a factor tree.

On the right is a factor tree for 48.

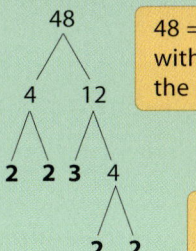

48 = 4 × 12 so we can start with this pair of factors at the ends of the branches.

Keep going until each branch ends with a **prime** factor.

The numbers at the ends of the branches give us a **product of prime factors**.

$48 = 2 \times 2 \times 2 \times 2 \times 3$

- Make two more factor trees for 48 that each start with a different pair of numbers. Do all the trees end with the same numbers?

F1 (a) Make a factor tree for 36.

(b) Copy and complete the statement below to write 36 as a product of prime factors.

$36 = \blacksquare \times \blacksquare \times \blacksquare \times \blacksquare$

F2 For each number below, make a factor tree and write the number as a product of primes.

(a) 28 (b) 40 (c) 45 (d) 300

We can use products of prime factors to find the highest common factor.

Example

Find the highest common factor of 84 and 120.

- Write each number as a product of prime factors.

    $84 = \underline{2} \times \underline{2} \times \underline{3} \times 7$
    $120 = \underline{2} \times \underline{2} \times 2 \times \underline{3} \times 5$

- Look for common prime factors.

    The factors 2, 2 and 3 are common to both products (underlined).

So the highest number that is a factor of 84 **and** a factor of 120 is $2 \times 2 \times 3$, which is **12**.

F3 (a) (i) Write 72 as a product of primes. (ii) Write 90 as a product of primes.

(b) Use your products to find the highest common factor of 72 and 90.

F4 Find the highest common factor of each pair of numbers by first writing each number as a product of prime factors.

(a) 72 and 180 (b) 90 and 105 (c) 165 and 154 (d) 104 and 234

We can also use products of prime factors to find the lowest common multiple.

Example

Find the lowest common multiple of 84 and 105.

- Write each number as a product of primes and look for common factors.

    $84 = 2 \times 2 \times \underline{3} \times \underline{7}$
    $105 = \underline{3} \times 5 \times \underline{7}$

- Look for common factors (underlined) and write down the product of the common factors.

    $\underline{3} \times \underline{7}$

- Multiply this product by all of the remaining (non-common) factors.

    $3 \times 7 \times 2 \times 2 \times 5$

So the lowest number that is a multiple of 84 **and** a multiple of 105 is $3 \times 7 \times 2 \times 2 \times 5$, which is **420**.

F5 **(a)** Write 18 and 42 as products of prime factors.

(b) Use your products to find the lowest common multiple of 18 and 42.

F6 Find the lowest common multiple of each pair of numbers by first writing each number as a product of prime factors.

(a) 12 and 20 **(b)** 14 and 15 **(c)** 28 and 42 **(d)** 84 and 120

Test yourself

T1 (a) Write down two multiples of 4.

(b) Write down two multiples of 7.

(c) Write down a number which is a multiple of both 4 and 7.

AQA

T2 Choose one number from this list to complete each sentence.

| 3 | 4 | 5 | 7 | 16 | 18 | 21 | 32 | 49 |

(a) …… is a factor of 8. **(b)** …… is a multiple of 6.

(c) …… is a common factor of 14 and 35.

OCR

T3 (a) Write down a number that is a multiple of 6 **and** a factor of 42.

(b) Write down a number that is a factor of 28 **and** prime.

T4 (a) Express the following numbers as products of their prime factors.

(i) 60 **(ii)** 96

(b) Find the highest common factor of 60 and 96.

(c) Work out the lowest common multiple of 60 and 96.

Edexcel

Review 1

1. Work out each of these.
   - (a) 4.7×10
   - (b) 2.375×100
   - (c) $425.6 \div 100$
   - (d) $278 \div 1000$

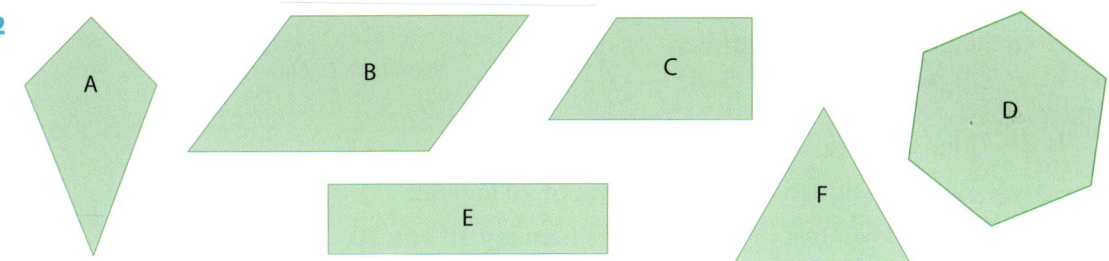

2.
   (a) Match the shapes above to these names.

   Equilateral triangle   Regular hexagon   Rectangle   Trapezium   Parallelogram   Kite

   (b) From the shapes above, name one that fits each of these descriptions.
   - (i) I have one line of reflection symmetry and no rotation symmetry.
   - (ii) All my angles are the same size and I have rotation symmetry of order 2.
   - (iii) I have two pairs of equal angles and no lines of symmetry.

3. (a) Maxine has 8 shades of eye-shadow. $\frac{3}{4}$ of them are blue. How many of her eye-shadows are blue?

   (b) She also has 10 pink lipsticks and 5 red lipsticks. In its simplest form, what fraction of her lipsticks are red?

4. What number does each of these arrows point to?

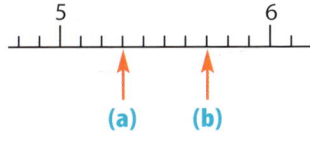

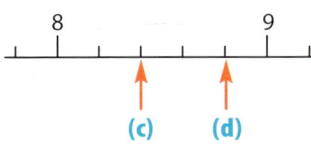

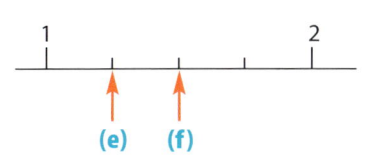

5. Solve each equation by drawing and reversing an arrow diagram.
   - (a) $4x + 1 = 29$
   - (b) $3p - 6 = 21$
   - (c) $\frac{w}{3} + 5 = 8$

6. Put these decimals in order, smallest first.   2.53   2.6   2.07

7. Calculate the missing angles in these diagrams.

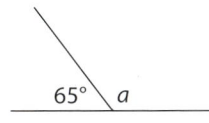

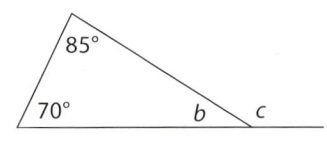

8 The dot plot shows the number of pictures remembered by students in a memory test.

  (a) How many students remembered 10 pictures?

  (b) How many students took part in the experiment?

  (c) Find the median number of pictures remembered.

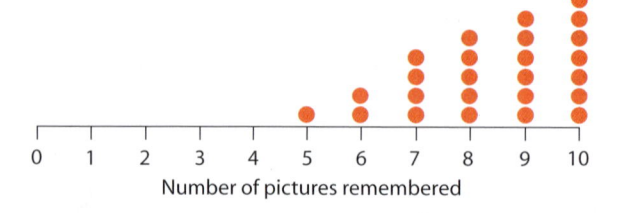

9 (a) Find a multiple of 7 between 10 and 20.

  (b) Write down two common factors of 20 and 32.

  (c) Write down two prime numbers between 10 and 20.

10 This graph is for conversion between Canadian dollars ($) and pounds (£).

  Use the graph to

  (a) change $150 into pounds (£)

  (b) change £40 into dollars ($)

  (c) change $80 into pounds (£)

  (d) change £50 into dollars ($)

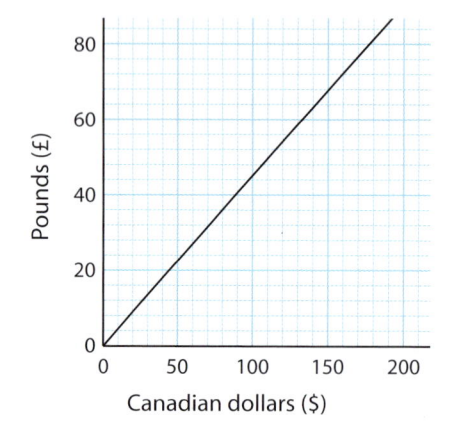

11 Katy drinks $\frac{1}{4}$ of a litre of orange juice every day. How much orange juice does she drink in a week?

12 (a) Round 6.139 to two decimal places.

  (b) Which is heavier, 6.25 kg or 6.139 kg?

13 This design has rotation symmetry of order 4. It is made from isosceles triangles.

  (a) Find the size of each marked angle.

  (b) How many lines of symmetry does the design have?

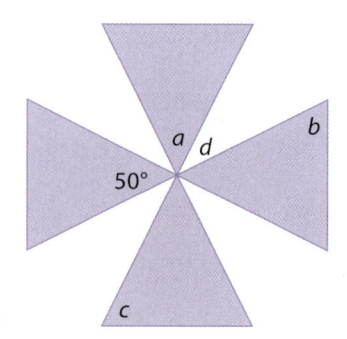

14 (a) Write 40 and 48 as products of prime factors.

  (b) Use your products to find the highest common factor of 40 and 48.

  (c) Find the lowest common multiple of 40 and 48.

9 Working with formulas 1

You should know

- if a stands for a number, you can write $4 \times a$ as $4a$
- the expression $4a + 6$ means 'multiply a by 4, then add 6'
- the expression $3(b + 5)$ means 'add 5 to b, then multiply by 3'

This work will help you

- find a formula or expression describing a pattern
- form an equation from a pattern and use it to solve a problem

A Review: expressions

Examples

Find the value of $2p$ when $p = 4$.

$2p = 2 \times 4 = 8$

Find the value of $q + 6$ when $q = 3$.

$q + 6 = 3 + 6 = 9$

Find the value of $3s + 2$ when $s = 5$.

$3s + 2 = 3 \times 5 + 2$
$= 15 + 2 = 17$

Find the value of $2(r + 1)$ when $r = 4$.

$2(r + 1) = 2 \times (4 + 1)$
$= 2 \times 5 = 10$

A1 Work out the value of each of these when $z = 6$.
   (a) $z + 4$ **(b)** $5z$ **(c)** $z - 4$ **(d)** $2z$

A2 What is the value of each of these expressions when $f = 5$?
   (a) $4f$ **(b)** $f + 4$ **(c)** $f - 4$ **(d)** $4 + f$

A3 Work out each of these when $g = 4$.
   (a) $2g + 1$ **(b)** $2(g + 1)$ **(c)** $2(1 + g)$ **(d)** $2 + g$

A4 Work out the value of the expression $4(m + 2)$ when
   (a) $m = 3$ **(b)** $m = 5$ **(c)** $m = 8$ **(d)** $m = 0$

A5 Work these out.
   (a) $10 - h$ when $h = 3$ **(b)** $4(j + 3)$ when $j = 1$ **(c)** $3k + 7$ when $k = 2$

A6 When $a = 5$, which is bigger, $2a + 1$ or $2(a + 1)$?

B Arranging tables and chairs

B1 Busby's Banquets organise meals.
They set out square tables in rows.
One of these tables needs 4 chairs.

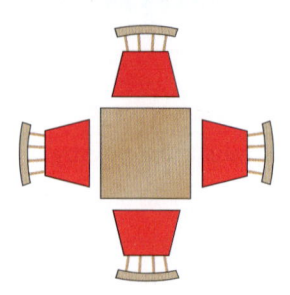

For 2 tables they need 6 chairs.

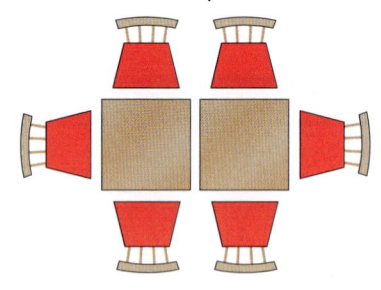

And for 3 tables they need 8 chairs.

(a) How many chairs do Busby's need for 4 square tables?

(b) How many do they need for 10 tables?

(c) How many do they need at 100 tables?

(d) Copy and complete this (mathematical) table.

Number of tables	1	2	3	4	5	6	10	100
Number of chairs	4	6	8					

(e) Which of these is correct for the rule connecting the number of square tables and the number of chairs?

number of chairs = number of tables + 2

number of chairs = number of tables × 4

number of chairs = (number of tables + 2) × 2

number of chairs = number of tables × 2 + 2

(f) Suppose t stands for the number of tables and c stands for the number of chairs.
Which of these rules is correct?

$c = t + 2$ $c = 2(t + 2)$ $c = 2t + 2$ $c = 4t$

64 9 Working with formulas 1

B2 Busby's Banquets also use rectangular tables.
Sometimes they set out the rectangular tables like this.

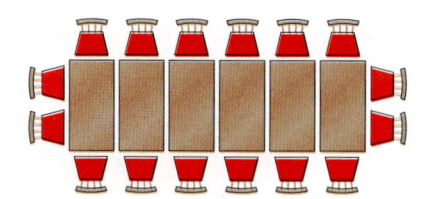

First they put out two chairs
with every table …

… then they put the four extra chairs
at the ends.

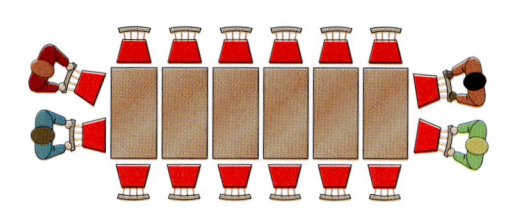

(a) How many chairs do Busby's need when they use
10 rectangular tables set out like this?

(b) How many do they need for 20 tables?

(c) For tables set out like this, copy and complete this table.

Number of tables (t)	1	2	3	4	5	6	10	100
Number of chairs (c)								

(d) Here are some rules written in words.
Which of the rules is correct?

number of chairs = (number of tables + 4) × 2

number of chairs = number of tables × 6

number of chairs = number of tables × 2 + 4

number of chairs = number of tables + 2

(e) Suppose t stands for the number of tables
and c stands for the number of chairs.

Look at these four formulas connecting c and t.

A **formula** is just
a rule using letters.

$c = t + 2$ $c = 2(t + 4)$ $c = 2t + 4$ $c = 6t$

Which of the formulas is correct?

9 Working with formulas 1   65

B3 Sometimes Busby's Banquets arrange their rectangular tables in a line.

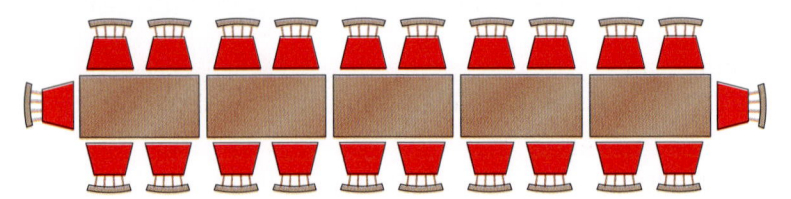

(a) If they use 10 tables in a line, how many chairs do they need?

(b) If they use 100 tables in a line, how many chairs do they need?

(c) Write a rule in words telling you the number of chairs you need when you know the number of tables.

Start your rule like this: number of chairs = ...

(d) Which of these formulas tells you the number of chairs (c) when you know the number of tables (t)?

$c = t + 2$ $c = 6t$ $c = t + 4$

$c = 4t + 2$ $c = 4(t + 2)$

B4 Here is another arrangement using larger tables.

(a) How many chairs does this arrangement need for 100 tables?

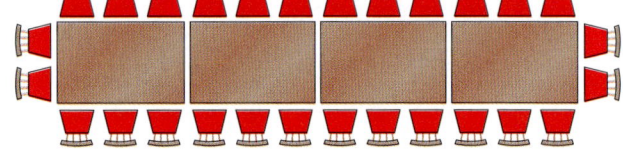

(b) Write a rule in words telling you the number of chairs you need when you know the number of tables.

(c) Write your rule as a formula, using letters. Use t to stand for the number of tables and c to stand for the number of chairs.

B5 This arrangement uses triangular tables.

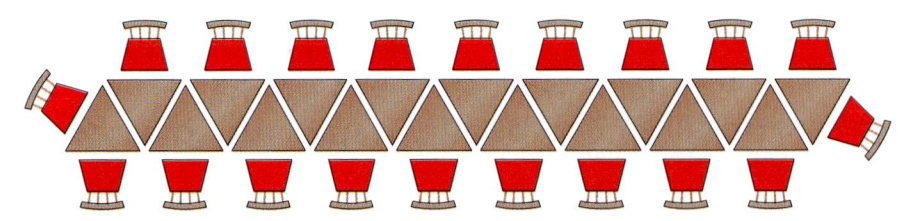

(a) For this arrangement, work out a rule in words telling you the number of chairs you need when you know the number of tables.

(b) Write your rule as a formula, where t stands for the number of tables and c stands for the number of chairs.

C Designing pendants

C1 James makes pendants in gold.
He links together small gold bars to make each pendant.

He makes different types of pendant.
These are SuperDrop pendants.

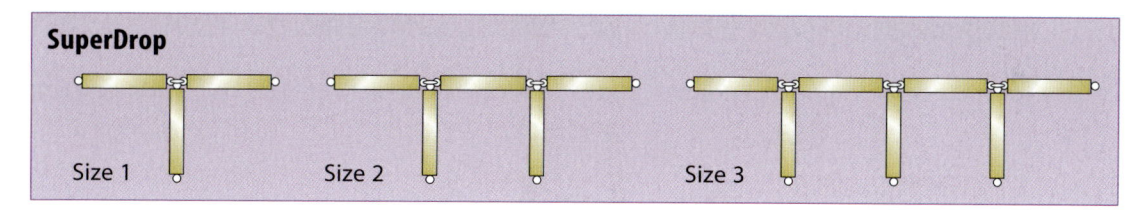

SuperDrop

Size 1   Size 2   Size 3

(a) How many gold bars are there in the size 1 SuperDrop?

(b) How many gold bars are there in   (i) a size 2   (ii) a size 3

(c) How many **extra** bars do you add to a size 3 SuperDrop to make a size 4?

(d) Without sketching, work out the number of gold bars in
   (i) a size 10 SuperDrop   (ii) a size 20 SuperDrop

(e) Copy and complete this table for the SuperDrop pendants.

SuperDrop size (n)	1	2	3	4	5	6	10	20
Number of bars (g)								

(f) Which of these rules is correct for the SuperDrops?

A number of gold bars = size number × 3

B number of gold bars = size number × 2 + 1

C number of gold bars = size number + 2

D number of gold bars = (size number + 1) × 2

(g) Write a formula using letters for the number of gold bars in the SuperDrops.
Use g to stand for the number of gold bars and n to stand for the size number of the SuperDrop.

C2 James also makes SuperSquare pendants.
Here is a size 3 and a size 5 SuperSquare.

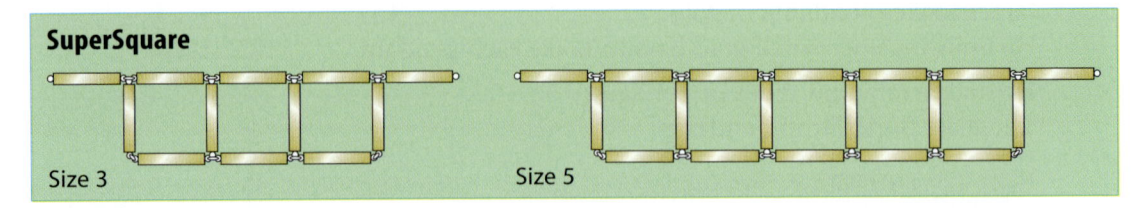

SuperSquare

Size 3   Size 5

To make SuperSquare pendants, James first makes up sets of bars in threes, like this.

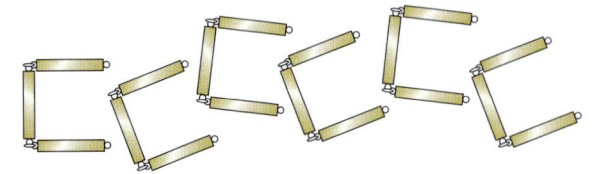

Then, if he wants a size 4 SuperSquare, he first joins together 4 of his sets.

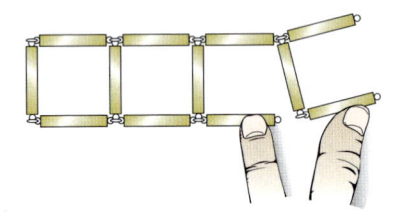

Then he adds the extra bars he needs to complete the pendant.

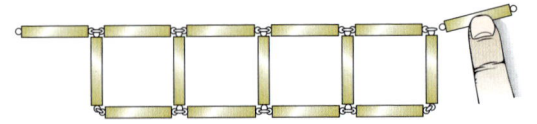

(a) How many gold bars does James use in a size 4 SuperSquare?

(b) How many gold bars are in a size 10 SuperSquare?

(c) If James made a size 100 SuperSquare, how many bars would he need?

(d) Explain how you can work out the number of gold bars needed when you know the size number.

(e) Choose one of the expressions on the right to complete this sentence.

If the size number of a SuperSquare is n then the number of gold bars in it is …

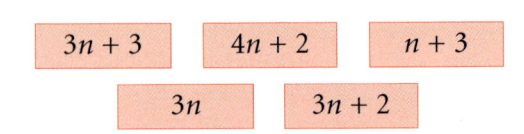

$3n + 3$ $4n + 2$ $n + 3$

$3n$ $3n + 2$

C3 These are two of James's Glissando pendants.
On the left is a size 2. On the right is a size 4.

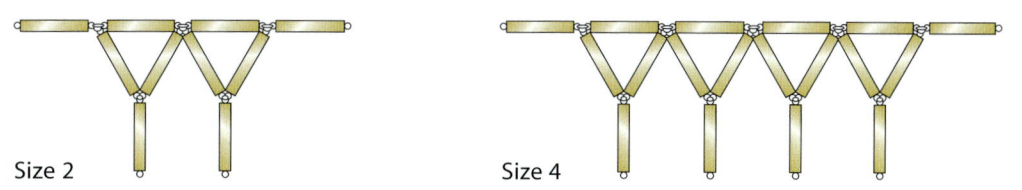

Size 2   Size 4

Which of these expressions tells you the number of gold bars
in a size n Glissando pendant?

| $4n$ | $4n - 2$ | $4n + 2$ | $6n$ | $4(n + 2)$ |

C4 Below are three more of James's pendant designs.
On the right are some expressions for
the number of gold bars in a size n pendant.

$3n + 1$ $6n + 2$

$5n + 3$

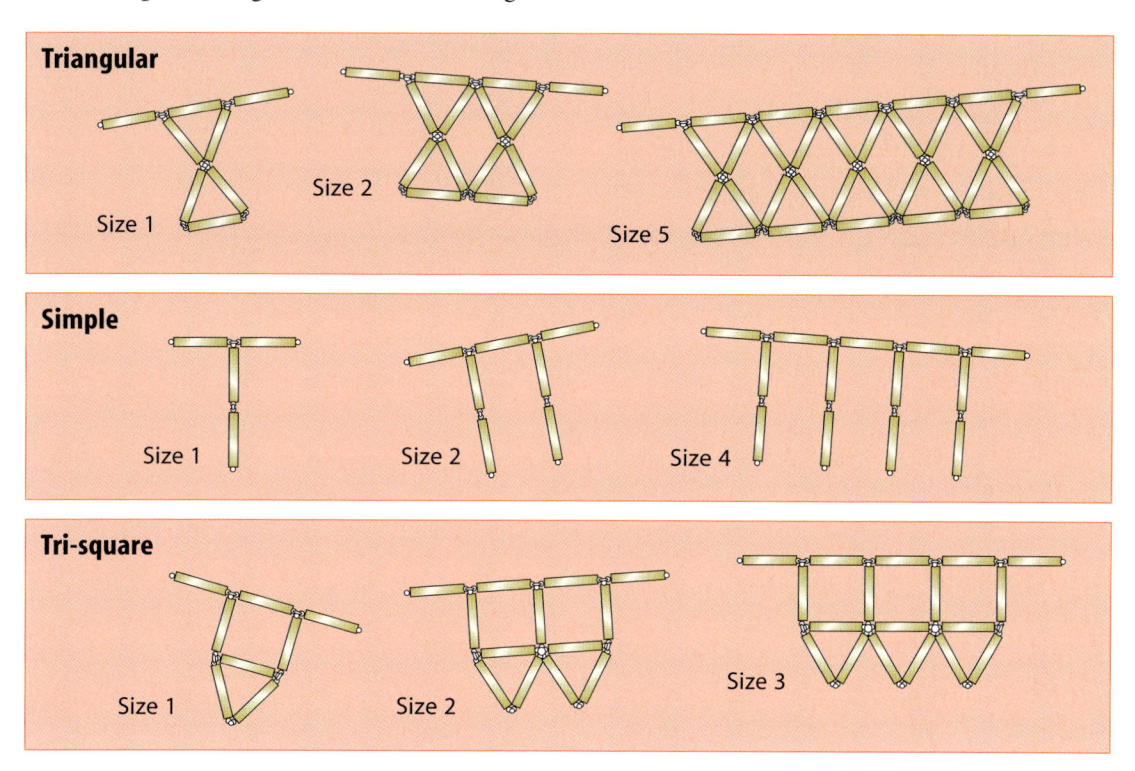

Which expression goes with which design?

Triangular

Size 1   Size 2   Size 5

Simple

Size 1   Size 2   Size 4

Tri-square

Size 1   Size 2   Size 3

C5 In James's Expressive pendant there are $3n + 2$ bars in a size n pendant.
  (a) How many bars are there in the size 1 pendant?
  (b) How many are there in the size 2 pendant?
  (c) Draw a sketch of what you think James's size 1 and
      size 2 Expressive pendants might look like.

9 Working with formulas 1

D Equations and arrow diagrams

Here are two of James's Janglie necklaces.

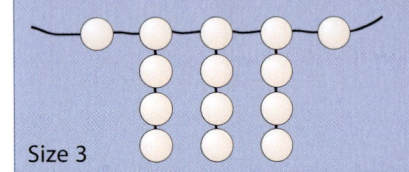

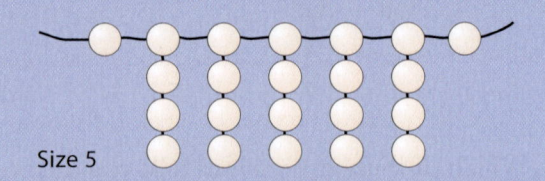

Size 3   Size 5

A size 3 Janglie has $4 \times 3 + 2$ pearls in it.
A size 5 Janglie has $4 \times 5 + 2$ pearls in it.

A size n Janglie will have $4 \times n + 2$ or $4n + 2$ pearls in it.

A customer wants a Janglie with 150 pearls in it!
Which size Janglie should James make?

We can solve this problem like this.

The number of pearls in a size n Janglie is $4n + 2$.
We want to find when the number of pearls is 150.

So we want to find when $4n + 2$ is 150.

We can write the equation $4n + 2 = 150$.
Now we can solve the equation using arrow diagrams.

- Draw an arrow diagram for the equation.

- Reverse the arrow diagram to find the value of n.

$4n + 2 = 150$

$n \xrightarrow{\times 4} 4n \xrightarrow{+ 2} 4n + 2$

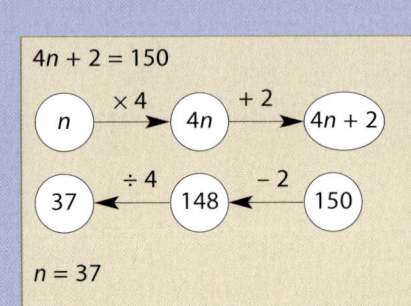

$37 \xleftarrow{\div 4} 148 \xleftarrow{- 2} 150$

$n = 37$

- Check that your value of n works in the original problem.

Check
When $n = 37$, the necklace needs
$4 \times 37 + 2$ pearls
$= 148 + 2$
$= 150$ pearls, which is correct.

D1 A size n Janglie necklace has $4n + 2$ pearls in it.
One size of Janglie has 70 pearls in it.

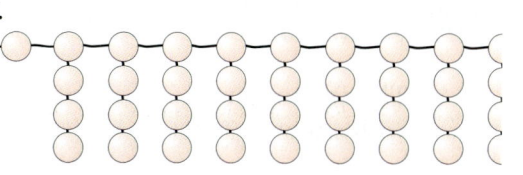

Copy and complete this working to work out which size Janglie it is.

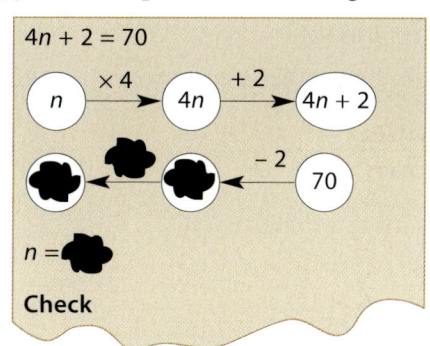

$4n + 2 = 70$

$n \xrightarrow{\times 4} 4n \xrightarrow{+2} 4n + 2$

$\blacksquare \xleftarrow{} \blacksquare \xleftarrow{-2} 70$

$n = \blacksquare$

Check

D2 A customer orders a Janglie necklace with 94 pearls.
Work out which size Janglie it is.
Show your working as in question D1.

D3 A size n Tribar pendant is made from $3n + 4$ gold bars.

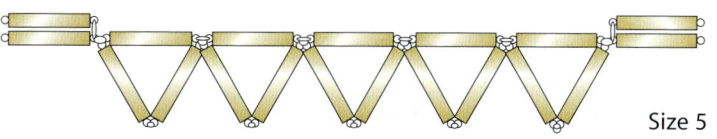

Size 5

James makes a Tribar using 55 gold bars.

Copy and complete this working to find out what size the Tribar is.

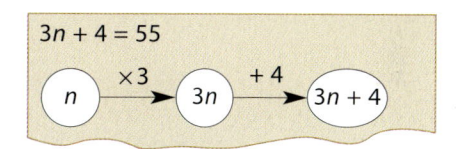

$3n + 4 = 55$

$n \xrightarrow{\times 3} 3n \xrightarrow{+4} 3n + 4$

D4 Below are three sizes of James's DeLuxe necklace.

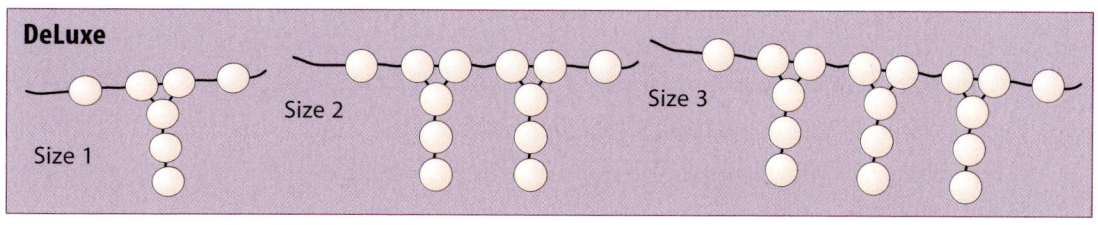

DeLuxe

Size 1   Size 2   Size 3

(a) Which of the expressions on the right tells you the number of pearls in a size n DeLuxe necklace?

$n + 2$ $7n$ $5n + 2$
$n + 5$ $2n + 5$

(b) A customer wants a DeLuxe necklace made from 122 pearls.
Work out what size it is.
Show all your working and check your answer.

9 Working with formulas 1   71

Test yourself

T1 This picture shows a table arrangement with a row of 3 tables

(a) How many chairs are there in this row of 3 tables?

(b) How many chairs will there be in a row of 4 tables?

(c) Work out the number of chairs needed for 100 tables set out in a row like this.

(d) Copy and complete this table for the arrangement.

Number of tables	1	2	3	4	100
Number of chairs	5	8	11		

(e) Which of these formulas tells you the number of chairs (c) when you know the number of tables (t)?

$c = 3t + 2$ $c = 2t + 3$ $c = 5t$ $c = t + 2$ $c = 2t - 1$

T2 Here are three sizes of Black Beauty necklaces. They are made from black pearls.

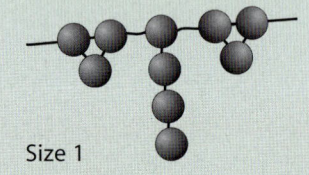

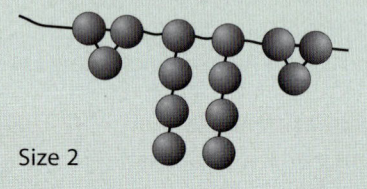

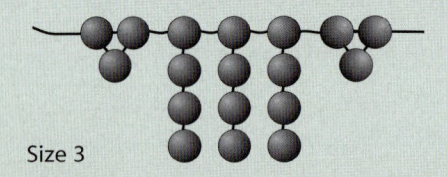

Size 1

Size 2

Size 3

(a) Which of these expressions tells you the number of black pearls in a size n Black Beauty necklace?

$4n$ $10n$ $4n + 6$ $n + 6$ $6n + 4$

One size of Black Beauty necklace uses 90 black pearls.

(b) Write down an equation that tells you this.

(c) Use arrow diagrams to work out which size necklace it is.

(d) Check that your answer is correct.

10 Representing 3-D objects

You will revise
- drawing three-dimensional objects
- drawing nets for three-dimensional objects whose faces are rectangles or equilateral triangles

This work will help you
- show three-dimensional objects in two dimensions using plans and views
- recognise reflection symmetry in three-dimensional objects

You need sheets F1–9, F1–10, F1–11, multilink cubes and a mirror.

A The Soma cube

This photograph shows the pieces of a Soma cube.
The pieces fit together to make a large cube.

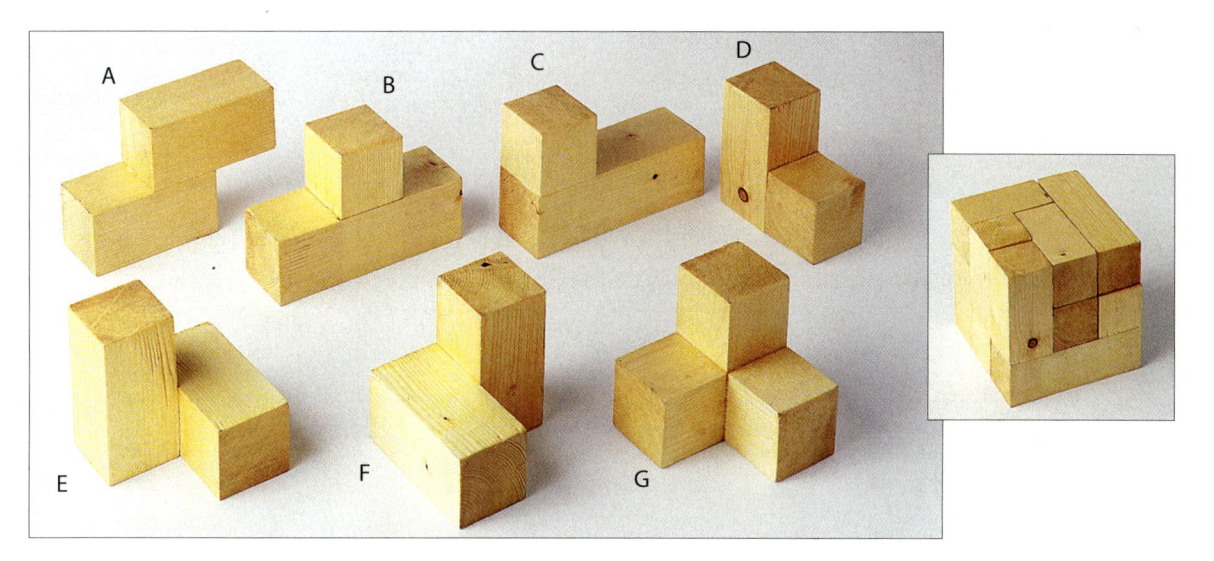

Each of these seven pieces can be made using cubes.
For example, piece A can be made with four cubes.

A1 (a) How many cubes would be needed to make each of the other pieces?

(b) Which pieces have the same volume?

A2 Here is piece E drawn on triangular dotty paper.
- Draw the rest of the pieces on triangular dotty paper.
- Shade sides that face the same direction in the same way, to help show the object more clearly.

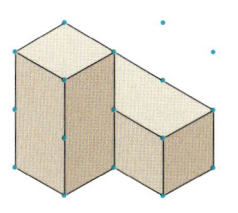

10 Representing 3-D objects   73

The Soma cube

The Soma cube puzzle was devised by the Danish mathematician Piet Hein in 1929.

Do a web search for Soma cube.
There are puzzles and other activities, some of them interactive.

B Plan and elevations

Another way of showing a 3-D object on paper is to draw the view from three different directions:

- a plan view
- a side view
- a front view

A front or side view can also be called an **elevation**.

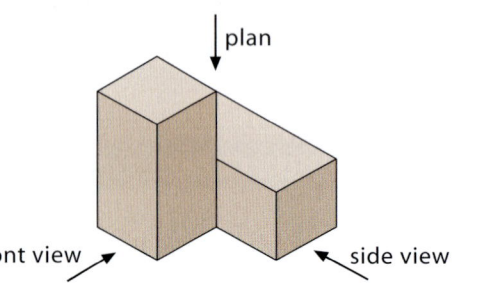

This is a front view of the Soma cube piece above.

This line is dotted because it is hidden in this view.

B1 Which of these are possible plan views of the Soma cube piece above?

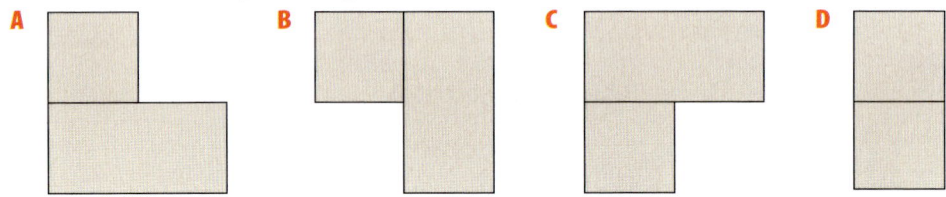

A   B   C   D

B2 Draw the side view of the Soma cube piece above.

B3 This is a plan view of one of the Soma cube pieces.

Which of these is the front view?

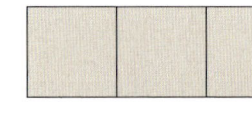

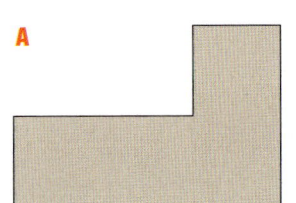

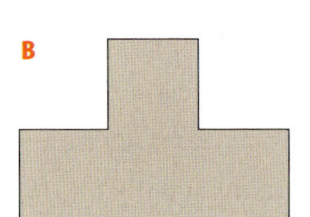

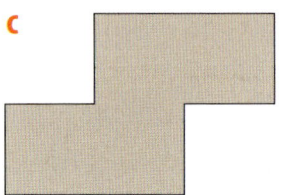

A   B   C

B4 Choose another Soma cube piece and draw the three views of it.

B5 This diagram shows a solid object with some measurements.

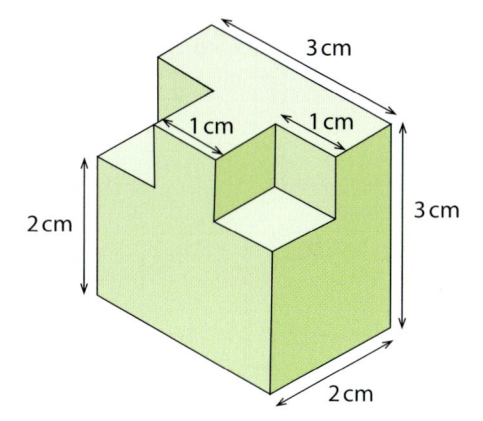

(a) Which one of the diagrams below is a full-scale view of this object?

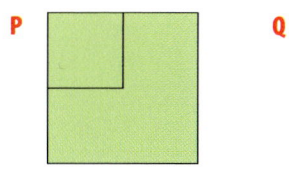

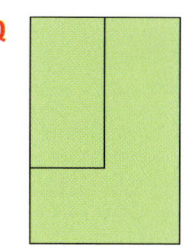

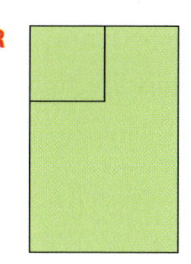

P   Q   R   S

Use centimetre squared paper.
(b) Draw a full-scale plan view of this object.
(c) Draw a full-scale front view of this object.

B6 This object has been made from seven centimetre cubes.

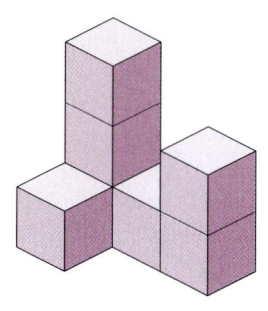

Draw full-size on centimetre squared paper
(a) a plan view
(b) a side view
(c) a front view

10 Representing 3-D objects 75

B7 These are views of some everyday objects.
For each object there are two views, which may be front, side or plan.
Identify the objects and sketch the missing view of each one.

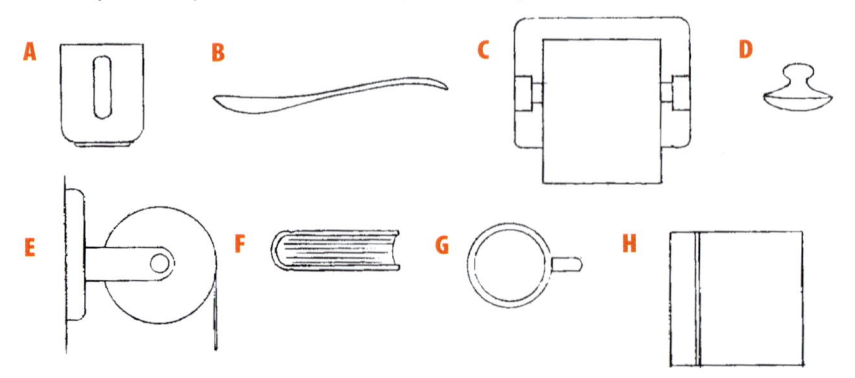

A B C D

E F G H

B8 Four views of this model are shown below.

(a) Match each view to one of the directions shown by arrows.

(b) The view from one direction is missing. Draw this view.

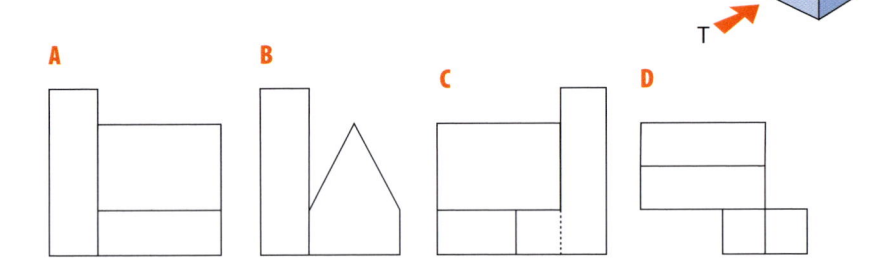

A B C D

B9 (a) Draw a full-size plan view of this shape.

(b) Draw a full-size side view of this shape from direction S.
Show any hidden edges with dotted lines.

(c) Use your drawings to measure the length of the sloping edge AB.

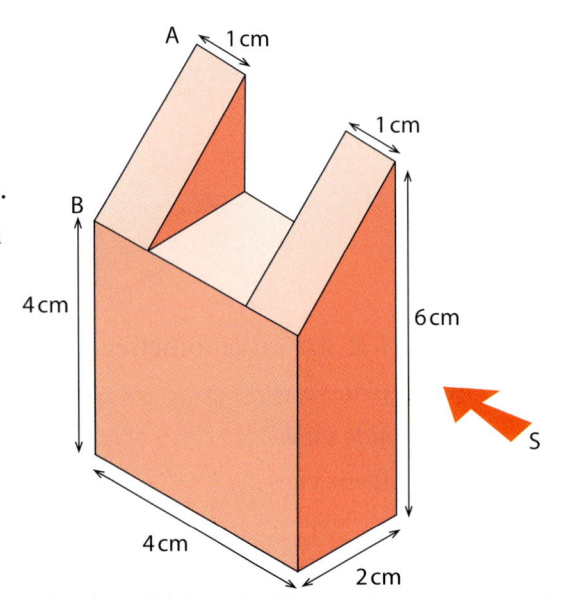

C Nets

This flat design can be folded together to make a cube.

A flat shape which makes up to a 3-D shape without overlapping is called a **net**.

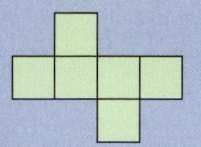

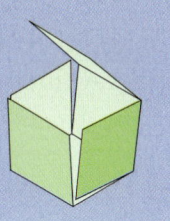

C1 Which of these are possible nets for a cube?

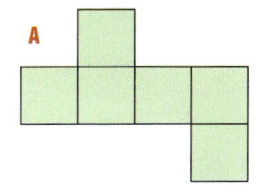

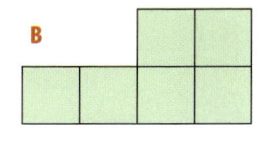

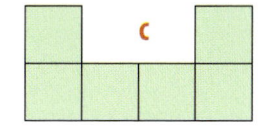

A   B   C

C2 There are 11 possible different nets of a cube.
Draw four of them on squared paper.

C3 This is a tetrahedron.
It has four faces that are all equilateral triangles.
Which of these are nets of a tetrahedron?

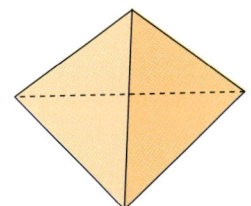

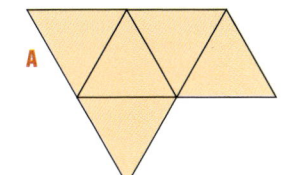

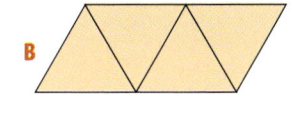

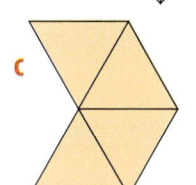

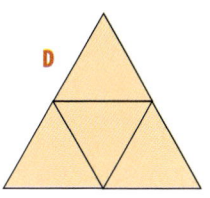

A   B   C   D

C4 This is a cuboid measuring 4 cm by 6 cm by 8 cm.
Draw an accurate net for this cuboid on centimetre squared paper.

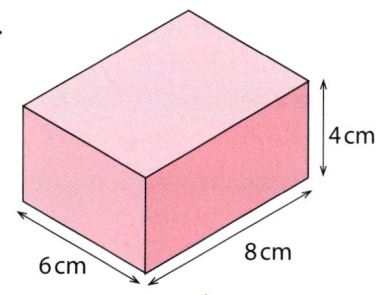

4 cm
6 cm
8 cm

*C5 This is an octahedron
It has eight faces that are all equilateral triangles.
Draw a net of an octahedron on triangular dotty paper.

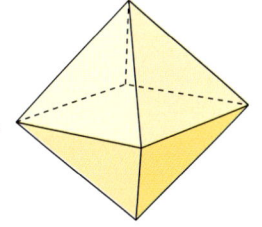

10 Representing 3-D objects 77

D Prisms

T A prism is a solid shape with a cross-section that is the same all the way through.

This cross-section is the same all the way through.

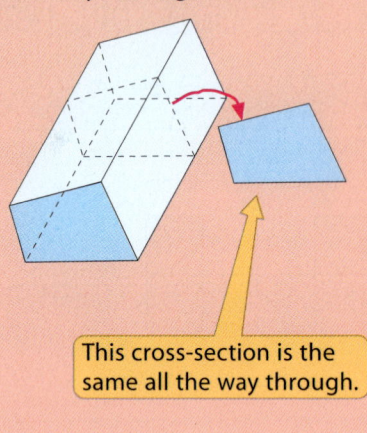

- For each prism here, what shape is the cross-section that is the same all the way through?

D1 (a) Which of these objects are prisms?

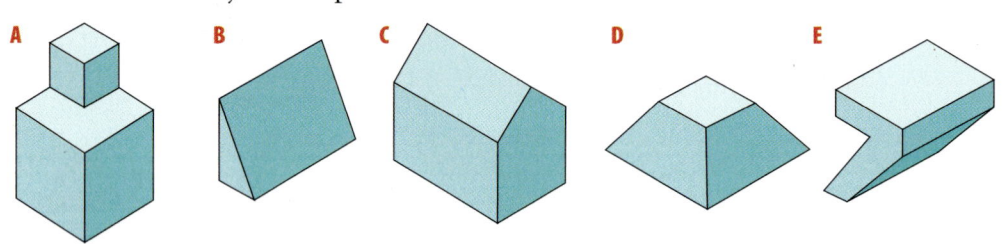

A B C D E

(b) For each object that is a prism, sketch the cross-section.

D2 This is a triangular prism.
The ends of the prism are equilateral triangles.

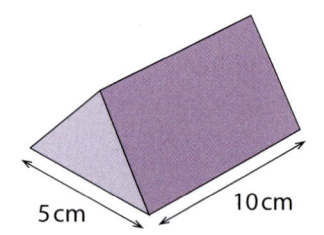

(a) Draw a rectangle 10 cm by 5 cm in the middle of a sheet of paper.

(b) Use this rectangle to complete an accurate net for this prism.

5 cm   10 cm

D3 This is a prism with a trapezium cross-section.
The front view is drawn full size on sheet F1–9.
On sheet F1–9…

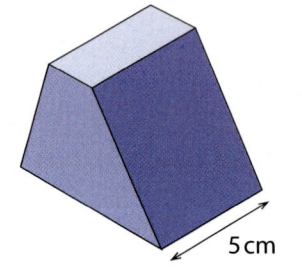

(a) Draw a full-size side view of this prism.

(b) Draw a full-size plan view of this prism.

5 cm

78   10 Representing 3-D objects

E Reflection symmetry

Mirror images

This shape is made from five multilink cubes.

What would the reflection of this shape in the mirror look like?
Can you make the shape that is the reflection?

Make some different shapes using five multilink cubes.
Ask a partner to make the reflection of your shape.
Check with a mirror.

Are any of the reflections identical to the original shape?

Do you get a different shape if you put the mirror in a different position?

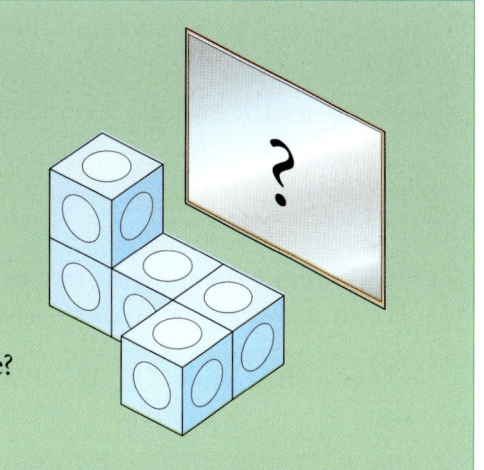

E1 This shape is made from five multilink cubes. Which of the shapes below is a mirror image of this shape?

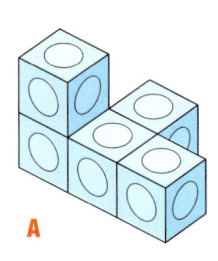

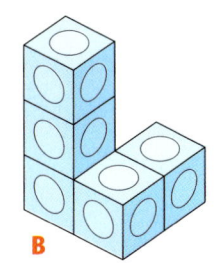

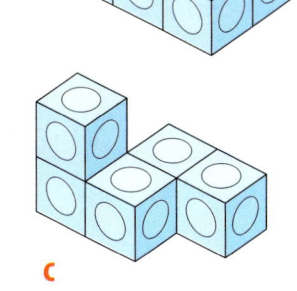

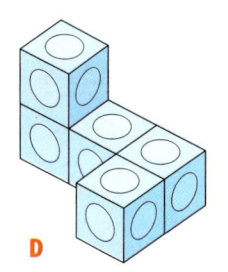

A   B   C   D

E2 Match each of these shapes to its mirror image.

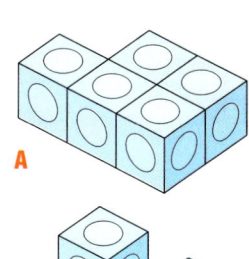

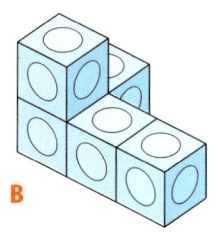

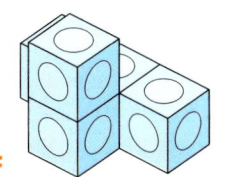

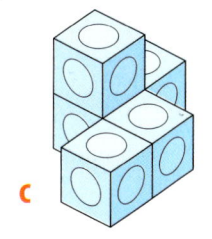

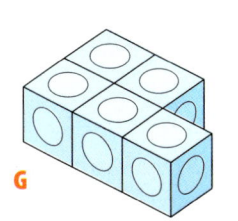

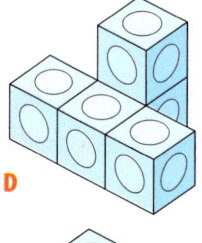

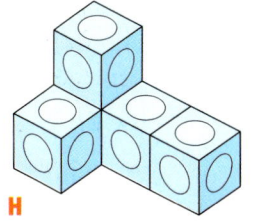

A   B   C   D

E   F   G   H

10 Representing 3-D objects   79

T This Soma cube piece has been cut in half and placed against a mirror.

The reflection makes the piece look whole again.
This whole shape has **reflection symmetry**.

Is there any other way this Soma piece could be cut so that half placed against a mirror gives the whole shape?

In a situation like this, the position of the mirror is called a **plane of symmetry** of the whole 3-D shape.

E3 On sheet F1–10 are some shapes shown cut by a mirror.
Draw the other half of each shape.

E4 How many planes of symmetry does each of these Soma cube pieces have?

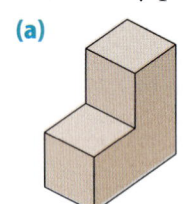

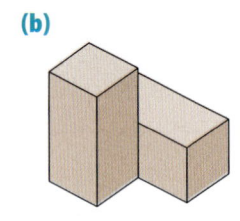

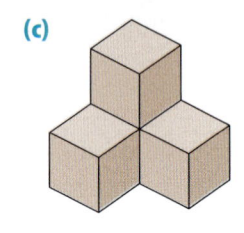

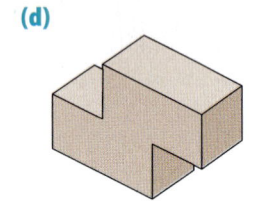

(a)   (b)   (c)   (d)

E5 This shape has been made from multilink cubes.
It has no planes of symmetry.

(a) Make this shape from multilink cubes.

(b) Add one cube to make it symmetrical.

(c) Sketch your shape on triangular dotty paper.

Make up some puzzles like these to try on a partner.

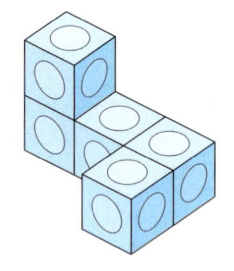

E6 How many planes of symmetry does each of these shapes have?

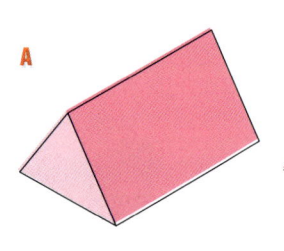

A Equilateral triangle prism

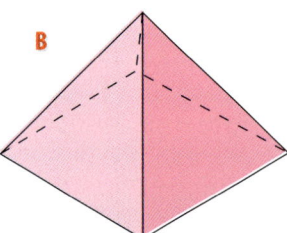

B Square-based pyramid

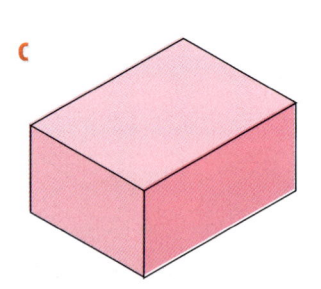

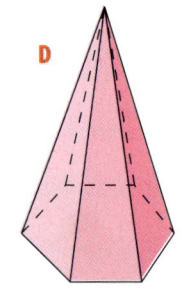

C Cuboid

D Regular-hexagon-based pyramid

80   10 Representing 3-D objects

Test yourself

T1 This diagram shows a box in the shape of a cuboid.
  (a) How many planes of symmetry does this box have?
  (b) Draw a full-sized net for this box.

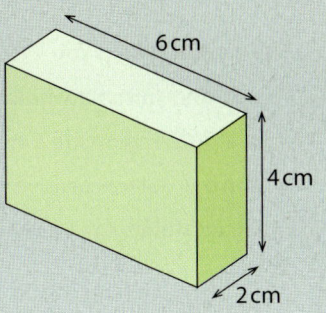

T2 A prism made from some centimetre cubes is drawn full-scale on centimetre dotty paper.
  (a) How many planes of symmetry does this prism have?
  (b) How many centimetre cubes are there in this prism?
  (c) Draw a full-size plan, front and side view of this solid.

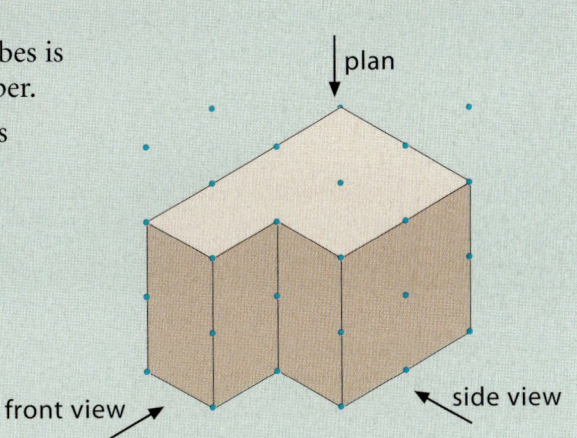

T3 This is a sketch of a house.

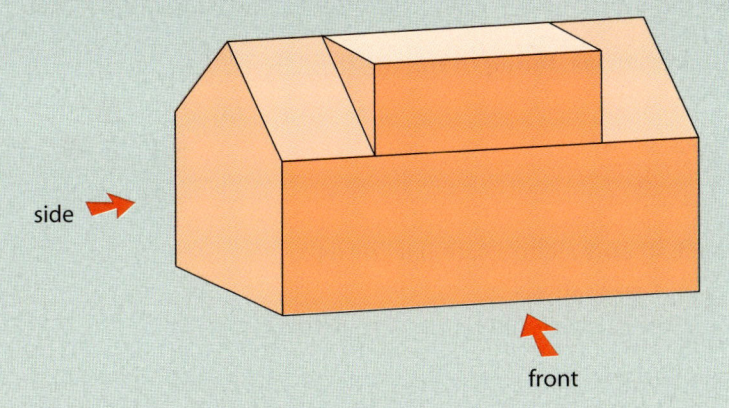

The front and side views are drawn accurately on sheet F1–11. Draw the plan view of the house on the sheet.

OCR

10 Representing 3-D objects 81

11 Written calculation 1

This work will help you
- add and subtract whole numbers and decimals
- multiply and divide a three-digit whole number or decimal by a one-digit number
- solve problems involving multiplication and division

You need sheets F1–12 and F1–13.

A Adding and subtracting whole numbers and decimals level 4

Examples

6.82 + 1.3 →
```
  6.82
+ 1.30
──────
  8.12
```

9.7 – 2.63 →
```
  9.⁶7̸¹0
– 2.6 3
──────
  7.0 7
```

Line up the decimal points. Putting in an extra zero can help.

A1 Work these out.
(a) 420 + 365 (b) 756 – 215 (c) 306 + 78 (d) 940 – 526 (e) 385 – 69

A2 Work these out.
(a) 1.65 + 2.31 (b) 8.34 – 5.12 (c) 4.2 + 2.68 (d) 7.43 – 2.6 (e) 9.8 – 3.65

A3 Copy and complete these calculations, filling in the missing digits.

(a)
```
   5 ■ 6
 + ■ 1 2
 ───────
   9 0 8
```

(b)
```
   3 5 ■
 – 2 6 8
 ───────
     ■ 2
```

(c)
```
   1 . 6
 + ■ . 5 2
 ─────────
   3 . ■ ■
```

(d)
```
   3 . ■ 1
 – 1 . 1 ■
 ─────────
   ■ . 4 8
```

A4 Tania buys a magazine for £3.50 and a chocolate bar for 64p.
(a) How much does she spend altogether?
(b) She pays with a £10 note. How much change does she get?

A5 Chris has a piece of wood 1.8 m long.
He cuts off 1.25 m to make a shelf.
How long is the piece he has left?

A6 Shohan makes fruit punch.
He mixes 0.6 litres of apple juice, 0.25 litres of mango juice and 0.3 litres of orange juice.
How much punch does he make altogether?

B Multiplying whole numbers   level 4

$$271 \times 6$$

```
  2 7 1
×     6
-------
1 6 2 6
    4
```

	200	70	1
6	1200	420	6

$1200 + 420 + 6 = 1626$

- Which method would you use?

B1 Work these out.

(a) 621×3 (b) 627×6 (c) 107×5 (d) 2×783 (e) 8×960

B2 Do the puzzles on sheet F1–12.

B3

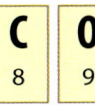

U	A	K	R	L	E	W	M	C	O
0	1	2	3	4	5	6	7	8	9

For each multiplication below, work out the answer and then use the code above to find a bird.
For example, 499×8 gives ROOK.

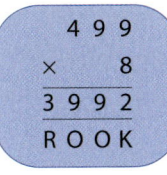

```
  4 9 9
×     8
-------
3 9 9 2
R O O K
```

(a) 6×17 (b) 114×5 (c) 241×4 (d) 2×199

(e) 4×1033 (f) 2099×4 (g) 8977×8 (h) $11\,875 \times 7$

B4 Copy these and fill in the missing digits.

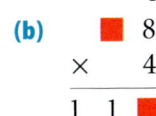

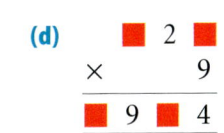

(a)
```
    1 ■
×     7
-------
  ■ 0 5
```

(b)
```
    ■ 8
×     4
-------
  1 1 ■
```

(c)
```
    ■ 7 ■
×       3
---------
  ■ 4 3 7
```

(d)
```
    ■ 2 ■
×       9
---------
  ■ 9 ■ 4
```

B5 There are 568 ml of milk in a pint.
How many ml of milk are in 3 pints?

B6 Tickets for a school play cost £4 each.
249 tickets are sold.
How much money is raised from the sale of tickets?

B7 The entry fee for a fun run is £8.
How much money is collected altogether if 265 people enter the run?

C Multiplying decimals

Examples

6.4×3 → $\begin{array}{r} 6.4 \\ \times 3 \\ \hline 19.2 \\ 1 \end{array}$

5.35×8 → $\begin{array}{r} 5.35 \\ \times 8 \\ \hline 42.80 \\ 24 \end{array}$ ← You could write this answer as 42.8.

C1 Work these out.

(a) 7.2×4 (b) 18.6×3 (c) 3.49×2 (d) 14.2×9

C2 Choose numbers from the loop to make these multiplications correct.
You can use each number more than once.

(a) ■ × ■ = 4.5 (b) ■ × ■ = 0.8
(c) ■ × ■ = 9.6 (d) ■ × ■ = 12
(e) ■ × ■ = 6   (f) ■ × ■ = 2

(0.4   0.1
  1.2 1.5 8
   5   3)

C3 Jane buys 6 sandwiches.
Each sandwich costs £1.52.
How much does she spend on sandwiches?

C4 Work these out.

(a) 6×2.15 (b) 2.09×8 (c) 4×3.25 (d) 12.48×7

C5 Do the puzzles on sheet F1–13.

C6 Nine cars are placed in a line, end to end.
Each car is 3.24 metres long.
How long is the line of cars?

C7 This table shows some approximate metric and imperial conversions.

Use these conversions to answer these questions.

(a) Two villages are 8 miles apart.
How far is this in kilometres?

(b) John cycles 7 kilometres to his evening class.
How far is this in miles?

(c) Gail's baby weighs 6 kg.
How heavy is her baby in pounds?

(d) Kate's weekend bag weighs 9 pounds.
Convert this weight to kg.

(e) Spen is making a patchwork quilt.
He is using square pieces that are 5 inches wide.
How wide are his pieces in cm?

Metric		Imperial
1 kg	=	2.2 pounds
0.45 kg	=	1 pound
1 km	=	0.6 mile
1.6 km	=	1 mile
2.54 cm	=	1 inch

D Dividing whole numbers level 4

Examples

$147 \div 3$ → $3\overline{)14^27}$ with quotient 49

$6751 \div 8$ → $8\overline{)67^35^31}$ with quotient 843 remainder 7

D1 Work these out.
- (a) 92 ÷ 4
- (b) 153 ÷ 3
- (c) 145 ÷ 5
- (d) 204 ÷ 6
- (e) 408 ÷ 2
- (f) 336 ÷ 7
- (g) 232 ÷ 8
- (h) 477 ÷ 9

D2 144 students divide into 9 equal groups.
How many students are in each group?

D3 Work these out.
- (a) 4740 ÷ 3
- (b) 2952 ÷ 8
- (c) 2268 ÷ 7
- (d) 4536 ÷ 9

D4 Find four matching pairs of divisions that give the same answer.
Which is the odd one out?

- **A** 2248 ÷ 4
- **B** 624 ÷ 6
- **C** 680 ÷ 5
- **D** 2810 ÷ 5
- **E** 208 ÷ 2
- **F** 789 ÷ 3
- **G** 225 ÷ 9
- **H** 1841 ÷ 7
- **I** 1088 ÷ 8

D5 Five teachers share 127 rulers.
- (a) How many rulers does each teacher get?
- (b) How many rulers are left over?

D6 Do each division below and find the remainder.
Then use the code to get a letter for each remainder.

Remainder	0	1	2	3	4	5	6	7	8	9
	I	L	M	U	P	O	V	E	R	A

Rearrange the nine letters to make the name of a city.

- (a) 389 ÷ 5
- (b) 673 ÷ 2
- (c) 293 ÷ 6
- (d) 5851 ÷ 7
- (e) 3209 ÷ 4
- (f) 2215 ÷ 8
- (g) 1133 ÷ 9
- (h) 5286 ÷ 3
- (i) 6785 ÷ 10

D7 A florist has 100 tulips.
She sells them in bunches of 8.
How many bunches can she make?

D8 167 people are going to a wedding by taxi.
Each taxi carries 5 people.
How many taxis will be needed?

E Dividing decimals

Examples

$7.44 \div 6$ → $6\overline{)7.^14^24}$ gives 1.24

$15.8 \div 4$ → $4\overline{)15.^38^20}$ gives 3.95

To divide you sometimes need to put in a zero.

E1 Work these out.
(a) $12.8 \div 2$
(b) $8.7 \div 3$
(c) $6.4 \div 4$
(d) $18.35 \div 5$
(e) $25.12 \div 8$
(f) $30.03 \div 7$
(g) $1.23 \div 3$
(h) $3.42 \div 9$

E2 A piece of cheese that weighs 5.28 kg is cut into four equal pieces. How heavy is each piece?

E3 Find four matching pairs of divisions that give the same answer. Which is the odd one out?

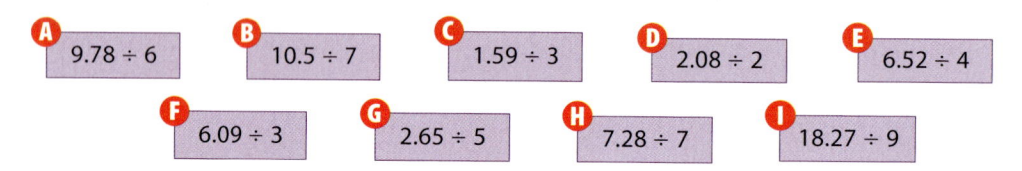

A $9.78 \div 6$ B $10.5 \div 7$ C $1.59 \div 3$ D $2.08 \div 2$ E $6.52 \div 4$
F $6.09 \div 3$ G $2.65 \div 5$ H $7.28 \div 7$ I $18.27 \div 9$

E4 Work these out.
(a) $7.3 \div 2$
(b) $5.4 \div 4$
(c) $17.2 \div 8$
(d) $1.3 \div 5$

E5 Marco shares 1.5 litres of orange juice equally between 4 glasses. How much juice is in each glass?

Example

$23 \div 4$ → $4\overline{)23.^30^20}$ gives 5.75

To divide you sometimes need to put in the decimal point and extra zeros.

E6 Work these out.
(a) $13 \div 2$
(b) $14 \div 4$
(c) $19 \div 5$
(d) $28 \div 8$

E7 Jane makes 12 litres of lemonade. She stores it in 8 identical bottles, with the same amount in each bottle. How much lemonade is in each bottle?

E8 Share £13 equally between 4 people.

E9 Work these out.
(a) $9 \div 4$
(b) $20 \div 8$
(c) $3 \div 4$
(d) $42 \div 8$

F Mixed questions

F1 Henry bought

2 pencils at 28p each,
4 pads of paper at £1.20 each and
1 magazine at £2.95.

He paid with a £10 note.
How much change should Henry get from £10?

Edexcel

F2 Find the area of this rectangle in cm².

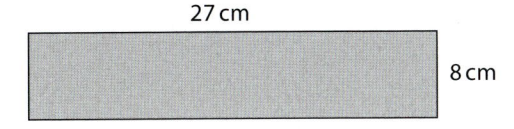

27 cm
8 cm

F3 To find the mean weight of a number of people, find the total of their weights and divide by the number of people.

(a) What is the total weight of these men?
(b) Find their mean weight.

Tom	Joe	Ken	Tim	Jack
70 kg	75 kg	76 kg	74 kg	80 kg

F4 Decide whether each statement is true or false.

(a) 5 is a factor of 756.
(b) 6 is a factor of 756.
(c) 7 is a factor of 756.
(d) 8 is a factor of 756.
(e) 9 is a factor of 756.

> The factors of 756 are numbers that divide into it exactly, with no remainder.

F5 The volume of a rectangular box is length × width × height.

Find the volume of this box in cm³.

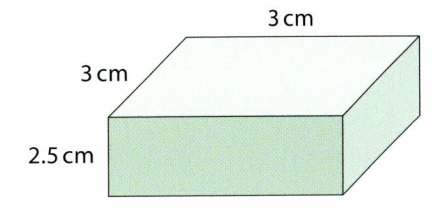

3 cm
3 cm
2.5 cm

F6 A lorry carries 9 tonnes of sand.
There are 156 tonnes of sand to be carried.
How many journeys will the lorry have to make?

F7 (a) A petrol station charges 82.9p for one litre of petrol.
Colin buys 6 litres.
How much does Colin pay for the petrol?
Write your answer to the nearest penny.

(b) Colin's motorcycle goes 92 km on 4 litres of petrol.
How far does the motorcycle go on 1 litre of petrol?

OCR

F8 This framework is made from steel bars.
Each steel bar is 1.45 metres long.

Calculate the total length of steel in this framework.

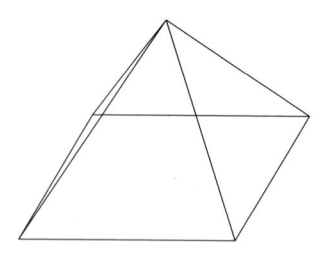

F9 Five friends go apple-picking. These are the amounts they pick.

   10.6 kg   12.45 kg   9.03 kg   11.2 kg   9.87 kg

They agree to put all the apples together and share out the weight equally.
How much do they each get?

Test yourself

T1 Cans of cola are sold in packs of six.
Each pack costs £2.18.
Sam buys eight packs of cola.

(a) How many cans does he buy altogether?

(b) How much does Sam pay for the eight packs?

(c) Sam pays for the packs with a £20 note.
How much change is he given?

AQA

T2 Work out the cost for

(a) one adult and two children

(b) three adults and ten children

Amusement park
Entrance charges
Adult £8.25
Child £6.15

OCR

T3 Three digits are missing in this multiplication.
Copy and complete it.

```
  ■ 6 ■
×     3
───────
■ 6 8 3
```

T4 Here is a rule for changing kilometres into miles.

| Multiply the number of kilometres by five and divide the answer by eight. |

Use this rule to change 120 kilometres into miles.

OCR

T5 A metal bar 5.8 metres long is cut into four equal pieces.
How long is each piece?

T6 Work these out.

(a) $5 - 3.5$ (b) 2.56×5 (c) $34.2 \div 9$

12 Frequency

You will revise
- the meaning of 'frequency' and how to use frequency tables
- how to draw a bar chart from frequency data
- how to find the mode or modal value

This work will help you
- put data into a stem-and-leaf table
- find the median and range from a stem-and-leaf table
- find the mean from a frequency table

A Stem-and-leaf tables

These are the times that some students from Mayfield School could hold their breath for.

Length of time breath held (s)   6   40   42   21   23   36   64   74   34   37   55   52   14   12
                                32   49   26   21   39   43   43   45   40   51   62   13   17   37

One way of recording the data is a **stem-and-leaf table** (or diagram).

The stem-and-leaf table is complete when the data is put in order in each row.

0	6
1	3 7 4 2
2	6 1 1 3
3	6 4 7 9 7 2
4	9 3 3 5 0 0 2
5	5 2 1
6	2 4
7	4

Stem: 10 s

This is the stem – it goes up in tens.

This is a time of 32 seconds.

These are the leaves and are units.

This tells you the scale of the stem.

0	6
1	2 3 4 7
2	1 1 3 6
3	2 4 6 7 7 9
4	0 0 2 3 3 5 9
5	1 2 5
6	2 4
7	4

Stem: 10 s

- How many students could hold their breath for 50 seconds or more?
- How many students could hold their breath for between 30 and 39 seconds?
- What was the shortest time anyone held their breath for? What was the longest?
- Which row of the table has the most students?
- How many students held their breath for less than 15 seconds?
- Collect data like this for your class. Compare it with the Mayfield School data. (Students with certain medical conditions will not be able to participate in the breath holding activity.)

A1 This data shows the weights in kilograms of patients in a children's ward at a hospital.

  51 46 27 28 18 16 38 37 24 40 42 30 44
  34 47 21 13 52 34 60 50 49 47 62 39

(a) Record this data is a stem-and-leaf table using this stem.
Rewrite the table putting the leaves in order.

```
1 |
2 |
3 |
4 |
5 |
6 |
```
Stem: 10 kg

(b) What was the weight of the lightest child?
(c) What was the weight of the heaviest child?
(d) Which row of the table has the children's weights?
(e) How many children weighed less than 35 kg?

A2 This data shows the number of hours of sunshine recorded at towns around the coast of the UK one day.

  7.4 7.1 5.4 7.3 11.0 8.5 3.3 8.0 5.0 6.5 6.3
  5.9 10.3 7.4 9.2 9.5 4.6 11.1 9.0 7.3 9.8

(a) Copy and complete this stem-and-leaf table for this data.
The first two pieces of data are already put on the table.
Rewrite the table putting the leaves in order.

(b) What was the most sunshine recorded by any of the coastal towns?
(c) Which row of the table contains the most recorded values?
(d) How many of the towns recorded less than 7 hours of sunshine?

```
 3 |
 4 |
 5 |
 6 |
 7 | 4 1
 8 |
 9 |
10 |
11 |
```
Stem: hours

A3 (a) Make an ordered stem-and-leaf table for this set of examination marks.
Use a stem of 10 marks.

Marks out of 80

  56 39 47 28 66 72 24 35 47 58
  63 70 30 49 56 44 68 41 55 47
  69 31 71 63 55 39 28 44 51 70

(b) What was the lowest mark?
(c) What was the highest mark?
(d) The pass mark for the examination was 45.
How many students passed?

B Median and range

The **median** of a set of data is the middle number when the numbers are put in order.
The **range** of a set of data is the difference between the largest and smallest values.
They are easy to find from a stem-and-leaf table once the leaves have been put in order.

This is the data for Mayfield School's breath holding experiment.

```
0 | 6
1 | 2 3 4 7
2 | 1 1 3 6
3 | 2 4 6 7 (7 9)
4 | 0 0 2 3 3 5 9
5 | 1 2 5
6 | 2 4
7 | 4
```
Stem: 10 s

Counting the leaves shows that there are 28 pieces of data.
The median lies between the 14th and 15th values.
It is halfway between 37 and 39.
So the median is 38 seconds.

The highest value is 74.
The lowest value is 6.
The range of the times is 74 – 6 = 68 seconds.

B1 This table shows the heights in centimetres of a group of students.

```
14 | 0 7
15 | 4 4 6 7 8
16 | 0 0 1 1 3 3 4 5 5 7 8
17 | 2 3 4 4 7
18 | 0 2
```
Stem: 10 cm

(a) How many students are between 150 and 159 cm tall?
(b) How many students are there in the group?
(c) Find the median height of the students in the group.
(d) Work out the range of students' heights in the group.

B2 Find the median and range of the data in question A1.

B3 Find the median and range of the data in question A2.

B4 This table shows the grip strength in kilograms of a group of students.

```
1 | 4
2 | 0 1 2 4 4 7 8 9
3 | 4 5 7 7
4 | 5 5 6
```
Stem: 10 kg

(a) How many students had a grip strength greater than 35 kg?
(b) Find the median and range of the grip strength of this group of students.

12 Frequency 91

C Comparisons

> **Pulse rate**
>
> A first-aider can feel a person's pulse on the carotid artery. This is found at the side of your neck.
>
> Measure your pulse rate by counting the number of beats per minute (b.p.m.).
>
> Now do some simple exercise such as stepping up and down on to a bench 20 times.
> Wait one minute and take your pulse rate again.
>
> Collect the results for the whole class.
> How does the pulse rate after exercise compare with the pulse rate before?

C1 These stem-and-leaf tables show the pulse rates of different groups of people.
All the pulse rates were taken after people had been sitting quietly for 15 minutes.

A: Class 10B at Southbury High School

```
 4 |
 5 | 7
 6 | 3 4 4 6 9
 7 | 0 1 4 4 5 7 8
 8 | 0 1 3 4 6 6
 9 | 3 7
10 |
11 |
```
Stem: 10 b.p.m.

B: Southbury Athletic Club

```
 4 | 8 9
 5 | 3 6 7
 6 | 2 2 3 4 5 6 9
 7 | 1 2 4 8
 8 | 0 0 4
 9 |
10 |
11 |
```
Stem: 10 b.p.m.

C: Babies at Southbury Post-Natal Clinic

```
 4 |
 5 |
 6 |
 7 | 4 5 8
 8 | 0 1 2 4 6 7 9
 9 | 0 3 5 5 7 8
10 | 3 5 6 6 7
11 | 5
```
Stem: 10 b.p.m.

D: Southbury Pensioners' Club

```
 4 | 3 7
 5 | 4 6
 6 | 3 4 6
 7 | 3 4 6 7
 8 | 2 5 6
 9 | 2 5
10 | 4
11 |
```
Stem: 10 b.p.m.

(a) Copy and complete these statements about the pulse rates of people in the groups using **one** of the words given.

(i) The babies at the Post-Natal Clinic generally had _____ pulse rates than the other groups. [higher / lower]

(ii) The people in the Pensioners' Club had a _____ range of pulse rates than the other groups. [wider / narrower]

(iii) The members of the Athletic Club had a _____ number of people with pulse rates less than 60 than the other groups. [larger / smaller]

(b) Find the median and range for each of the four groups.

C2 The results below show the pulse rates of a group of college students in Australia. They are split into those who smoked and those who didn't.

```
     Smoke     | Do not smoke
               | 5 | 0 8 9
         9 8 5 | 6 | 0 4 4 5 6 6 6 8 8
     6 6 5 0 0 | 7 | 0 1 1 8
     8 8 6 3 0 | 8 | 0 1 6 8 8
             2 0 | 9 |
                 | 10 | 4
```

Stem: 10 b.p.m.

(a) Find the median and range of the pulse rates of the group who smoked.

(b) Find the median and range of the pulse rates of the group who did not smoke.

(c) Which of these statements are true?

A The median pulse rate of the students who smoked was higher, so their pulses were on average higher.

B The student with the highest pulse rate was a non-smoker, so non-smokers have higher pulse rates on average.

C The range of pulse rates for the smokers was smaller, so the pulse rates of smokers were less on average.

(d) It turned out that the student with a pulse of 104 had been late for his class and had been running shortly before his pulse was taken.
If his pulse is not counted, how would this affect the median and the range of the students who do not smoke?

D Grouping

This information shows the numbers of eggs laid by a group of 38 chickens in a particular week.

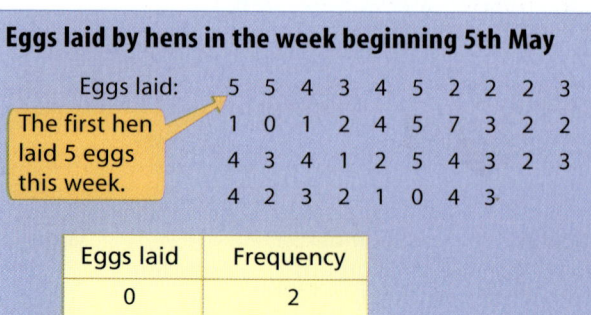

Eggs laid by hens in the week beginning 5th May

Eggs laid:
5 5 4 3 4 5 2 2 2 3
1 0 1 2 4 5 7 3 2 2
4 3 4 1 2 5 4 3 2 3
4 2 3 2 1 0 4 3

The first hen laid 5 eggs this week.

Eggs laid	Frequency
0	2
1	4
2	10
3	8
4	8
5	5
6	0
7	1
Total	38

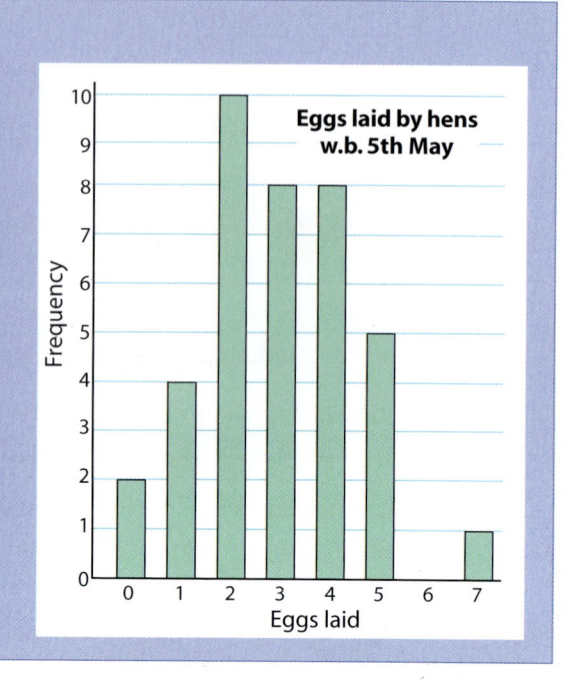

Here are the numbers of eggs laid by the same group of hens over a one-month period.

Eggs laid in May: 5 7 8 23 23 18 17 19 21 13 11 12 13 12 14 10 12 11 8
9 11 13 12 11 3 26 28 8 20 24 25 15 16 19 16 17 15 16

These can be put into a **grouped frequency table** and a bar chart drawn from this.

Eggs laid	Tally	Frequency
0–4	I	1
5–9	IIII I	6
10–14	IIII IIII III	13
15–19	IIII IIII	10
20–24	IIII	5
25–29	III	3
	Total	38

The **modal group** is the group with the highest frequency.

In this case the modal group is 10–14 eggs.

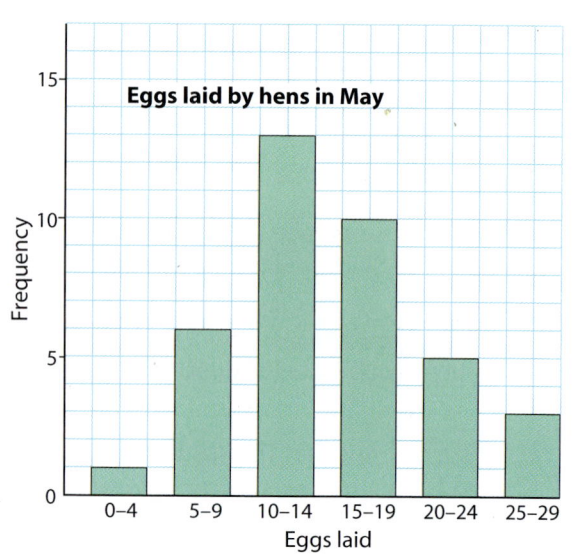

94   12 Frequency

D1 A postman counts the number of letters he delivers to the houses in one street.
These are

0 4 2 3 1 0 2 3 4 7 4 3 2 3 5 1 1 2 5 3 4 2 3 3

(a) Put this data into a frequency table like the one shown here.

Letters	Frequency
0	
1	
2	

(b) Use your frequency table to draw a bar chart of the information.

(c) What was the modal number of letters delivered in this street?

(d) How many houses got 4 or more letters?

(e) How many houses are there in the street?

(f) How many houses did the postman deliver letters to?

D2 A charity has a group of workers selling its magazine in a town.
They record the number of magazines sold by each worker on one day.

Number of magazines sold

7 34 45 23 18 15 22   9 34 30 27 16
25 33 40 36 41 27 24 26 37 19 12 31
26 23 14 35 31 25 17 29 34 27 25 38
53 51 33 16 43 23 34 20 36 28 27 31

(a) Put the data into a grouped frequency table using these groups.

Number of magazines sold	Tally	Frequency
0–9		
10–19		
20–29		
30–39		
40–49		
50–59		

(b) Use your table to draw a bar chart of the information.

(c) How many workers were selling the magazines?

(d) What was the modal group of the number of magazines sold?

(e) How many workers sold fewer than 20 magazines?

(f) How many workers sold 40 or more magazines?

D3 The ages of people using a small local library on a Saturday morning were recorded as

61 72 63 74 33 29 37 28 81 83 14 16 11 10 9 40 53 56 48
41 42 71 65 62 60 68 5 7 12 15 15 71 65 62 60 68 84 80

(a) Record this data in a frequency table using these groups.

Ages
0–19
20–39
40–59
60–79
80–99

(b) Use your table to draw a bar chart of the people using the library that morning.
(c) How many people used the library altogether?
(d) What was the modal age group of those using the library?
(e) How many people over the age of 60 used the library?
(f) How many people under the age of 20 used the library?

D4 This graph shows the ages of people using the same local library on the following Monday morning.

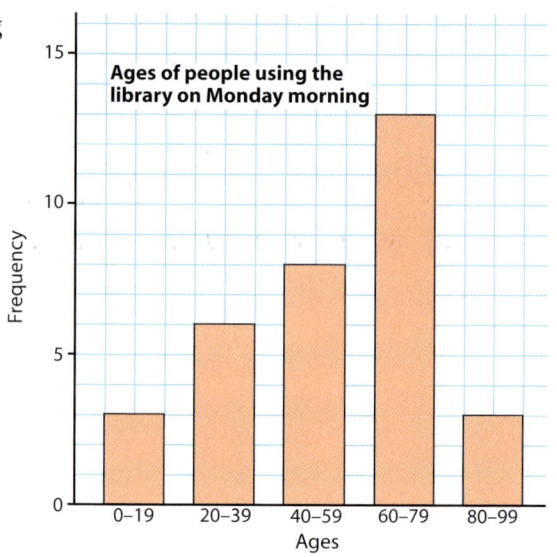

(a) How many people used the library altogether on Monday morning?
(b) What was the modal age group of those using the library that morning?
(c) Make two statements about the differences between the ages of people who used the library on Saturday morning and on Monday morning.

*D5 Which of these questions cannot be answered by using the graph above?

A How many people between the ages of 12 and 19 used the library on the Monday morning?

B How many people aged 60 or over used the library on the Monday morning?

C What is the range of ages of people using the library on the Monday morning?

E Mean

For a set of data, the mean is $\frac{\text{the sum of the values}}{\text{the number of values}}$.

Andrew goes on a walking holiday.

He records the number of kilometres he walks each day.

20 km   24 km   15 km   27 km   12 km   21 km   24 km

Sum of the values = 20 + 24 + 15 + 27 + 12 + 21 + 24 = 143

Number of values = 7

Mean distance = $\frac{143}{7}$ = 20.428 57…

The mean doesn't work out exactly, so the answer needs to be rounded.

The mean distance walked each day is 20.4 km to one decimal place (1 d.p.).

E1 One year, students are given six French tests, each marked out of 50.

| Helen's marks | 40 | 36 | 42 | 38 | 48 | 46 |
| Leah's marks | 34 | 38 | 40 | 45 | 46 | 46 |

(a) Work out the mean of Helen's marks, correct to 1 d.p.

(b) Work out the mean of Leah's marks, correct to 1 d.p.

(c) On average, who did better in the tests?

E2 Gina and Grace play a computer game called 'Snake'.
One day, they write down all their scores.

| Gina | 236 | 103 | 65 | 126 | 198 |
| Grace | 132 | 138 | 141 | 160 | 152 | 140 |

(a) Work out the mean and range of Gina's scores.

(b) Work out the mean and range of Grace's scores.

(c) On this evidence, who would you say is better at 'Snake'?
Give reasons for your decision.

E3 (a) Nathan is practising for the long jump.
His coach records the lengths of Nathan's jumps.

6.85 m   6.62 m   6.94 m   6.78 m   6.48 m   6.67 m   6.90 m   6.71 m

Work out the mean and range of these lengths.

(b) Steve is also practising for the long jump.
His mean length is 6.70 m and the range of his lengths is 0.58 m.

Who should the coach pick for the team?
Give reasons for your decision.

This table shows the number of people in some cars passing a particular set of traffic lights one morning.

Number of people in a car	Number of cars
1	29
2	12
3	7
4	2

This row tells us there were 7 cars with 3 people in each.
There were 21 people altogether in these 7 cars.

The total number of cars in the survey is 29 + 12 + 7 + 2 = 50

The total number of people in these cars is (1×29) + (2×12) + (3×7) + (4×2) = 82

The mean number of people in a car is $\frac{82}{50}$ = 1.64

- What is the modal number of people in a car?
- What is the median number of people in a car?

E4 Jan recorded the number of students present in each class of Highbury School one day.

(a) How many classes are there in the school?

(b) Find the total number of students at school.

(c) Work out the mean number of students in a class, correct to 1 d.p.

Number of students	Number of classes
27	8
28	11
29	6
30	3

E5 Greg surveys some people to find out how many television sets there are in their homes.

(a) How many homes had 3 television sets?

(b) How many homes were surveyed in total?

(c) Work out the mean number of television sets in a home.

(d) What was the modal number of television sets in a home?

Number of TV sets	Number of homes
0	8
1	20
2	37
3	29
4	6

E6 A survey asked people to estimate how many eggs they had eaten in the previous week.

(a) What is the modal number of eggs?

(b) Work out the mean number of eggs eaten per person.

(c) What is the median number of eggs?

Number of eggs	Number of people
0	3
1	16
2	28
3	25
4	18
5	11
6	4
7	2

Test yourself

T1 These are the numbers of visits to the library by women members in one year.

12 43 24 0 37 32 8 15 14 21 36 14 23 33 15 0 34
13 13 3 16 3 38 29 22 16 44 12 41 18 26 8 12 15

(a) Record this data in a stem-and-leaf table like this one. Put the leaves in order.

(b) Use your stem-and-leaf table to find the median and range of the number of visits made.

Library visits by women

0 |
1 |
2 |
3 |
4 |

Stem: 10 visits

T2 Here are the times, in minutes, taken to change some tyres.

5 10 15 12 8 7 20 35 24 15
20 33 15 25 10 8 10 20 16 10

Draw a stem-and-leaf diagram to show these times.

Edexcel

T3 Simon keeps a record of the points scored by his rugby team in each match.
The points scored this season are shown in this stem-and-leaf diagram.

0 | 6 7
1 | 2 4 5
2 | 1 2 4 8 9
3 | 0 2 2 6
4 | 3 7
5 | 2

Key: 4 | 3 = 43

(a) Write down

   (i) the range   (ii) the median

(b) The points scored by his team last season had a range of 38 and a median of 35. Make one comment comparing the points scored in these two seasons.

OCR

T4 Gareth recorded the temperature at midday every day for a week.

26°C 28°C 24°C 30°C 30°C 27°C 28°C

Work out the mean midday temperature, correct to 1 d.p.

T5 The number of goals scored in 15 hockey matches is shown in the table.

Calculate the mean number of goals scored.

Number of goals	Number of matches
1	2
3	1
5	5
6	3
9	4

AQA

13 Fractions, decimals and percentages

You should know how to
- use equivalent fractions
- order decimals
- find a fraction of a number

This work will help you
- convert between fractions, decimals and percentages
- convert a fraction to a decimal using short division

You need sheet F1–14.

A Fractions and percentages

- Match each fraction with an equivalent percentage.

  $\frac{1}{2}$ $\frac{1}{10}$ 10%   25%

  $\frac{3}{4}$ $\frac{1}{4}$ 75%   50%

Example

Work out $\frac{9}{10}$ as a percentage.

$\frac{1}{10}$ of 100% is 10%

$\frac{9}{10}$ is $9 \times \frac{1}{10}$

so $\frac{9}{10} = 9 \times 10\% = 90\%$

A1 For each shape, write down

(i) the fraction shaded   (ii) the percentage shaded

(a)   (b)   (c)

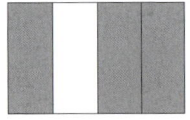

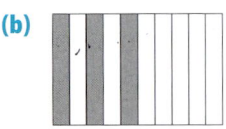

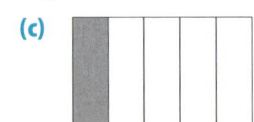

A2 (a) Copy and complete this working to change $\frac{3}{5}$ into a percentage.

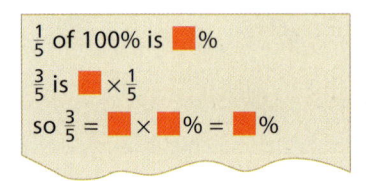

$\frac{1}{5}$ of 100% is ■%

$\frac{3}{5}$ is ■ $\times \frac{1}{5}$

so $\frac{3}{5}$ = ■ $\times$ ■% = ■%

(b) Change $\frac{4}{5}$ into a percentage.

A3 Change each of these fractions into a percentage.

(a) $\frac{1}{4}$ (b) $\frac{7}{10}$ (c) $\frac{9}{10}$ (d) $\frac{1}{20}$ (e) $\frac{7}{20}$

A4 Which is bigger, $\frac{2}{5}$ or 60%?
Explain your answer.

A5 Write each of these lists in order of size, starting with the smallest.

(a) $\frac{1}{2}$ 30% $\frac{1}{5}$ 40% $\frac{3}{4}$

(b) $\frac{2}{5}$ 50% $\frac{1}{4}$ $\frac{3}{10}$ 10%

(c) 25% $\frac{1}{5}$ $\frac{1}{2}$ 30% $\frac{2}{5}$

(d) 60% $\frac{3}{4}$ $\frac{1}{20}$ $\frac{4}{5}$ 70%

B Decimals and percentages

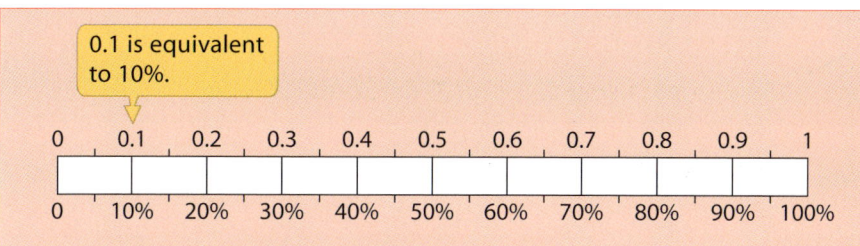

0.1 is equivalent to 10%.

- What decimal is equivalent to 70%?
- What percentage is equivalent to 0.35?
- Which is bigger, 0.8 or 85%?

B1 Write each of these decimals as a percentage.

(a) 0.2   (b) 0.5   (c) 0.25   (d) 0.6   (e) 0.75

B2 Write each of these percentages as a decimal.

(a) 10%   (b) 70%   (c) 90%   (d) 30%   (e) 45%

B3 Find four matching pairs.
What could match the odd one out?

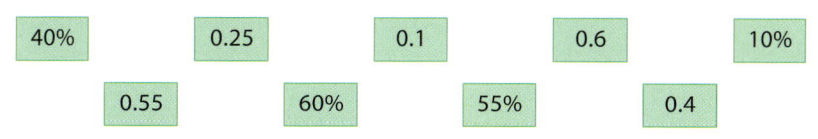

40%   0.25   0.1   0.6   10%
    0.55   60%   55%   0.4

B4 Which is smaller, 15% or 0.2?
Explain your answer.

B5 Write these in order of size, starting with the smallest.

50%   0.4   25%   0.7   10%

13 Fractions, decimals and percentages   101

C Fractions and decimals

- Match each fraction with an equivalent decimal.

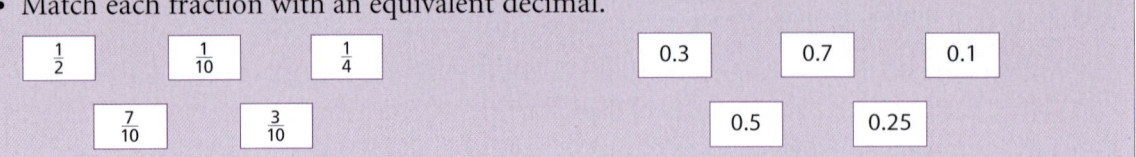

  $\frac{1}{2}$ $\frac{1}{10}$ $\frac{1}{4}$ 0.3   0.7   0.1

  $\frac{7}{10}$ $\frac{3}{10}$ 0.5   0.25

You can change any fraction to a decimal using division.

Change $\frac{1}{5}$ to a decimal. $\frac{1}{5}$ means '1 whole one divided by 5'.

So to change $\frac{1}{5}$ to a decimal you divide 1 by 5.

$$5\overline{)1.0}^{0.2}$$

- How would you change $\frac{2}{5}$ to a decimal using division? What about $\frac{7}{8}$?

C1 Fill in the fractions on sheet F1–14.

C2 Find three matching pairs.
What could match the odd one out?

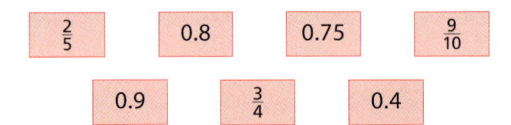

$\frac{2}{5}$ 0.8   0.75 $\frac{9}{10}$

0.9 $\frac{3}{4}$ 0.4

C3 Which is smaller, 0.1 or $\frac{1}{5}$? Explain your answer.

C4 Change each fraction to a decimal using division.

(a) $\frac{3}{5}$ (b) $\frac{4}{5}$ (c) $\frac{1}{8}$ (d) $\frac{3}{8}$

C5 Write each of these lists in order of size, starting with the smallest.

(a) $\frac{1}{4}$ 0.2 $\frac{1}{10}$ 0.3 $\frac{2}{5}$ (b) $\frac{7}{10}$ 0.6 $\frac{4}{5}$ $\frac{1}{2}$ 0.75

D Thirds

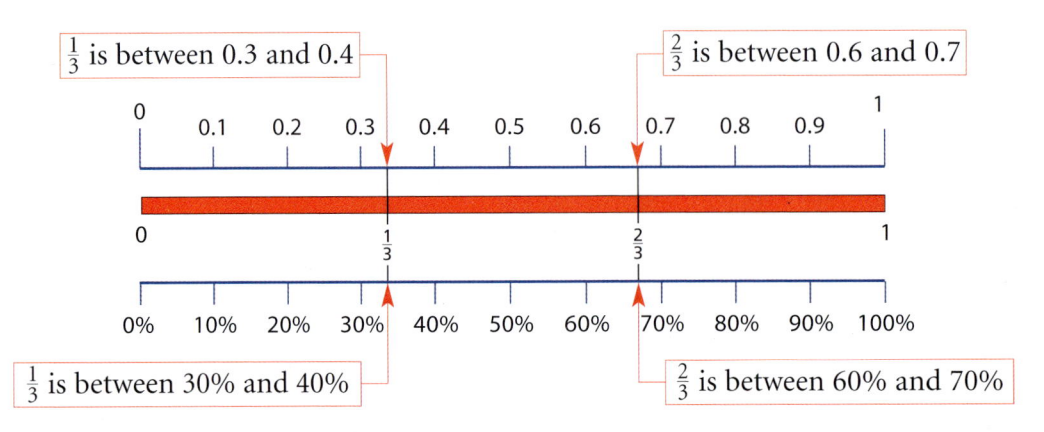

$\frac{1}{3}$ is between 0.3 and 0.4

$\frac{2}{3}$ is between 0.6 and 0.7

$\frac{1}{3}$ is between 30% and 40%

$\frac{2}{3}$ is between 60% and 70%

102   13 Fractions, decimals and percentages

$\frac{1}{3}$ as a percentage

From the diagram, $\frac{1}{3}$ is about 33%.
But 3 times 33% is only 99%.
$\frac{1}{3}$ is $33\frac{1}{3}$% (because 3 times $33\frac{1}{3}$ is 100).

$\frac{2}{3}$ as a percentage

$\frac{2}{3}$ is $66\frac{2}{3}$%.

$\frac{1}{3}$ as a decimal

3 means '1 whole one divided by 3'.

$3 \overline{)1.00000}$ 0.33333...... (goes on forever!)

$\frac{2}{3}$ as a decimal

$\frac{2}{3}$ is 0.66666......

D1 Write each of these in order of size, smallest first.

(a) $\frac{1}{2}$ 40%   0.45 $\frac{1}{3}$ 30%

(b) 70%   0.65 $\frac{3}{4}$ $\frac{2}{3}$ 0.8

(c) $\frac{1}{3}$ 20% $\frac{1}{4}$ 0.35   50%

(d) 0.3 $\frac{2}{5}$ 0.5 $\frac{1}{3}$ 25%

E Converting between fractions, decimals and percentages

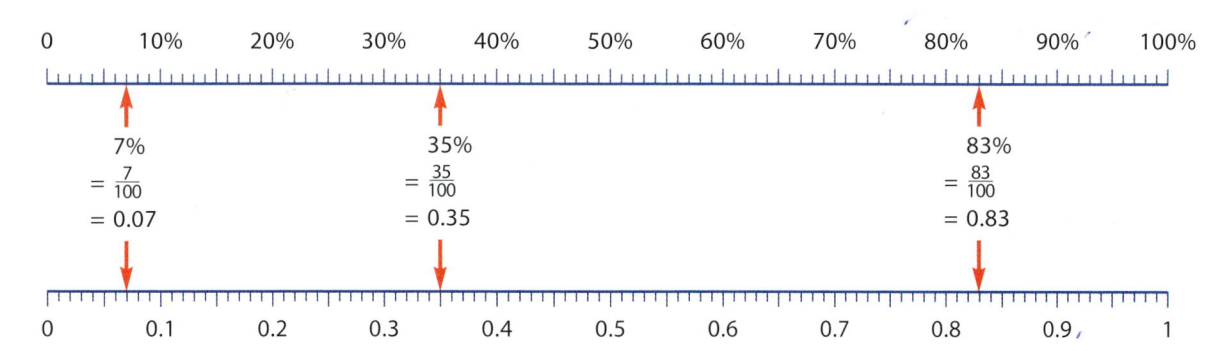

7% = $\frac{7}{100}$ = 0.07

35% = $\frac{35}{100}$ = 0.35

83% = $\frac{83}{100}$ = 0.83

E1 Copy and complete this table.

Percentage	Fraction	Decimal
21%	$\frac{21}{100}$	
	$\frac{57}{100}$	
		0.41
9%		
	$\frac{3}{100}$	
		0.08

E2 Write each of these percentages as a decimal.

(a) 65%   (b) 73%   (c) 8%   (d) 80%   (e) 94%

E3 Write each of these decimals as a percentage.

(a) 0.85   (b) 0.17   (c) 0.33   (d) 0.02   (e) 0.1

E4

A	E	M	N	R	S	T	U	V
$\frac{1}{2}$	30%	$\frac{1}{4}$	0.8	0.6	0.2	75%	40%	$\frac{7}{10}$

Use this code to find a letter for each fraction, decimal or percentage below.
Rearrange each set of letters to spell a planet.

(a) $\frac{1}{5}$ 0.25 $\frac{5}{10}$ 60%
(b) 80% $\frac{2}{5}$ $\frac{6}{10}$ 20% $\frac{3}{4}$ 0.5
(c) $\frac{4}{5}$ 0.7 $\frac{2}{10}$ 0.3   0.4
(d) 0.4   50% $\frac{3}{5}$ $\frac{2}{10}$ $\frac{2}{5}$ 80%

E5 (a) Write 15% as a decimal.
(b) Write the fraction $\frac{2}{5}$ as a decimal.
(c) Use your answers to (a) and (b) to help you write these in order, smallest first.
   0.2   15%   0.09 $\frac{2}{5}$

E6 Write each of these lists in order of size, smallest first.
(a) 0.3   28% $\frac{1}{4}$ 0.18
(b) 8%   0.6 $\frac{7}{10}$ 0.55
(c) 78% $\frac{3}{4}$ 0.09   0.8
(d) $\frac{1}{2}$ 48%   0.4   0.19

E7 A theatre was 82% full for an afternoon show and $\frac{9}{10}$ full for the evening show. Which attendance was better? Explain how you decide.

E8 Which of these would give the bigger discount? Explain how you decide.

Special offer save 20%

SALE $\frac{1}{3}$ off everything

Test yourself

T1 Write down each number that is less than one half.
   0.21   52% $\frac{1}{3}$ 0.78 $\frac{3}{4}$ 35%

AQA

T2 Copy and complete the table.

Fraction	Decimal	Percentage
$\frac{1}{2}$	0.5	
	0.7	70%
$\frac{3}{100}$		3%

AQA

T3 (a) Write $\frac{1}{5}$ as a decimal.
(b) Write 0.25 as a fraction.
(c) Write 17% as a decimal.
(d) Write $\frac{1}{5}$, 0.25, 17% in ascending order.

WJEC

T4 Change $\frac{5}{8}$ to a decimal using division.

104   13 Fractions, decimals and percentages

14 Area of a parallelogram

You need to know how to find the area of a rectangle.

This work will help you

- understand what the perpendicular height of a parallelogram is
- calculate the area of a parallelogram

You need sheets F1–15 and F1–16.

A Changing a parallelogram into a rectangle

Sheet F1–15 has some parallelograms on it.

What special properties does a parallelogram have?

Can you see how each of these parallelograms can be cut **once only** and put back together to make a rectangle?

- Draw the cutting line on each parallelogram
- Cut the parallelogram and put the two pieces together to make a rectangle.
- Stick the rectangle on to centimetre square paper. Find the area of the rectangle and write it on.

Can you do this for all the parallelograms?

Did everyone in the class do it the same way?

A1 This question is on sheet F1–16.

When you cut across a parallelogram and make the pieces into a rectangle, the area of the parallelogram and the rectangle are the same.

A2 (a) If this parallelogram is cut and made into a rectangle, what will the rectangle's dimensions (width and height) be?

(b) What will the rectangle's area be?

(c) What is the area of the parallelogram?

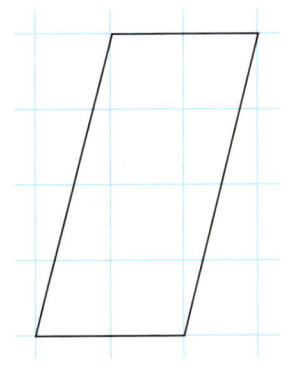

A3 Find the area of each of these parallelograms.

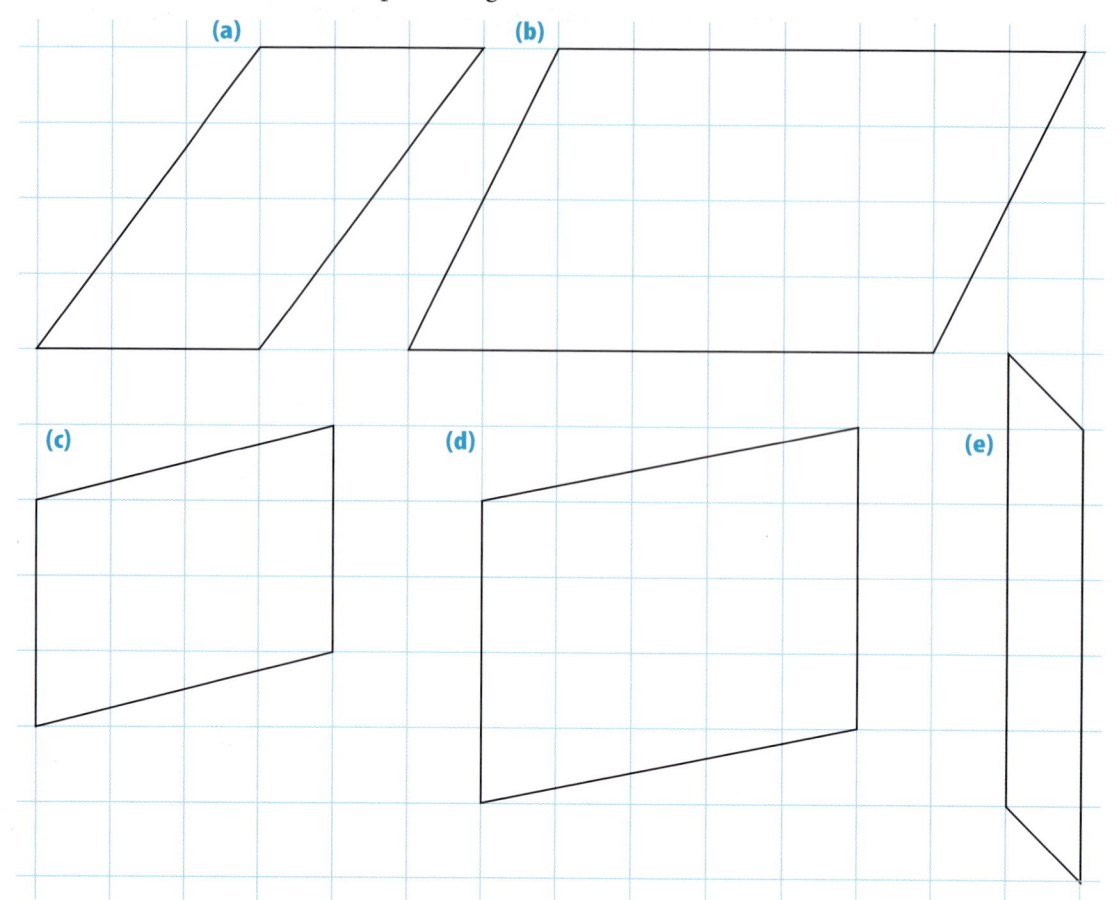

(a) (b) (c) (d) (e)

A4 On centimetre squared paper draw parallelograms of your own with the following areas.

(a) 9 cm²   (b) 14 cm²   (c) 16 cm²   (d) 5 cm²

B Using the formula

The area of a parallelogram is given by this formula.

   area = length of base × perpendicular height

The **base** does not have to be horizontal. It can be any of the sides.

The **perpendicular height** is the height measured at right angles to the base you have chosen.

- How does this formula come from the area of a rectangle that has been made from a parallelogram?

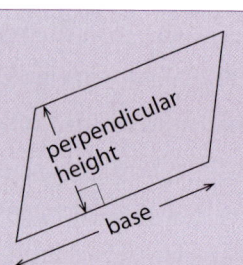

B1 (a) Below, there are two copies of the same parallelogram.
In each case, measure the base and perpendicular height that are marked, then set out your working like this.

> Area = base × perpendicular height
> = ... cm × .... cm
> = ... cm²

(i)

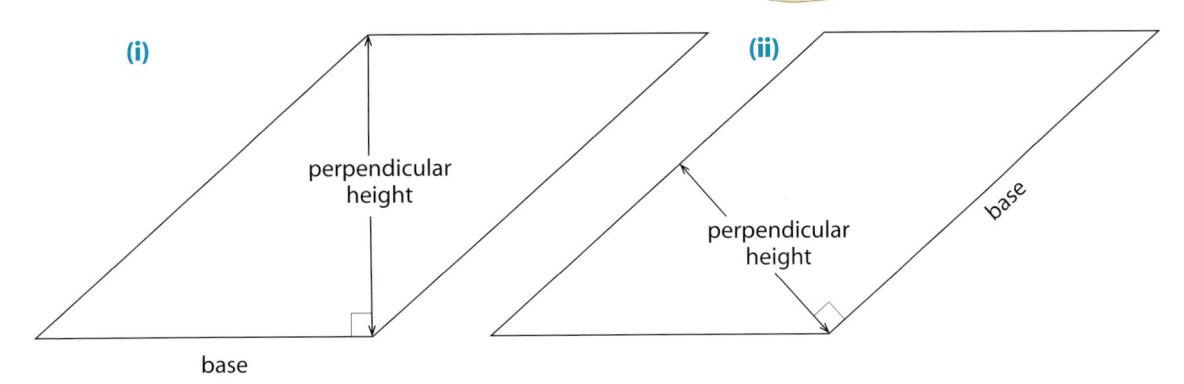

perpendicular height

base

(ii)

perpendicular height

base

(b) Comment on your two answers.

B2 By measuring and calculation, find the area of this parallelogram.
Decide which side you will use as the base.
Use a set square or the corner of a piece of paper to help you measure the perpendicular height.

Set out your working the same way as in question B1.

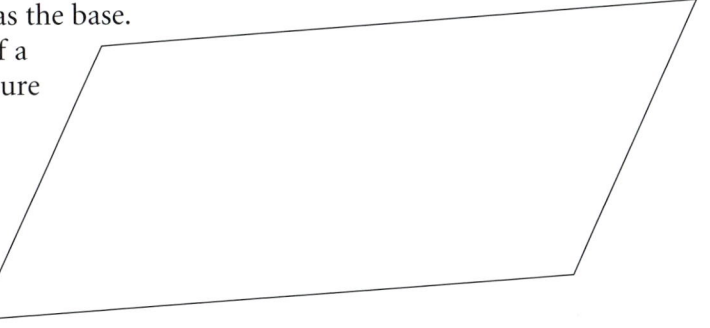

B3 Find the area of each of the parallelograms sketched here.

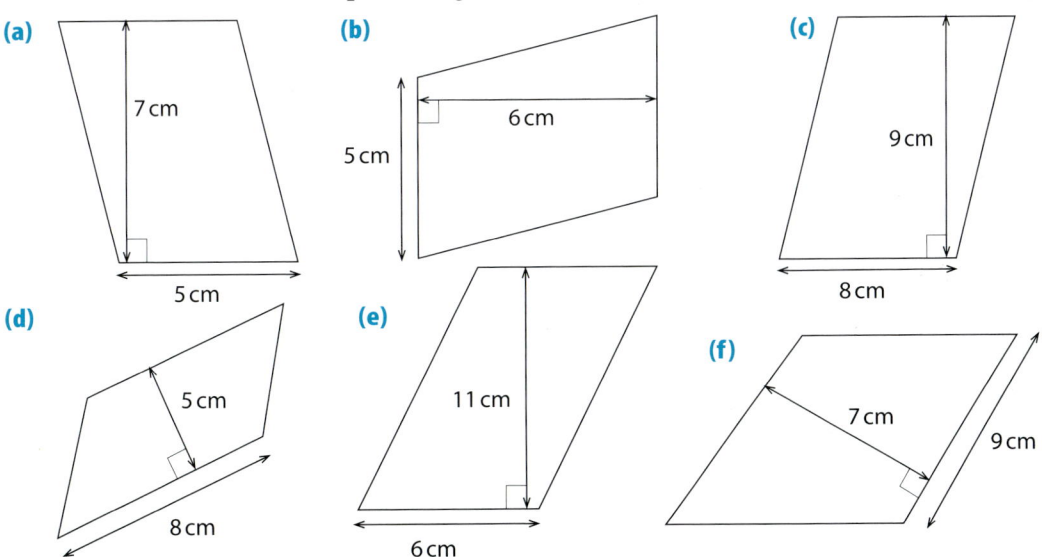

(a) 7 cm, 5 cm

(b) 6 cm, 5 cm

(c) 9 cm, 8 cm

(d) 5 cm, 8 cm

(e) 11 cm, 6 cm

(f) 7 cm, 9 cm

14 Area of parallelogram 107

T A parallelogram that 'overhangs' cannot be changed into a rectangle by making one vertical cut. But it can be changed into a rectangle by making more than one cut – so the formula still works – as in this example.

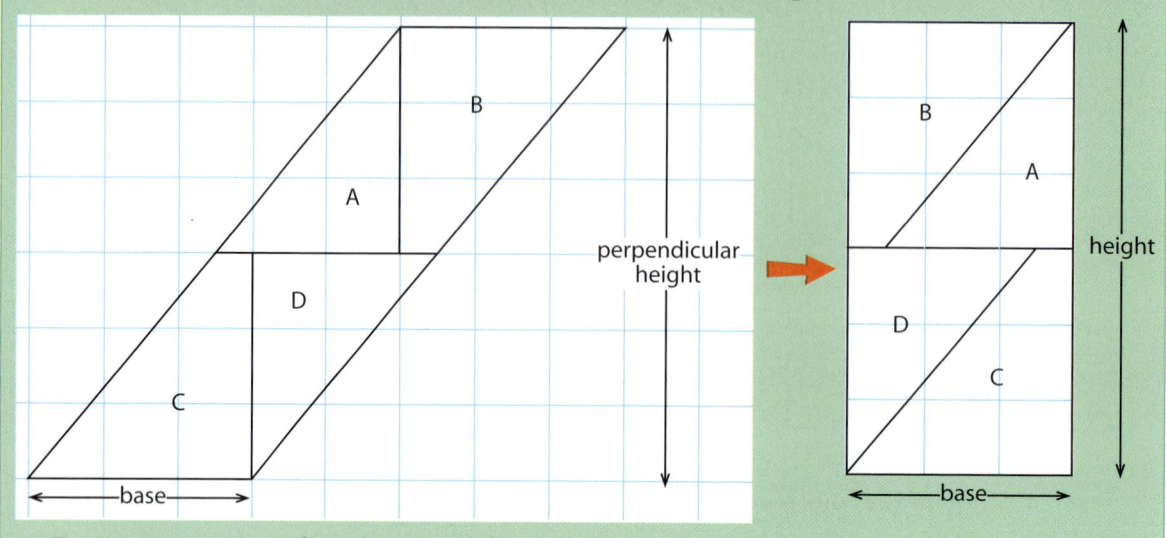

- Draw your own overhanging parallelogram on squared paper and work out how to cut it to make it into a rectangle.

B4 Find the area of each of these parallelograms.

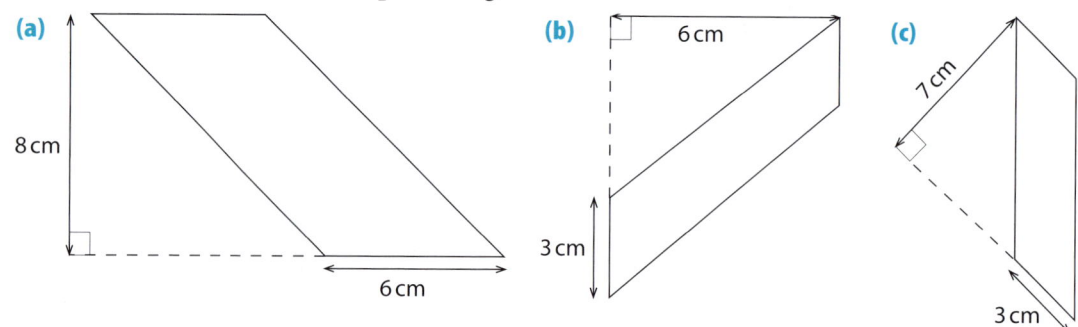

(a) 8 cm, 6 cm

(b) 6 cm, 3 cm

(c) 7 cm, 3 cm

Test yourself

T1 A parallelogram is drawn on a centimetre square grid.

Calculate the area of the parallelogram.

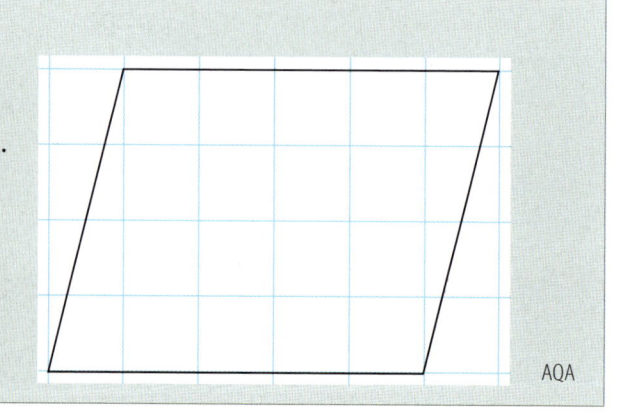

AQA

108 14 Area of parallelogram

15 Negative numbers

You will revise using negative numbers for temperatures.

This work will help you
- add and subtract negative numbers
- multiply a negative number by a positive number

You need dice of two different colours, some counters, and sheets F1–17 and F1–18.

A Temperature changes

A1 Write down the lower temperature in each pair.
(a) ⁻2°C   1°C
(b) ⁻3°C   ⁻6°C
(c) ⁻3°C   ⁻3.5°C
(d) ⁻9°C   3°C
(e) ⁻12°C ⁻7°C
(f) ⁻16°C ⁻20°C

A2 Write each list of temperatures in order, lowest first.
(a) ⁻4°C 3°C 10°C ⁻7°C 0°C
(b) 6°C ⁻5°C 7.5°C ⁻4.5°C ⁻1°C

A3 The temperature was 5°C in the morning.
In the evening it was ⁻4°C.
How many degrees did the temperature fall between morning and evening?

A4 When Rob went to bed, the temperature was 3°C.
When he woke up, it had gone down by 8 degrees.
What was the temperature when he woke up?

A5 Is each of these a rise or a fall?
Write down how many degrees the temperature rises or falls.
(a) From 5°C to ⁻1°C
(b) From ⁻3°C to 2°C
(c) From ⁻10°C to ⁻3°C
(d) From 8°C to 3°C
(e) From 6°C to ⁻4°C
(f) From ⁻13°C to 7°C

A6 Work out the finishing temperature.
(a) Start at 4°C, rise 7 degrees.
(b) Start at ⁻4°C, rise 6 degrees.
(c) Start at 2°C, fall 6 degrees.
(d) Start at ⁻5°C, fall 4 degrees.
(e) Start at ⁻10°C, rise 8 degrees.
(f) Start at 2°C, fall 12 degrees.

A7 Work these out.
(a) 2 – 7 (Start at 2, go down 7)
(b) ⁻14 + 1
(c) ⁻8 – 3
(d) ⁻13 + 8
(e) ⁻10 + 2
(f) ⁻11 – 5
(g) 3 – 20
(h) ⁻15 + 4
(i) ⁻12 – 4

15 Negative numbers   109

B Adding negative numbers

Sarah and Afza are judging a talent contest.

Afza thinks Peter is good. He gives him a score of 5.
Sarah thinks he is awful. She gives him ⁻3.

Peter's total score is 5 + ⁻3 = 2.

5 + ⁻3 = 2

Adding ⁻3 is the same as subtracting 3.

B1 Work these out.

(a) 4 + ⁻3 (b) 5 + ⁻2 (c) 7 + ⁻8 (d) 4 + ⁻10 (e) ⁻3 + ⁻4
(f) ⁻4 + ⁻2 (g) ⁻8 + ⁻7 (h) ⁻20 + ⁻5 (i) 6 + ⁻3 (j) 7 + ⁻5

B2 Work out the answers and write them in order, lowest first.
The letters will spell a make of car.

(a)
G	A	R	A	J	U
2 + ⁻3	1 − 4	⁻2 + 7	5 + ⁻1	⁻2 + ⁻3	2 + ⁻2

(b)
B	U	R	S	U	A
6 + ⁻8	10 + ⁻4	12 + ⁻7	⁻5 + ⁻4	⁻4 − 2	5 + ⁻2

(c)
T	E	R	O	N	I	C
5 + ⁻9	7 + ⁻4	6 + ⁻7	6 + ⁻4	⁻4 + 8	⁻5 + ⁻3	⁻4 − 7

B3 From the numbers in the loop, find two numbers that add up to

(a) 1 (b) ⁻6 (c) ⁻1 (d) 3

(⁻5 ⁻1 2 4)

B4 Work these out.

(a) 8 + ⁻2 + ⁻1 (b) ⁻3 + ⁻2 + ⁻4 (c) 5 − 2 − 4 (d) ⁻10 + 3 + ⁻2
(e) 3 + ⁻4 − 7 (f) ⁻2 + 5 + ⁻1 (g) 3 + ⁻8 + ⁻2 (h) 6 − 8 + ⁻4

Target practice   a game for two players

Make a copy of the grid.

⁻3	5	⁻1	2
7	⁻4	3	⁻5

- Agree a target number between ⁻3 and 5.
- Take turns to cross off a number.
  As you go, add up the numbers you cross off.

The winner is the player whose final total is closer to the target.

Three in a row games   These are on sheet F1–17.

C Subtracting a negative number

Sue and Joe enter a fancy dress competition.
Here are the scores the judges give them.

- What are their total scores?
  Who has won?

Sue: 4, ⁻3, 2, ⁻1
Joe: 4, ⁻1, 3, ⁻4

It is then decided to disregard their lowest scores.

- What are their new scores?
  Who has won now?

Discard it! a game for two players

You need cards numbered ⁻5 to 5 (11 cards).

⁻5 ⁻4 ⁻3 ⁻2 ⁻1 0 1 2 3 4 5

- Deal three cards to each player.
- Each player finds the total of their three cards, shows their cards and says their total.
- The player with the **lower** total now discards their lowest scoring card and says their new total.
- The player who now has the higher total wins.

Subtracting a negative number 7 − ⁻2 is the same as adding a positive number 7 + 2.

C1 Work these out.

(a) 2 − ⁻7 (b) ⁻4 − ⁻1 (c) ⁻6 − ⁻3 (d) 3 − ⁻8 (e) ⁻10 − ⁻2
(f) ⁻6 − ⁻5 (g) 3 − ⁻10 (h) ⁻5 − ⁻4 (i) 7 − ⁻4 (j) ⁻5 − ⁻9

C2 Match these in pairs with the same answer.

⁻4 + 6   ⁻3 − 2   3 − ⁻2   5 − 8   ⁻2 + 7   1 − ⁻1   ⁻6 − 3   ⁻10 + 5

C3 Work these out.

(a) ⁻7 + ⁻3 (b) ⁻3 − ⁻7 (c) ⁻7 − 3 (d) 3 − ⁻7 (e) ⁻7 − ⁻3
(f) 7 − ⁻3 (g) ⁻7 + 3 (h) ⁻3 + ⁻7 (i) 3 + ⁻7 (j) 3 − 7

C4 Work out (a) 4 + ⁻3 − ⁻2 (b) 6 − ⁻5 + ⁻3 (c) ⁻8 + ⁻4 − ⁻7 (d) ⁻3 − ⁻4 − 5

C5 Work out (a) 15 + ⁻25 (b) ⁻3 + ⁻21 (c) ⁻10 − 15 (d) ⁻12 − ⁻20

Dominoes for practice in adding and subtracting negative numbers

These are on sheet F1–18.
The rules are as usual for dominoes.

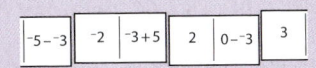

⁻5−⁻3 | ⁻2   ⁻3+5 | 2   0−⁻3 | 3

D Multiplying a negative by a positive number

3 lots of ⁻2 = ⁻6	⁻2 ⁻2 ⁻2 Total ⁻6	⁻2 multiplied by 3 = ⁻6
3 × ⁻2 = ⁻6		⁻2 × 3 = ⁻6

D1 Work these out.

(a) 4 × ⁻2   (b) 5 × ⁻3   (c) 7 × ⁻5   (d) 6 × ⁻4   (e) 9 × ⁻1

D2 Work these out.

(a) ⁻4 × 3   (b) ⁻5 × 8   (c) ⁻1 × 6   (d) ⁻3 × 9   (e) ⁻7 × 8

D3 Work these out.

(a) 7 × ⁻10   (b) 20 × ⁻3   (c) ⁻14 × 2   (d) ⁻5 × 16   (e) 15 × ⁻4

D4 Copy and complete these.

(a) ? × ⁻6 = ⁻12   (b) 4 × ? = ⁻8   (c) ⁻5 × ? = ⁻25   (d) 8 × ? = ⁻24

(e) 2 × ? = ⁻2   (f) ⁻20 × ? = ⁻100   (g) ? × 7 = ⁻28   (h) ? × ⁻6 = ⁻30

D5 Work out the answers to the questions below.
Use the code to change them to letters.
Rearrange the letters to make some animals.

A	B	C	E	G	H	I	M	O	P	R	S	T	W
⁻12	⁻24	⁻28	⁻36	24	30	⁻18	48	20	⁻20	36	28	⁻60	⁻48

(a) ⁻6 × 8   (b) 4 × ⁻5   (c) ⁻6 × 4   (d) 5 × ⁻12   (e) 12 × 4
    7 × ⁻4   3 × 10   9 × ⁻2   5 × 4   6 × ⁻6
    4 × 5   ⁻6 × 6   3 × ⁻8   3 × 8   2 × 14
                 4 × 7   ⁻10 × 6   ⁻4 × 3   5 × 6
                 ⁻9 × 4   ⁻2 × 6   2 × 18
                              4 × 9   ⁻3 × 4
                                                             15 × ⁻4

***D6** Work out the answers and write them in order, lowest first.
The letters will spell the name of a city.

(a)
A	R	R	E	P	I	T	O
⁻1 + 3	⁻4 + ⁻2	⁻4 × 4	⁻10 − 3	3 × ⁻6	2 × ⁻2	⁻6 × 2	⁻14 + 4

(b)
K	A	L	C	U	N	D	A
⁻2 × 3	3 × ⁻4	⁻7 − ⁻2	1 − 9	⁻8 − 2	5 + ⁻5	⁻3 + 7	⁻1 + ⁻3

(c)
M	O	H	I	S	H	R	I	A
2 − ⁻3	2 − 10	⁻16 + 5	2 + ⁻7	⁻9 − ⁻2	⁻1 + ⁻5	⁻3 × 3	5 × ⁻2	⁻2 + 8

Test yourself

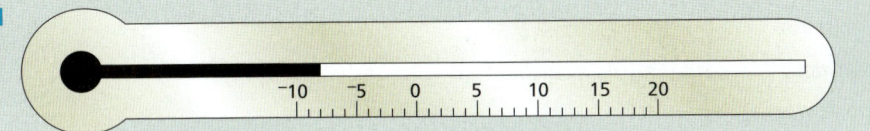

T1

(a) Write down the temperature shown on the picture of the thermometer.

(b) At 6 a.m., the temperature in Fred's garden was ⁻3 °C.
By noon, the temperature had risen by 12 degrees.
Work out the temperature at noon.

(c) By midnight, the temperature in Fred's garden had fallen to ⁻7 °C.
Work out the fall in temperature from noon to midnight.

Edexcel

T2 The top of Mount Kenya, in Africa, is about 5000 metres above sea level.
When you climb a mountain the temperature drops by 6 degrees for every 1000 metres climbed.

When the temperature at sea level is 26 °C, what will the temperature be on the top of Mount Kenya?

OCR

T3 Work these out.

(a) 3 + ⁻7
(b) 2 − ⁻8
(c) ⁻1 − 4
(d) ⁻2 + ⁻6
(e) 4 × ⁻5
(f) ⁻8 × 7
(g) 6 − 9 + ⁻3
(h) ⁻10 − ⁻4 − 6

T4 In a dance competition the three judges can each award a score between ⁻5 and 5.

(a) The judges give Parveen these scores. ⁻2 3 1
What is her total score?

(b) The judges give Stuart these scores. ⁻4 0 ⁻1
What is his total score?

(c) The winner of the competition has a total score of 3.
These were the scores from two of the judges. 4 1
What score did the third judge give?

T5 John uses this rule to change a temperature from °C into °F.

> Multiply the temperature in °C by 2 and add 30 to the answer.

Use this rule to change   (a) 19 °C into °F   (b) ⁻3 °C into °F

OCR

16 Metric units

This work will help you
- use metric units to estimate lengths, weights and volumes
- convert between metric units

A Using metric units

Baked beans are usually sold in cans that have
- a weight of about 470 grams (including the beans)
- a height of about 11 centimetres
- a capacity of about 400 millilitres

Estimate
- the weight of this book
- the length of your arm from the elbow to the tip of your longest finger
- the capacity of a mug

A1 This book is roughly 19 centimetres wide.
Use this to estimate these in centimetres.

(a) How wide your desk is
(b) The height of this book
(c) Your handspan
(d) How high your chair seat is above the floor

A2 Sugar is usually sold in bags that weigh 1 kilogram.
Estimate the weight of these in kilograms.

(a) Your school bag
(b) Your chair
(c) A pile of class exercise books

A3 An apple weighs about 150 grams.
Estimate the weight of these in grams.

(a) Your exercise book
(b) A full pencil case
(c) Your ruler

A4 A large carton of orange juice contains 1 litre of juice.

Estimate how much these contain in litres.
(a) Your school bag
(b) The rubbish bin in your classroom

A5 A normal teaspoon can hold about 5 millilitres of liquid.
Estimate the amount of
- **(a)** yogurt in a small yogurt pot
- **(b)** liquid in a full mug of tea
- **(c)** ink in a ballpoint pen

A6 For each statement, what is the missing metric unit of length: millimetres, centimetres, metres or kilometres?
- **(a)** The distance from Glasgow to Leeds is 359 ....
- **(b)** The width of my thumbnail is 14 ....
- **(c)** The height of my apple tree is 3 ....
- **(d)** The length of my middle finger is 8 ....

A7 What metric units of length would you use to measure these?
- **(a)** The length of a lorry
- **(b)** The distance from your school to the nearest beach
- **(c)** The length of your foot
- **(d)** The length of a fly

A8 For each statement, what is the missing metric unit of weight: grams or kilograms?
- **(a)** The weight of a one pound coin is 12 ....
- **(b)** The weight of an adult chimpanzee is about 60 ....

A9 A tonne is 1000 kilograms.
What units would you use – grams, kilograms or tonnes – to estimate the weight of these?
- **(a)** A large dog
- **(b)** A hamster
- **(c)** A van

A10 For each statement, what is the missing metric unit of volume: millilitres or litres?
- **(a)** A tube of my favourite hand cream contains 50 ....
- **(b)** The capacity of my rucksack is 25 ....

A11 What is the missing metric unit in each statement?
- **(a)** The weight of a banana is 225 ....
- **(b)** The average height of a male giraffe is 530 ....
- **(c)** The volume of milk in a glass is 300 ....
- **(d)** The diameter of the Moon is 3476 ....

A12 Write down the metric unit you would use to measure
- **(a)** the length of a person's hand
- **(b)** the weight of a mouse
- **(c)** the distance from Manchester to London
- **(d)** a teaspoon of medicine

Edexcel

A13 The average height of a 16-year-old girl is about 1.6 metres.
In metres, estimate the height of
- **(a)** your classroom
- **(b)** an 11-year-old girl

16 Metric units 115

B Converting between metric units

Length

There are
- 10 millimetres in 1 centimetre
- 100 centimetres in 1 metre
- 1000 metres in 1 kilometre

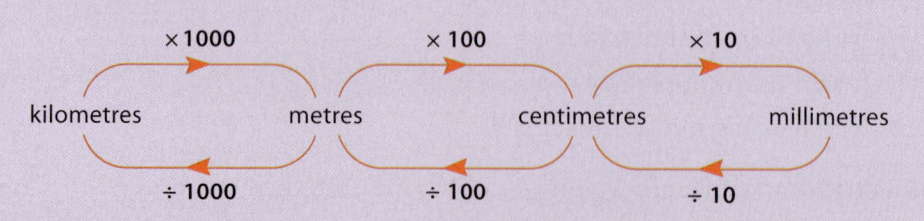

kilometres ×1000→ metres ×100→ centimetres ×10→ millimetres
kilometres ←÷1000 metres ←÷100 centimetres ←÷10 millimetres

Shorthand for millimetres, centimetres, metres and kilometres are mm, cm, m and km.

B1 Change 6 cm into millimetres.

B2 Change these lengths into centimetres.
(a) 5 m (b) 23 m (c) 50 mm (d) 200 mm

B3 Change these lengths into metres.
(a) 800 cm (b) 1500 cm (c) 7 km (d) 25 km

B4 Change 9000 m into kilometres.

B5 How many millimetres are there in 3.6 cm?

B6
A 452 × 100
B 452 × 1000
C 452 ÷ 1000
D 452 ÷ 100

(a) Choose the correct calculation to change 452 km to metres.
(b) Choose the correct calculation to change 452 cm to metres.

B7 Change these lengths into metres.
(a) 486 cm (b) 607 cm (c) 3.2 km (d) 14.9 km

B8 Change these lengths into centimetres.
(a) 4.5 m (b) 1.25 m (c) 72 mm (d) 129 mm

B9 Change 87 200 m into kilometres.

B10 Put each set of lengths in order, shortest first.
(a) 400 m   500 cm   2 km
(b) 3 m   3 cm   40 mm
(c) 0.3 m   8.1 cm   62 mm
(d) 1.5 km   900 m   0.4 km

B11 A certain tropical bamboo plant grows 33 cm every day.
  (a) In centimetres, how much does it grow in 10 days?
  (b) Give your answer in metres.

B12 The smallest recorded marine fish is the dwarf goby at 8.6 mm long.
  (a) In millimetres, how long is a line of 100 dwarf goby fish, placed end to end?
  (b) Give your answer in centimetres.

B13 Vincent's car is 4.5 m long.
  (a) How long is a line of 1000 of these cars, placed end to end?
  (b) York is 39 km from Leeds. Would the line of cars stretch this far?

B14 A specimen of *Dioon edule*, a Mexican evergreen shrub, was found to be growing only 0.76 mm in a year.
At this rate, how many centimetres would it grow in a thousand years?

B15 The full stops in this book are 0.5 mm wide.
How wide will a hundred of these full stops be if they are printed side by side?
Give your answer in centimetres.

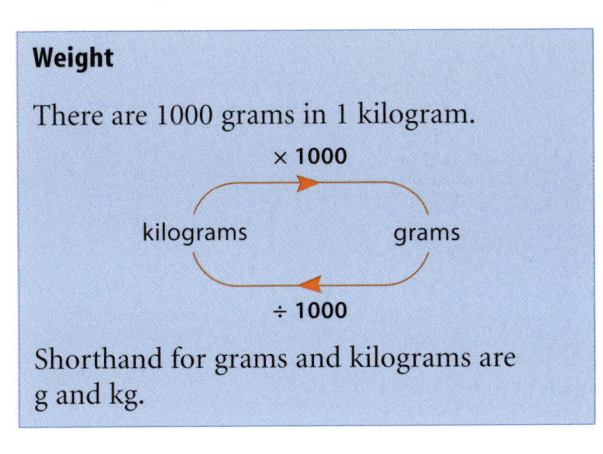

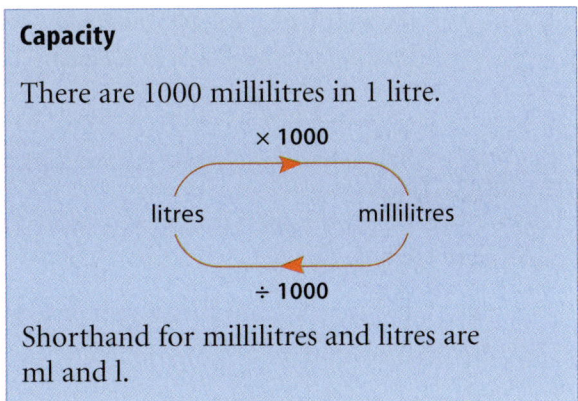

Weight

There are 1000 grams in 1 kilogram.

× 1000
kilograms → grams
÷ 1000

Shorthand for grams and kilograms are g and kg.

Capacity

There are 1000 millilitres in 1 litre.

× 1000
litres → millilitres
÷ 1000

Shorthand for millilitres and litres are ml and l.

B16 (a) Change 2450 g to kilograms.   (b) Change 1.2 litres to millilitres.
  (c) Change 890 ml to litres.   (d) Change 0.3 kg to grams.

B17 Which is heavier: 2.58 kg or 785 g?

B18 A house mouse weighs 12 g.
How much would 100 of these mice weigh in kilograms?

B19 Jane has two cartons of milk.
One carton holds 500 ml and the other holds 250 ml.
How many **litres** of milk does she have altogether?

B20 Helen buys 6 bags of flour, each holding 250 grams.
How many kilograms of flour does she buy altogether?

B21 Which holds more: a glass that holds 0.2 litre or a glass that holds 125 ml?

B22 Sue has a bottle that holds 0.3 litre of medicine.
She takes 5 ml of this medicine every day.
How long will her medicine last?

B23 Put these weights in order, smallest first.

   300 g   0.5 kg   0.07 kg   67 g   892 g   1.04 kg   0.985 kg

Test yourself

T1 Estimate the height of your classroom door.

T2 (a) Copy and complete the table by writing a sensible metric unit on each dotted line. The first one has been done for you.

The distance from London to Birmingham	179 kilometres
The weight of a twenty pence coin	5 ....
The height of the tallest living man	232 ....
The volume of lemonade in a glass	250 ....

(b) Change 5000 metres to kilometres.

Edexcel

T3 Write down the **metric** unit you would use to measure
   (a) the weight of a car
   (b) the distance from Birmingham to Glasgow
   (c) the amount of lemonade in a glass
   (d) the length of a bus

Edexcel

T4 Change 64 000 metres to kilometres.

T5 A hairdresser buys a large bottle of shampoo that holds 1.5 litres.
How many millilitres of shampoo is this?

T6 Which length is longer: 165 cm or 2.4 m?

T7 Chetna has two bags of rice.
One weighs 1.5 kg and one weighs 750 g.
How much rice does she have altogether in kilograms?

17 Working with expressions 1

This work will help you
- substitute into expressions such as $7 - 3n$
- simplify expressions such as $2 + 6n + 5 - 7n$

A Simplifying expressions such as $4 + 2n - 3 + n$

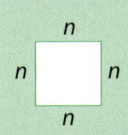

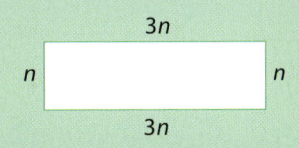

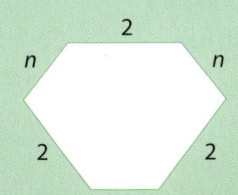

[Shapes with side labels: square with sides n, n, n, n; rectangle with sides $3n, n, 3n, n$; hexagon with sides $2, n, 2, n, 2, n$.]

- Find an expression for the perimeter of each shape. Write each expression in its simplest form.
- What is the perimeter of each shape when $n = 2$?

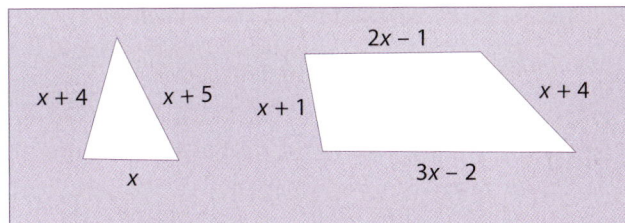

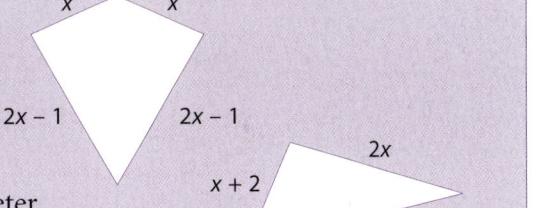

[Shapes with side labels: triangle with sides $x + 4$, $x + 5$, x; quadrilateral with sides $2x - 1$, $x + 1$, $3x - 2$, $x + 4$; kite with sides x, x, $2x - 1$, $2x - 1$; triangle with sides $x + 2$, $2x$, $3x - 5$.]

- Find and simplify an expression for each perimeter.
- What is the perimeter of each shape when $x = 10$?

A1 Work out the value of each expression when $n = 4$.

(a) $3n$ (b) $n + 5$ (c) $2n + 1$ (d) $4n - 3$ (e) $5n + 2$

A2 There are seven expressions below.
There are three pairs of equivalent expressions and one left over.

(a) Find the three equivalent pairs.

A $6 + 3a + a + 5$ **B** $2a + 2 + a + 1$ **C** $a + 2a + 1 + 2$ **D** $2a + 4 + 2a + 5$

E $a + 2 + a + 1$ **F** $7 + 2a + 2a + 4$ **G** $a + 3 + a$

(b) Work out the value of each expression when $a = 5$.

A3 Simplify each of these expressions.
- (a) $p + p + p$
- (b) $e + e + 2 + 1$
- (c) $h + h + 2 + h + 3$
- (d) $f + 1 + f + 2 + f$
- (e) $10 + g + 3 + g + g$
- (f) $y + 2 + y + 3 + y + y$

A4 Write down an expression for the perimeter of each shape.
Write each expression as simply as possible.

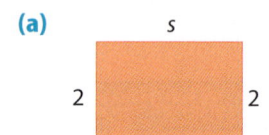

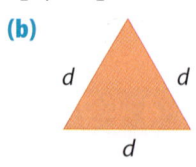

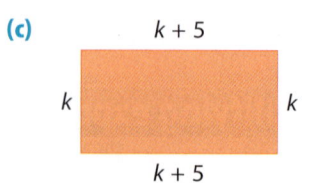

(a) Rectangle with sides s and 2.

(b) Triangle with all sides d.

(c) Rectangle with sides $k + 5$ and k.

A5 Simplify each of these.
- (a) $2a + 3a + 4a$
- (b) $2b + 12 + 3b + 1$
- (c) $30 + c + 3c + 12 + 2c$
- (d) $3d + 10 + 2d + 8$
- (e) $12e + 13 + 4e + 10$
- (f) $10f + 2 + 2f + 13 + 7f$

A6 Work out an expression for each length marked ?.

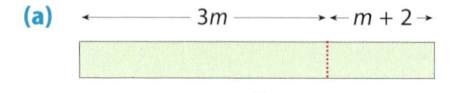

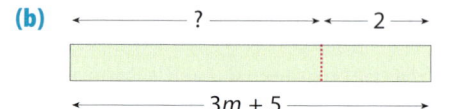

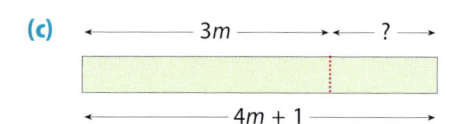

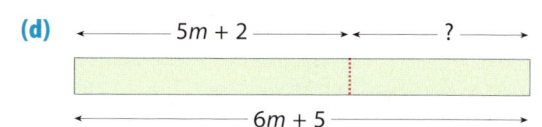

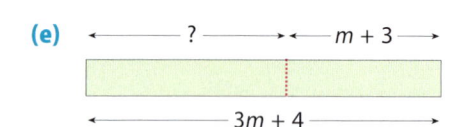

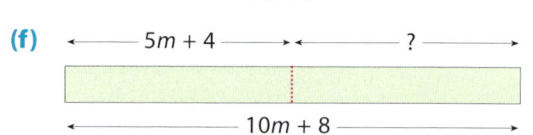

(a) Top: $3m$ and $m + 2$; bottom: ?

(b) Top: ? and 2; bottom: $3m + 5$

(c) Top: $3m$ and ?; bottom: $4m + 1$

(d) Top: $5m + 2$ and ?; bottom: $6m + 5$

(e) Top: ? and $m + 3$; bottom: $3m + 4$

(f) Top: $5m + 4$ and ?; bottom: $10m + 8$

A7 The perimeter of this triangle is $7n + 8$.
Write an expression for the missing length.

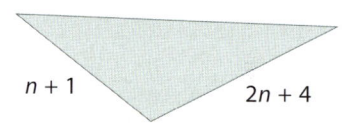

Triangle with sides $n + 1$ and $2n + 4$.

A8 Simplify each of these.
- (a) $5x + x + 4 - 1$
- (b) $4x + 3x + 9 - 3$
- (c) $2x + 5 + 3x - 2$
- (d) $6x + 8 + 3x - 5$
- (e) $5 + 2x + 3x - 2$
- (f) $2x + 6x - 1 + 2$
- (g) $x + 8x - 3 + 5$
- (h) $10x - 4 + x + 7$
- (i) $3x - 10 + 2x + 15$

A9 Simplify each of these.
- (a) $4n + 3n + 2 - 5$
- (b) $n + 8n + 1 - 3$
- (c) $7n + 4 + 2n - 5$
- (d) $n + 2n - 3 - 2$
- (e) $5n - 3 + 5n - 8$
- (f) $3n - 5 + 7n - 2$
- (g) $5n + n - 6 + 4$
- (h) $3n - 5 + 4n + 4$
- (i) $8n - 3 + 4n + 1$

B Substituting into expressions such as 7 – 2n

Examples

Find the value of 7 – x when x = 3.

7 – x = 7 – 3
     = 4

Find the value of 11 – 3b when b = 2.

11 – 3b = 11 – (3 × 2)
       = 11 – 6
       = 5

You can use brackets to remind you to do the multiplication first.

B1 What is the value of 10 – n when n = 3?

B2 What is the value of each expression when n = 5?
(a) 6 – n (b) 15 – n (c) 8 – n (d) 5 – n

B3 Find the value of 15 – 2x when x = 4.

B4 Find the value of each expression when x = 2.
(a) 7 – 2x (b) 11 – 3x (c) 9 – 4x (d) 10 – 5x

B5 What is the value of each expression when a = 8?
(a) 20 – a (b) 50 – 3a (c) 60 – 5a (d) 100 – 4a

B6 When n = 3 find the value of
(a) 5 – n (b) n – 5 (c) 9 – n (d) n – 9

B7 The ground clearance of a lorry or car is the distance between the bottom of the lorry or car and the ground.

For this lorry the rule for the ground clearance is
  d = 100 – 5w
where d is the ground clearance in centimetres and w is the weight the lorry is carrying in tonnes.

(a) Work out d when w = 10.
(b) What is the value of d when w = 3?
(c) What is the ground clearance when the lorry is carrying 8 tonnes of sand?
(d) Can the lorry carry a weight of 30 tonnes? Explain your answer.

B8 Evaluate each expression when x = 5.
(a) 20 – 3x (b) 3x – 20 (c) 3 – 2x (d) 3x – 3

*B9 Evaluate each expression when a = ⁻2.
(a) 1 – a (b) a – 1 (c) 10 – a (d) a – 10

C Simplifying expressions such as $4 + 2n - 3 - 5n$

When simplifying expressions it can often help to reorder the parts of the expression first.
For example,

$$2 - 5x + 8 - 3x = 2 + 8 - 5x - 3x$$

5x and 3x are both subtracted so they must be subtracted in the reordered expression.

$$= 10 - 8x$$

Subtracting 5x and then 3x is the same as subtracting 8x.

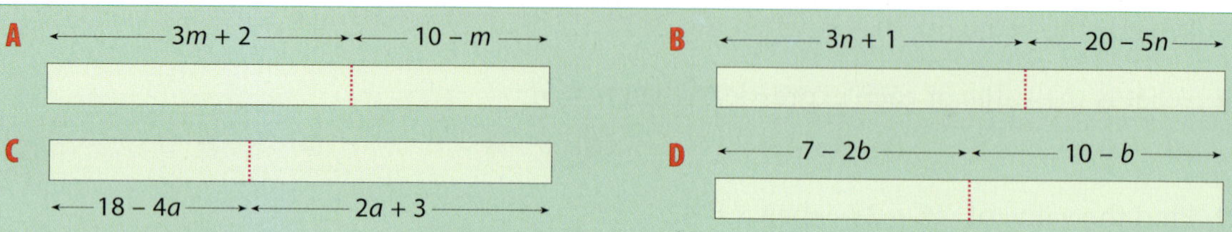

A ←——— $3m + 2$ ———→ ←——— $10 - m$ ———→

B ←——— $3n + 1$ ———→ ←——— $20 - 5n$ ———→

C ←——— $18 - 4a$ ———→ ←——— $2a + 3$ ———→

D ←——— $7 - 2b$ ———→ ←——— $10 - b$ ———→

- Find an expression for the length of each bar.
  Write each expression as simply as possible.

C1 Simplify each of these.

(a) $7a - 3a$ (b) $8x - 3x$ (c) $3n - n$
(d) $2b + 7b - 3b$ (e) $8c - 4c + 2c$ (f) $5y - y + 5y$
(g) $10p - 3p - 5p$ (h) $8g - 3g - 4g$ (i) $7h - h - 3h$

C2 Find three pairs of equivalent expressions.

A $3 + 8x - 6x$ **B** $7x - 3 - 5x$ **C** $3 - x + 5x$
D $3 + 4x$ **E** $2x - 3$ **F** $3 + 2x$

C3 Simplify each of these.

(a) $6 + 7y - 3y$ (b) $4x + 5 - x$ (c) $8f - 1 - 5f$
(d) $10 - 2g + 7g$ (e) $8 - k + 5k$ (f) $2a - 9 - a$

C4 Find four pairs of equivalent expressions.

A $7 + 2a - 7a$ **B** $7 - 4a + a$ **C** $7 - 5a$ **D** $a + 7 - 3a$
E $7 - 2a$ **F** $7 - 5a - 3a$ **G** $7 - 8a$ **H** $7 - 3a$

C5 Simplify each of these.

(a) $1 + 2x - 5x$
(b) $6 + y - 8y$
(c) $7 + 2f - 4f$
(d) $3 - 7g + 3g$
(e) $2 - 9k + k$
(f) $5 - 2n - 7n$
(g) $1 - g - 3g$
(h) $5 - m - m$
(i) $2a + 9 - 3a$

C6 Simplify each of these.

(a) $7a - 4a + 8 + 1$
(b) $10x - 7x + 4 - 5$
(c) $3n + 5 - n + 5n$
(d) $6b + 3 - 2b + 1$
(e) $5 + 7c + 3 - 6c$
(f) $7y + 5 - 2y - 4$
(g) $7 + 3p - 3 - 7p$
(h) $4 - 2g + 3 - 3g$
(i) $10 - 3h - 7 - h$

C7 (a) Write down and simplify an expression for the length of each bar.

(i) ⟵ $5n + 3$ ⟶ ⟵ $20 - 3n$ ⟶

(ii) ⟵ $8n - 4$ ⟶ ⟵ $10 - 2n$ ⟶

(b) What is the length of each bar when $n = 2$?

C8 Write down and simplify an expression for the perimeter of each shape.

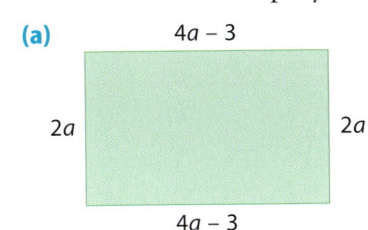

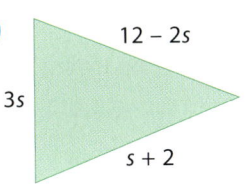

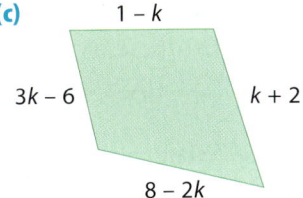

(a) rectangle with sides $4a - 3$ and $2a$

(b) triangle with sides $12 - 2s$, $3s$, $s + 2$

(c) quadrilateral with sides $1 - k$, $k + 2$, $8 - 2k$, $3k - 6$

Test yourself

T1 Simplify each of these expressions.

(a) $t + t + t + t$
(b) $r + 2 + r - 1$
(c) $1 + u + 2 + u + 2$
(d) $2f + 5f + 3f$
(e) $2a + 3 + a + 5$
(f) $2g + 4 + 5g - 3$

T2 Simplify each of these expressions.

(a) $n + n + n - n$
(b) $9x + 5 - 2x + 1$
(c) $7m - 3m + 2m$
(d) $9 + 8k - 7 - 3k$
(e) $1 + h + 3 - 6h$
(f) $1 - 3y + 5 - 2y$

T3 (a) Find and simplify an expression for the perimeter of this shape.

triangle with sides $3x + 1$, $10 - x$, $5x - 6$

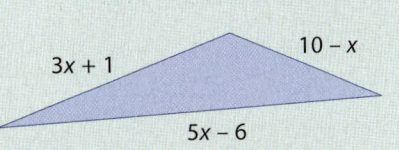

(b) Find the perimeter when $x = 4$.

Review 2

1. Here are three of Anna's bracelets.

   (a) Size 1 is made from 5 silver bars. How many bars would be needed to make a size 4 bracelet?

   (b) Copy and complete this table.

Size of bracelet (n)	1	2	3	4	5	10
Number of bars (b)	5	9				

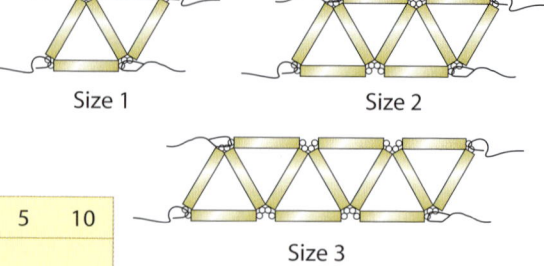

   (c) Which of these expressions is correct for the number of bars in a size n bracelet?

   $3n + 2$ $2n + 3$ $5n$ $4n + 1$ $4n - 1$

   (d) What size bracelet will use 49 silver bars? Show your working clearly.

2. This solid is made from five centimetre cubes.

   (a) Does the solid have any planes of symmetry? If so, how many?

   (b) On squared paper, draw a plan view, a front view and a side view of the solid.

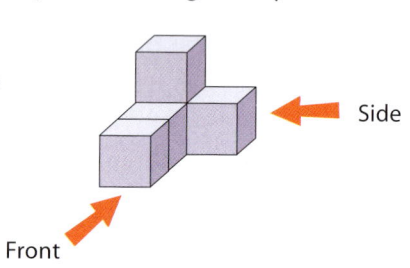

3. Do these in your head, without writing down any working.

   (a) 46×5 (b) 18×4 (c) $68 \div 4$ (d) $120 \div 4$ (e) $120 \div 5$

4. Write

   (a) $\frac{2}{5}$ as a decimal   (b) 0.25 as a fraction   (c) 60% as a decimal

5. Arica, in Chile, has the lowest annual rainfall in the world.
   It has on average only 0.7 mm of rain in a year.
   How many centimetres of rain would it have on average in 100 years?

6. Work out the area of each parallelogram.
   You will not need to use all the measurements each time.

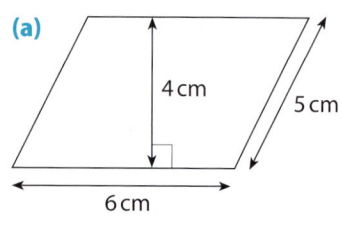

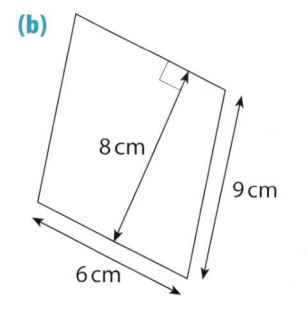

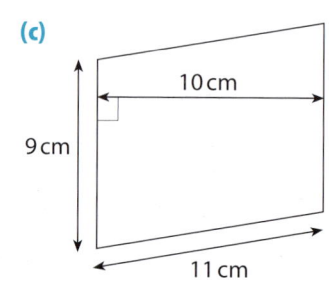

   (a) 4 cm, 5 cm, 6 cm

   (b) 8 cm, 9 cm, 6 cm

   (c) 10 cm, 9 cm, 11 cm

7 Work these out.

(a) $8 + {}^-4$ (b) ${}^-2 + {}^-3$ (c) $3 - 10$ (d) $3 - {}^-6$ (e) $4 \times {}^-3$

8 Choose the most appropriate unit from the ones below for giving

(a) the weight of a railway engine
(b) the weight of a piece of paper
(c) the weight of a sheep
(d) the height of the Eiffel tower
(e) the distance from London to Paris
(f) the width of a pencil

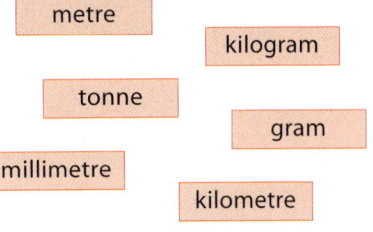

metre   kilogram   tonne   gram   millimetre   kilometre

9 Simplify each of these expressions.

(a) $f + f + f + f + f$ (b) $2x + 5 + x - 7$ (c) $7 + a + 1 - 4a$

10 Work out each of these. Show your working clearly.

(a) $315 + 109$ (b) $315 - 109$ (c) 68×6 (d) $1442 \div 7$

(e) $1.85 + 1.3$ (f) $2.1 - 0.34$ (g) 7.45×4 (h) $7.45 \div 5$

11 Find and simplify an expression for the perimeter of this shape.

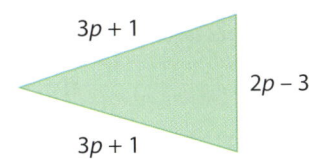

Triangle sides: $3p + 1$, $2p - 3$, $3p + 1$

12 Michelle is making curtains and needs 1.4 m of material for each curtain.

(a) How much material does she need to make 4 curtains?
(b) Michelle bought a piece of material 6 m long.
How much material does she have left after making the 4 curtains?

13 Write these in order, starting with the smallest. 28% 0.2 $\frac{1}{4}$ 0.36 $\frac{1}{3}$

14 This table shows the weights of some slimmers before taking a 6-week slimmers' course.

Weight in kg	89	98	75	79	88	75	88	70	93	76
	82	73	69	96	81	99	68	65	87	77

(a) Work out the mean weight of these slimmers.
(b) Copy and complete this stem-and-leaf table.
The first two weights have been put into the table.
Rewrite the table, putting the leaves in order.
(c) What is the median weight of the slimmers?
(d) What is the range of weight of the slimmers?

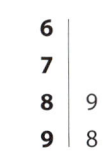

6	
7	
8	9
9	8

Stem: 10 kg

18 Graphs of changes over time

This work will help you

- describe what is happening on a graph
- sketch a graph for a real-life situation

You need sheet F1–19.

A Noise level

Noise probe call   City Mail

Residents near City's ground called for action against noise on match days. They recorded the noise at last Saturday's match against Ribchester Rovers, saying it was far above permitted levels.

Blonde mother of six Mrs Betty Bowland, City resident for 15 years, said 'It's not me I worry about, it's all us with young kids. Can't sleep at all, they can't, on match days.'

Last Saturday City turned out 25,000 fans against Ribchester Rovers' 10,000. It was a lively crowd, said our reporter Tom Drivel, and the noise was about average for a Saturday game.

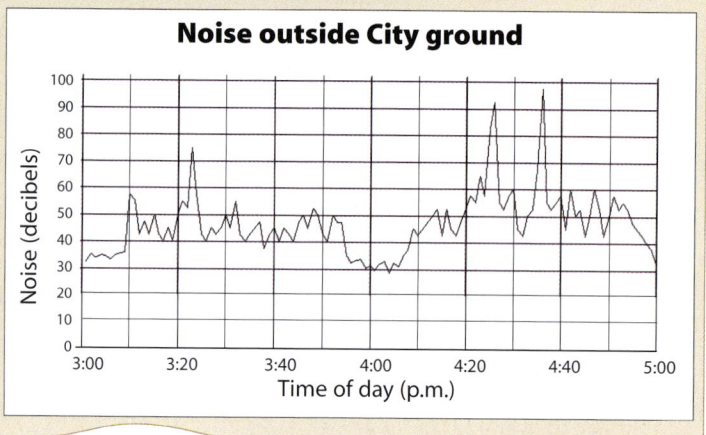

Noise outside City ground

(graph of Noise (decibels) vs Time of day (p.m.) from 3:00 to 5:00)

A1 Look at the graph of the noise from the football match.

  (a) At about what time do you think the match actually started? (It was not 3 o'clock.)

  (b) Roughly when did half-time begin?

  (c) About what time did the match end?

A2 (a) How many goals do you think were scored?

  (b) City had 25 000 fans at the match. Ribchester Rovers had 10 000. What do you think the score was at the end of the match?

A3 Noise is regularly monitored at rock concerts.
Here is a noise chart and a newspaper cutting about a rock concert.

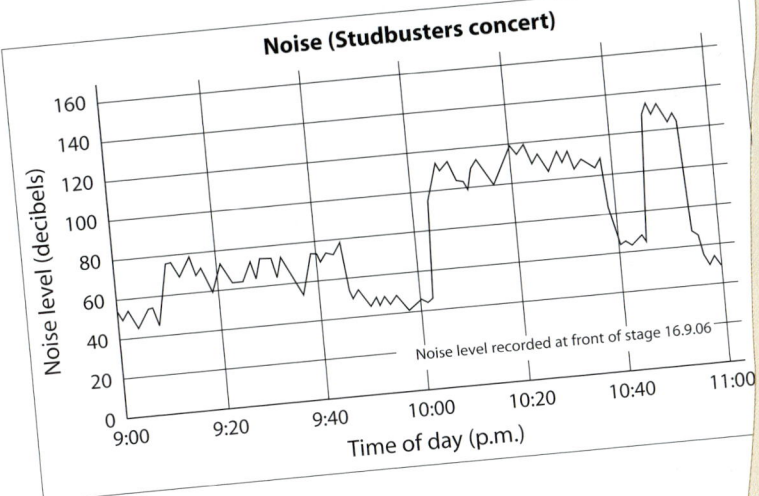

Noise (Studbusters concert) — Noise level recorded at front of stage 16.9.06

> Never have the Studbusters played better. Last night's concert at Heathcote Park was just brilliant. A noisy and energetic crowd gave them a huge welcome and just kept on cheering. As the concert drew to a close, the quiet ballad 'Down Mine' was followed by the ear-bending 'Deep Fruit' – f a n t a s t i c ! In the first half, the support band Stargaggle were a bit quiet, but OK. All told an amazing night.

Read the newspaper cutting carefully.
Use the cutting and the noise chart to answer these questions.

(a) About what time do you think Stargaggle came on?

(b) There was an interval in the concert.
Roughly how long did it last?

(c) What time did the Studbusters start playing?

(d) Between what times did the Studbusters play 'Down Mine'?

(e) 'Deep Fruit' was earbending. When?

(f) About when did Studbusters go off?

(g) A noise level of 120 decibels may cause damage to a person's hearing within a few minutes.
Was this level of noise exceeded at the concert? If so, when?

A4 The noise in a playground changes during the day. When everyone is in lessons it is quiet. At other times it is noisier.

On squared paper, draw axes like these.

Sketch the noise level in your school playground during the day.

Don't worry about decibels!
Just draw a sketch.

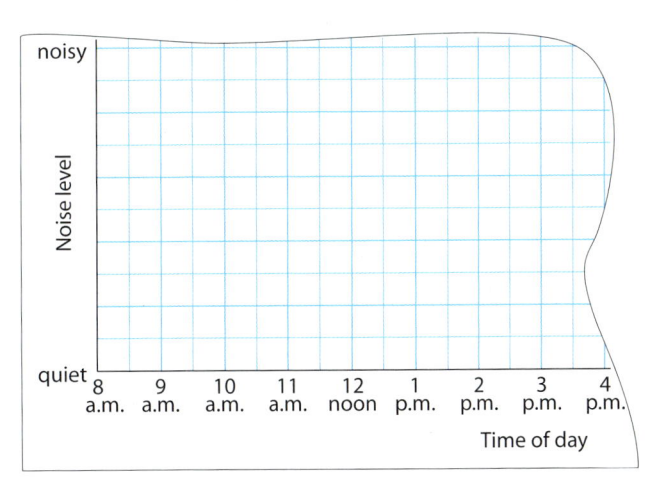

18 Graphs of changes over time   127

B Pulse rate

Ellie works out at a gym.
She has a pulse meter that records her pulse rate every 10 seconds.

Here is a printout and graph of her pulse rate when she was using a rowing machine.

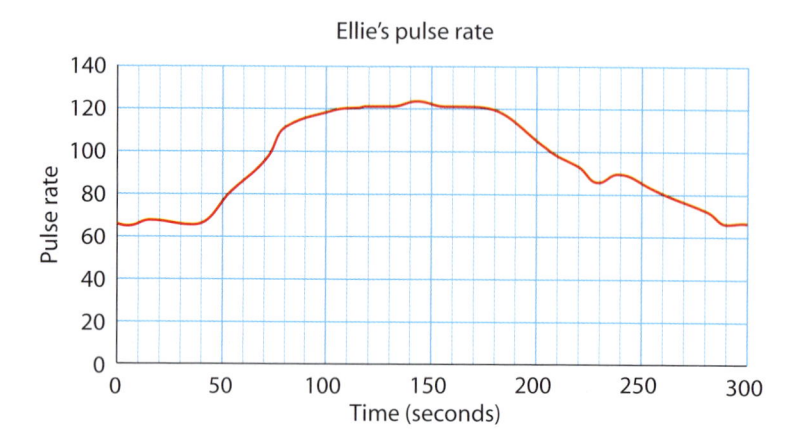

Time (s)	Pulse rate (beats per min)
0	65
10	65
20	66
30	65
40	65
50	73
60	85
70	93
80	110
90	115
100	118
110	119
120	121
130	120
140	123
150	122
160	120
170	121
180	119
190	114
200	104
210	99
220	93
230	85
240	89
250	84
260	80
270	76
280	72
290	69
300	67

Look carefully at the graph of Ellie's pulse rate.
She switched the meter on when the time was 0.
She waited a bit, then started rowing hard, and then stopped.

B1 **(a)** About how long did Ellie wait before she started rowing?

(b) What was the time on the graph when she stopped rowing?

(c) For about how long was she rowing?

(d) Roughly how long did it take Ellie's pulse to get back to normal?

B2 **(a)** The maximum pulse rate (p) for a person aged n years can be worked out using the formula $p = 220 - n$.
Ellie is aged 50.
What is her maximum pulse rate?

(b) When training hard, your pulse rate should get up to 80% of your maximum pulse rate.
Do you think Ellie is training hard enough?
Give your reasons.

B3 This question is on sheet F1–19.

C Temperature

C1 The graph shows the temperature inside a new fridge.
The temperature was taken every minute over a two-hour period.

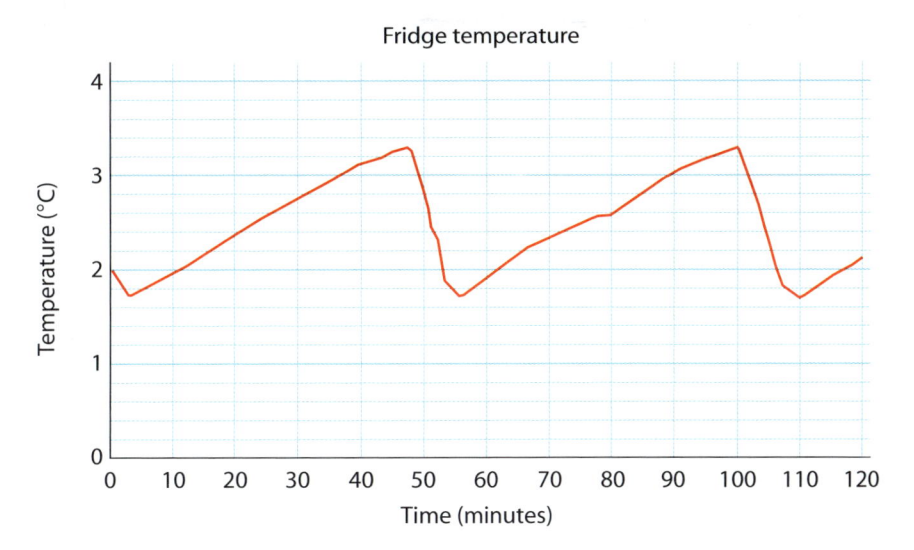

Fridge temperature

Temperature (°C) vs *Time (minutes)*

The fridge has a motor which cools down the inside.
The motor is switched on and off by a thermostat.

(a) What happens to the temperature in a fridge when the motor is running?

(b) At what temperature does the thermostat switch the motor on?

(c) What happens to the temperature when the motor is not running?

(d) At what temperature does the thermostat switch the motor off?

(e) For about how long does the motor run each time it is switched on?

C2 This graph shows the temperature in a greenhouse during 24 hours in summer.

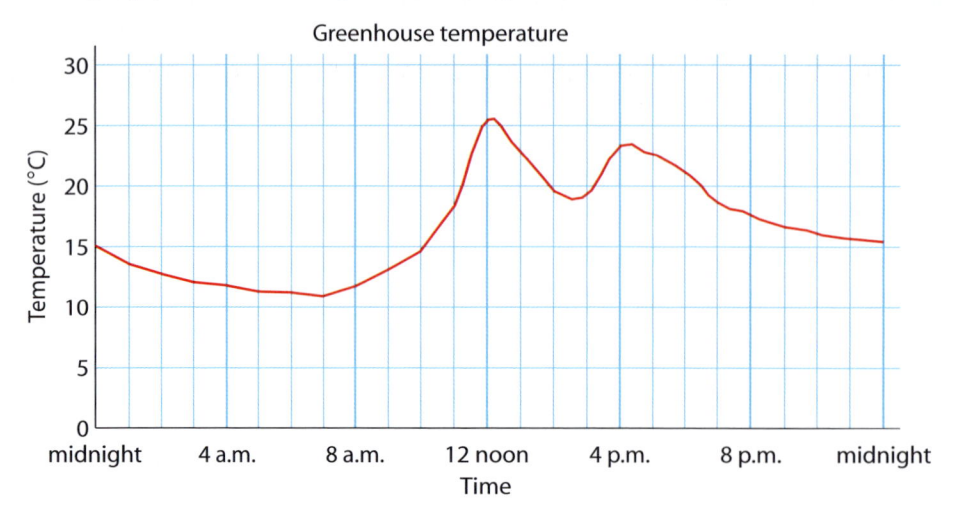

Greenhouse temperature

The temperature in a greenhouse falls during the night and rises during the day. There are windows in this greenhouse to help keep the temperature down when it gets too hot.

(a) At roughly what time in the morning does the temperature in the greenhouse start to go up?

(b) About when during the day is the temperature going up fastest?

(c) About when is it going down fastest?

(d) Because it was getting too hot, the gardener opened a window in the greenhouse. Later she closed it again.

  (i) About what time do you think she opened the window?

  (ii) Roughly when did she close it?

(e) What was the highest temperature in the greenhouse during the day?

(f) What was the lowest temperature in this 24 hours?

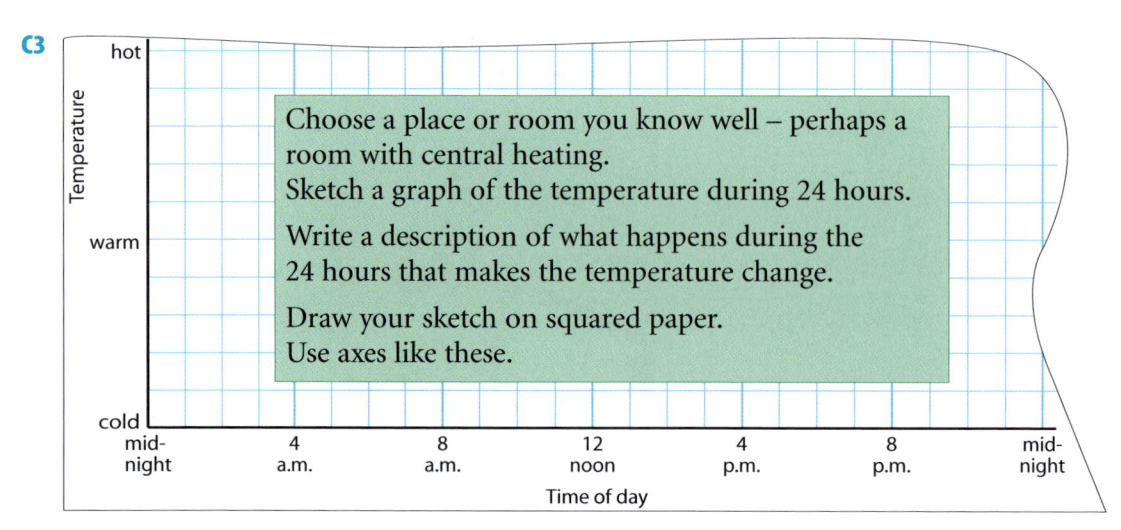

C3 Choose a place or room you know well – perhaps a room with central heating.

Sketch a graph of the temperature during 24 hours.

Write a description of what happens during the 24 hours that makes the temperature change.

Draw your sketch on squared paper. Use axes like these.

130 18 Graphs of changes over time

Test yourself

T1 This graph shows the number of people in a shopping centre one day near Christmas.

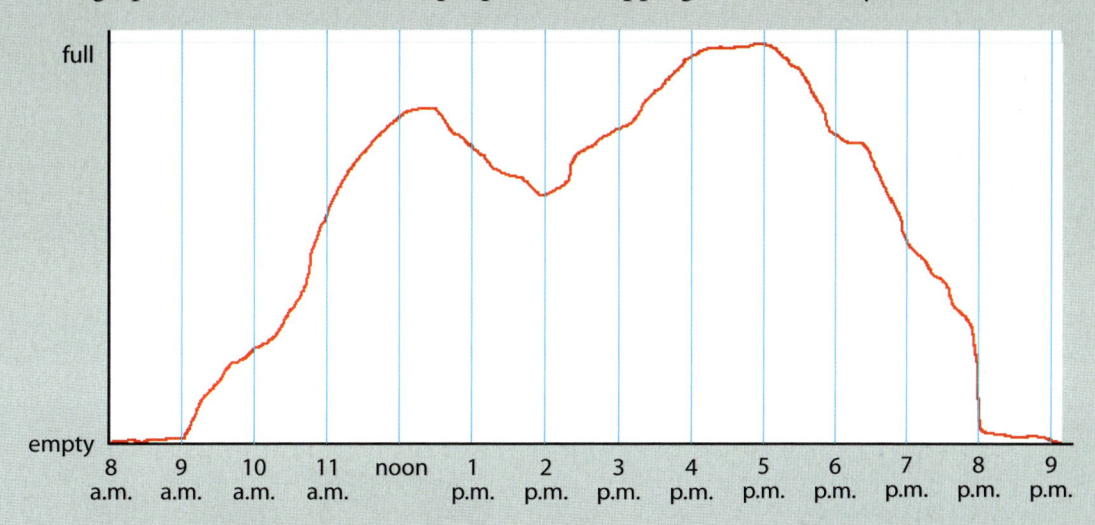

(a) What time do you think the shopping centre opened?
(b) What time do you think it closed?
(c) At roughly what time were there most people in the centre?
(d) At 1 p.m. was the centre empty, fairly empty, fairly full or full?
(e) Between noon and 6 p.m. when was it least full?

T2 This is part of the diary of Abir, who works in the shopping centre. On squared paper, sketch a graph for Abir's day.

Number your across axis like in question T1.
Label your up axis 'cold' at the bottom and 'hot' at the top.

> Got to work about 8 a.m. – it was really cold in the centre.
>
> The heating didn't come on until 10, and it only got warm by noon.
>
> By about 1 p.m. it was quite hot – and by 2 p.m. it was so hot they put the air-conditioning on to cool off a bit.
>
> At 4 p.m. we complained because it was now too cold! So they put the heating back on. But the heating broke down at 6 p.m. and by the time I left at half past 7 it was freezing again.
>
> Let's just hope they get it right tomorrow!

18 Graphs of changes over time

19 Chance

This work will help you

- write a probability as a fraction
- list all the outcomes in a given situation
- calculate probabilities from a list of outcomes
- use a grid to show all the outcomes

You need sheet F1–20, dice and counters.

A Probability as a fraction

You shuffle these five cards and pick one at random.

Wolf   Sheep   Goat   Rock   Tree

One of the cards is a sheep.
The probability of picking a sheep is $\frac{1}{5}$.

What is the probability that the card you pick

- is a wolf
- is an animal
- is a goat or a sheep
- is not a wolf
- is not an animal
- is a rabbit

A1 This fair spinner is spun once.

(a) On which colour is it most likely to stop?

(b) What is the probability it stops on

(i) white (ii) blue

(iii) yellow (iv) yellow or white

(c) What is the probability that it stops on a colour that is not white?

A2 There are 3 yellow beads and 5 blue beads in a bag.

(a) How many beads are there altogether?

A bead is taken from the bag without looking.

(b) What is the probability of taking a yellow bead?

(c) What is the probability of taking a blue bead?

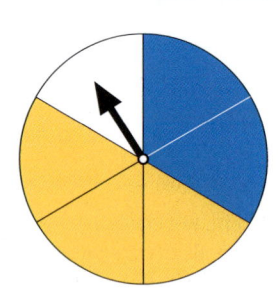

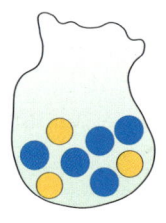

A3 For each of these bags find the probability of choosing

        (i) a yellow bead   **(ii)** a blue bead

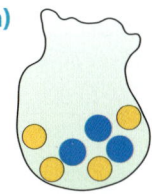

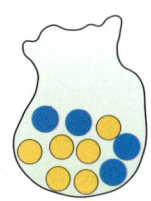

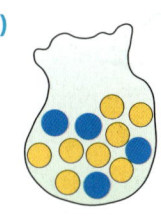

(a)   **(b)**   **(c)**   **(d)**

A4 The names Alan, Brian, Catherine, David and Eleanor are written on pieces of paper and put in a bag.

A piece of paper is chosen at random.
What is the probability that the name is

  (a) Catherine   **(b)** a boy's name   **(c)** a girl's name

A5 A box contains 5 blue pens, 3 black pens and 2 red pens.
A pen is taken from the box at random.

  (a) Which colour of pen has the best chance of being taken?

  (b) What is the probability that the pen is

      (i) blue   **(ii)** black   **(iii)** red   **(iv)** not black

> An **unbiased** dice is a fair dice where all the faces are equally likely to be rolled.

A6 An unbiased six-sided dice is rolled once.
What is the probability that the number on the dice is

  (a) 1   **(b)** less than 3

  (c) more than 2   **(d)** 5 or 6

A7 A bag contains four numbered discs that are all the same size.
A disc is taken from the bag at random.
What is the probability that the number on the disc is

  (a) 2   **(b)** greater than 5

  (c) even   **(d)** 3

A8 Two bags contain yellow and blue beads.
Katie will pick a bead at random from one of the bags.

Katie thinks that she has more chance of getting a blue bead with bag B.
She says that her chance is better because there are more blue beads in bag B than there are in bag A.

Explain why Katie is wrong.

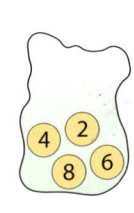

Bag A   Bag B

19 Chance 133

B Listing outcomes

T George runs a vegetarian café.
This is his menu.

He lists all the possible meals there are with a starter and a main course.

To make this easier he uses the first letter of each dish. He starts the list by writing all the meals with Avocado as a starter.

The Green Café

Starters
Avocado with mayo
Beetroot soup

Main courses
Cauliflower cheese
Deep fried tofu
Enchiladas

Starter	Main
A	C
A	D
A	

Copy and complete George's list.

Each different meal is called an **outcome**.

How many different outcomes are there?

One customer likes every dish and always chooses a starter and a main course **at random**.

What is the probability that this customer chooses

- beetroot soup and enchiladas
- avocado as a starter
- cauliflower cheese as a main course
- tofu or enchiladas as a main course

B1 Each section on this unbiased spinner is the same size.
The arrow is spun twice.

(a) Copy and complete this list to show all the possible outcomes where the arrow could land.

First spin	Second spin
Red	Red
Red	Blue

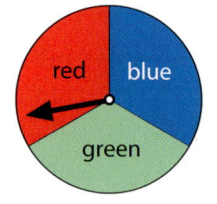

(b) How many outcomes are there altogether?
(c) What is the probability that the arrow lands on red both times?
(d) What is the probability the arrow lands on the same colour both times?
(e) What is the probability the arrow lands on a different colour each time?

B2 The arrows on both these unbiased spinners are spun.

(a) Copy and complete this list of all the possible outcomes.

First spinner	Second spinner
1	5
1	6

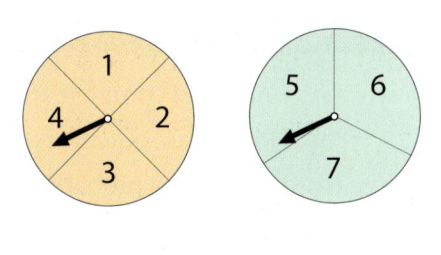

(b) How many outcomes are there altogether?

(c) What is the probability that

   (i) the arrows point to 3 and 5   (ii) both arrows point to odd numbers

   (iii) both point to even numbers

B3 These cards are placed face down and shuffled.
A player chooses a card and turns it over.
The card is returned to the pack and it is shuffled again.
A second player now chooses a card and turns it over.

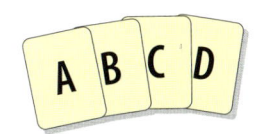

(a) Make a list to show the possible pairs of letters they could have chosen.

(b) What is the probability that both players choose the same letter?

B4 There are two sets of cards as shown here.
Julie picks one card from set A and one from set B.
Her score is the sum of the two cards.

(a) Copy and complete this list.

Set A	Set B	Score
1	6	7
1	7	8

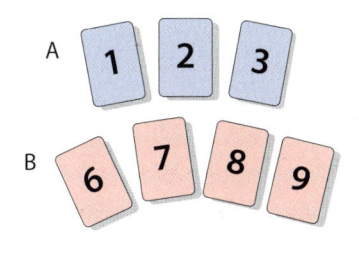

(b) What is the probability of Julie getting a score of 10?

(c) What is the probability of Julie getting a score of 11?

(d) What is the probability of getting a score that is 10 or more?

(e) What is the probability of getting a score of 6?

B5 A 2p and a 10p coin are flipped together.

(a) Copy and complete this list of outcomes.

2p coin	10p coin
H	H

(b) How many outcomes are there altogether?

(c) What is the probability both coins show heads?

(d) What is the probability that you get one head and one tail?

19 Chance 135

B6 A 2p, a 5p and a 10p coin are flipped together.

2p coin	5p coin	10p coin
H	H	H
H	H	T

(a) Copy and complete this list for the outcomes.
(b) How many outcomes are there altogether?
(c) What is the probability that all three coins show tails?
(d) What is the probability that two coins show tails and one coin shows a head?

C Using a grid

Skyscraper a game for up to six players

You need two dice, sheet F1–20 and six counters.

- Each player chooses a different number between 0 and 5 and places a counter on their number at the bottom of a skyscraper.
- Each player takes it in turn to roll the two dice.
  The score is the **difference** in the numbers on the two dice.
  For example a 2 and a 5 would give a score of 5 − 2 = 3.
  Whichever player has the number equal to that score can move their counter up one floor of their skyscraper.
- The winner is the first person to reach the top of their skyscraper.

Do you think this game is fair?

C1 (a) Copy and complete this grid to show all the possible outcomes in the 'Skyscraper' game.
(b) How many outcomes are there altogether?
(c) On your grid, colour in all the outcomes where the score is 0.
What is the probability of a score of 0?
(d) In a different colour, shade in the outcomes where the score is 1.
What is the probability of a score of 1?
(e) Work out the probability of each of the other possible scores.
(f) Which score is least likely?
(g) Which number skyscraper would you choose to get the best chance of winning?

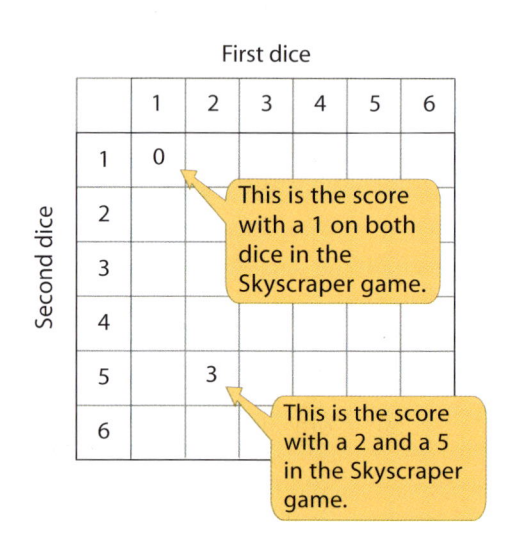

First dice

	1	2	3	4	5	6
1	0					
2						
3						
4						
5		3				
6						

Second dice

This is the score with a 1 on both dice in the Skyscraper game.

This is the score with a 2 and a 5 in the Skyscraper game.

C2 In a different game the score is the **sum** of the numbers on two unbiased dice.

(a) Copy and complete this grid to show the possible scores in this game.

(b) On your grid colour in all the scores where the sum is 10.
What is the probability of scoring 10?

(c) Use a different colour to colour in all the scores where the sum is 6.
What is the probability of scoring 6?

(d) Use a different colour to colour in all the scores where the sum is greater than 10.
What is the probability of scoring **more than** 10?

(e) Which score is the most likely in this game? What is the probability of this score?

First dice

+	1	2	3	4	5	6
1						
2						
3						
4			6			
5						
6						

Second dice

C3 A bag contains five discs that are numbered 1, 2, 3, 4 and 5.

Rachel takes a disc at random from the bag. She notes the number and puts the disc back. She shakes the bag and picks again. She adds the number to the first number.

(a) Copy and complete the table to show all the possible totals.

(b) Find the probability that Rachel's total is

   (i) 10   (ii) 1   (iii) 3 or 4

First number

+	1	2	3	4	5
1	2				
2					
3				7	
4					
5					

Second number

OCR

C4 In a game, both these unbiased spinners are spun and the score is the numbers added together.

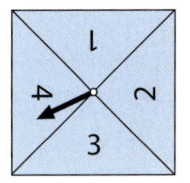

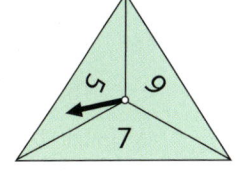

(a) Copy and complete this table to show all the possible scores.

(b) Find the probability that the score is 8.

(c) Find the probability that the score is more than 8.

(d) Find the probability that the score is an even number.

Square spinner

+	1	2	3	4
5				9
6	7			
7				

Triangular spinner

19 Chance 137

Test yourself

T1 Shreena has a bag of 20 sweets.
10 of the sweets are red.
3 of the sweets are black.
The rest of the sweets are white.

Shreena chooses one sweet at random.
What is the probability that Shreena will choose a

  (a) red sweet   **(b)** white sweet?

Edexcel

T2 In a raffle 200 tickets are sold.
There is only one prize.

Mr Key buys 10 tickets.
Mrs Key buys 6 tickets.
Their children, Robert and Rachel, buy 2 tickets each.

  (a) Which member of the family has the best chance of winning the prize?
  Give a reason for your answer.

  (b) What is the probability that Mrs Key wins the prize?

  (c) What is the probability that **none** of the family wins the prize?

AQA

T3 Sarah is choosing from this menu.

Starters	Main courses
Tomato soup [T]	Beef [B]
Salmon salad [S]	Duck [D]
Prawns [P]	Lasagne [L]
	Chicken [C]

She chooses a starter and a main course.

  (a) Copy and complete the table below showing all her possible choices.
  One has been done for you.

Starter	Main course
T	B

  (b) She chooses at random.
  What is the probability that she chooses
   (i) Prawns and Duck
   (ii) Tomato soup or Salmon salad as a starter

OCR

T4 Two bags, A and B, each contain four numbered discs that are all the same size.

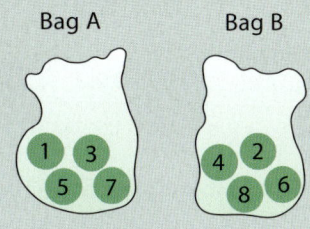

Bag A: 1, 3, 5, 7
Bag B: 2, 4, 6, 8

(a) A disc is drawn at random from bag A and a disc is drawn at random from bag B.
A score is obtained by adding the numbers on the two discs.
Copy and complete the table to show all the possible scores.

Bag A

+	1	3	5	7
2	3	5		
4				
6				
8				

Bag B

(b) Find the probability of scoring less than 9. *AQA*

T5 A red dice and a blue dice are rolled together. Both dice are unbiased.
The **difference** between the two scores is recorded in a table.

Score on red dice

	1	2	3	4	5	6
1	0	1	2	3	4	5
2	1			2		
3	2			1		
4	3			0		
5	4			1		
6	5	4	3	2	1	0

Score on blue dice

(a) Copy and complete the table.
(b) Find the probability that the difference in the scores is 2.
(c) Find the probability that the difference in the scores is **greater than 3**. *OCR*

20 Area of a triangle and of composite shapes

You need to know how to find the area of a parallelogram.

This work will help you
- find the area of a triangle
- find the area of composite shapes (shapes made from simpler shapes)

You need sheets F1–21 and F1–22.

A Area of a triangle

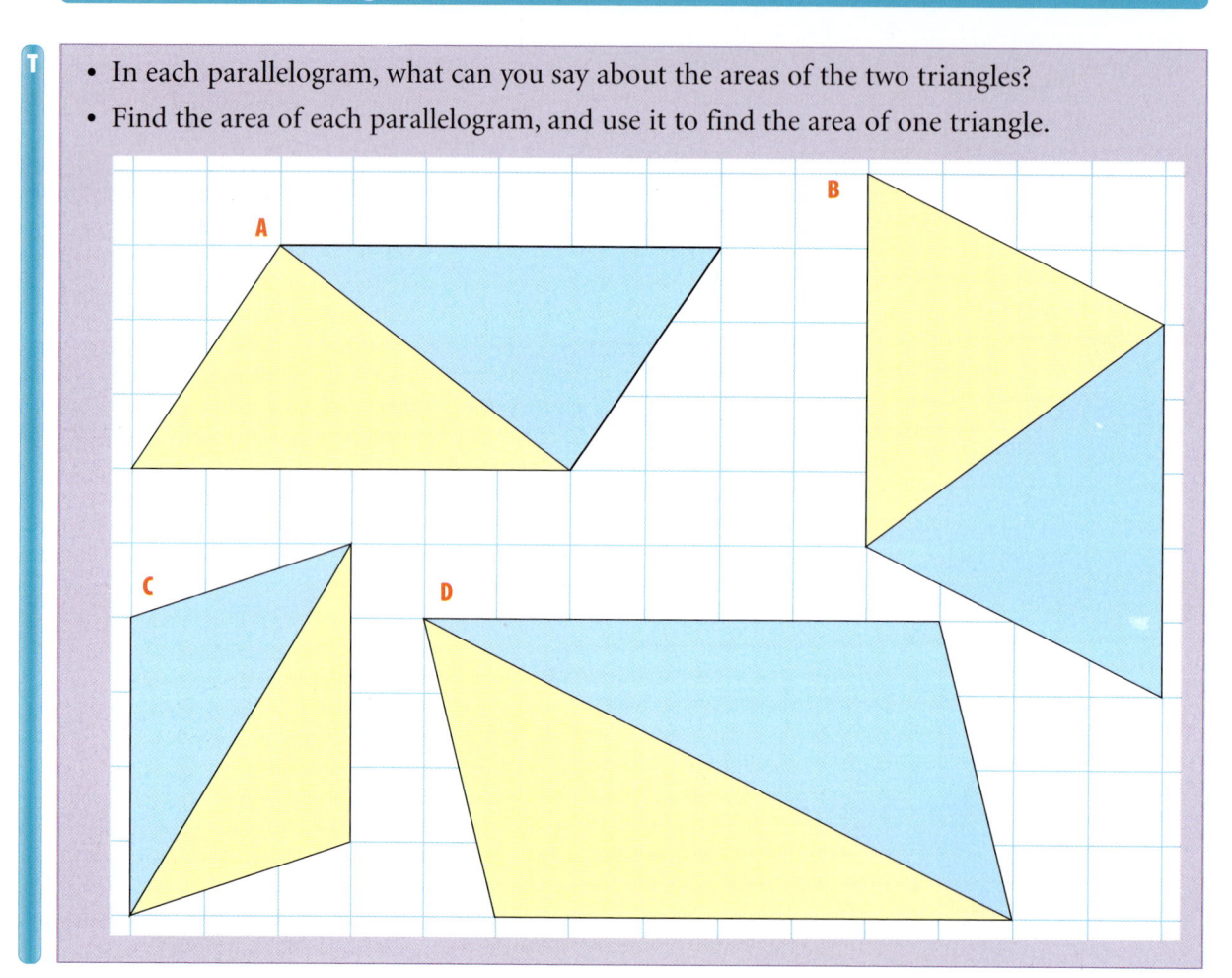

T
- In each parallelogram, what can you say about the areas of the two triangles?
- Find the area of each parallelogram, and use it to find the area of one triangle.

A1 This question is on sheet F1–21.

Formula for the area of a triangle

Any triangle is exactly half a parallelogram with the same base and perpendicular height.

The area of a triangle is found by

area = $\frac{1}{2}$(base length × perpendicular height)

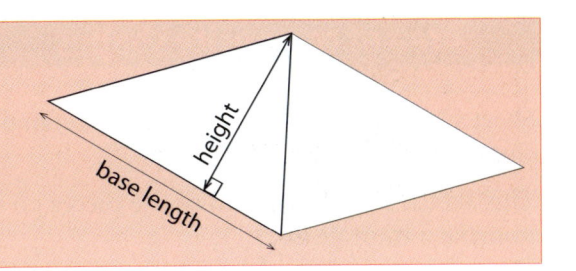

A2 (a) Below, there are two copies of the same triangle.
In each case, measure the base and perpendicular height that are marked, then set out your working like this.

Area = $\frac{1}{2}$(base × perpendicular height)
= $\frac{1}{2}$(...... cm × ...... cm)
= ...... cm²

(i)

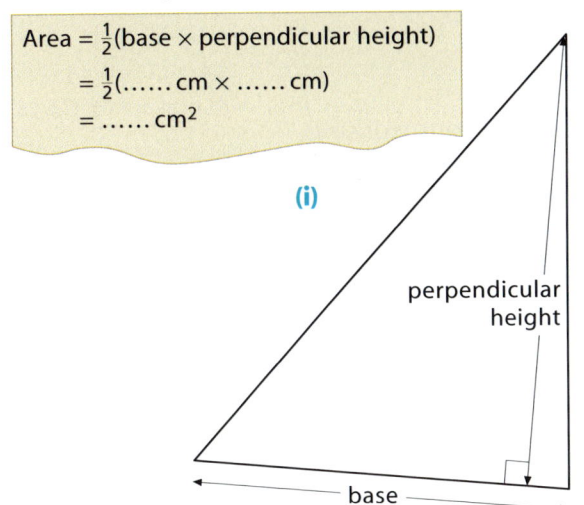

(ii)

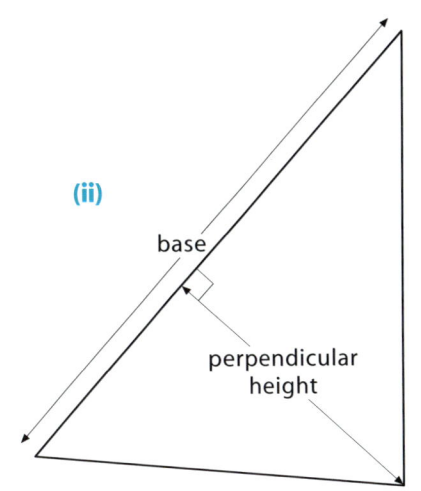

(b) Comment on your two answers.

A3 Find the area of each of these triangles.
You will not need all the measurements for some triangles.

(a) 6 cm, 8 cm

(b) 7 cm, 8 cm, 10 cm

(c) 18 cm, 20 cm, 12 cm

(d) 7.5 cm, 7 cm, 9 cm

(e) 4.5 cm, 6 cm

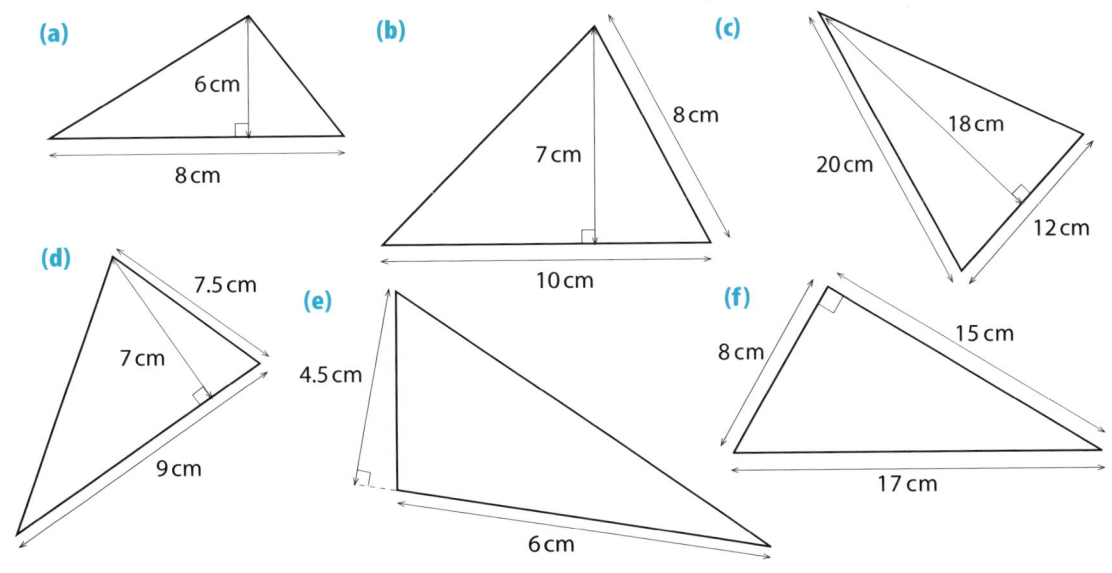

(f) 8 cm, 15 cm, 17 cm

B Area of composite shapes

Sheet F1–22 has some triangles and rectangles on a grid of centimetre squares.
Cut out all these pieces.

This sketch shows how two of the pieces go together to make a trapezium.
The working for the area of the trapezium is shown.

Area C = $\frac{1}{2}(3 \times 4)$ = 6 cm²
Area D = 3×4 = 12 cm²
Total area = 6 + 12 = 18 cm²

B1 Find a different pair of pieces that make a trapezium.
Sketch how they go together.
Find the area of the trapezium, showing your working.

B2 Find three pieces that make a trapezium.
Sketch how they go together.
Find the area of the trapezium, showing your working.

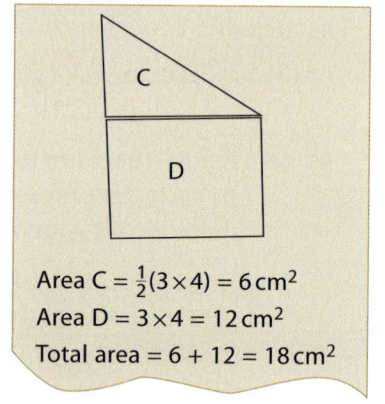

B3 The same way, sketch two pieces that make a kite and find the kite's area.

B4 Make some other shapes with the pieces. Sketch each shape and find its area.

B5 These shapes are drawn on centimetre squared paper.
Find the area of each shape. Draw a sketch to show how you did it.

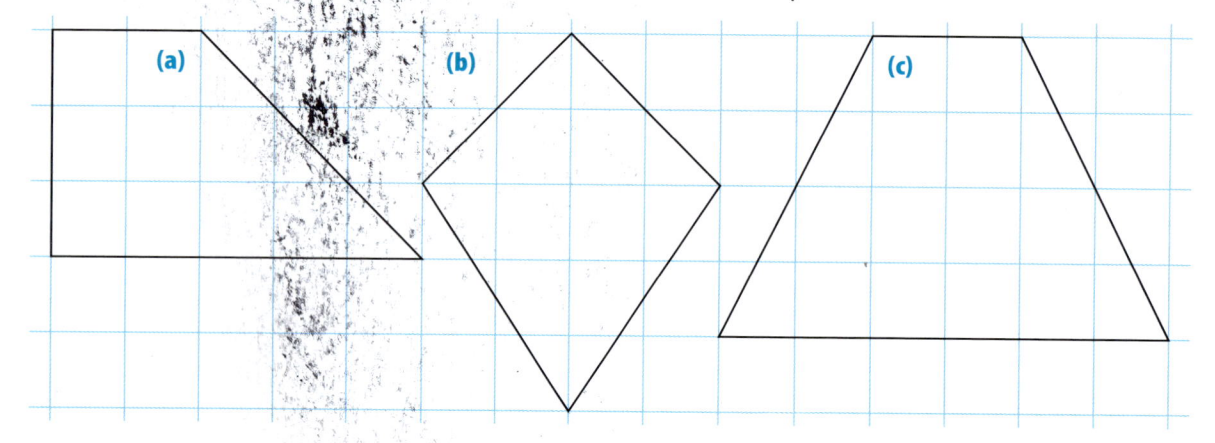

(a) (b) (c)

B6 Find the areas of these shapes.
Draw a sketch to show how you did each one.

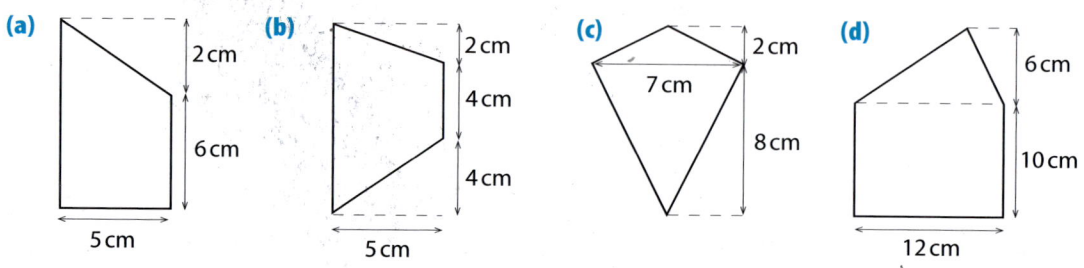

(a) 2 cm, 6 cm, 5 cm
(b) 2 cm, 4 cm, 4 cm, 5 cm
(c) 2 cm, 7 cm, 8 cm
(d) 2 cm, 6 cm, 10 cm, 12 cm

142 20 Area of a triangle and of composite shapes

Sometimes you need to work out a missing length before you can find the area of part of a composite shape.

B7 For each of these,
- draw a sketch
- work out each length shown by a '?' and mark it on your sketch
- find the area of the composite shape

(a) 6 cm, 8 cm, 9 cm, ?

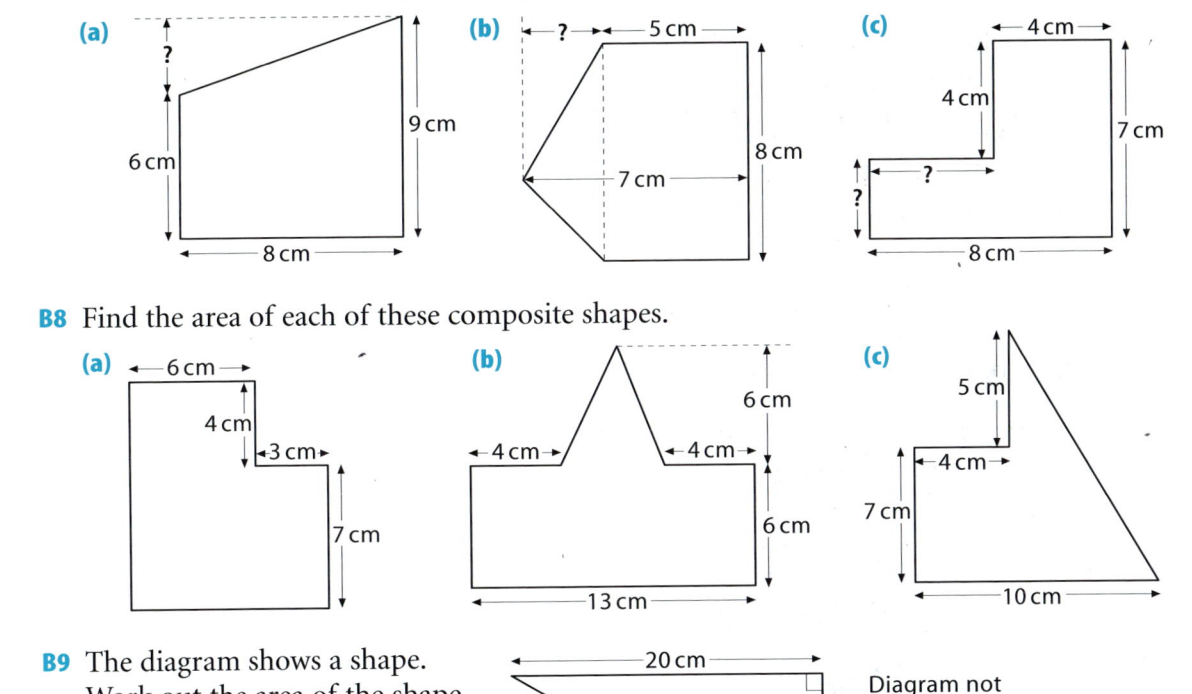

(b) ?, 5 cm, 7 cm, 8 cm

(c) 4 cm, 4 cm, 7 cm, 8 cm, ?

B8 Find the area of each of these composite shapes.

(a) 6 cm, 4 cm, 3 cm, 7 cm

(b) 4 cm, 4 cm, 6 cm, 6 cm, 13 cm

(c) 5 cm, 4 cm, 7 cm, 10 cm

B9 The diagram shows a shape. Work out the area of the shape.

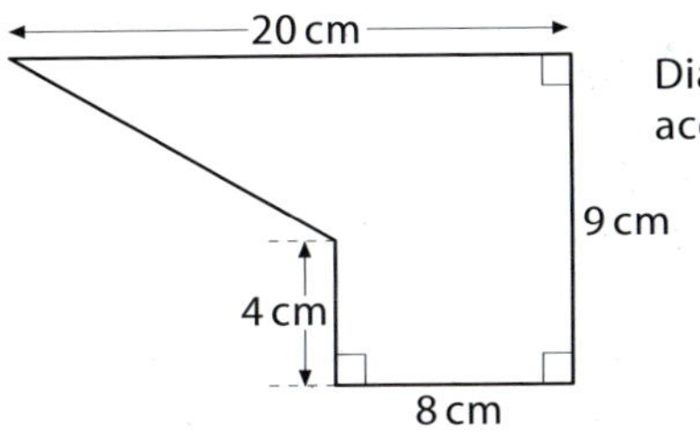

20 cm, 9 cm, 4 cm, 8 cm

Diagram not accurately drawn

Edexcel

Sometimes you can find the area of a composite shape by finding the area of one shape then **subtracting** the area of a smaller shape.

B10 Find the area of each of these shaded shapes.

(a) 6 cm, 5 cm, 8 cm, 10 cm

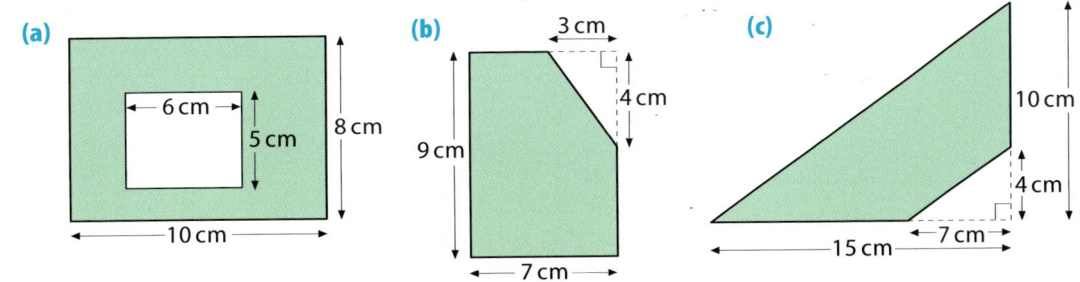

(b) 3 cm, 4 cm, 9 cm, 7 cm

(c) 10 cm, 4 cm, 7 cm, 15 cm

20 Area of a triangle and of composite shapes 143

Test yourself

T1 Find the area of each of these triangles.

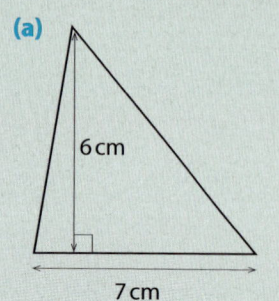

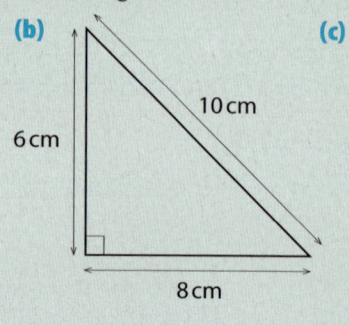

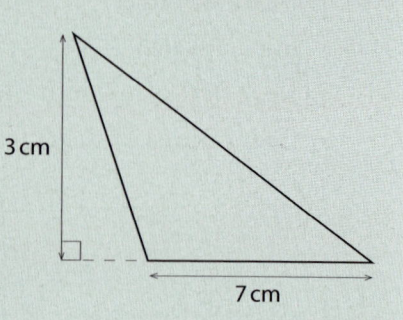

(a) 6 cm, 7 cm

(b) 6 cm, 10 cm, 8 cm

(c) 3 cm, 7 cm

T2 Calculate the area of each of these shapes.

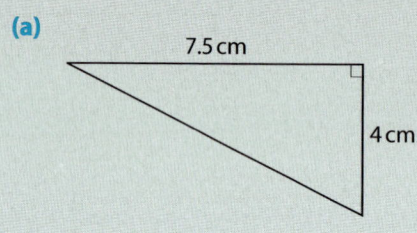

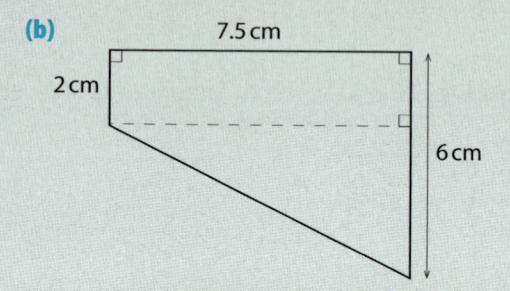

(a) 7.5 cm, 4 cm

(b) 7.5 cm, 2 cm, 6 cm

OCR

T3 Find the areas of these shapes.
Use a sketch to show how you worked out each answer.

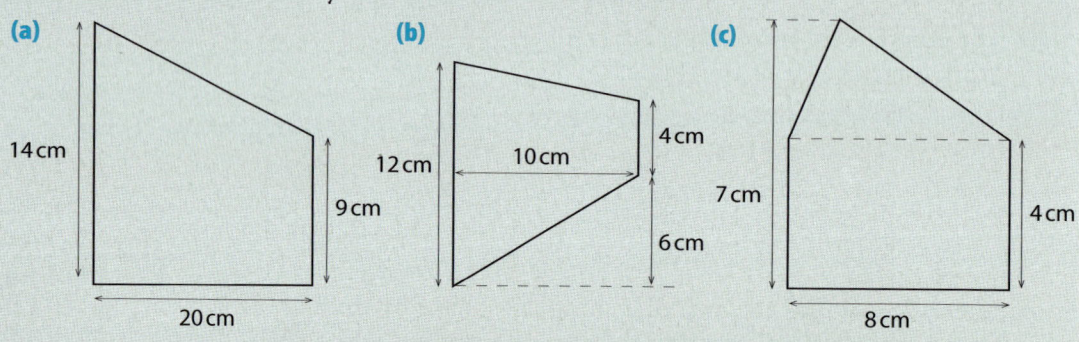

(a) 14 cm, 9 cm, 20 cm

(b) 12 cm, 10 cm, 4 cm, 6 cm

(c) 7 cm, 4 cm, 8 cm

T4 Calculate the area of each of the shaded shapes.

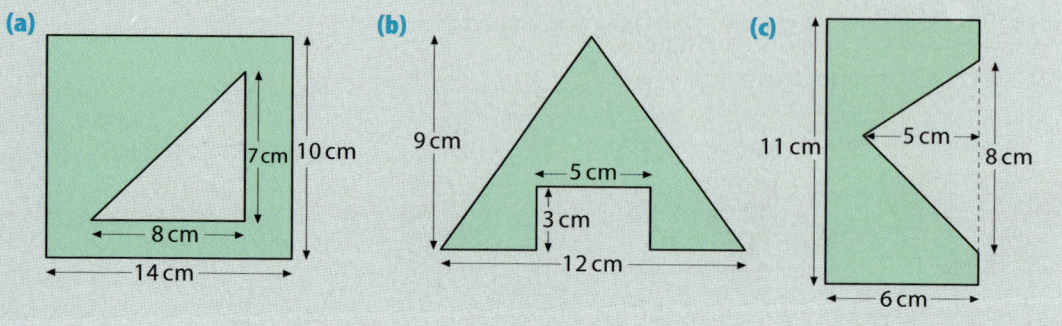

(a) 7 cm, 10 cm, 8 cm, 14 cm

(b) 9 cm, 5 cm, 3 cm, 12 cm

(c) 11 cm, 5 cm, 8 cm, 6 cm

144 20 Area of a triangle and of composite shapes

21 Working with percentages

You should know how to use equivalent fractions.

You will revise how to change between fractions, decimals and percentages.

This work will help you
- find percentages of different amounts
- write one number as a percentage of another

A Review: fractions, decimals and percentages

A1 Some of these signs mean the same thing.

A $\frac{1}{3}$ more!

B Extra $\frac{1}{4}$ free!

C 20% bonus

D 25% more!

E Half extra free!

F 50% more – same low price!

G $33\frac{1}{3}$% extra free!

(a) Match the pairs that say the same thing.

(b) Write a sign to match the odd one out.

A2 Write these percentages as decimals.
(a) 28%   (b) 40%   (c) 16%   (d) 1%   (e) 8%

A3 Write these decimals as percentages.
(a) 0.55   (b) 0.07   (c) 0.8   (d) 0.61   (e) 0.9

A4 Write these fractions as percentages.
(a) $\frac{89}{100}$ (b) $\frac{7}{100}$ (c) $\frac{3}{4}$ (d) $\frac{7}{10}$ (e) $\frac{2}{5}$

A5 Write these percentages as fractions. Simplify them if possible.
(a) 37%   (b) 9%   (c) 25%   (d) 20%   (e) 15%

A6 Copy and complete these statements.
(a) $\frac{3}{50} = \frac{\ }{100} = \ \%$
(b) $\frac{12}{25} = \frac{\ }{100} = \ \%$
(c) $\frac{68}{200} = \frac{\ }{100} = \ \%$

A7 Write each set of fractions, decimals and percentages in order, smallest first.
(a) 0.5 $\frac{1}{10}$ 49% $\frac{1}{4}$ 20%
(b) $\frac{4}{5}$ 76%   0.9   0.08   5%
(c) $\frac{1}{3}$ $\frac{2}{5}$ 45%   33%   0.03
(d) $\frac{1}{5}$ 5%   0.4   4%   51%

B Finding a percentage of an amount (mentally)

Useful facts

50% is the same as $\frac{1}{2}$.

25% is the same as $\frac{1}{4}$.

75% is 50% + 25% and is the same as $\frac{3}{4}$.

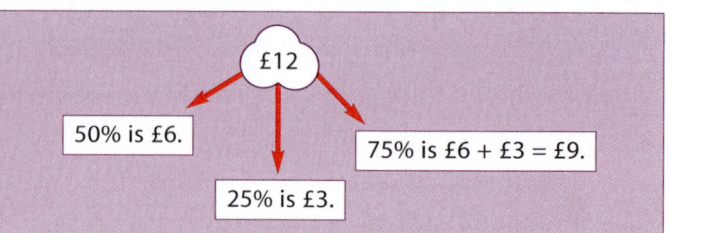

£12 → 50% is £6.
£12 → 25% is £3.
£12 → 75% is £6 + £3 = £9.

B1 Work out 50% of
- (a) £40
- (b) 84p
- (c) 30 kg
- (d) 200 ml
- (e) 70 litres

B2 Work out 25% of
- (a) £16
- (b) 40 kg
- (c) 64p
- (d) 500 g
- (e) 30 cm

B3 Work out 75% of
- (a) £20
- (b) 80 kg
- (c) 200 ml
- (d) 24p
- (e) 18 m

B4 Work these out.
- (a) 50% of £50
- (b) 25% of 36 kg
- (c) 75% of 60 pens
- (d) 75% of 160 g

B5 Sanjay earns 25% commission on every secondhand car he sells.
How much will he earn on selling these cars?
- (a) Ford Fiesta £500
- (b) Jeep £8000
- (c) Skoda £1800

10% is the same as $\frac{1}{10}$.
To work out 10% of something, divide by 10.
10% of 80 = 80 ÷ 10 = 8

Once you know what 10% is, you can easily work out 20%, 30%, …
20% of 80 = 2 × 8 = 16
60% of 80 = 6 × 8 = 48

B6 Work out 10% of
- (a) £70
- (b) 300 ml
- (c) 150 g
- (d) 50 litres
- (e) £8.50

B7 Work these out.
- (a) 10% of £60
- (b) 20% of £60
- (c) 90% of £60
- (d) 40% of £60

B8 Work these out.
- (a) 20% of £90
- (b) 70% of 30 kg
- (c) 10% of 120 g
- (d) 60% of 80 g

B9 How much **extra** do you get in these offers?
- (a) A 200 g tube of tomato puree with 30% extra
- (b) A 250 g bag of pasta with 20% extra
- (c) A 750 ml bottle of wine with 10% extra

> 5% is half of 10%. This helps to work out other percentages.
> 10% of 80 = 8   30% of 80 = 3 × 8 = 24
> 5% of 80 = 8 ÷ 2 = 4   so 35% of 80 = 24 + 4 = 28

B10 Work these out.
  (a) 10% of 120 g   (b) 5% of 120 g   (c) 35% of 120 g   (d) 85% of 120 g

B11 Work these out.
  (a) 5% of £60   (b) 5% of £200   (c) 5% of 140 g   (d) 5% of 240 ml

B12 Work these out.
  (a) 15% of 20 kg   (b) 35% of 300 g   (c) 65% of 60 eggs   (d) 45% of 160 g

B13 These labels show the percentage of fat in some foods.

  Pizza 10% fat
  Chips 15% fat
  Doughnuts 20% fat
  Stilton cheese 35% fat
  Butter 80% fat
  Dry roast peanuts 50% fat

  How much fat is there in
  (a) a 250 g pizza   (b) a 30 g doughnut   (c) 120 g of dry roast peanuts
  (d) 200 g of butter   (e) 400 g of chips   (f) 250 g of dry roast peanuts
  (g) 500 g of stilton cheese   (h) 60 g of chips   (i) 300 g of stilton cheese

B14 A cake is described as '85% fat free'.
  (a) What percentage of the cake is fat?
  (b) If the cake weighs 400 g, how much fat does it contain?

B15 Liam gets £5 pocket money each week.
  On his birthday, his pocket money is increased by 10%.
  (a) How much extra pocket money does he get each week?
  (b) How much pocket money does Liam get each week after his birthday?

B16 When Luigi bought some pasta he got '15% extra free'.
  (a) A normal pack weighs 500 g. How much extra did he get?
  (b) What was the **total** weight of the pack he bought?

B17 In a sale all prices are reduced by 20%.
  Jasmine buys a jacket which originally cost £45.
  (a) What is 20% of £45?
  (b) How much does Jasmine pay for the jacket?

C Finding a percentage of an amount (with a calculator)

T Calculate 36% of £450.

Method 1

Find 1% of £450. → Multiply by 36 to find 36%.

$$\frac{450}{100} \times 36 = £162$$

On a calculator 450 ÷ 100 × 36 = 162

Method 2

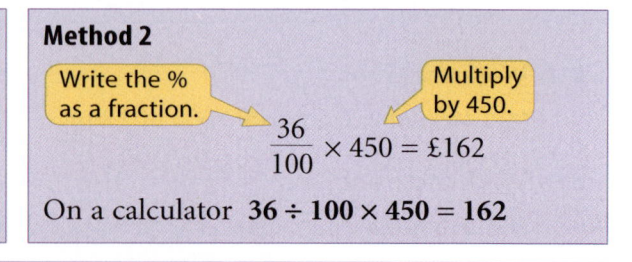

Write the % as a fraction. → Multiply by 450.

$$\frac{36}{100} \times 450 = £162$$

On a calculator 36 ÷ 100 × 450 = 162

Method 3

$36\% = \frac{36}{100} = 0.36$ so on a calculator $0.36 \times 450 = 162$

- How would you calculate 24% of £160?

C1 Calculate these.
  (a) 36% of 200 (b) 74% of 250 (c) 44% of 350 (d) 72% of 550

C2 Calculate these.
  (a) 22% of 80   (b) 64% of 120 (c) 48% of 70   (d) 86% of 340
  (e) 17% of 240 (f) 39% of 880 (g) 23% of 420 (h) 92% of 820

C3 Find these.
  (a) 23% of £85 (b) 47% of £56 (c) 33% of £84 (d) 83% of £54

C4 Find these.
  (a) 36% of 94 litres (b) 84% of 450 g (c) 17% of 350 ml (d) 93% of 150 km

C5 This is some nutritional information about different foods.

Food	Water	Fat	Protein	Carbohydrate
Cheddar cheese	36%	34%	26%	0%
Tofu	51%	18%	24%	2%
Cornflakes	3%	1%	8%	86%

How much is there of
  (a) water in 250 g of cheddar cheese
  (b) protein in 225 g of tofu
  (c) carbohydrate in 35 g of cornflakes
  (d) fat in 120 g of cheddar cheese
  (e) fat in 280 g of tofu
  (f) water in 750 g of cornflakes

C6 Josh earns £5.50 per hour. He gets a pay rise of 8%.
  (a) Calculate 8% of £5.50.
  (b) How much does Josh earn per hour after the pay rise?

D Expressing one number as a percentage of another

7 out of a class of 25 students cycle to school. What percentage is this?

Write as a fraction and make the denominator 100.

$\frac{7}{25}$ cycle. $\frac{7}{25} = \frac{28}{100} = 28\%$ (×4)

Out of 200 tyres checked, 90 were found to be faulty. What percentage is this?

$\frac{90}{200}$ are faulty. $\frac{90}{200} = \frac{45}{100} = 45\%$ (÷2)

D1 Write these as percentages.

(a) 7 out of 20 (b) 12 out of 25 (c) 13 out of 50 (d) 13 out of 20
(e) 150 out of 200 (f) 75 out of 500 (g) 650 out of 1000 (h) 160 out of 400

D2 Ray takes 20 bottles to the bottle bank.
4 of the bottles are brown. What percentage are brown?

D3 A pack contains 10 pens of which 5 are black, 3 are blue and 2 are red.
What percentage of the pens are

(a) black (b) blue (c) red (d) not red

D4 A 25 g cereal bar has these listed under 'nutrition'.

Protein 3 g   Carbohydrate 16 g   Fat 4 g   Fibre 2 g

What percentage of the bar is

(a) protein (b) carbohydrate (c) fat (d) fibre

D5 Write the following as percentages, and put them in order, smallest first.

A 164 out of 200   B 420 out of 500   C 43 out of 50
D 19 out of 20   E 8 out of 10   F 22 out of 25

D6 Tina scored 30 out of 50 in her maths exam.
Mel scored 65% in the same maths exam.
Who got the better score? Explain your answer.

D7 In a survey on holidays 160 out of 200 people said they preferred to go abroad.
What percentage preferred to go abroad?

D8 Highfield School awards attendance certificates to all students who attend at least 95% of the time.
Which of these students get a certificate?

Martin	Rani	Amy
$\frac{192}{200}$	$\frac{190}{200}$	$\frac{180}{200}$

21 Working with percentages   149

E Expressing one number as a percentage of another (with a calculator)

Jason had £125 birthday money and spent £45 of it on a computer game.
What percentage of his money did he spend?

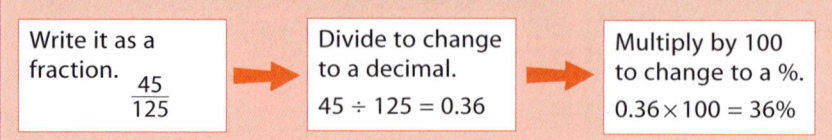

| Write it as a fraction. $\frac{45}{125}$ | Divide to change to a decimal. $45 \div 125 = 0.36$ | Multiply by 100 to change to a %. $0.36 \times 100 = 36\%$ | On a calculator $45 \div 125 \times 100 = 36$ So 45 out of 125 is 36%. |

E1 Work these out as percentages.
(a) 56 out of 160   (b) 63 out of 225   (c) 54 out of 72   (d) 364 out of 560
(e) 36 out of 40   (f) 75 out of 250   (g) 3 out of 75   (h) 228 out of 240

E2 A triathlon had 120 entries but only 78 finished the race.
(a) What percentage finished the race?   (b) What percentage dropped out?

E3 Ms King marks her art exam out of 80. Change these marks out of 80 to percentages.
Miriam 68   Charles 36   Adam 56   Tak Man 72   Celia 44

E4 A survey of 150 students on their choice of school uniform colour gave these votes.
Black 81   Blue 27   Grey 30   Green 12
What percentage voted for each option?

E5 Patrick and Carlos are practising taking penalties.
Patrick scores 34 out of 40 penalties.
Carlos scores 28 out of 35 penalties.
Who is better at taking penalties? Explain your answer.

E6 Azmat's garden is a rectangle measuring 15 m by 10 m.
In the garden he digs a rectangular vegetable patch 3 m by 7 m.
(a) What is the area of   (i) his whole garden   (ii) his vegetable patch
(b) What percentage of his garden is taken up by his vegetable patch?

Example
A 27 g crunchy bar contains 7 g of fat.
Find, to the nearest 1%, the percentage of the bar that is fat.

$7 \div 27 \times 100 = 25.92592592$ which is 26% to the nearest 1%

E7 Write these as percentages to the nearest 1%.
(a) 27 out of 48   (b) 43 out of 80   (c) 35 out of 78   (d) 23 out of 75
(e) 45 out of 56   (f) 28 out of 65   (g) 210 out of 560 (h) 25 out of 48

E8 Pauline lists how many hours each day she spends on different activities.

    Sleeping 8   School 7   Eating 2   Homework 3   Television 4

Work these out as percentages of the whole day. Check that they add to 100%.

E9 During netball training on Tuesday, Sheena got the ball through the net 22 times out of 30 attempts.
On Wednesday 69% of her attempts were successful.
Which day did she do better?

E10 Peter asked students in years 10 and 11 whether they were satisfied with school meals.
In year 10, 108 out of 180 were satisfied.
In year 11, 98 out of 150 were satisfied.

Which year group was less satisfied? Explain how you decide.

F Mixed questions

F1 Fried fish fingers contain

    55% water   15% protein   15% fat   15% carbohydrate

(a) How much fat is there in 250 g of fried fish fingers?

(b) How much water is there in 250 g of fried fish fingers?

F2 Dermot's garden is a rectangle measuring 15 metres by 5 metres.

(a) What is the total area of the garden?

(b) The lawn takes up 55% of the garden. What is the area of the lawn?

(c) A flower bed is a rectangle measuring 3 m by 2 m.
What percentage of the garden is this?

F3 In a survey a group of people were asked how they learned to use a computer.
The answers were listed as

Method	Number of people
Self-taught	33
Through work	18
From family or friend	5
At school	21
Other	3

(a) How many people were asked in the survey in total?

(b) What percentage of this total were self-taught?

(c) What percentage learned at school?

F4 These are the results of a survey on students who had passed their driving test.

	Passed first time	Took more than one test
Male	7	17
Female	9	16

(a) What is the total number of females in the survey?

(b) What percentage of the females passed first time?

(c) Were males or females more likely to pass first time?
Explain your answer.

Test yourself

T1 (a) Write $\frac{3}{4}$ as a percentage.

(b) Write 30% as a fraction.

Edexcel

T2 Which is the larger amount?
You **must** show your working.

| 60% of £40 | $\frac{2}{5}$ of £55 |

AQA

T3 (a) These are Tanya's results for her German tests.

Vocabulary	Writing	Speaking	Listening	Reading
$\frac{15}{20}$	63%	$\frac{3}{5}$	$\frac{7}{10}$	55%

Put the results in order, highest first.

(b) Tanya scored 60% in the history test.
She gets a grade based on the test result.

Which grade does she get in history?
Give a reason for your choice.

Score	Grade
0.9 and above	A
0.7 and less than 0.9	B
0.5 and less than 0.7	C
less than 0.5	D

OCR

T4 (a) A frozen curry weighs 380 g.
The curry contains 25% meat.
What weight of meat does it contain?

(b) An individual frozen pie weighs 160 g.
The pie contains 28% meat.
What weight of meat does it contain?

OCR

T5 In an election there were three candidates.
The candidates were Alan Archer, Priti Patel and Simon Smith.

Alan Archer got 25% of the votes, Priti Patel got 35% of the votes and Simon Smith got the rest.

(a) What percentage of the votes did Simon Smith get?

(b) Who won the election?

Altogether 40 000 people voted in the election.

(c) How many people voted for Priti Patel?

OCR

T6 Jo did a maths test.
There was a total of 40 marks for the test.
Jo got 65% of the marks.

(a) Work out 65% of 40.

Jo got 36 out of 80 in an English test.

(b) Work out 36 out of 80 as a percentage.

Edexcel

22 Representing data

You will revise how to

- read information from a two-way table
- draw and interpret bar graphs and line graphs

This work will help you understand time series graphs and index numbers.

A Two-way tables

Elisa is doing a survey of the types of houses in her area.
She surveys houses in the town and in the surrounding country.

	Type of house			Total
	Detached	Semi-det.	Terraced	
Town	120	180	200	
Country	80	100	70	
Total				

I think there are more detached houses in the town than there are in the country.

- Work out the totals for Elisa's table.
- What percentage of the houses in the town are detached?
- What percentage of the houses in the country are detached?
- Was Elisa right?

A1 Jake is doing a survey of how students get to school.
This table shows his results with some numbers missing.

	How they get to school			Total
	Walk/cycle	Bus	Car	
Boys	32	48		100
Girls	12		10	50
Total		44		150

(a) Copy and complete the table.

(b) What percentage of the boys in the survey walk or cycle to school?

(c) What percentage of the girls walk or cycle to school?

(d) Who in the survey are more likely to walk or cycle to school, boys or girls?

A2 (a) In Jake's survey who are more likely to use a bus to get to school, boys or girls?
Give a reason for your answer.

(b) What can you say about the proportion of boys and girls who come to school by car?

A3 This table shows some results from a class survey. Some of the numbers have been left out.

	Wear glasses	Don't wear glasses	Total
Boys	5		13
Girls		10	
Total	12		30

(a) Copy and complete this table.

(b) What fraction of the boys wear glasses?

(c) How many girls were there altogether?

(d) What fraction of the girls wear glasses?

A4 These results are for all the houses in a village.

	Number of bedrooms			
	2	3	4	5
Detached	0	10	8	2
Semi-detached	2	8	5	0
Terraced	10	15	0	0

(a) Copy this table and add row and column totals.

(b) How many detached houses have 4 bedrooms?

(c) How many terraced houses are there?

(d) What percentage of the detached houses have 3 bedrooms?

A5 This table shows the number of bedrooms and living rooms for the houses in the village.

		Number of bedrooms			
		2	3	4	5
Number of living rooms	1	3	5	0	0
	2	9	20	10	1
	3	0	8	3	1

(a) How many houses have 2 living rooms?

(b) How many houses have 3 bedrooms and 3 living rooms?

(c) How many houses have more living rooms than bedrooms?

A6 Dan carried out a survey of the students in his year group to find out whether they had a computer or a games console at home.

(a) The results for the boys are shown in this table.

	Computer	No computer
Console	11	13
No console	12	9

  (i) How many boys had a computer and a games console?

  (ii) How many boys altogether had a games console?

  (iii) How many boys did he ask?

(b) Here are his results for the girls.
He wrote C for 'computer only', G for 'games console only', B for 'both' and N for 'neither'.

G	C	C	B	N	N	G	N	B	C	G	C	C	N
G	B	N	C	C	G	G	N	N	C	C	G	C	N
B	N	C	G	C	N	C	G	N	C	C	N	B	C

Make a table like the one above for the girls' results.

154   22 Representing data

B Two-way tables with grouped data

This table shows the gender and age breakdowns for the population of a small town.

	Age 0–59	Age 60+	Total
Male	358	82	
Female	309	112	
Total			

- Copy the table and complete the totals.
- What is the total population of the town?
- How many males are there?
- How many females aged 60+ are there?

B1 Pete is doing a survey of the people using his local library. He records their gender and their age group.

	Age 0–17	Age 18–59	Age 60+	Total
Male	27	41	38	
Female	21	52	49	
Total				

(a) Copy the table and complete the totals.
(b) How many males were there?
(c) How many people aged 60+ were there?
(d) How many people did he survey altogether?

B2 Kate is doing a survey of the visitors at a theme park. She records their gender and their height.

	Under 140 cm	140 cm and over
Male	120	424
Female	204	252

(a) How many of the visitors were male and under 140 cm?
(b) How many of the visitors were 140 cm and over?
(c) How many people did she survey altogether?
(d) What percentage of the visitors were under 140 cm?
(e) What percentage of the visitors were female?

C Pictograms and bar charts

This data shows the number of homes of different types in a small town.

Type of home	Detached	Bungalow	Semi-det.	Terraced	Flat
Number	60	15	122	97	53

Two ways we could present the data are
a **pictogram** or … … a **bar chart**.

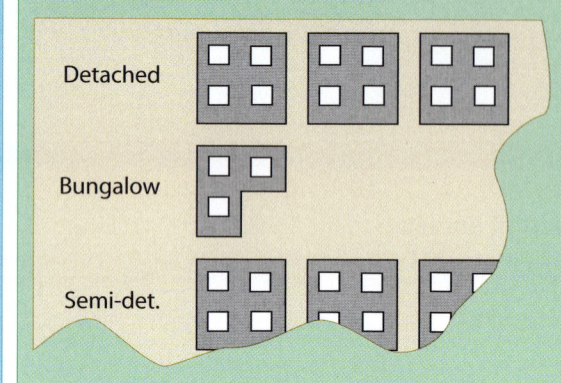

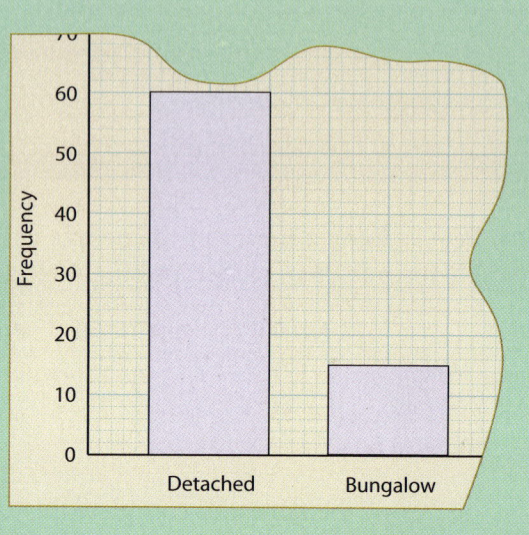

- What does ▨ represent on the pictogram?
- Copy and complete the pictogram for the homes. Remember to give it a key.
- Copy and complete the bar chart for the homes.
- Which diagram gives the most information?

C1 This pictogram shows the number of parcels posted at the high street post office on Monday, Tuesday and Wednesday.

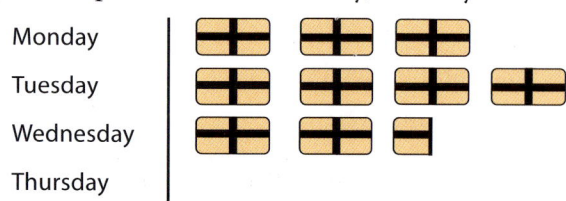

▦ represents 20 parcels

(a) How many parcels were posted on

 (i) Monday (ii) Wednesday

(b) 25 parcels were posted on Thursday. Show this on a copy of the pictogram.

Edexcel

C2 Nasser has carried out a survey of the number of bedrooms in homes in his area. His results are shown in this bar chart.

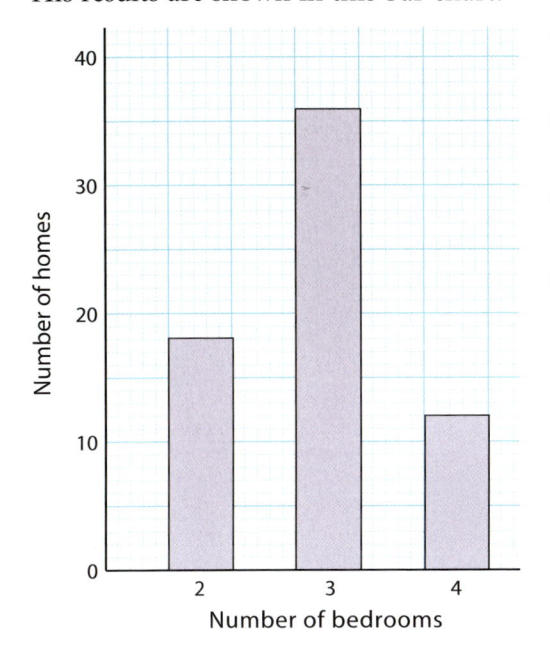

(a) What is the modal number of bedrooms in a home?

(b) How many homes did Nasser use in his survey?

(c) How many more 2-bedroom homes were there than 4-bedroom homes?

(d) How many bedrooms were there altogether in the homes surveyed?

C3 A number of students were asked how many times they had used the canteen that week. The results were

Number of visits	0	1	2	3	4	5
Students	10	24	18	15	8	32

(a) Draw a suitable diagram for this data.

(b) Explain why you chose this type of diagram.

C4 Give two reasons why this diagram may be misleading.

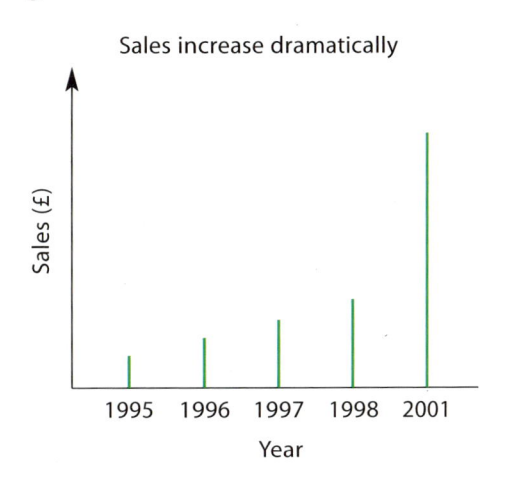

Sales increase dramatically

OCR

22 Representing data   157

D Dual bar charts

When you have more than one set of data it can be useful to show them on a **dual bar chart**.

This dual bar chart shows the percentage of different types of houses in a town and the surrounding country.

D1 (a) What is the modal type of house in the town?

(b) What is the modal type of house in the country?

D2 Which types of house did the survey show were more common in the town than in the country?

D3 This diagram shows the number of people in the armed forces between 1968 and 1998.

(a) Over the thirty years were the numbers in the armed forces going up, going down or staying about the same?

(b) Which was the biggest of the armed forces in 1968?
Was it still biggest in 1998?

(c) Between what years does the chart show that the numbers in the Air Force increased?

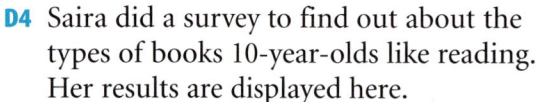

D4 Saira did a survey to find out about the types of books 10-year-olds like reading. Her results are displayed here.

(a) What was the modal type of book for boys?

(b) What was the modal type of book for girls?

(c) Use the results of the survey to make two comments comparing the reading habits of boys and girls.

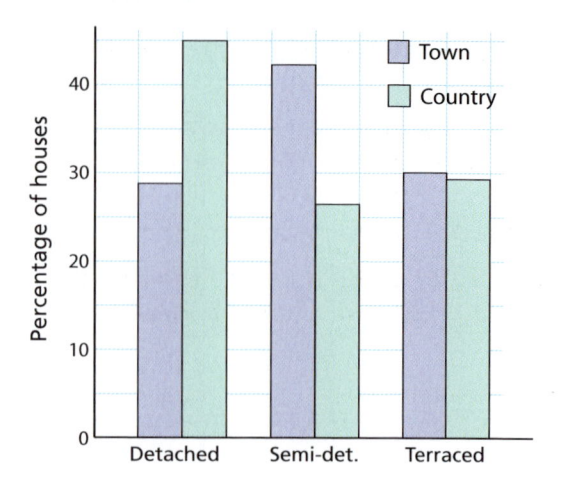

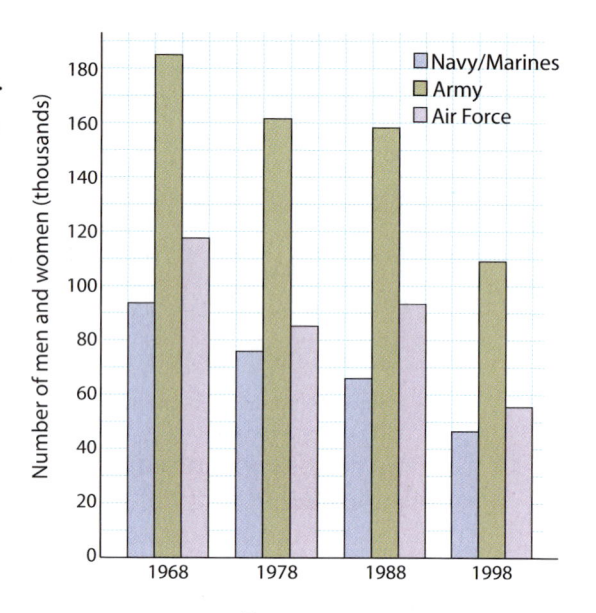

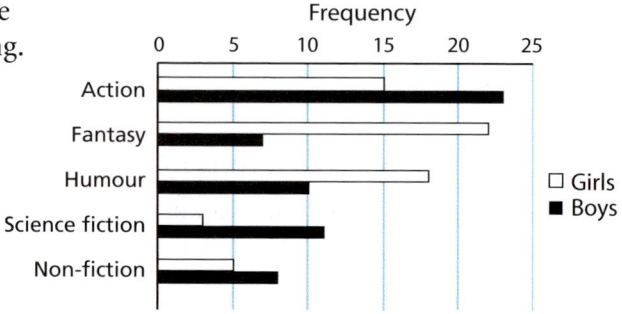

E Line graphs for time series

A line graph is useful to show how an amount changes over a period of time.

This line graph shows the average amount of pocket money received by 6- to 9-year-old children between 1989 and 1999.

A line graph with time on the horizontal axis is called a **time series graph**.

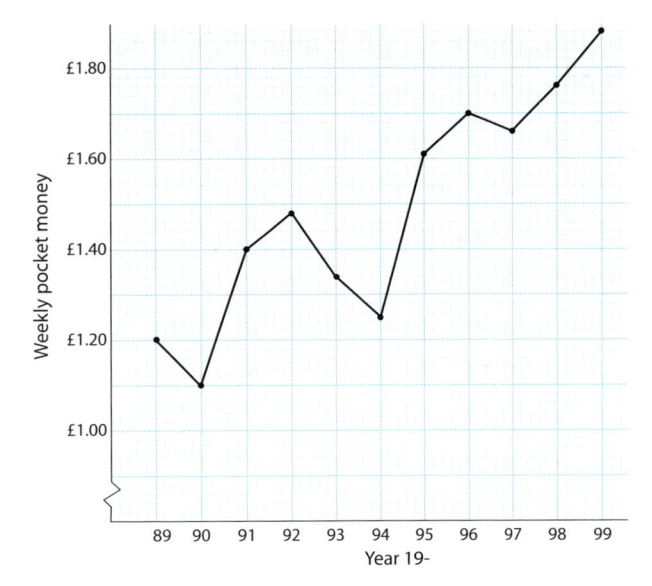

E1 Why has a jagged line been drawn at the bottom of the pocket money axis?

E2 What was the average amount of pocket money given to 6- to 9-year-olds in

(a) 1989   (b) 1994   (c) 1999

E3 (a) Between which two consecutive years did the amount of pocket money go up most?

(b) Only once did the average amount go down for two consecutive years. Between which years was this?

E4 Which of these statements describes what the graph shows about 6- to 9-year-olds' average pocket money?

It generally got less between 1989 and 1999.

It generally went up between 1989 and 1999.

It stayed about the same between 1989 and 1999.

E5 This table shows the number of cinema tickets sold between 1986 and 1999.

Year	1986	1987	1988	1989	1990	1991	1992	1993	1994	1995	1996	1997	1998	1999
Tickets (millions)	73	75	78	88	89	93	98	113	124	115	123	139	135	139

(a) On axes like these, draw a line graph of the figures.

(b) Make two statements about what the graph tells you about sales of cinema tickets.

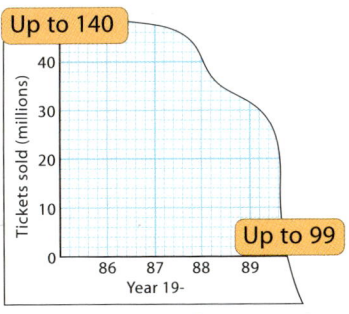

Up to 140

Up to 99

22 Representing data

E6 This graph shows the number of journeys made by passengers on British airlines each month.

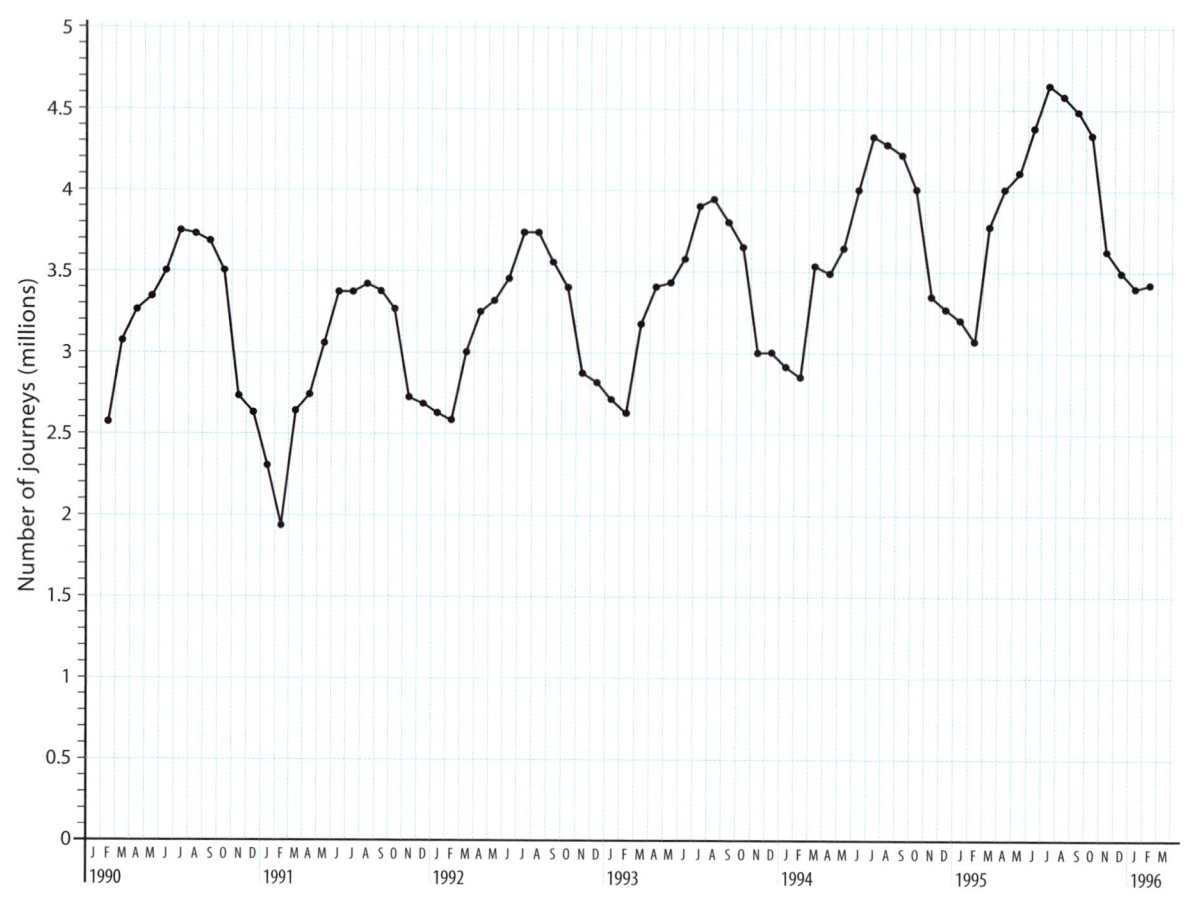

(a) What do the letters JFMAMJJASOND stand for?
(b) On the graph, which months are usually the busiest?
(c) Which month is usually the least busy?
(d) Between 1990 and 1996 did airline business generally get better, get worse or stay the same?
(e) Was there an unusual pattern in any of the years?

> You can find up-to-date line graphs on many subjects by searching on the web. The website www.statistics.gov.uk has a great deal of useful data. You could find a line graph and comment on what it is showing.
>
> By putting data you have collected into a spreadsheet, you can use the spreadsheet's charting facility to display the data quickly and accurately. Investigate the different types of chart that can be produced by a spreadsheet and discuss which are the most useful.

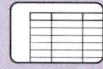

160   22 Representing data

F Index numbers

When people want to look at how an amount changes over a period of time they sometimes use an **index number**.

A starting point in time is made to be 100% of the amount.

At any time after this, the amount is written as a percentage of what it was at the start.

In this table the populations of birds were set at 100% in 1970.

In 1990 the population of the Song Thrush was 51% of what it was in 1970.

Indexes of bird populations

Year	1970	1980	1990	1998
Song Thrush	100	67	51	45
Spotted Flycatcher	100	105	55	32
Tree Sparrow	100	74	17	13

F1 Answer these questions from the table.

(a) What percentage of the 1970 population was the Spotted Flycatcher population in 1998?

(b) Which bird had the biggest percentage drop in population between 1970 and 1998?

(c) Which bird population increased between 1970 and 1980?

The Retail Price Index

The government keeps a check on prices of goods and services in the UK.
Each month they check the prices of a wide range of things people spend money on.
This is recorded as an index called the **Retail Price Index** (**RPI**).

The RPI was set at 100 in April 1987.
When the news talks about a rise in inflation it means the RPI is increasing faster than before.

F2 This table shows the annual RPI from 1990 to 2000.

Year	1990	1991	1992	1993	1994	1995	1996	1997	1998	1999	2000
RPI	126	134	139	141	144	149	153	158	163	165	170

(a) By what percentage had the RPI increased from the start in 1987 to 1997?

(b) Draw a line graph of the RPI between 1990 and 2000 using these scales.

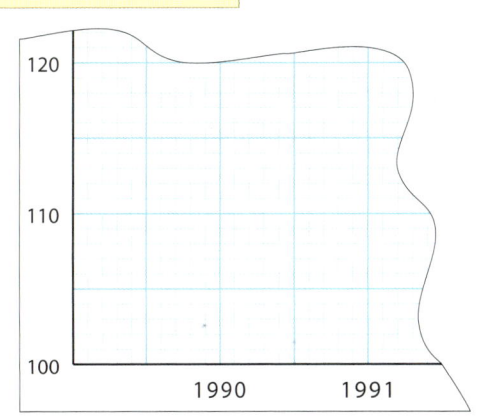

22 Representing data

Test yourself

T1 A group of 40 children are asked how many dogs and cats they own.
The results are shown in the table.

Number of dogs

	0	1	2	3
0	5	7	3	1
1	6	3	2	0
2	7	2	1	0
3	2	1	0	0

Number of cats

(a) How many children own two cats but no dog?

(b) How many children own two dogs?

(c) How many children own a total of three of these animals?

AQA

T2 80 students each study one of three languages.
The two-way table shows some information about these students.

	French	German	Spanish	Total
Female	15			39
Male		17		41
Total	31	28		80

Copy and complete the two-way table.

Edexcel

T3 A school carried out a survey one day of the numbers of pupils wearing trainers.
The dual bar chart shows the results.

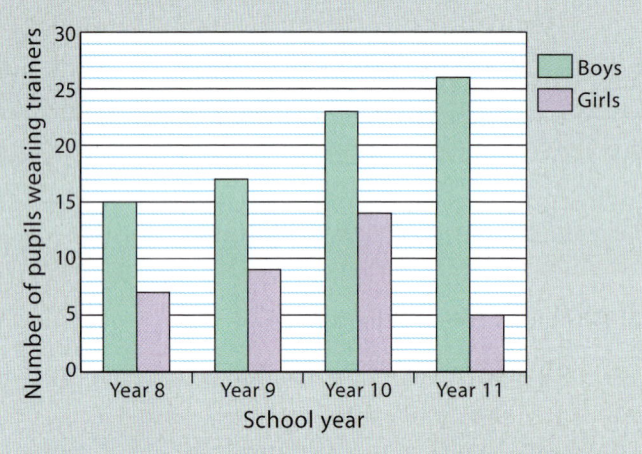

(a) How many girls in year 8 were wearing trainers?

(b) Work out the total number of pupils in year 11 wearing trainers.

(c) Which school year had the greatest total number of pupils wearing trainers?

(d) Describe one general difference between the number of boys and the number of girls wearing trainers.

AQA

T4 Ray and Clare are pupils at different schools. They each did an investigation into their teachers' favourite colours.

Here is Ray's bar chart of his teachers' favourite colours.

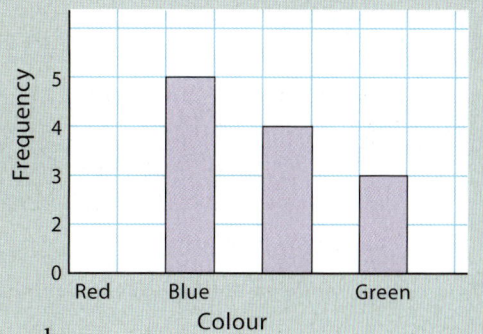

(a) Write down two things that are wrong with Ray's bar chart.

Clare drew a bar chart of her teachers' favourite colours. Part of her bar chart is shown.

4 teachers said that yellow was their favourite colour.
2 teachers said that green was their favourite colour.

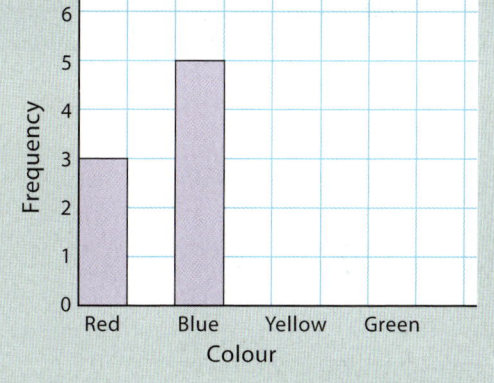

(b) Copy and complete Clare's bar chart.
(c) Which colour was the mode for the teachers that Clare asked?
(d) Work out the number of teachers that Clare asked.
(e) Write down the fraction of the number of teachers that Clare asked who said red was their favourite colour.

Edexcel

T5 This table shows the number of miles Chris drove on business each month for six months.

Month	April	May	June	July	Aug	Sept
Business miles	280	245	210	55	190	225

(a) On axes like these, draw a line graph of this data. 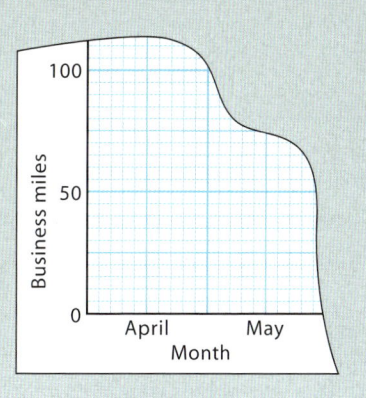
(b) Why do you think Chris's average mileage was least in July?

22 Representing data 163

23 Ratio and proportion

This work will help you

- scale a recipe up or down
- use the unitary method to solve proportion problems
- use unit cost to compare prices
- use and simplify ratios written in the form $a:b$

A Recipes

Lemon ice cream
(makes 6 servings)
10 egg yolks
200 g caster sugar
50 ml lemon juice
400 ml double cream

Gooseberry jam
(makes about 5 kg)
2 kg gooseberries
3 kg sugar
1 litre water

Fish pie
(serves 4)
500 g haddock
400 ml milk
60 g butter
200 ml single cream
2 eggs
800 g potatoes

Spinach and panir curry
(serves 4)
30 ml oil
200 g panir (Indian cheese)
400 g spinach
3 tomatoes

Nice Nosh Catering buffet menu
(quantities needed for 50 people)
4 sliced loaves or 12 French sticks
1.8 kg of butter
10 tomatoes

Basic fillings for 12 sandwiches
400 g canned tuna fish
or 240 g coleslaw
or 10 hard boiled eggs
1 large sliced loaf can make 12 sandwiches.
100 g of butter can be spread on 12 sandwiches.

How many egg yolks would you need to make 12 servings of ice cream?

How much caster sugar would you need to make ice cream for 24 people?

How much double cream would you need to make ice cream for 3 people?

If you had plenty of all the other ingredients, but only 100 ml of lemon juice, how many people could you make ice cream for?

Use the recipes opposite to answer these questions.

A1 How many eggs would you need to make fish pie for 8 people?

A2 How many of these would you need to make the food described?
- (a) Tomatoes to make spinach and panir curry for 12 people
- (b) Hard boiled eggs to make 48 sandwiches
- (c) Tomatoes for Nice Nosh Catering to give a buffet for 150
- (d) Eggs to make fish pie for 2 people
- (e) Hard boiled eggs to make 6 sandwiches
- (f) Tomatoes to make spinach and panir curry for 2 people

A3 How much would you need of these ingredients to make the food described?
- (a) Butter to make a fish pie to serve 8 people
- (b) Panir to make a spinach and panir curry for 12 people
- (c) Coleslaw to make 48 sandwiches
- (d) Sugar to make 20 kg of jam
- (e) Butter for Nice Nosh to run a buffet for 25 people
- (f) Spinach to make spinach and panir curry for 2 people

A4 Copy and complete these recipes.

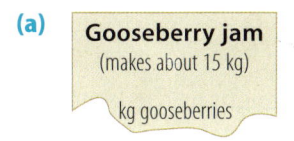

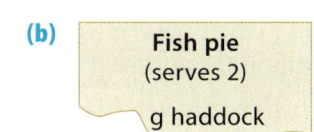

(a) Gooseberry jam (makes about 15 kg)
☐ kg gooseberries

(b) Fish pie (serves 2)
☐ g haddock

A5 What number of people could you make fish pie for if you had plenty of all the other ingredients but only had
- (a) 180 g of butter
- (b) 10 eggs
- (c) 1 kg of haddock

A6 What number of people could you make spinach and panir curry for if you had plenty of all other ingredients but only had
- (a) 90 ml of oil
- (b) 18 tomatoes
- (c) 1 kg of panir

A7 (a) How much butter would you need to make a fish pie for one person?
(b) Use this to find the amount of butter you would need to make a fish pie for
- (i) 6 people
- (ii) 10 people
- (iii) 14 people

A8 (a) How much tuna fish would you need to make 3 tuna sandwiches?
(b) How much tuna fish is needed to make
- (i) 9 sandwiches
- (ii) 15 sandwiches
- (iii) 30 sandwiches

B Comparing prices

In a supermarket packets of Lingos can be bought for 27p.

They can also be bought in a multipack with 6 packets costing £1.50.

- What would 6 packets of Lingos cost if they were bought separately?
- Is the multipack better value?

27p   Special price £1.50

B1 In each of these examples
- find the cost of buying the items in the multipack separately
- decide whether the multipack gives you more for your money

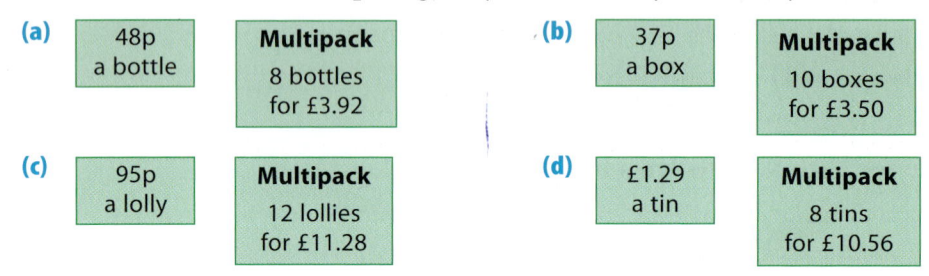

(a) 48p a bottle | Multipack 8 bottles for £3.92

(b) 37p a box | Multipack 10 boxes for £3.50

(c) 95p a lolly | Multipack 12 lollies for £11.28

(d) £1.29 a tin | Multipack 8 tins for £10.56

B2 A large pack of Roquefort cheese weighs 500 g and costs £7.
A small pack weighs 100 g and costs £1.50.

(a) How many small packs would you need to get the same weight as the large pack?
(b) What is the cost of buying this number of small packs?
(c) Do you save money by buying one of the larger packs?

B3 In each of these cases
- find out how many smaller units make up the larger one
- find out whether it saves money to buy the larger unit

(a) 200 ml of cream costs 85p
    600 ml costs £3.25

(b) 200 g of rice costs £1.20
    1 kg (1000 g) costs £6.25

(c) 125 g of tea costs £1.30
    500 g costs £4.99

(d) 100 g of sweets cost 80p
    250 g costs £1.95

B4 Packets of fish fingers are sold in two sizes

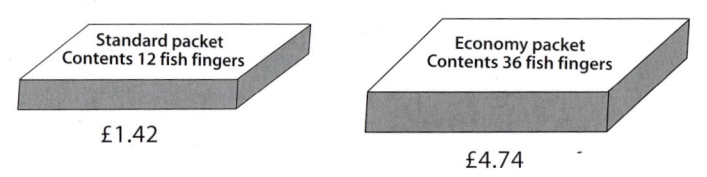

Standard packet
Contents 12 fish fingers
£1.42

Economy packet
Contents 36 fish fingers
£4.74

Which size packet is the better value for money?
You must show all your working.

AQA

166 23 Ratio and proportion

C Unitary method

To solve a recipe-type problem, it often helps to calculate first how much is needed for one person or unit.

3 litres of paint cover 36 m². What area will 5 litres of the same paint cover?

3 litres covers 36 m²
÷ 3
1 litre covers 12 m²
× 5
5 litres covers 60 m²

This is called the **unitary method**.

C1 A garden centre uses 30 kg of compost to fill 6 tubs.
   (a) How much compost do they use to fill one tub?
   (b) How much compost do they need to fill 10 tubs?

C2 150 g of dried peas is needed to make pea soup for 5 people.
   (a) What weight of peas is needed to make enough soup for one person?
   (b) What weight of peas is needed to make soup for 20 people?

C3 A woman walks 6 miles in 2 hours.
   If she walks at the same pace, how far can she walk in 5 hours?

C4 Amy and Tom make bird tables. To make 3 bird tables they need these materials.

15 m of wood
3 wooden trays
36 nails

Write out a list of materials they would need to make 7 bird tables.

C5 An expedition company has lists of suggested meals.
This is a list of food for one meal for 5 people.

20 veggie sausages
750 g rice
5 litres of water

Make a list of food they would need for 7 people.

C6 This is a recipe for pastry to make mince pies.
   (a) To make 30 mince pies what weight would you need of
      (i) flour   (ii) sugar   (iii) butter
   (b) How many egg yolks would you need for 30 mince pies?

Pastry for mince pies
(makes 20 pies)

500 g wholewheat flour
180 g brown sugar
240 g of butter (chopped)
4 egg yolks
2–3 drops of vanilla essence

23 Ratio and proportion 167

D Unit cost

D1 These are two offers for paving slabs at different garden centres.

Trimleys Special offer
6 paving slabs for only £48

Hedges & Co
This week only
4 paving slabs for only £28

(a) At Trimleys', what is the cost of each paving slab?

(b) At Hedges & Co, what is the cost of each slab?

(c) Which offer gives you more slabs for your money?

D2 Here are two bags of potatoes at a supermarket.

(a) Work out the cost of 1 kg in the Family Pack.

(b) Work out the cost of 1 kg in the Value Pack.

(c) Which pack gives you more for your money?

Value Pack: POTATOES 3kg £1.47
Family Pack: POTATOES 5kg £2.60

The cost of an item for 1 kilogram, 1 litre, 1 metre or whatever the item is measured in is called the **unit cost**.

Supermarkets often put a unit cost underneath a price label to help customers decide what is the best way to buy the product.

POTATOES, King Ed. 10kg
Item Code: 4456
15.3p per kg

D3 Here are some more labels from different shops.
In each part use unit cost to decide which works out cheaper.

(a) 3 litres 135p | 2 litres 94p

(b) 5 kg £1.50 | 2 kg 62p

(c) 3 kg £2.16 | 5 kg £3.25

(d) 12 metres £6.60 | 14 metres £8.40

D4 A standard bottle of mineral water contains 1.5 litres and costs 96p.
A large bottle contains 2.5 litres and costs £1.50.

(a) What is the cost of one litre of water in the standard bottle?

(b) What is the cost of one litre in the large bottle?

(c) In which bottle does the water work out cheaper?

(d) Why might you prefer to buy the standard bottle?

D5 Ecowash washing liquid can be bought in four sizes.

| Large 3 litre £4.32 | Standard 1 litre £1.49 | Economy 1.5 litre £2.13 | Travel 0.5 litre 78p |

(a) Find the cost of 1 litre for each size.

(b) Write the sizes in order of price per litre, the cheapest first.

D6 Ambreen wants to find the unit cost of a 3 kg pack of bacon costing £2.42.
Her calculator gives the answer to 2.42 ÷ 3 as ➡ `0.8066666`

(a) Round this number to two decimal places.

(b) What is the cost of 1 kg of bacon to the nearest penny?

D7 Find the unit cost of each of these to the nearest penny.

(a) 6 litres of oil costing £5.48   (b) 7 metres of cable costing £4.99

(c) 9 kg of potatoes costing £3.99   (d) Ice cream costing £3.95 for 1.5 litres

D8 A supermarket sells milk in four different sizes

A 1 litre for 93p   **B** 0.5 litre for 48p   **C** 1.5 litres for £1.37   **D** 3 litres for £2.75

(a) Find the cost of 1 litre of each size.

(b) Which size works out cheapest at this supermarket?

When items are measured in millilitres or grams
it is easier to use a larger unit than 1.

For the medium size   200 g costs £1.32
                  ÷ 2 ↘   ↙ ÷ 2
                     100 g costs 66p

	Medium	Large
	200 g £1.32	500 g £3.36

For the large size   500 g costs £3.36
                  ÷ 5 ↘   ↙ ÷ 5
                     100 g costs 67p

So the medium size works out cheaper.

D9 A wholefood store sells ground almonds in four sizes:

S 200 g for 90p   **M** 300 g for £1.15   **L** 500 g for £2.05   **EL** 800 g for £3.50

Find the cost for 100 g in each size and decide which works out cheapest.

D10 Softskin hand cream is sold in two sizes.
The small size contains 300 ml and costs £3.75.
The large size contains 500 ml and costs £6.30.

Which size is the better value for money? Explain why.

D11 Simla tea is sold in these two sizes.   Small: 100 g for £1.64   Large: 250 g for £4.25

(a) Find the cost of 50 g of tea for both sizes.

(b) Which of the sizes gives you more for your money?

D12 A shop sells mayonnaise in two sizes.
Which jar gives better value for money?
Show how you decide.

MAYO 400 g £1.19   MAYO 250 g 69p

OCR

E Mixtures and ratio

A drama club is mixing up orange squash for the interval of the school play.
The students mixed the drinks up in different ways.
These trays show how much squash each student mixed with water.

- Which students made drinks with the same strength?
- Which trays had the strongest concentration of orange squash? Which had the weakest?

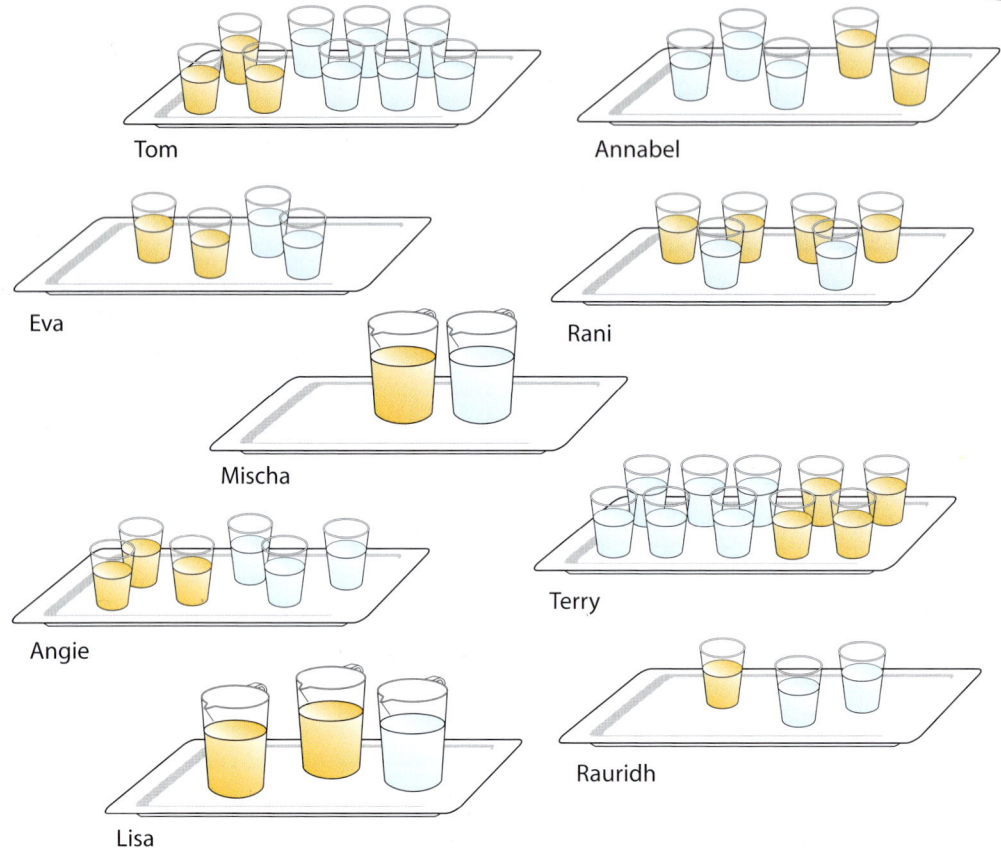

- Nina wants to make a drink the same strength as Rauridh.
  She has two mugs of squash. How much water does she need?

Ratio

If the squash is mixed so that every unit of squash is mixed with 4 of water, we say

> The **ratio** of squash to water is 1 to 4.

This is written as 1:4.
It tells you the **proportions** of squash and water in the mixture.

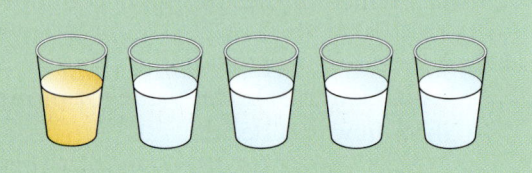

E1 Which of these mixtures show a ratio for squash to water of 1:4?
Where they do not, give the true ratio.

(a)

(b)

(c)

(d)

(e)

(f) ½ full

E2 Karl is making up some lemon squash.
He needs to use 6 parts of water for every part of juice.
Write 'True' or 'False' for each of these statements.

(a) The ratio of water to juice is 1:6.
(b) The ratio of juice to water is 6:1.
(c) The ratio of water to juice is 6:1.
(d) The ratio of juice to water is 1:6.

E3 To make porridge Moragh uses a ratio of oats to water of 1:3.

(a) How much water would she need to go with
   (i) 4 cups of oats
   (ii) 10 cups of oats
   (iii) $1\frac{1}{2}$ cups of oats

(b) How much oats would she need to go with
   (i) 6 cups of water
   (ii) 15 cups of water
   (iii) 600 ml of water

E4 To make shortcrust pastry you use flour and margarine in the ratio 2:1.

(a) How much margarine would you need to go with 500 g of flour?
(b) If you only had 150 g of margarine, how much flour would you need to use?
(c) If you used 400 g of flour…
   (i) How much margarine do you need?
   (ii) What will be the weight of the flour and margarine mixed together?

E5 Concrete is made by mixing ballast and cement.
Different mixtures are used for different types of job.

Job	Cement	Ballast	Ratio of cement to ballast
General	1 part	5 parts	1 : 5
Foundations	1 part		1 : 6
Paving	1 part	4 parts	

(a) Copy and complete the table above.

(b) What job would these mixtures be used for?
  (i) 2 buckets of cement and 10 of ballast
  (ii) 3 bags of cement and 12 bags of ballast

(c) How much ballast would you need with
  (i) 3 buckets of cement to make concrete for foundations
  (ii) 10 wheelbarrows of cement to make concrete for general use

(d) How much cement would you need with
  (i) 12 shovels of ballast to make concrete for foundations
  (ii) 20 bags of ballast to make concrete for general use

(e) Charlie is making concrete for paving and uses 12 buckets of cement.
  (i) How much ballast does she need?
  (ii) How many buckets of the mixture will she have in total?

E6 In a three-legged race the ratio of 'legs' to people is 3 : 2.
(a) How many people are there if there are 9 'legs'?
(b) How many 'legs' are there if there are 18 people?
(c) What is the ratio of heads to 'legs'?
(d) What is the ratio of arms to 'legs'?

*E7 To make wholemeal flaky pastry you use flour and fat in the ratio 4 : 3.
(a) How much fat would you use with 400 g of flour?
(b) How much flour would you use with 600 g of fat?
(c) How much fat would you use with 200 g of flour?
(d) How much flour would you use with 60 g of fat?
(e) How much fat would you use with 1 kg of flour?
(f) How much flour would you use with 1 kg of fat?

F Writing a ratio in its simplest form

T Which pairs of these mixtures have the same ratio?

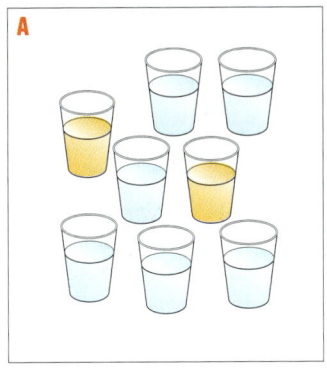

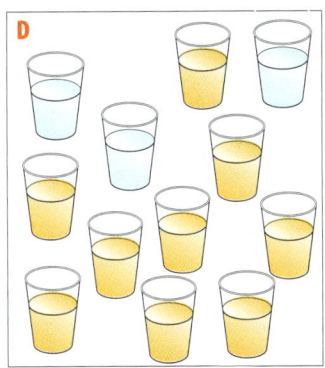

A B C

D E F

It is often useful to write a ratio in its **simplest form**.

You can do this in the same way as a fraction by dividing both sides by common factors.

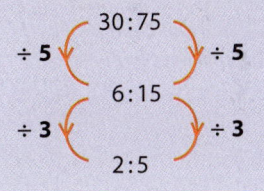

30:75 ÷5→ 6:15 ←÷5
6:15 ÷3→ 2:5 ←÷3

F1 Write these ratios in their simplest form.
- (a) 8:24
- (b) 21:15
- (c) 18:36
- (d) 24:60
- (e) 144:60
- (f) 28:84
- (g) 120:300
- (h) 500:2400

F2 A recipe says that you should use 150g of fat and 250g of flour.
Write the ratio of fat to flour in its simplest form.

F3 Write these as ratios in their simplest form.
- (a) A school has 240 boys and 300 girls.
- (b) A school has 60 teachers and 900 pupils.
- (c) A football match had 2700 United supporters and 3600 City supporters.
- (d) A cat charity has 200 female members and 25 males.

23 Ratio and proportion 173

Test yourself

T1 A recipe for chocolate mousse for 2 people uses these ingredients.

> 100 g of chocolate
> 10 g unsalted butter
> 2 large eggs

(a) How much chocolate would be needed for 1 person?
(b) Write the ingredients needed for 6 people.
(c) John makes some mousse and uses 150 g chocolate.
How many people is he making the recipe for?

OCR

T2 Michael buys 3 files.
The total cost of these 3 files is £5.40.
Work out the total cost of 7 of these files.

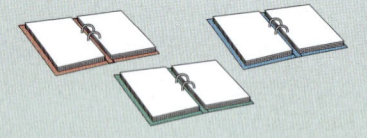

Edexcel

T3 (a) A DIY shop sells cement in two sizes:

   10 kg sack for £8.95   3 kg handy-pack for £2.95

   Which is the best value for money? Explain your answer.

(b) Varnish is sold in two sizes of tin

   200 ml for £4.65   500 ml for £11.95

   Which is the best value for money? Explain your answer.

T4 The same type of crystal glasses is sold in two different packs.

> Small pack
> Contents
> 4 glasses
> £3.20

> Large pack
> Contents
> 12 glasses
> £10.20

Which size is the better value for money?
You must show your working.

AQA

T5 Sea blue paint is made by mixing blue and green paint in the ratio 3:1.

(a) Copy and complete this mixing table.
(b) George mixes 4 litres of blue paint with 2 litres of green paint.
Has he made sea blue paint?
Explain your answer.

Blue paint	Green paint
3 litres	1 litre
	2 litres
15 litres	
	10 litres

T6 A company employs 80 full-time staff and 60 part-time staff.
Write the ratio of full-time staff to part-time staff in its simplest form.

24 Cuboids

This work will help you

- find the volume of a cuboid
- find the surface area of a cuboid
- find the volume of a shape made from cuboids

A Volume of a cuboid

T The net for this box has been drawn on centimetre squared paper. The box measures 6 cm by 4 cm by 3 cm.

- How many 1 cm cubes would it take to make a layer to cover the bottom of this box?
- How many layers would you need to fill the box to the top?
- How many centimetre cubes would it take to fill the box to the top?

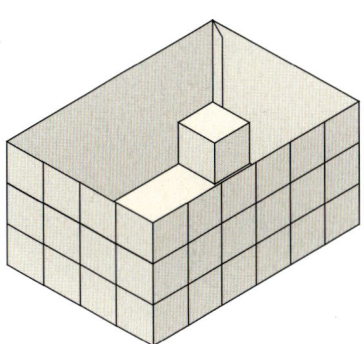

A1 For each of these boxes, work out how many 1 cm cubes it would take to

(i) make a layer to cover the bottom

(ii) completely fill the box

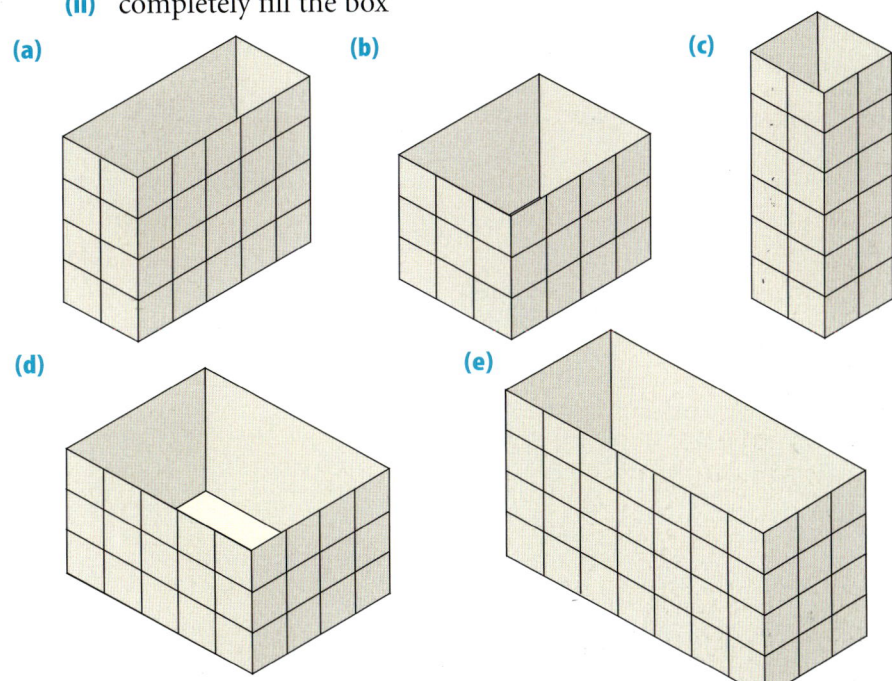

(a)

(b)

(c)

(d)

(e)

24 Cuboids 175

Counting the number of 1 cm cubes that will fit inside a cuboid gives the **volume**.

The volume of a cuboid can be found by multiplying the height (h), length (l) and width (w) together.

volume = $h \times l \times w$

If the measurements are in centimetres then the volume is measured in **cubic centimetres** (cm^3).

The volume of the cuboid here is $3\,\text{cm} \times 7\,\text{cm} \times 4\,\text{cm} = 84\,\text{cm}^3$.

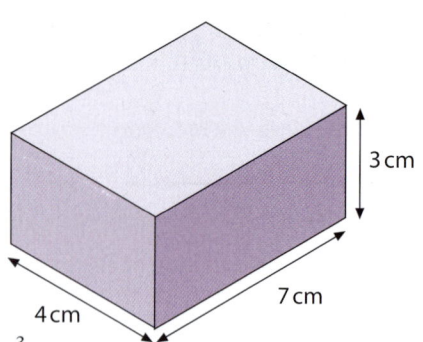

A2 Find the volume of each of these cuboids.

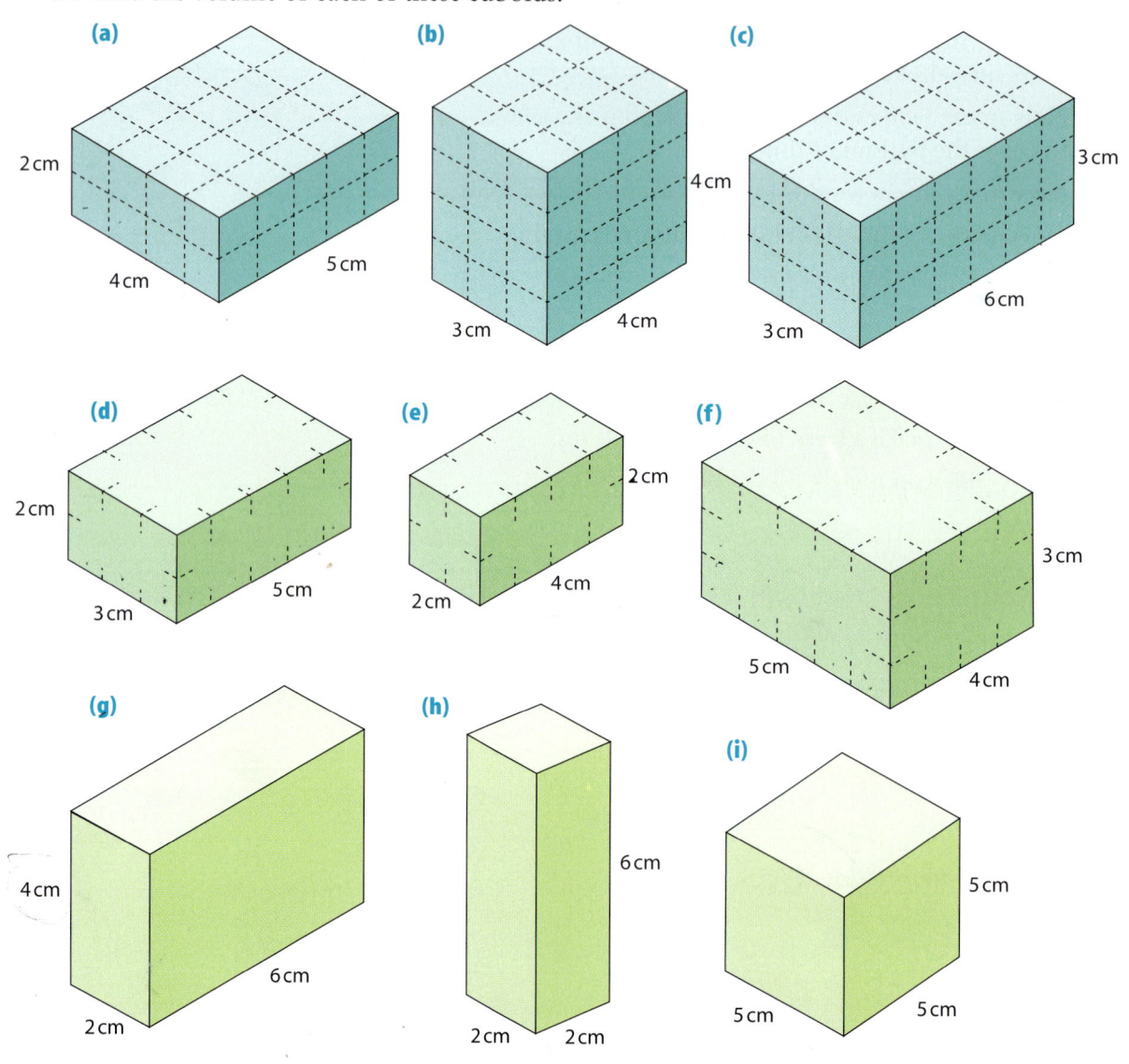

(a) 2 cm, 4 cm, 5 cm

(b) 4 cm, 3 cm, 4 cm

(c) 3 cm, 3 cm, 6 cm

(d) 2 cm, 3 cm, 5 cm

(e) 2 cm, 2 cm, 4 cm

(f) 3 cm, 5 cm, 4 cm

(g) 4 cm, 2 cm, 6 cm

(h) 6 cm, 2 cm, 2 cm

(i) 5 cm, 5 cm, 5 cm

A3 The height, length and width of four cuboids are given below.
Find the volume of each cuboid. (You may sketch them.)

(a) 6 cm, 2 cm, 5 cm
(b) 2 cm, 3 cm, 6 cm
(c) 1 cm, 7 cm, 4 cm
(d) 3 cm, 3 cm, 4 cm

A4 Work out the volume of each of these cartons.

(a) Totley's TEA — 13 cm, 5 cm, 7 cm

(b) Colour-run Remover — 14 cm, 1 cm, 9 cm

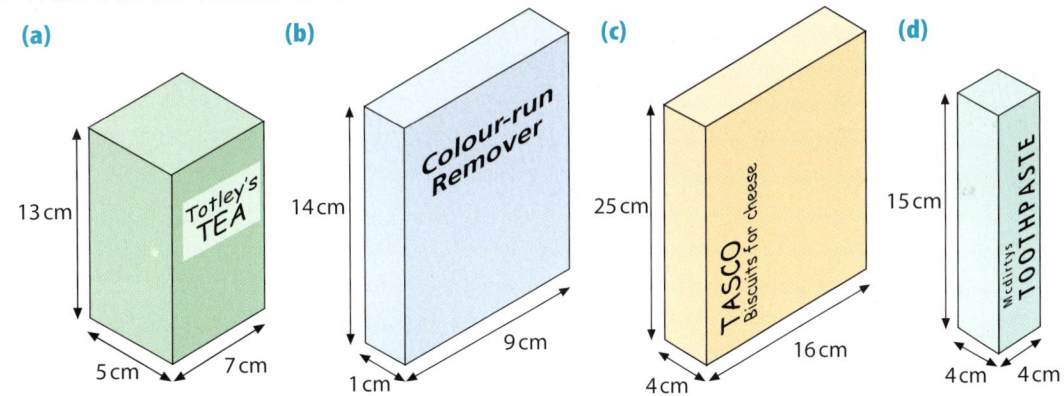

(c) TASCO Biscuits for cheese — 25 cm, 4 cm, 16 cm

(d) McdirtysTOOTHPASTE — 15 cm, 4 cm, 4 cm

A5 Jeni is making a range of metal vases.

One vase, in the shape of a cuboid, has the measurements shown.

What volume of water can it hold?
State the units of your answer.

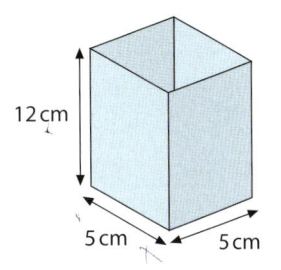

12 cm, 5 cm, 5 cm

OCR

A6 Find the volume of each of these cuboids.

(a) 8 cm, 4.5 cm, 0.25 cm

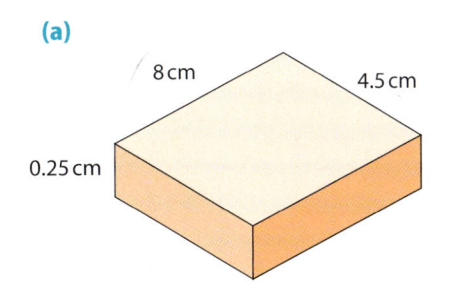

(b) 3 cm, 2.2 cm, 6.5 cm

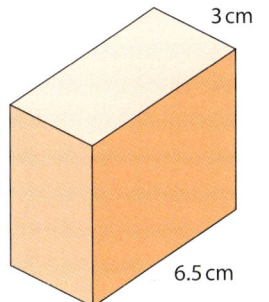

(c) 0.6 cm, 2.4 cm, 5.5 cm

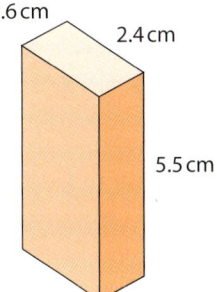

A7 The volume of this cuboid is 24 cm³.
What is the height of the cuboid?

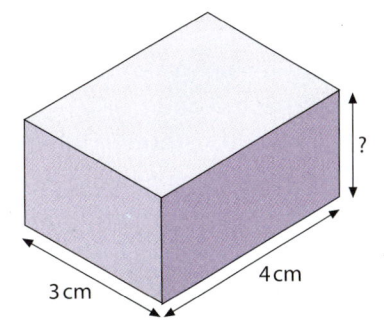

3 cm, 4 cm, ?

24 Cuboids 177

A8 These cuboids all have the same volume.
Find the missing measurements.
(The diagrams are not drawn to scale.)

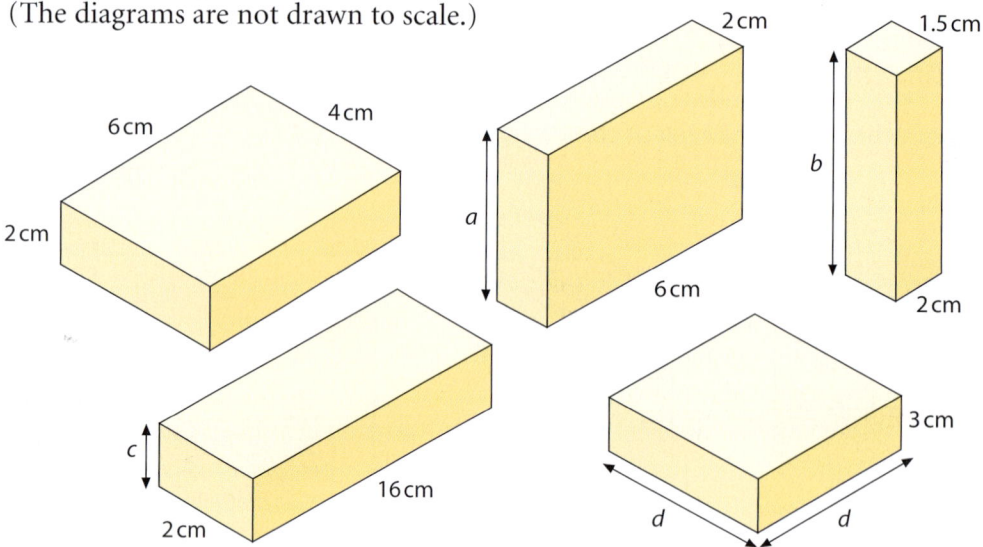

A9 A cuboid has a volume of 7.2 cm³.
The cuboid is 3 cm long and 2 cm wide.
What is the height of the cuboid?

A10 A block of pastry has a volume 300 cm³.
How thick will it be if it is rolled out to form a rectangle

(a) 15 cm by 10 cm (b) 25 cm by 24 cm

Filling boxes

You will need some empty packets that are cuboids and a few centimetre cubes.

Try to estimate how many centimetre cubes will fit inside each box.

Now measure the dimensions of each box to the nearest centimetre.
Use these to find the volume of each box.

How good were your estimates?

Maximum volume

Cut a rectangle 25 cm by 18 cm out of centimetre squared paper.
Cut a 1 cm square from each corner.
Fold the net to form a cuboid without a lid.

What is the volume of this cuboid?

If you cut a 2 cm square at each corner what would be the volume of the cuboid you made?

What size square cut from each corner gives the greatest volume?

B Cubic metres

Living in a box

Large volumes are measured in **cubic metres** (m^3).

A cube 1 m by 1 m by 1 m has a volume of $1 m^3$.

How many students could you get in the metre cube shown in this picture?

What do you think the volume of each of these is roughly in m^3?

- Your classroom
- A swimming pool
- A home freezer
- A container on a lorry
- Your school hall

B1 Find the volume of these cuboids in m^3.

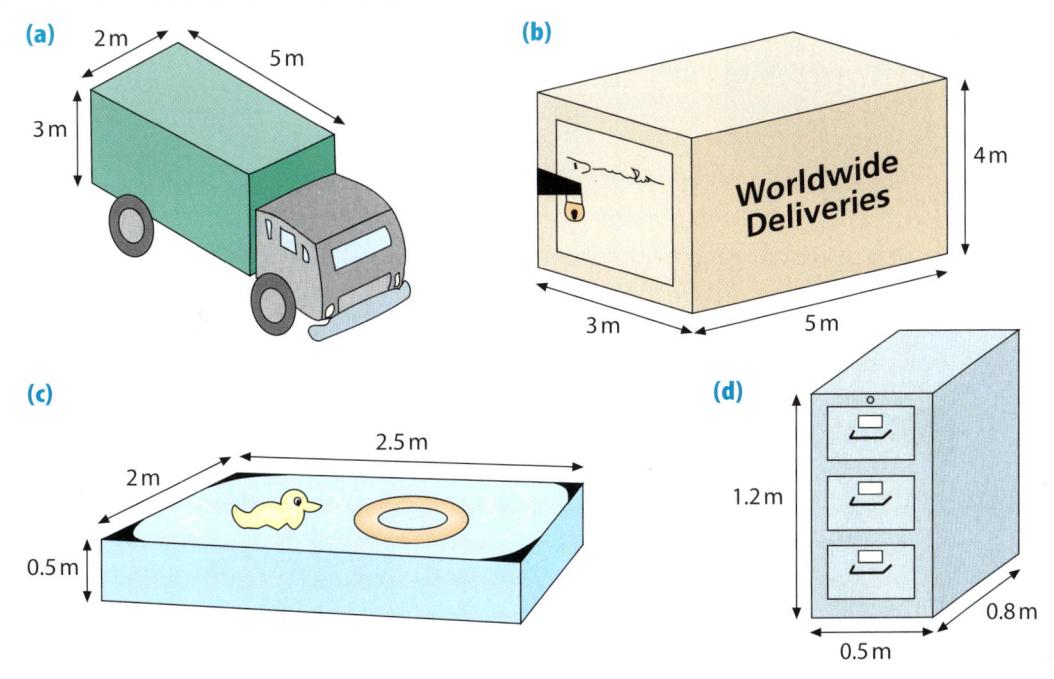

(a) 2 m, 5 m, 3 m

(b) 3 m, 5 m, 4 m — Worldwide Deliveries

(c) 2 m, 2.5 m, 0.5 m

(d) 1.2 m, 0.5 m, 0.8 m

B2 A swimming pool is 25 m long and 10 m wide.

(a) What is the volume of water in the swimming pool if the water is 1.5 m deep?

(b) How deep would the water be if the pool was filled with $200 m^3$ of water?

24 Cuboids 179

C Surface area

The **surface area** of a shape is the total area of all of the outside faces.
It can be useful to sketch the net of a shape and write the area of each face on it.

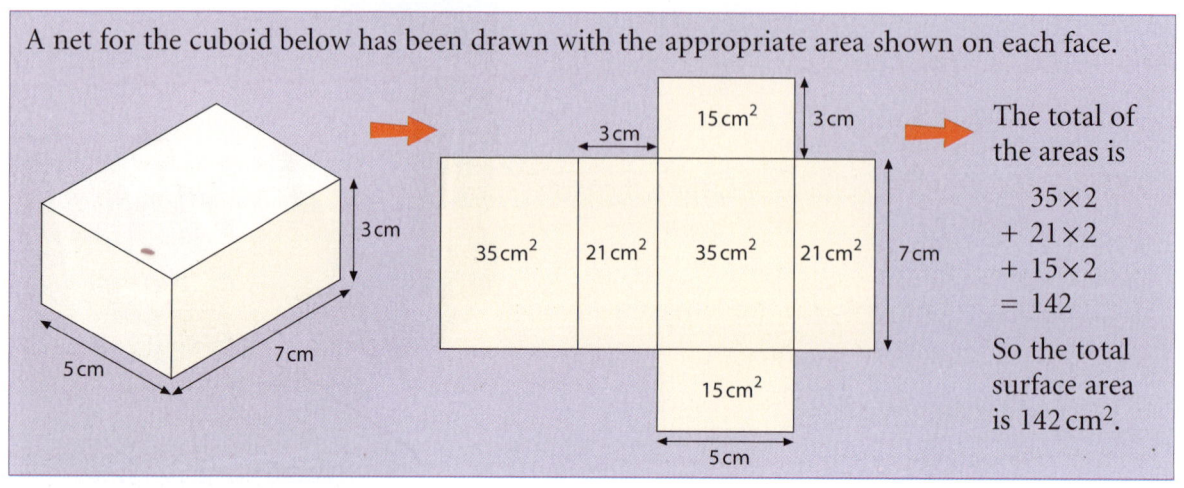

A net for the cuboid below has been drawn with the appropriate area shown on each face.

The total of the areas is

35×2
$+ 21 \times 2$
$+ 15 \times 2$
$= 142$

So the total surface area is 142 cm².

C1 Find the surface area of each of these cuboids.

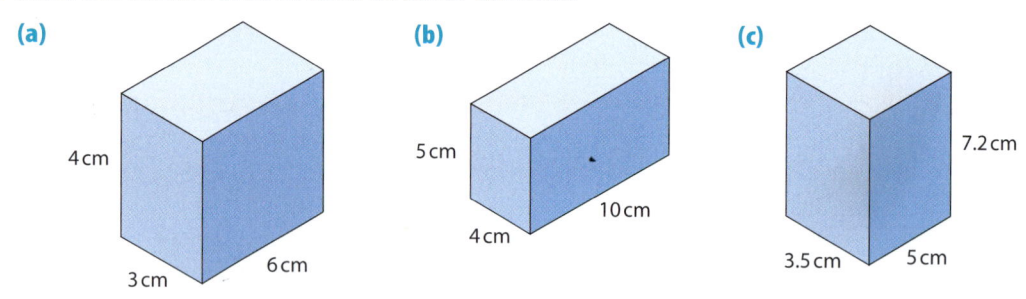

(a) 4 cm, 3 cm, 6 cm

(b) 5 cm, 4 cm, 10 cm

(c) 7.2 cm, 3.5 cm, 5 cm

C2 Find the surface area of each of these cartons.

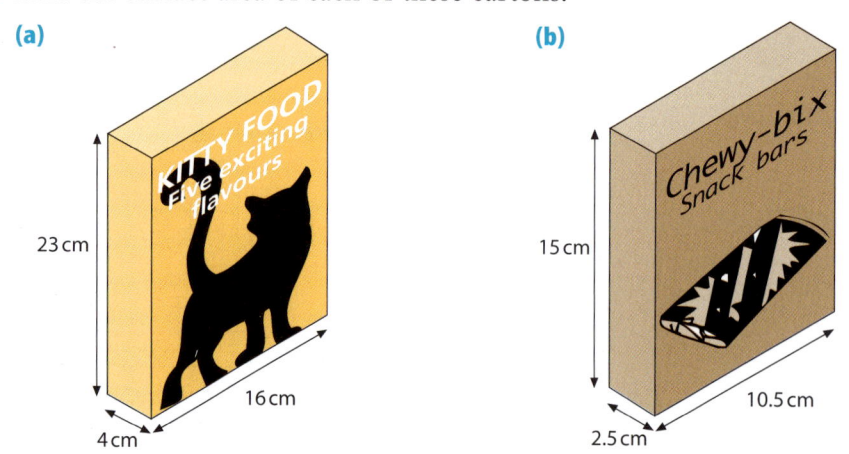

(a) KITTY FOOD — Five exciting flavours — 23 cm, 16 cm, 4 cm

(b) Chewy-bix Snack bars — 15 cm, 10.5 cm, 2.5 cm

C3 A freight company uses containers that are cuboids measuring 3 m by 4 m by 8 m. What is the surface area of one of these containers?

C4 A metal waste bin measures 30 cm by 10 cm by 40 cm.
The bin is painted on all the outside faces except the bottom.
What is the area of painted metal?

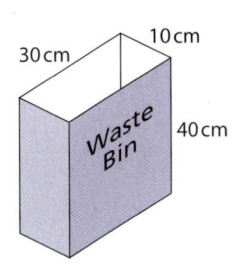

D Volume of a solid made from cuboids

T A solid is made by joining two cuboids together as shown.
- What are the dimensions (length, width and height) of each cuboid?
- Find the volume of each cuboid.
- What is the volume of the whole solid?

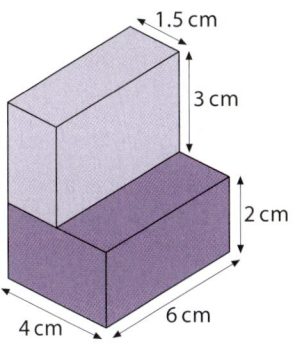

D1 Find the total volume of each solid.
(It might help to write down the length, width and height of each cuboid first.)

(a)

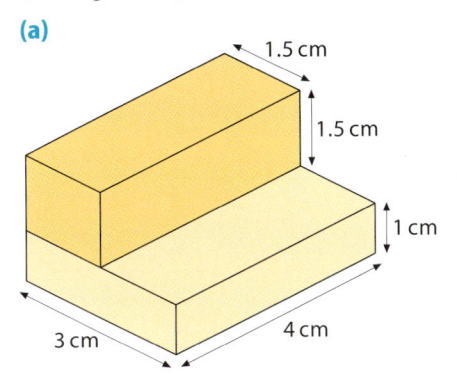

(b)

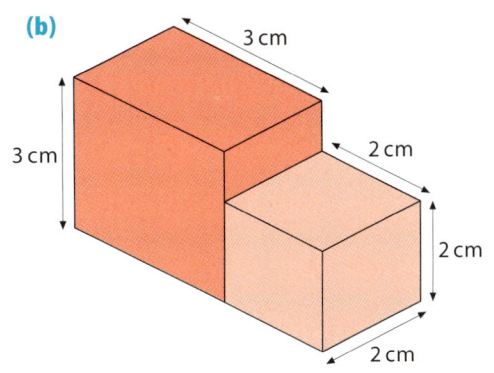

D2 This solid has been made from two cuboids as shown.
(a) What is the height of the smaller cuboid?
(b) Find the total volume of the solid.

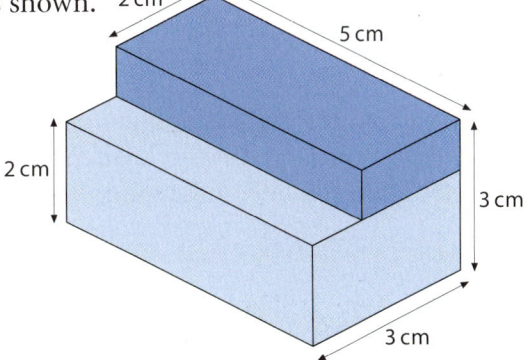

24 Cuboids 181

D3 The solid below can be split up in two different ways as shown.

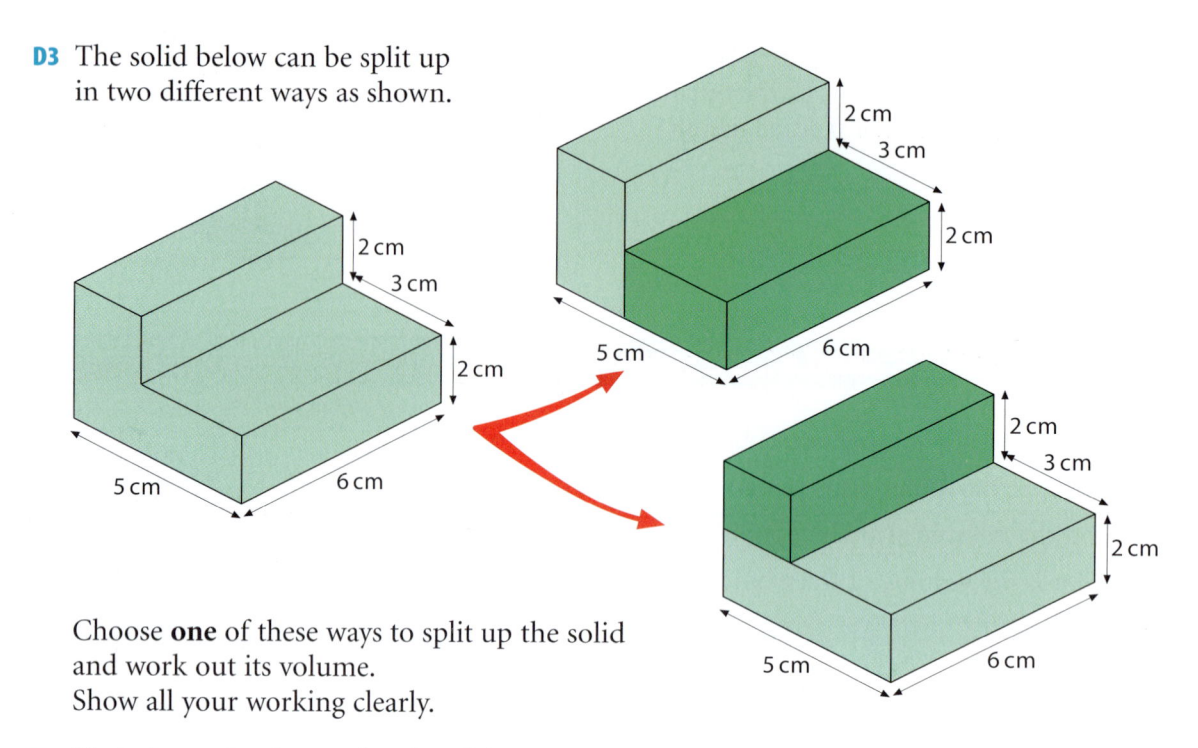

Choose **one** of these ways to split up the solid and work out its volume.
Show all your working clearly.

D4 Find the total volume of each solid.

(a)

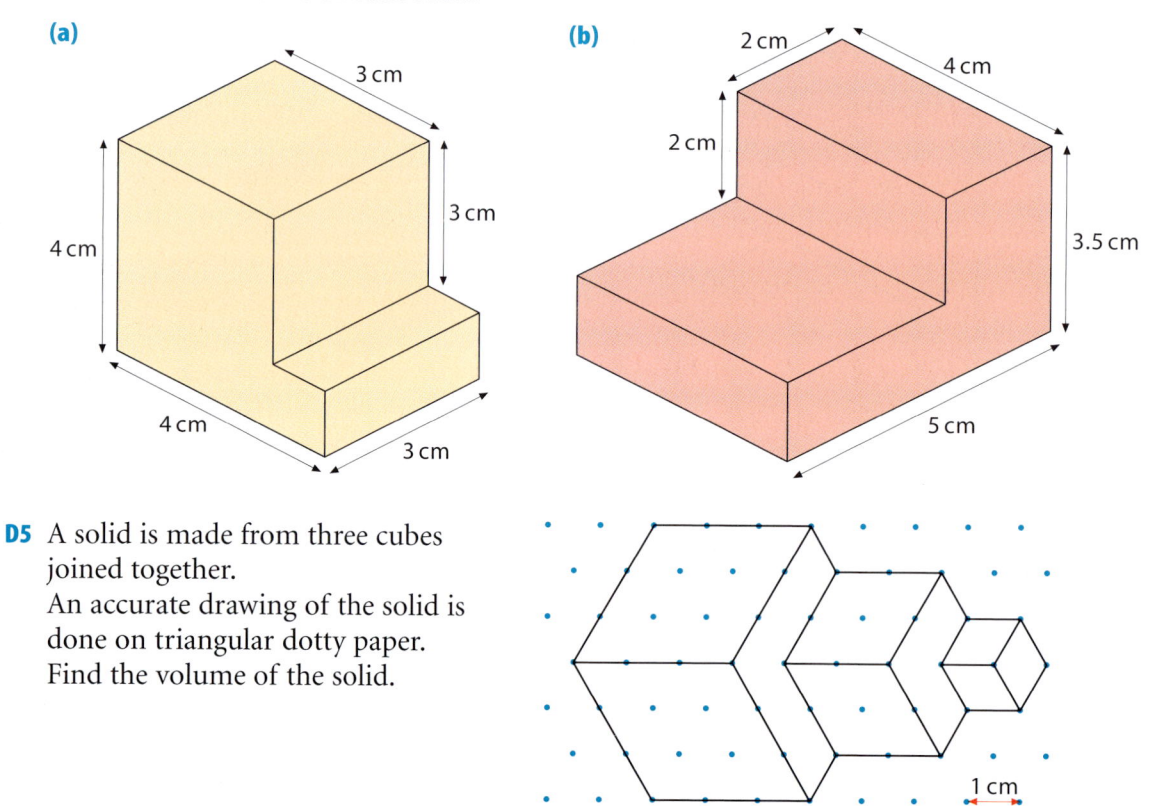

(b)

D5 A solid is made from three cubes joined together.
An accurate drawing of the solid is done on triangular dotty paper.
Find the volume of the solid.

182 24 Cuboids

Test yourself

T1 (a) Find the area of this rectangle.

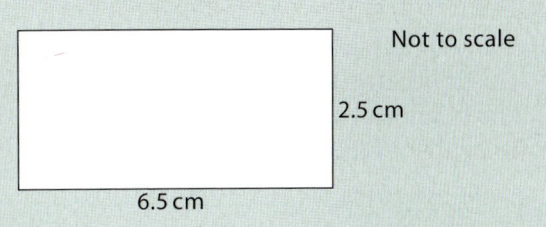

2.5 cm
6.5 cm

Not to scale

(b) Find the volume of this cuboid.

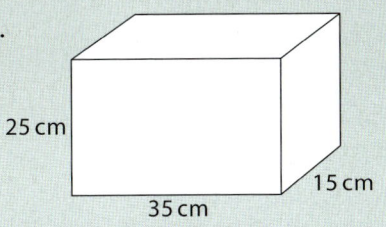

25 cm
35 cm
15 cm

OCR

T2 (a)

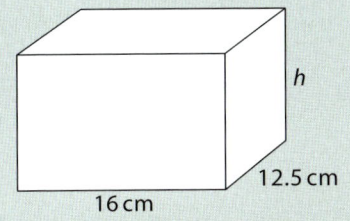

h
12.5 cm
16 cm

The base of a cuboid has length 16 cm and width 12.5 cm.
The volume of the cuboid is 1880 cm^3.
Find the height, h, of the cuboid.

(b) The volume of another cuboid is 36 cm^3.
The length, width and height of the cuboid are all **different whole** numbers.
Give one set of possible values of the length, width and height.

OCR

T3 A room is in the shape of a cuboid.
It is 8 m long, 6 m wide and 3 m high.

(a) Calculate the volume of the room.

(b) Calculate the total area (including any doors or windows) of the **four walls** of the room.

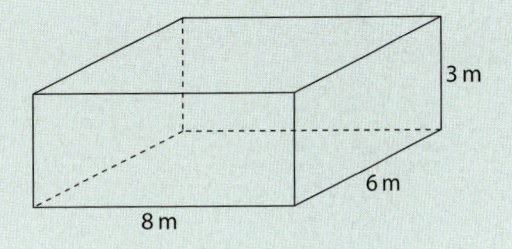

3 m
6 m
8 m

T4 This solid can be split up into two cuboids.
Find the total volume of the solid.

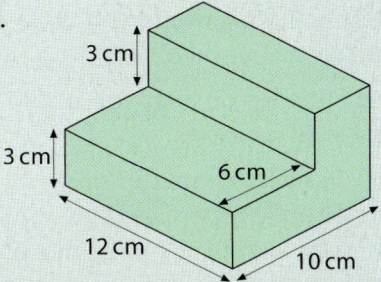

3 cm
3 cm
12 cm
6 cm
10 cm

24 Cuboids 183

Review 3

1 A lot of electrical power is used in the intervals of any popular TV show. This is because people use appliances like kettles during the intervals. The graph shows the power used in an area of the UK one evening.

A megawatt (MW) is a million watts.

(a) The show started at 9:30 and there were two intervals. At roughly what times were these?

(b) What do you think happened between 10:45 and 11:15?

(c) For roughly how long was the amount of power being used greater than 30 MW?

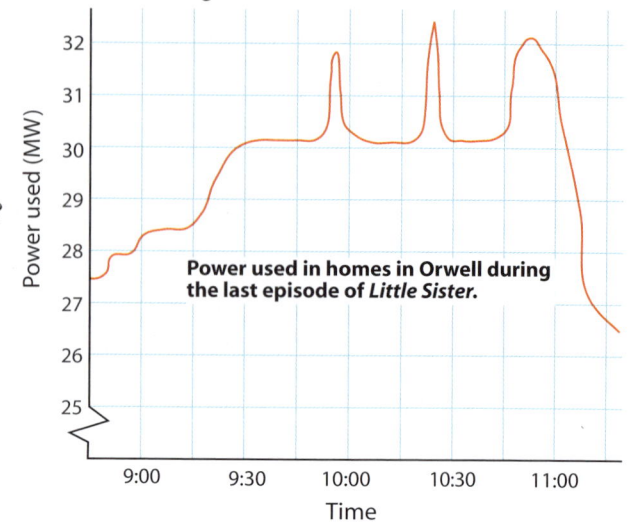

Power used in homes in Orwell during the last episode of *Little Sister*.

2 Work these out.

(a) 50% of £3.00   (b) 25% of 600 ml   (c) 75% of 400 g   (d) 10% of 60 kg

3 Kemal buys 5 pencils for £1.65.
What would be the cost of 8 of these pencils?

4 Calculate the area of each of these shapes.

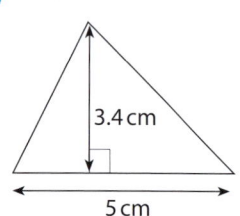

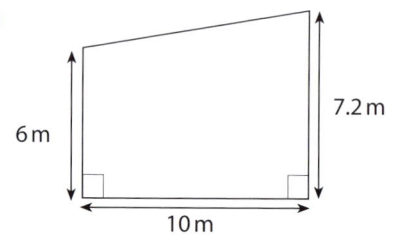

(a) triangle: base 5 cm, height 3.4 cm

(b) trapezium: parallel sides 6 m and 7.2 m, width 10 m

5 This recipe makes 5 pancakes.

(a) How much flour would you need to make one pancake?

(b) Write out a list of what you would need to make 10 pancakes.

(c) Harry has a kilogram of flour, a litre of milk, 6 eggs and lots of salt. How many pancakes can he make?

Plain pancakes

100 grams plain flour
250 ml milk
1 egg
½ teaspoon salt
Method: sift the flour and salt into a bowl, make a well in the centre

6 A teacher has a set of 30 calculators.
12 of them are made by Cosio, 10 by Taxos and the rest by Shirp.
She picks out a calculator at random.
What is the probability that she picks   **(a)** a Taxos   **(b)** a Shirp

7 This table shows information about the eye colour of boys and girls in one class.

(a) How many boys are there in this class?
(b) How many girls are there?
(c) Copy and complete the table.
(d) What fraction of the girls have blue eyes?
(e) What percentage of the boys have brown eyes?
(f) What is the ratio of boys to girls in this class? Give the ratio in its simplest form.

	Brown	Blue	Total
Boys	8	2	
Girls	15		
Total			30

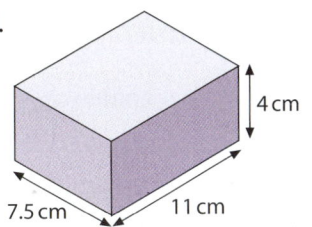

8 Calculate the volume of this cuboid.

(7.5 cm, 11 cm, 4 cm)

9 Calculate these.
(a) 24% of £150   (b) 16% of 35 g   (c) 48% of 550 m   (d) 98% of 15 km

10 Two unbiased spinners, each numbered from 1 to 4, are spun.
The numbers shown on the spinners are multiplied together to give a score.

(a) Copy and complete this grid to show all the possible scores.
(b) Find the probability that the score is
    (i) 9   (ii) greater than 8

Second spinner

×	1	2	3	4
1				4
2				
3			6	
4				

First spinner

11 Harry and Carl are practising hitting the centre of a dartboard.
Harry hits the centre 37 out of 55 times.
Carl hits the centre 34 out of 45 times.
Who do you think is better at hitting the centre? Explain your answer.

12 Sue makes salad dressing by mixing oil and vinegar in the ratio 3 : 1.
How much vinegar would she need to mix with 90 ml of oil?

13 A fish tank is 60 cm long and 40 cm wide.
It contains 72 000 cm^3 of water.
What is the depth of water in the tank?

Review 3   185

25 Scatter diagrams and correlation

This work will help you
- draw a scatter diagram from data
- identify types of correlation
- draw a line of best fit on a scatter diagram
- use a line of best fit to make estimates

You need sheets F1–23 and F1–24.

A Scatter diagrams

Some people are good at word puzzles such as crosswords and word searches.
Sheet F1–23 has two different word puzzles to be done in a time limit.

Word search

Twenty words are hidden in the word square.
Find as many words as you can in 7 minutes.

Anagrams

There are twenty words with the letters mixed up.
How many words can you write out correctly in 10 minutes?

- Record the number of correct answers you get in each puzzle.
- On a grid like this, plot a point for each member of your class.
  We call this a **scatter diagram**.

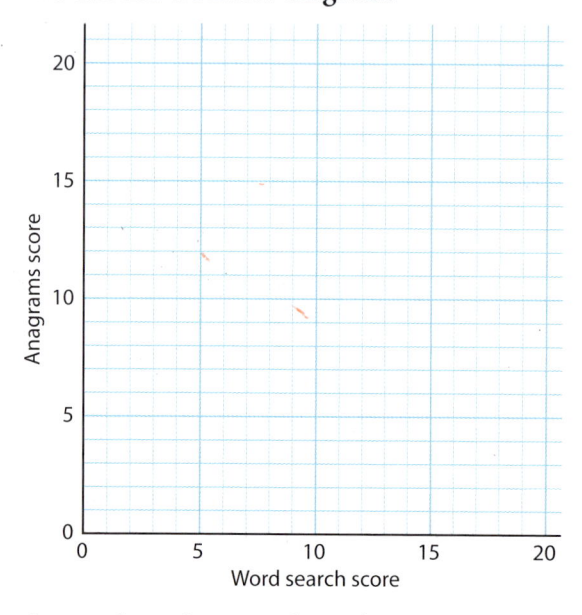

- Are students in your class who are good at one puzzle also good at the other?

A1 A group of students tried both the word search and the anagrams.
They recorded their results as follows.

Student	Ann	Bob	Cath	Dave	Erin	Fran	Guy	Hal	Iain	Jay
Word search score	14	7	9	17	10	14	11	19	16	12
Anagrams score	14	9	12	20	15	16	10	19	17	14

(a) Who scored the lowest on the word search?
Did the same person score the lowest on the anagrams?

(b) Who scored the highest on the word search?
Did the same person score the highest on the anagrams?

(c) Who had the second lowest score on the anagrams?

(d) Draw a scatter diagram for these results on a grid like this.

(e) 'The students who were good at the word search were also good at the anagrams.'
Does the scatter diagram suggest this is true for these students?

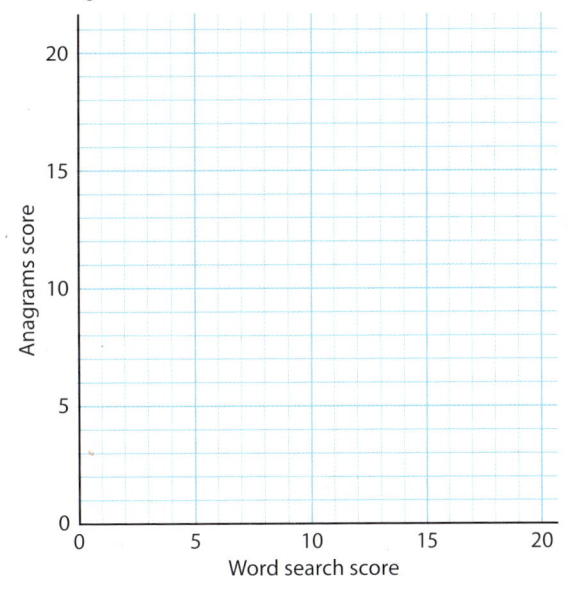

A2 A sweet-taster judges eight different brands of wine gums.
He gives each brand scores out of 10 on colour and on flavour.
These were the results.

Brand	A	B	C	D	E	F	G	H
Colour score	7	10	6	5	9	7	9	4
Flavour score	4	7	2	3	4	3	6	1

(a) Draw a scatter diagram with both scales going from 0 to 10 on squared paper.
Mark a cross for each brand.

(b) Which of these statements best describes how the judge scored these brands?

A The brands with higher colour scores got lower flavour scores.

B The brands with higher colour scores also got the higher flavour scores.

C There is no connection between the scores for flavour and colour.

25 Scatter diagrams and correlation 187

A3 Some children are given two tests to complete.
One test involves some number puzzles.
The other test involves spotting mistakes in pictures.
The table shows the children's scores in the tests.

Child	Anna	Ben	Carol	Donna	Eric	Fred	Gus	Haji	Izzy	Jo
Number puzzle score	12	7	10	3	7	10	5	5	12	14
Picture puzzle score	3	12	7	16	10	5	14	12	5	1

(a) Plot these results on a scatter diagram on squared paper using the scales below.

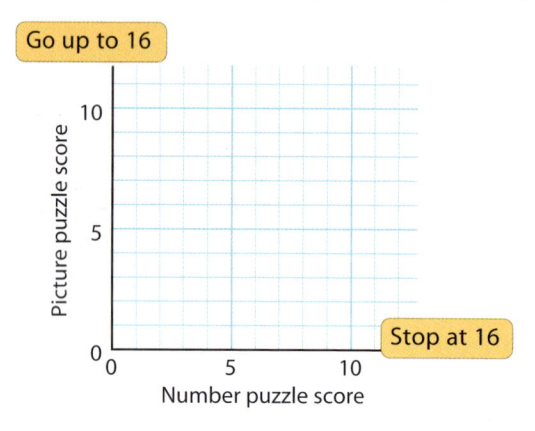

Go up to 16

Stop at 16

(b) What does the scatter diagram tell you?

A4 The scatter diagram shows the heights of some year 8 girls and their mothers.
The jagged lines show that the scales do not start at zero.

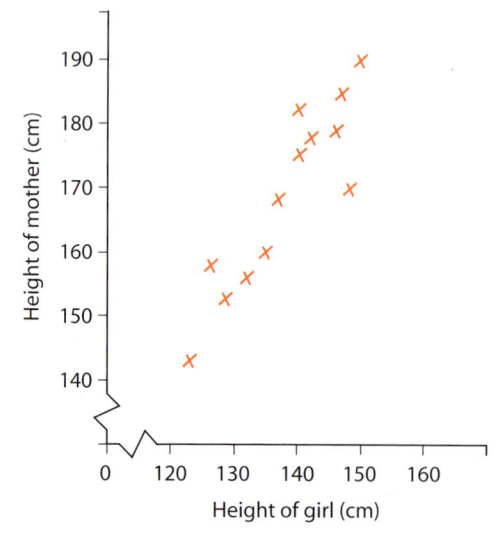

What does the scatter diagram tell you about the connection between the heights of these girls and their mothers?

188 25 Scatter diagrams and correlation

B Correlation

There are three basic patterns that can occur in a scatter diagram.

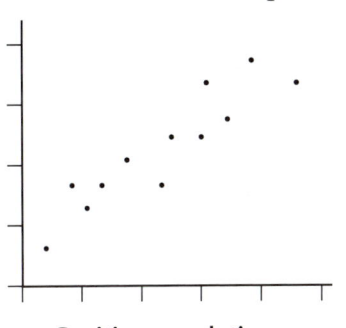

Positive correlation
Both measurements increase together.

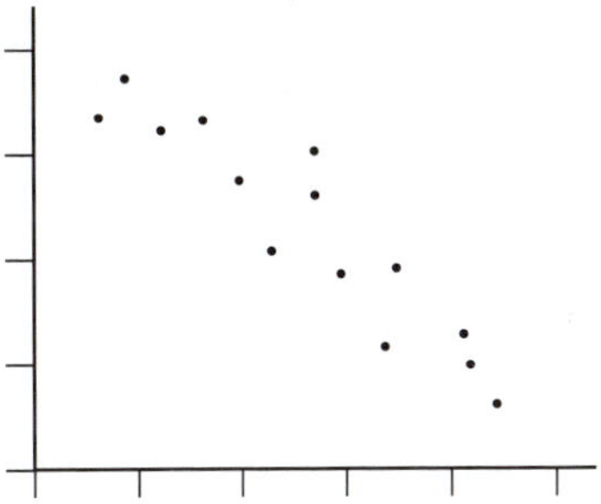

Negative correlation
One measurement goes down when the other goes up.

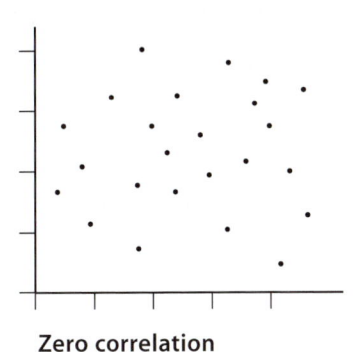

Zero correlation
There is no simple linear link between the two measurements.

B1 This scatter diagram shows the heights and weights of some students.

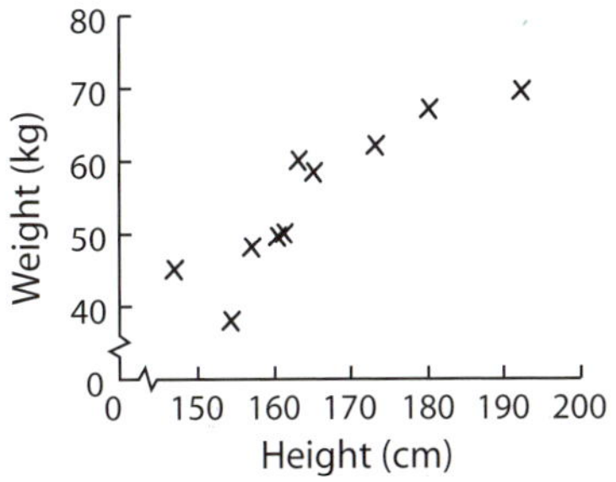

The pattern shows positive correlation.
It shows that the taller students generally weighed more and shorter students weighed less.

For each of the scatter diagrams below
- describe the correlation,
- write a short sentence about any connection the diagrams show.

(a) Engine size and top speed of some cars

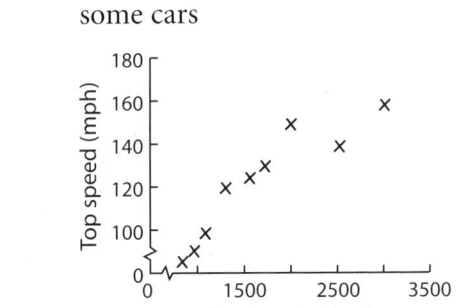

(b) Leg length of students and time to run 100 m

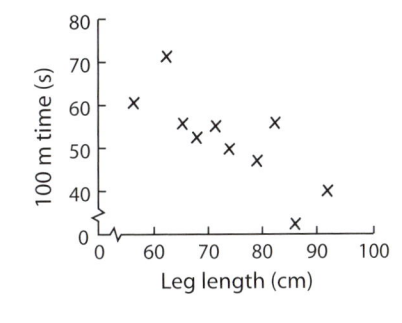

(c) Height and maths tests results of some students

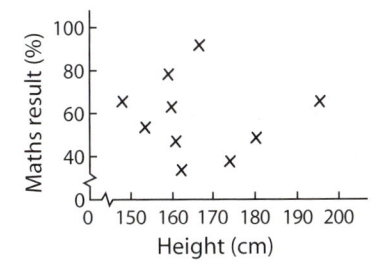

25 Scatter diagrams and correlation 189

B2 Some students carried out an experiment by asking people to do a 'standing jump'. This meant standing against a wall with a piece of chalk in their hands and jumping to make a chalk mark on the wall as high as possible.
They also measured the height of those who took part.

| Height (cm) | 163 | 168 | 147 | 140 | 192 | 156 | 180 | 177 | 158 | 160 | 174 | 172 |
| Jump (cm) | 231 | 244 | 209 | 212 | 293 | 222 | 268 | 254 | 240 | 217 | 262 | 241 |

(a) Draw a scatter diagram on graph paper using these scales.

(b) Does this show positive, negative or zero correlation?

(c) Write a short sentence describing the connection between people's heights and their standing jumps.

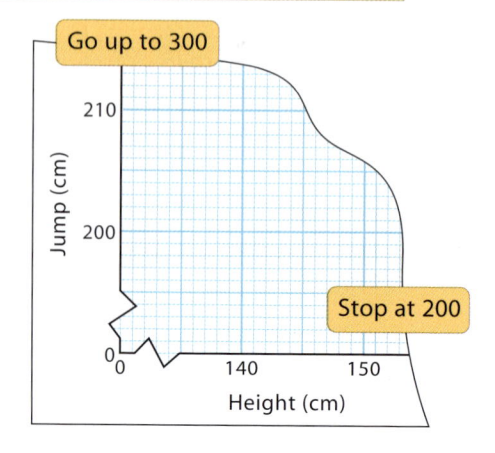

B3 A house owner records the outside temperature at 7 p.m. on some evenings over a period of time.
She also notes how many units of electricity she uses on those days.

| Temperature at 7 p.m. (°C) | 12 | 8 | 6 | 0 | 4 | 1 | 3 | 9 | 11 | 13 |
| Electricity units used that day | 21 | 27 | 31 | 39 | 32 | 35 | 38 | 24 | 26 | 18 |

(a) Draw a scatter diagram on graph paper using these scales.

(b) What type of correlation does the graph show?

(c) Describe the connection between the temperature at 7 p.m. and the amount of electricity the house owner uses.

(d) At 7 p.m. on another day, the house owner records the temperature as 2°C. Roughly how many units of electricity do you think were used on that day?

(e) On another day, the house owner notes that 29 units of electricity were used. Estimate the temperature on that day at 7 p.m.
How accurate do you think your estimate is?

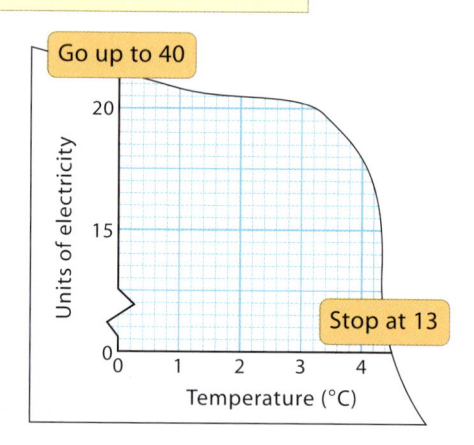

C Line of best fit

Forensic scientists sometimes have to decide what someone looked like by examining the bones of a skeleton.

This scatter diagram shows the heights of some males and the length of their femur (thigh bone).

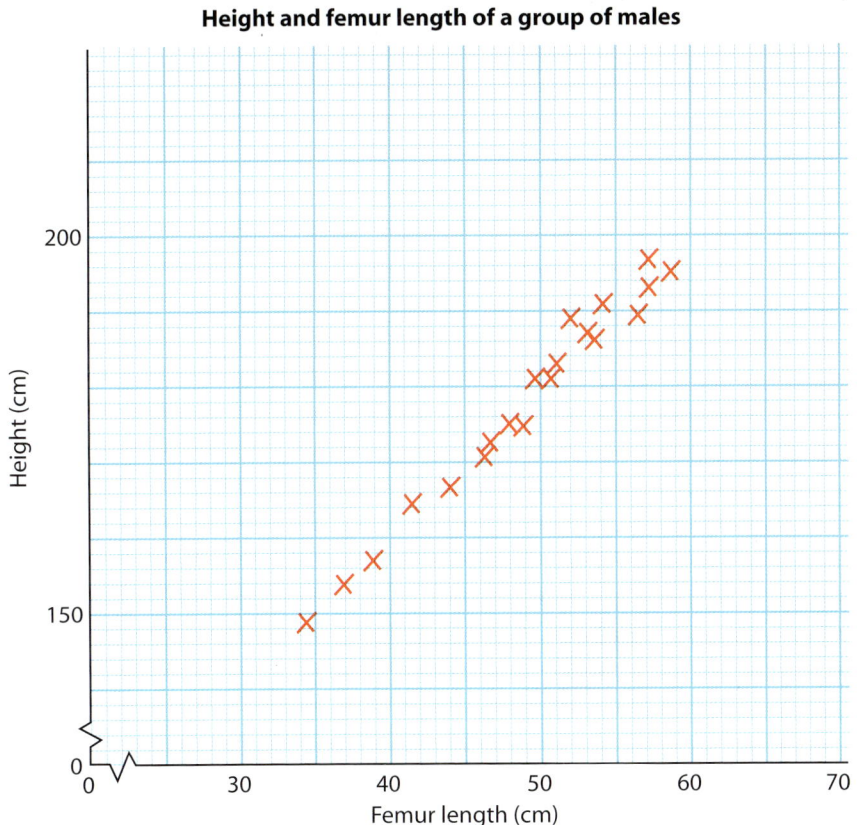

Height and femur length of a group of males

- What type of correlation is there between femur length and height? Is this a strong or a weak correlation?
- Police find a male femur in a pit.
  It is 42 cm long.
  How tall would you estimate the person to whom this belonged was?
  How accurate do you think your estimate is?
- A man is 180 cm tall.
  How long would you expect his femur to be?
  How accurate do you think your estimate is?
- A femur is found that is 65 cm long.
  Can you accurately estimate the height of the man?
- A boy is 140 cm tall.
  Can you accurately estimate the length of his femur?

When paired data has a strong correlation, it is useful to draw a straight line through the points on the scatter diagram.
This is called a **line of best fit**.

Try to draw the line that fits best through the points. You should aim to have roughly the same number of points on either side of your line.

The line can be used to estimate other values. However, estimating values where the line has been extended above or below the given points is less reliable.

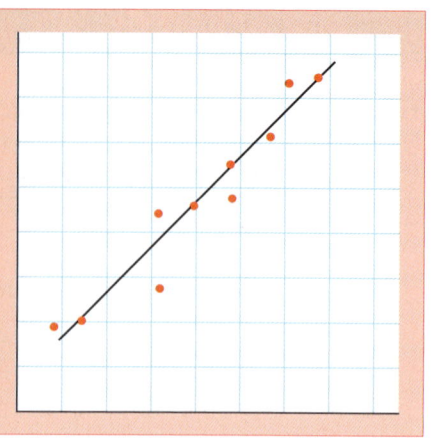

C1 Below is a copy of the femur graph with the line of best fit added.

Height and femur length of a group of males

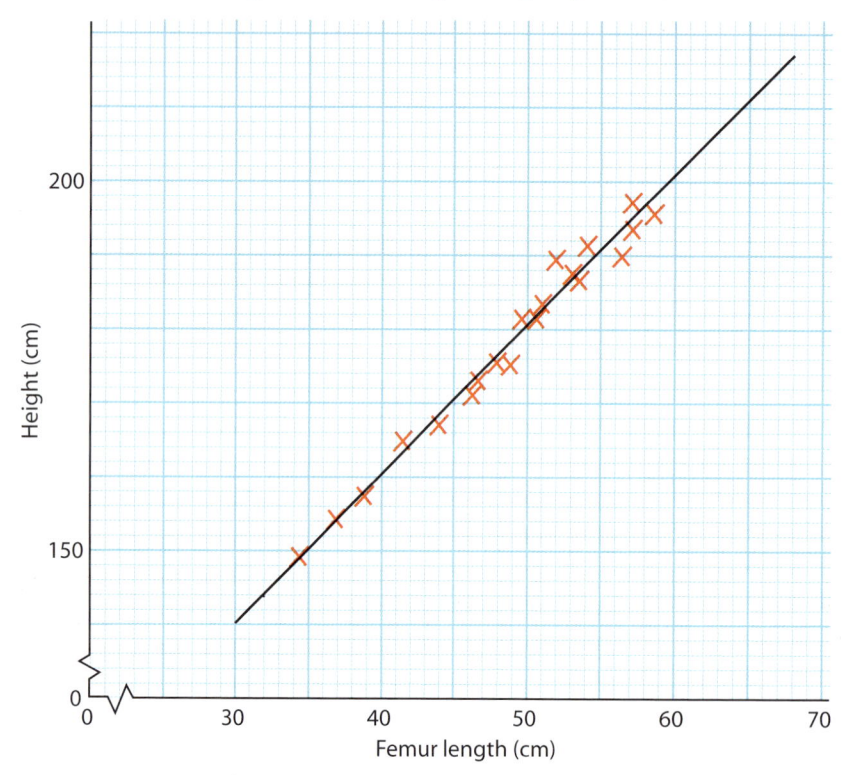

(a) Use the line to estimate the height of a male whose femur length was

 (i) 45 cm (ii) 55 cm (iii) 60 cm (iv) 33 cm

(b) Use your line to estimate the length of femur in a male whose height was

 (i) 180 cm (ii) 160 cm (iii) 150 cm (iv) 178 cm

(c) Archaeologists unearth a male femur bone that is 67 cm long.
Use the graph to estimate the height of the man to whom this belonged.
How reliable do you think this estimate is?

C2 This table shows the engine size and the fuel economy of some older petrol cars.

Engine size (litres)	1.6	1.4	3.0	1.2	1.1	1.0	2.0	1.7	1.3	4.0	3.5
Fuel economy (m.p.g.)	37	41	32	43	46	49	34	35	44	18	25

(a) Show this information on a scatter diagram using the scales shown.

(b) Describe the correlation between the engine size and fuel economy of these cars.

(c) Draw the line of best fit on your scatter diagram.

(d) Use your graph to estimate the fuel economy of a car whose engine capacity is 2.5 litres.

(e) What capacity engine do you estimate would have a fuel economy of more than 50 m.p.g.?

(f) A Lamborghini Diablo has a 5.7 litre engine. Use your graph to estimate the fuel economy of this car. How reliable do you think this estimate is?

Go up to 50
Stop at 6.0

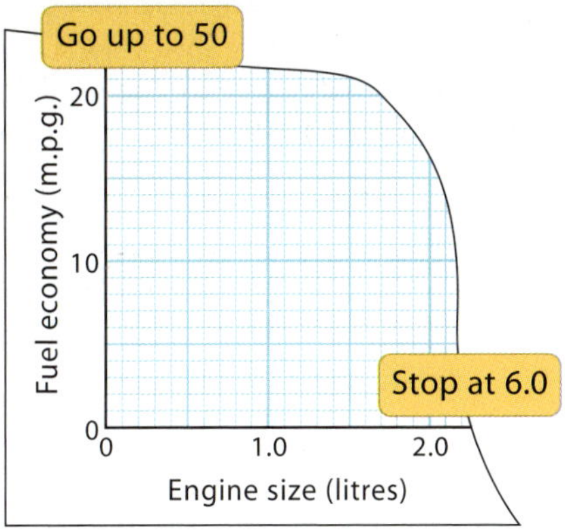

C3 A fish farmer collected this information about salmon.

Weight (kg)	5.0	3.3	4.3	5.1	3.4	5.1	4.7	4.2	3.1	2.9	4.5	4.9	3.4	5.0	5.0
Length (cm)	74	49	62	67	54	74	71	57	54	48	69	69	58	79	71

(a) Show this information on a scatter diagram using these scales.

(b) Draw a line of best fit.

(c) Measuring the length of a live salmon is difficult. Weighing is easier, using a net with scales attached. Estimate the length of a salmon weighing

   (i) 4 kg   (ii) 3 kg   (iii) 3.7 kg   (iv) 5.5 kg

(d) Estimate the weight of a salmon of length 75 cm.

(e) The largest salmon ever caught was about 1 m long. Use your diagram to estimate the weight of this salmon.
How reliable do you think this estimate is?

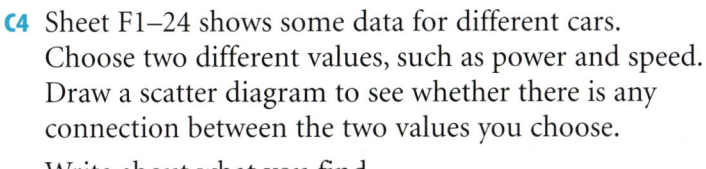

Go up to 100
Stop at 7.0

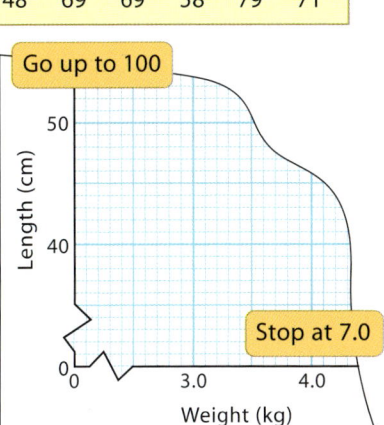

C4 Sheet F1–24 shows some data for different cars. Choose two different values, such as power and speed. Draw a scatter diagram to see whether there is any connection between the two values you choose.
Write about what you find.

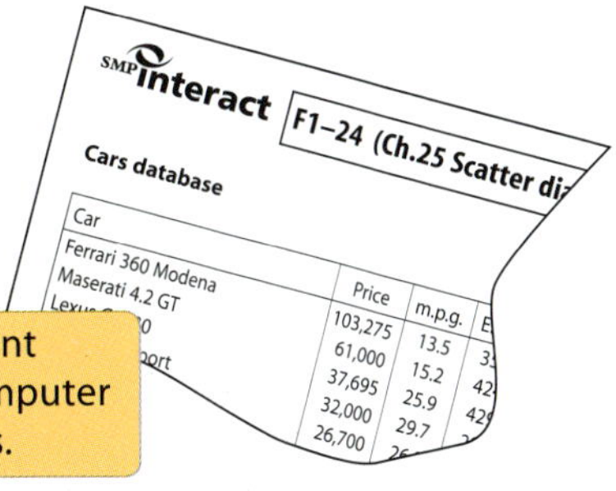

You could investigate different pairs of values and use a computer to draw the scatter diagrams.

25 Scatter diagrams and correlation   193

By searching on the web you can find many sets of paired data that are worth investigating for correlation. Where you find correlation you can consider whether it would be useful to draw a line of best fit.

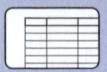

By putting paired data on a spreadsheet in two adjacent columns with each pair in its own row, you can use the spreadsheet's charting facility to draw a scatter diagram quickly and accurately.

Test yourself

T1 At a gym 10 men are asked to spend 5 minutes on a running machine. Two minutes after they finish, their pulses are recorded. Their ages and pulse rates are shown in the table.

Age (years)	39	43	22	27	47	48	55	61	21	30
Pulse rate (per minute)	96	97	76	81	101	106	105	112	80	90

(a) Use this information to draw a scatter diagram using these scales.

(b) What type of correlation is there between the ages and pulse rates of these men?

(c) Draw a line of best fit.

(d) Use your diagram to estimate the pulse rate of a 35-year-old man after 5 minutes on the running machine.

(e) An 80-year-old man joins the gym. Use your graph to estimate his pulse rate after 5 minutes on the running machine. How reliable do you think this estimate is?

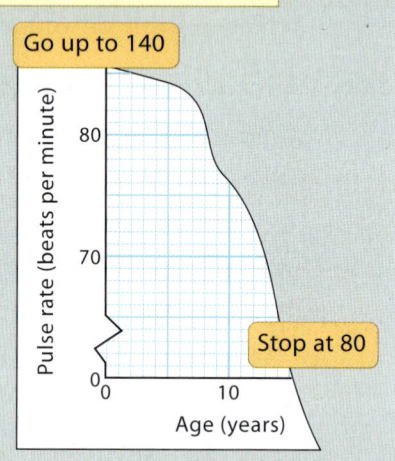

Go up to 140
Stop at 80
Pulse rate (beats per minute) — Age (years)

T2 Here are the results of two papers in a mathematics exam taken by 10 students. Each paper is out of a maximum of 100 marks.

Paper 1 mark	65	35	56	59	50	44	25	70	22	75
Paper 2 mark	77	41	66	64	55	50	31	83	27	85

(a) Plot these values on a scatter diagram using these scales.

(b) What does your scatter diagram tell you about the connection between the marks for Paper 1 and Paper 2 for these students?

(c) A student is ill for Paper 2. She scored 40 on Paper 1. Estimate her mark for Paper 2.

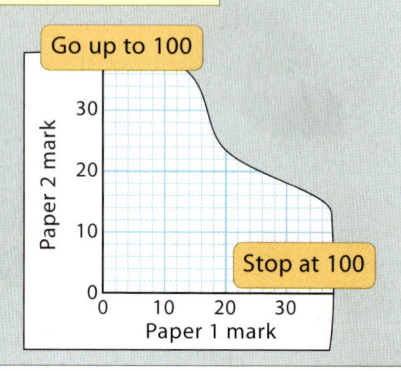

Go up to 100
Stop at 100
Paper 2 mark — Paper 1 mark

26 Square and cube numbers

This work will help you
- identify square and cube numbers
- find square roots and cube roots
- use simple index notation

A Squares and square roots

We can arrange 25 square tiles to make a square.
This shows us that 25 is a **square number**.

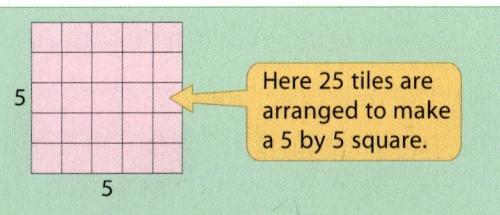

Here 25 tiles are arranged to make a 5 by 5 square.

When we multiply any whole number by itself we get a square number.

25 is a square number because $5 \times 5 = 25$

We can write this in shorthand as $5^2 = 25$

We say '5 **squared** is 25'.

25 is called the **square** of 5.

5 is called the **square root** of 25.

In shorthand $\sqrt{25} = 5$

A1 Which of the following numbers are square numbers?

8   4   144   80   49   13   1

A2 Choose one number from the box to complete each sentence.

| 2 | 3 | 4 | 8 | 10 | 16 | 18 | 50 | 81 |

(a) The square of 4 is ...... (b) 9 squared is ......
(c) The square root of 100 is ......

A3 Work these out.

(a) The square of 8   (b) 4 squared   (c) The square root of 1

A4 Work these out.

(a) 6^2 (b) 10^2 (c) 7^2 (d) 12^2 (e) 1^2

A5 Find these.

(a) $\sqrt{36}$ (b) $\sqrt{49}$ (c) $\sqrt{9}$ (d) $\sqrt{81}$ (e) $\sqrt{64}$

26 Square and cube numbers 195

A6 121 counters are arranged to make a square.
This diagram shows a corner of the square.
How many counters are there along one edge?

A7 (a) Which of the calculations below gives the area of this square?

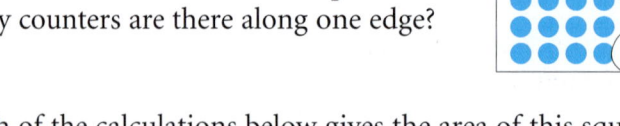

  A 13×2 B 13^2 C 13×4

  13 cm
  13 cm

  (b) What is the area of this square in cm^2?

A8 Which of the numbers in the loop are square numbers?

  240   94   225   196
     144   200   160

A9 Use your calculator to work these out.

  (a) The square of 16 (b) 19 squared (c) The square root of 289 (d) 23^2
  (e) 31^2 (f) $\sqrt{400}$ (g) $\sqrt{625}$ (h) $\sqrt{484}$

A10 Use the clues to find each number.

  (a) I am a two-digit number.
      I am a square number.
      I am a multiple of 7.

  (b) I am between 200 and 500.
      I am a square number.
      I am a multiple of 100.

A11 Find a square number between 300 and 350.

How many squares?

- How many squares can you find altogether in a 3 by 3 grid like the one on the right? (Some are shown outlined in red.)

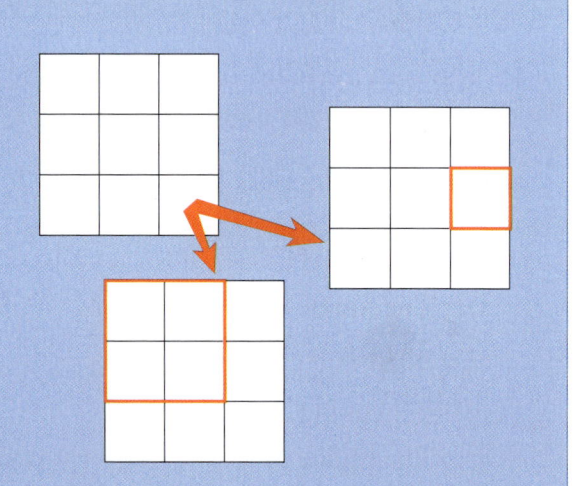

- Try larger and smaller square grids. How many squares can you find altogether?
- Can you find any rules or patterns for your results?
- Use any rules or patterns you have found to decide how many squares there are altogether in a 10 by 10 grid.

B Cubes and cube roots

We can arrange 8 small cubes to make a large **cube**.
This shows us that 8 is a **cube number**.

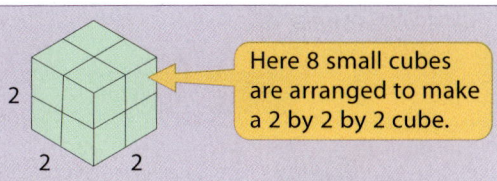

Here 8 small cubes are arranged to make a 2 by 2 by 2 cube.

When we multiply any whole number by itself and by itself again we get a cube number.

8 is a cube number because $2 \times 2 \times 2 = 8$

We can write this in shorthand as $2^3 = 8$ *We say '2 **cubed** is 8'.*

8 is called the **cube** of 2.

2 is called the **cube root** of 8.

B1 (a) What is the value of $1 \times 1 \times 1$?

(b) List the first four cube numbers.

B2 Choose one number from the box to complete each sentence.

| 1 | 6 | 9 | 12 | 15 | 25 | 27 | 100 | 125 |

(a) The cube of 3 is ...... (b) 5 cubed is ......

B3 (a) Write down the value of 4 cubed.

(b) Write down the cube root of 64.

B4 Work these out.

(a) 5^3 (b) 10^3 (c) 6^3 (d) 9^3

B5 What is the cube root of 729?

B6 Which of the following are cube numbers?

3   125   100   216   300   1000   1331

B7 A cube has a volume of 27 m^3.
How long is each edge?

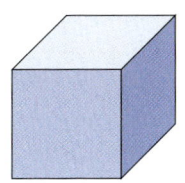

B8 What is the value of n^3 when $n = 7$?

B9 (a) Find n if $n^3 = 1728$. (b) Find x if $x^3 = 8000$.

26 Square and cube numbers   197

C Squares, cubes and higher powers

C1 Match these up.

- A 2^3
- B 3^3
- C 4^2
- D 8^2
- E 3^2

- P 9
- Q 8
- R 16
- S 27
- T 64

C2 Work these out.

(a) 12^2 (b) 8^3 (c) 14^2 (d) 13^3

C3 Copy and complete: $5^3 + 4^2 = 125 + \blacksquare$
$= \blacksquare$

C4 Work these out.

(a) $10^2 + 3^2$ (b) $2^3 - 1^3$ (c) $3^3 + 5^2$ (d) $3^2 - 2^3$

C5 Write down the numbers in the loop that are

(a) square numbers
(b) cube numbers

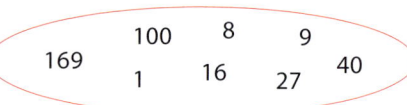

(169   100   8   9   1   16   27   40)

C6 Find all the numbers between 100 and 200 that are

(a) square numbers   (b) cube numbers

C7 Find the value of

(a) the cube of 7   (b) 14 squared   (c) 11 cubed

C8 Use the clues to find each number.

(a) I am a two-digit number.
I am a square number.
I am a cube number.

(b) I am a three-digit number.
I am a cube number.
I am a multiple of 6.

We know that $2^3 = 2 \times 2 \times 2 = 8$.

This shorthand can be used for longer multiplications.

For example, $2^4 = 2 \times 2 \times 2 \times 2 = 16$.

C9 Copy and complete the multiplication below to evaluate 2^5.

$2^5 = 2 \times 2 \times 2 \times 2 \times 2 = \blacksquare$.

C10 Evaluate these.

(a) 3^4 (b) 2^6 (c) 10^4 (d) 1^5 (e) 10^5

*C11 Copy and complete this cross-number puzzle.

Across
1 A square number
3 A square number
5 A square number
6 A square number between 30 and 40
7 A cube number
8 A square number

Start with this clue.

Down
2 A cube number between 4500 and 5000
4 A cube number

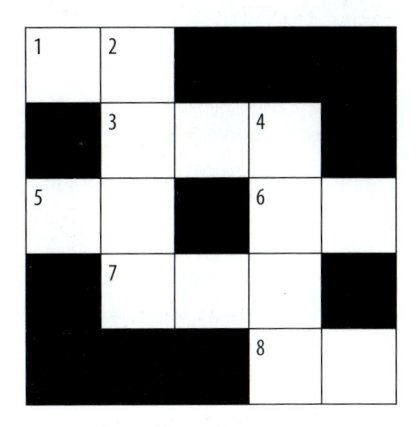

Test yourself

T1

Cloud contains: 8, 12, 27, 4, 6, 16, 5, 3

Using only the numbers in the cloud, write down
(a) all the multiples of 6
(b) all the square numbers
(c) all the factors of 12
(d) all the cube numbers

Edexcel

T2 Work out the difference between the two square numbers in this list of numbers.

  6   11   15   21   27   36   48   64

AQA

T3 Work out the value of $9^2 + 5^2$.

T4 Work out
(a) $\sqrt{81}$
(b) 5^3

OCR

T5 Write down the cube of 10.

T6 (a) Write down the values of the following
  (i) 8^2
  (ii) $\sqrt{36}$
(b) Work out $7^2 - 2^3$.

OCR

T7 Find the value of (a) 3 cubed (b) 2^5

T8 What is the cube root of 8?

26 Square and cube numbers

27 Surveys

This work will help you design a questionnaire, choose a sample to take part in a survey and report your results.

You need a pie chart scale in section D.

A Starting a project

When choosing a project you must decide on a question or statement that you can test.

A statement like this is sometimes called a **hypothesis**.

Here are some questions and statements that could be tested in a project.

| Are teachers more likely to be in favour of a school uniform than students? |

| Mobile phones improve your social life. |

| More students would use the school library if it had different opening times. |

| Are roads in the UK safer than on the continent? |

| It is easier being a vegetarian in the UK than in other European countries. |

| Are young people more likely to smoke if their parents smoke? |

| Do students work better when listening to music? |

| Organically grown tomato plants give more fruit than non-organic ones. |

| The Sun is easier to read than The Times. |

| Do teenagers have a more healthy lifestyle than their parents? |

| Students who live further away from school are less likely to walk to school. |

A **survey** is one way of collecting data.
What other ways could you use?

Which of the above statements and questions could be tested by carrying out a survey of the people in your school or local area?

Think of a statement or question of your own to test.
Discuss whether it could be answered by carrying out a survey of people or by some other means.

> **Primary data** is data that you collect yourself from a survey or experiment.
> **Secondary data** is data that someone else has collected and organised.

B Designing a questionnaire

A school's student council is looking at changing the school uniform.
They design a questionnaire to give to students in their school.

School uniform survey

The student council is looking at changing the school uniform policy.
We would like your views on school uniform.
Please complete the questionnaire below and hand it to your form rep.

Name _____

1	What year group are you in? (Please ring.)	Y7 Y8 Y9 Y10 Y11
2	Are you male or female?	Male Female
3	Do you think there should be a school uniform?	Yes No
4	If there has to be a school uniform, would you prefer	Blazer Sweatshirt
5	What colours would you like the school uniform to be?	☐

6   'Students should be allowed to wear jewellery.' What do you think?

Strongly agree   Agree   Not sure   Disagree   Strongly disagree

---

What do you think of these questions?
- Are they easy to answer?
- Are they clear – will they mean the same to everyone?
- Will the answers be easy to sort out?

B1 Write a better question to replace question 5 about colours.
Say why you think your question is better.

B2 The council wondered whether 'jewellery' was too vague.
Write a question which asks about different types of jewellery.

B3 The council wanted to ask a question about what action the school should take on anyone who did not follow the school uniform policy.
Write a question which asks this.

Things to avoid in a questionnaire

- Don't ask questions that might be embarrassing.
  Don't ask for names: people will be more honest if they know their name is not on the survey.
- Don't ask questions that try to persuade people to give a particular answer: 'In view of the appalling number of accidents outside the school, should traffic be banned on this road?' These are called **leading questions**.
- Don't ask questions that are difficult to answer precisely, such as 'How many hours of TV do you usually watch each week?'

B4 These questions were written for a school uniform survey.
Say why you think they are unsuitable.

(a) How much do you or your parents spend on school clothes in a year?   £ ☐

(b) How do you think the school uniform makes you look?
Not attractive ☐   Attractive ☐   Very attractive ☐

(c) School uniform is never fashionable so we should not be made to wear it.
Do you agree?   Yes ☐   No ☐

B5 The following were suggested as 'multiple-choice' questions on uniform colour.

A. What do you think should be the main school uniform colour?
Black ☐   Grey ☐   Red ☐   Blue ☐
Purple ☐ Brown ☐ Green ☐ Yellow ☐

B. What do you think should be the main school uniform colour?
Black ☐   Blue ☐   Red ☐

C. What do you think should be the main school uniform colour?
Black ☐   Grey ☐   Red ☐   Blue ☐   Other (specify) ☐

Which question do you think is the most useful?
Why do you prefer this to the other questions?

B6 Design a questionnaire to test one of the questions or statements in section A.
Ask one person to complete it.
Discuss with them whether they think the questions are suitable.

Pilot surveys

Before carrying out a large survey it is always a good idea to try out the questionnaire on a small number of people. This will usually tell you if all the questions are suitable. You can also find out what choices you should give in a multiple-choice question.

This is called a **pilot survey**.

C Choosing a sample

The student council are discussing who they should ask to take part in the survey.
Here are some of the suggestions.

- I could stand outside the canteen at dinner time and ask the first twenty people who come in.
- I could ask all my friends.
- We could give a questionnaire to everyone in the school and ask them to give it to their form tutor.
- Leave a pile of questionnaires by the front entrance with a box for replies.
- Ask all the form tutors in the school to give the survey to 5 students during registration.

How useful are these suggestions?

- Are the samples representative?
- Are the samples large enough?

C1 Karen works on Saturdays in a pet shop and is carrying out a survey.

She wants to test the statement 'Cats are easier to keep than dogs.'

She has written a questionnaire to ask cat and dog owners how easy they find looking after their pet.

These are some suggestions about how she should get questionnaires filled in.

(a) Ask 10 students in her class to fill in the questionnaire.

(b) Give a questionnaire to each customer she serves one Saturday and ask them to fill it in at home and post it to her.

(c) Ask the questions in person to 25 people who buy dog food, and 25 who buy cat food.

For each of these suggestions say whether you think it is a good or bad idea.
If it is a bad idea, say why.

C2 Jordan is doing a survey to test the statement

'Manchester United is the most popular football team in our school.'

(a) About how many people would you choose to take part?

(b) Describe how you would choose who to take part in this survey.

The right choice?

In the 1980s a local council wanted to find out what local residents would like to be done with a piece of reclaimed wasteland in the area.
Close to the wasteland was a golf course on which houses were planned to be built.

The council put about 50 000 questionnaires in a free local newspaper.
People were asked to post the survey back to the council.

Just over 100 people sent back replies, nearly all of whom wanted a golf course.

Was this a good survey? How would you have done it?

D Summarising results

In a survey about school uniform students were asked four questions.

> 1 Are you male or female?
> 2 Do you think school uniform should be compulsory?
> 3 Which colour would you prefer for a school sweatshirt?
>   Black   Blue   Grey   Red   Other
> 4 How many brothers and sisters do you have at this school?

1	2	3	4
M	Yes	Black	2
F	Yes	Blue	0
F	Yes	Grey	2
M	No	Black	4
M	Yes	Other	2
F	Yes	Blue	1
F	No	Blue	1
F	Yes	Grey	2
M	No	Grey	3
F	Yes	Other	2
M	Yes	Black	2
F	Yes	Blue	2
F	Yes	Grey	1
F	No	Red	1
M	No	Black	3
M	Yes	Black	2
F	Yes	Blue	1
F	Yes	Red	2
F	Yes	Red	0
F	Yes	Other	2
M	Yes	Black	2
F	No	Blue	2
F	Yes	Red	1
M	No	Red	5
M	Yes	Black	2

A pilot survey was carried out on the 25 students in one class. The results are shown in the table.

D1 (a) How many students in the class were male?

(b) What is this as a fraction of the whole class?

(c) Write this fraction as a percentage.

(d) What percentage of the class were female?

D2 (a) What percentage of the class thought that school uniform should not be compulsory?

(b) What percentage of the class thought it should be compulsory?

D3 (a) Copy and complete this two-way table about whether school uniform should be compulsory.

Should school uniform be compulsory?

	Yes	No	Total
Male	6		
Female			
Total			25

(b) (i) What fraction of the males said yes?

(ii) What fraction of the females said yes?

(c) (i) What fraction of those who said yes were male?

(ii) What fraction of those who said yes were female?

(d) What fraction of the class said no?

204   27 Surveys

D4 **(a)** Copy and complete this frequency table for the colour preferences.

(b) What was the most popular colour?

(c) What was the frequency of blue being chosen?

(d) Draw a frequency chart to show these results.

Colour	Tally	Frequency
Black		
Blue		
Grey		
Red		
Other		
Total		

D5 **(a)** Find the mean and range of the number of brothers and sisters boys had at the school.

(b) Find the mean and range of the number of brothers and sisters girls had at the school.

(c) Who, on average, had more brothers and sisters at the school, boys or girls?

D6 The same survey was given to five students in every class at the school. The percentage choosing each colour were

Black 28%   Blue 48%   Grey 18%   Red 4%   Other 2%

(a) Draw a pie chart to show these results.

(b) There are 800 students in the whole school. Roughly how many would you expect to choose blue?

E Writing a report

Use the following tips to help you when you write a report on your survey.
- State clearly the question or statement you are testing.
- Describe how you carried out your survey and any difficulties you found.
- Include the final version of your questionnaire.
- Say how you chose who took part and how they returned the questionnaire.
- Summarise the answers to each question using tables and charts. Decide on the best way to show the results for each question.
- Is the statement you tested true or false? What is the answer to your question? Explain why you think your results show this.

> I think that my statement that parents watch more television than their children is true because only 42% of the students that I asked said that they watched TV on 3

Choose your own statement that you can carry out a survey on.
Do the survey and write up your report.

28 Imperial measures

You will change between imperial units such as feet, pounds and gallons and appropriate metric units.

A Length

Centimetres, metres and kilometres are all part of the **metric** system. Until the 1970s most people in the UK used **imperial** measurements such as feet and miles.

A ruler which measures up to 30 cm long used to be called a **foot** ruler. About how many foot rulers can you fit alongside a metre rule? In imperial measurements 3 feet is a **yard**.

- What can you say about a metre and a yard?
- Do you know any other imperial measurements that are still used? About how big are they in metric units?

A1 Roughly how long are these distances in metres?

(a) A long jump of 27 feet
(b) A pole vault of 18 feet
(c) A discus throw of 210 feet
(d) A race of 100 yards

A2 Roughly how many feet are there in each of these?

(a) 10 m
(b) 25 m
(c) 100 m
(d) 1.5 m

A3 A distance of 5 miles is very close to 8 kilometres.

(a) 10 miles is double 5 miles, so what is 10 miles in kilometres?

(b) Copy and complete this 'ready reckoner' table for changing from miles to kilometres.

Miles	5	10	20	50	100	200
Kilometres	8					

(c) Use your table to change these distances between cities into kilometres.

(i) York to Leeds 25 miles
(ii) London to Dover 75 miles
(iii) Bristol to London 120 miles
(iv) Glasgow to Inverness 165 miles
(v) Norwich to Liverpool 215 miles

A4 To change miles into kilometres without a ready reckoner table use this rule.

miles ⟶ | Divide by 5 | ⟶ | Multiply by 8 | ⟶ kilometres

Use the rule to change these distances into kilometres.

(a) 15 miles   (b) 35 miles   (c) 55 miles   (d) 125 miles

A5 These are the distances in miles from London to various places in the UK.

Salisbury 88   Brighton 59   Cardiff 152   York 211   Newcastle 285

(a) Round these distances to the nearest ten miles.
(b) Change the rounded distances into kilometres.

A6 (a) Copy and complete this rule for changing kilometres into miles.

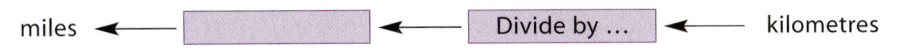

miles ⟵ | | ⟵ | Divide by … | ⟵ kilometres

(b) Use this rule to change these distances into miles.

(i) 24 km   (ii) 48 km   (iii) 88 km   (iv) 136 km

A7 Change these speed limits in kilometres per hour to miles per hour.

(a) 40   (b) 80   (c) 120

A8 James lives 25 miles from where he works.
Jaqueline lives 32 kilometres from her workplace.
Who lives further from their work, James or Jaqueline?

A9 Emma is driving from Calais to Paris, a distance of 280 kilometres.
When she leaves Calais, the mileometer in her car reads 1550 miles.

001550 miles

What will the mileometer read when she gets to Paris?

*A10 For many years running a mile was a popular event in athletics.

(a) Use a calculator to find what 1 mile is in kilometres.
(b) What is this in metres?
(c) In modern athletics runners can take part in a 1500 m race.
Is this more or less than a mile?

28 Imperial measures   207

B Weight

In the UK food is now weighed using the metric units grams or kilograms by law.
In the United States food is still sold in pounds (lb).
A kilogram is just over 2 pounds.

- What do these items of food weigh roughly in pounds?

  Rice 500 g   Sweets 250 g   Tea 125 g

- Gemma's baby weighs 8 pounds. How much is this roughly in kilograms?

B1 What are these weights roughly in kilograms?
(a) 10 lb (b) 56 lb (c) 180 lb (d) 5000 lb
(e) 3 lb (f) half a pound (g) one-and-a-half pounds

B2 Work out roughly what each of these weights is in pounds.
(a) 6 kg (b) 12 kg (c) 25 kg (d) 2.5 kg
(e) 7.5 kg (f) 0.5 kg (g) 600 g (h) 750 g

B3 (a) In boxing a Heavyweight is someone weighing over 190 lb. What is this roughly in kilograms?
(b) A Flyweight weighs less than 112 lb. What is this roughly in kilograms?

B4 Mavis has a recipe for apricot jam but her scales only weigh in pounds. Change these amounts roughly into pounds.
Preserving sugar 4 kg   Dried apricots 1.5 kg   Almonds 400 g

B5 In 2000, the Olympic weightlifting record for women was 660 lb. How much is this roughly in kilograms?

A more exact method

Hospitals weigh babies in kilograms but parents often want to know the weight in pounds.

A kilogram is very close to 2.2 pounds (lb).
So this is an easy way to change kilograms into pounds.

Can you see how it works?

Use this method to find the weight in pounds of these babies.

Maddi 4.1 kg   Andrew 2.7 kg   Roxanne 1.8 kg   Tulip 6.5 kg

Do you know how much you weighed at birth?

Baby Jennifer weighs 3.5 kg
Write down the kg weight   3.5
… and again   3.5
Write down the kgs ÷ 10   0.35
… and again   0.35
Now add these together   7.70
So the weight in pounds is 7.7 lb

C Liquid measure

A metric measurement for liquids is a litre.
There are 1000 millilitres (ml) in one litre.

Liquids such as milk and beer are sometimes sold in pints.
A pint is slightly more than half a litre.
So a litre is roughly two pints.

Panic in the pub
Is beer drinking going to pot? Many regulars up and down the country are angry at what they see as the end of the traditional pint. EU plans to go metric would mean that the pint glass would become half a litre. This would mean that instead

C1 A milkman records how many pints he sells to some of his customers.
How many litres roughly are there in
- (a) 8 pints
- (b) 20 pints
- (c) 7 pints
- (d) 15 pints

C2 How many pints are there roughly in
- (a) 6 litres
- (b) 15 litres
- (c) $2\frac{1}{2}$ litres
- (d) $12\frac{1}{2}$ litres

C3 Roughly how many millilitres are there in
- (a) 1 pint
- (b) $\frac{1}{2}$ pint
- (c) $\frac{1}{4}$ pint
- (d) $\frac{3}{4}$ pint

C4 There are exactly 8 pints in a gallon.
A landlord records how many gallons he sells of different beers in a week.

Witney's Pale	12 gallons
Adlard's Old Socks	4 gallons
Khronicberg	15 gallons
Bugwiper	$8\frac{1}{2}$ gallons

- (a) Find how many pints he has sold of each beer.
- (b) Roughly how many litres of each beer has he sold?

C5 A more accurate way of converting gallons into litres is to multiply by 4.5.
Use a calculator to change these amounts into litres.
- (a) 10 gallons
- (b) 5 gallons
- (c) $2\frac{1}{2}$ gallons
- (d) 16 pints
- (e) 48 pints
- (f) 36 pints

Big hats?

Who says that everything in the USA is bigger than in the UK?
A US gallon is only 3.8 litres!

Cowboys often wear what is called a 'ten-gallon' hat.

How many litres would 10 UK gallons be?

How many litres would 10 US gallons be?

D Mixed questions

Remember these useful facts to compare metric and imperial measures.

| A foot is about 30 cm. So 3 feet are about one metre. | 5 miles is very close to 8 km. |

| There are roughly 2 pounds (lb) in 1 kilogram. | There are roughly 2 pints in 1 litre. |

D1 Change these measurements roughly into centimetres.
  (a) 5 feet   (b) 2 feet   (c) 6 feet   (d) 10 feet

D2 Change these measurements roughly into metres.
  (a) 150 feet   (b) 30 feet   (c) 90 feet   (d) 6000 feet

D3 Pam's jam recipe uses 6 pounds of raspberries.
  About how many kilograms of raspberries is this?

D4 Scott has a casserole dish that holds 8 pints.
  About how many litres is this?

D5 About how many pounds are there in $4\frac{1}{2}$ kg?

D6 Jane needs about 500 ml of cream.
  About how many pints of cream is this?

D7 These road signs are in miles.
  Convert them into kilometres.

| Detford | 40 |
| Malpeth | 25 |

| Walford | 15 |
| Ardale | 50 |

| Midworth | 20 |
| Frotton | 10 |

D8 Fiona weighs 10 stone 3 pounds.
  (a) There are 14 pounds in one stone.
      Estimate her weight in kilograms.

  Fiona is 5 feet 2 inches tall.

  (b) There are 12 inches in one foot.
      Take one inch as 2.5 centimetres.
      Work out her height in metres.

OCR

Test yourself

T1 What is the approximate weight in kilograms of these items?

(a) 50 lb

(b) 112 lb

(c) 7 lb

T2 (a) Roughly how many pints of milk does this container hold? (3 Litres)

(b) Roughly how many kilograms of rice does this bag of rice contain? (2 lb)

OCR

T3 Roughly how many litres are there in 4 pints?

T4 Jamie is 6 feet tall. About how tall is he in metres?

T5 This road sign gives distances in miles.
Write out the sign with the distances in kilometres.

| Truro | 15 |
| St Austell | 35 |

T6 Fiona has a container that holds 3 gallons of water.
Which one of these is closest to this amount?

$1\frac{1}{2}$ litres   3 litres   6 litres   12 litres   24 litres

T7 Marlene and Roy travelled from London to Edinburgh by car.
The distance from London to Edinburgh is 400 miles.

(a) Estimate the number of kilometres in 400 miles.

The car used 45 litres of petrol on the journey.

(b) Estimate the number of gallons in 45 litres.

Edexcel

T8 (a) Harry runs 15 miles in a road race.
Henri walks 20 kilometres in a walking race.
Whose race is further, Harry's or Henri's? Show how you decided.

(b) Harriet claims that 28 lb of apples weigh the same as 10 kg of flour.
Is she right? Show how you decided.

28 Imperial measures   211

29 Navigation

You will revise how to
- use a scale on a map or plan
- give directions using compass points

This work will help you
- use four-figure grid references
- use bearings to give a position or to describe a journey

You need an angle measurer, and sheets F1–25, F1–26 and F1–27.

A Four-figure grid references and points of the compass

This is a map of the island of Tiree off the north-west coast of Scotland.

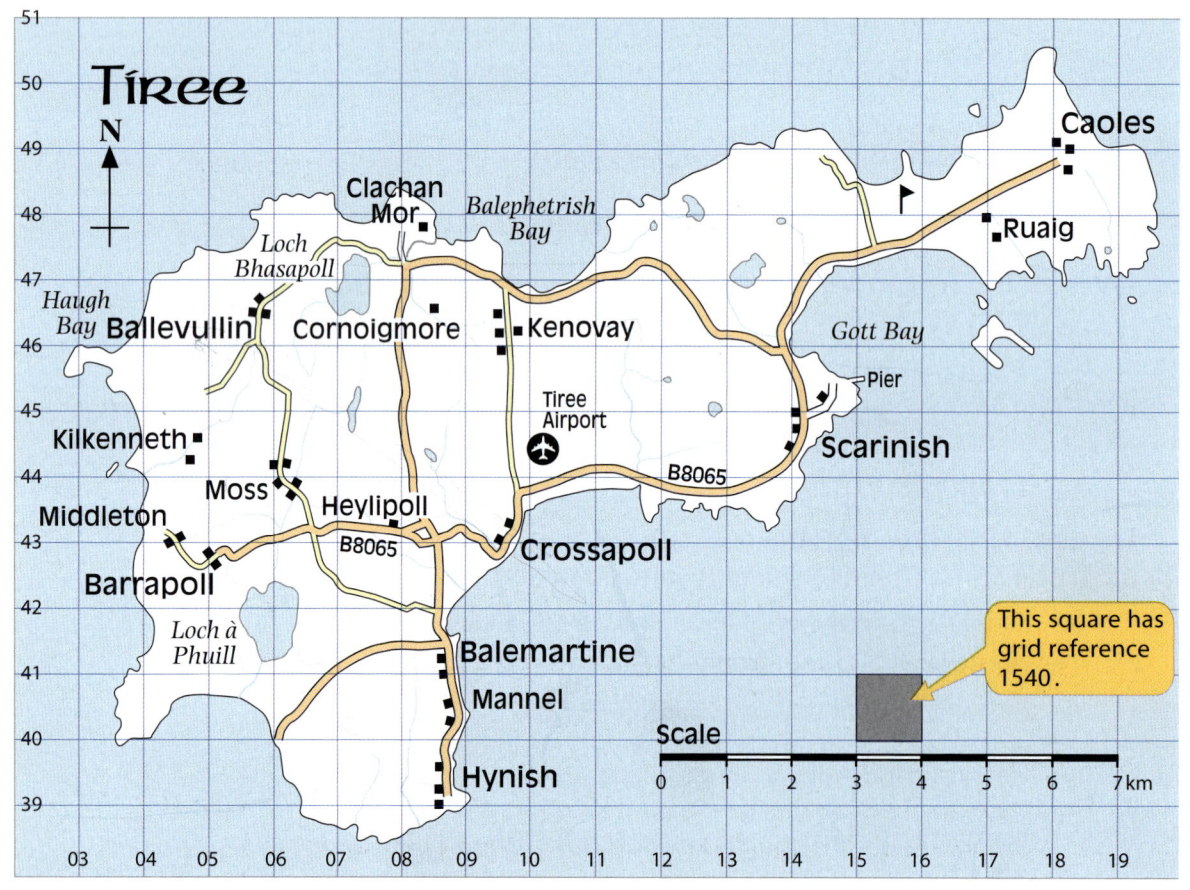

Based on Ordnance Survey mapping with the permission of the Controller of Her Majesty's Stationery Office, © Crown copyright. All rights reserved. Licence no. 100001679

212 29 Navigation

> **T** On the map opposite, like many others, the grid lines are 1 km apart.
>
> To give the position of a place on the map, a **grid reference** can be used.
>
> The shaded square on the map opposite has grid reference 1540.
> The reference across the page is always given first.

A1 Give the name of the village in each of these grid squares.

    (a) 0839   (b) 1747   (c) 0546   (d) 1444

A2 In what grid square is each of these?

    (a) The end of the pier   (b) The airport (shown by a plane)

    (c) Mannel   (d) The golf course (shown by a flag)

A3 Sketch a copy of this compass rose and add the missing points of the compass.

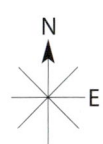

A4 A helicopter takes off from the airport.
In which compass direction would it fly to go over

    (a) Balephetrish Bay   (b) Scarinish   (c) Kilkenneth

    (d) Loch à Phuill   (e) Loch Bhasapoll   (f) the golf course

A5 In which compass direction would a helicopter be flying if it went directly between these places?

    (a) Clachan Mor to Hynish   (b) Ruaig to Scarinish

    (c) Moss to Kenovay   (d) Ballevullin to Crossapoll

A6 Use the scale and the edge of a piece of paper to find these distances as the crow flies.
Give each answer to the nearest kilometre.

    (a) The airport to the golf course   (b) Middleton to Crossapoll

    (c) Clachan Mor to Hynish village   (d) Kilkenneth to Ruaig

A7 Roughly how far is it between Middleton and Scarinish along the B8065?

A8 A canoeist wants to canoe around this island keeping close to the coast.
Find the rough distance around the island.

A9 Name the features in these locations.

    (a) 3 km due west of Balemartine   (b) 5 km due north of Crossapoll

    (c) 4 km north-west of the airport   (d) 3 km south-west of Ruaig

A10 Give the distance and compass direction for a helicopter to fly

    (a) from Ruaig to Hynish   (b) from Middleton to Clachan Mor

B Scales and points of the compass

B1 This is a plan of a school playground and sports area. It is drawn to a scale where 1 cm represents 10 m.

What are these measurements in real life, to the nearest 5 m?

(a) The length and width of the playground

(b) The length and width of the sports area

(c) The distance in a straight line between the two gates to the sports area.

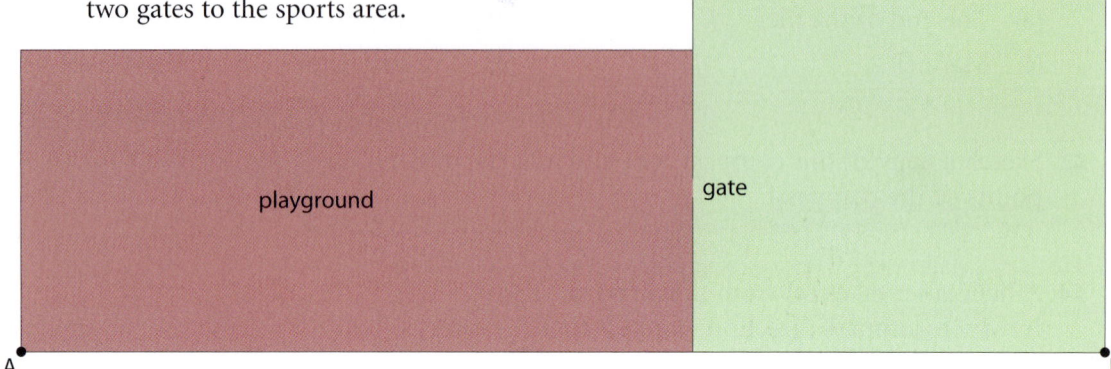

B2 (a) A fence is to be erected from A to B. How long will this fence be?

(b) Fencing costs £8 per metre. What will the cost be for the whole fence?

B3 A cycle shelter 5 m wide by 15 m long is put in the corner of the playground. How big would this be when shown on the plan?

The map opposite shows the whole of Great Britain and part of Ireland.
The map is scaled so that 1 cm represents 50 km.

B4 In what compass direction would you be travelling if you flew directly

(a) from Cardiff to London (b) from London to Belfast

(c) from Cardiff to Land's End (d) from Edinburgh to John o'Groats

B5 By measuring to the nearest centimetre, find these real-life distances.

(a) From Dublin to Cardiff (b) From London to Glasgow

(c) From Belfast to Leicester (d) From Land's End to John o'Groats

B6 A courier firm in Manchester says it will guarantee same-day delivery to anywhere within 300 km. Which of the places on the map are within 300 km of Manchester as the crow flies?

Map of the United Kingdom and Ireland

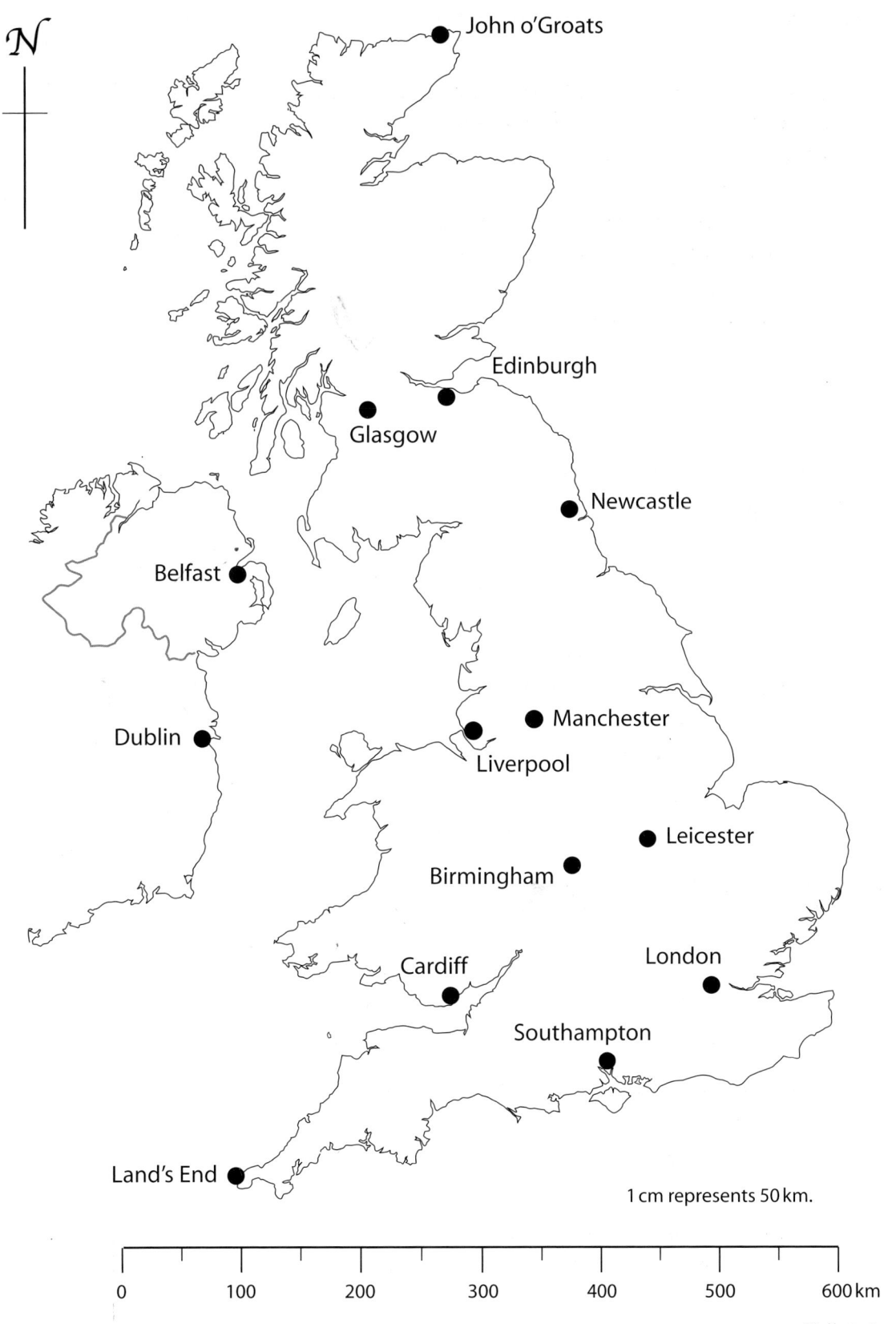

N

- John o'Groats
- Edinburgh
- Glasgow
- Newcastle
- Belfast
- Dublin
- Manchester
- Liverpool
- Leicester
- Birmingham
- Cardiff
- London
- Southampton
- Land's End

1 cm represents 50 km.

| 0 | 100 | 200 | 300 | 400 | 500 | 600 km |

29 Navigation 215

Opposite is part of an Ordnance Survey map of Great and Little Cumbrae in Scotland.

B7 What features can be found in these grid squares?

(a) 1855 (b) 1452 (c) 1759 (d) 1658

B8 On this map 1 cm represents $\frac{1}{2}$ km.
How far apart are the grid lines on this map in real life?

B9 Find the distance, to the nearest $\frac{1}{2}$ kilometre, in a straight line

(a) from Trail Isle (1551) to Clashfarland Point (1856)
(b) from Sheriff's Port (1555) to Skate Point (1658)

B10 What feature will you find

(a) 3 km north of Broad Islands (1551)
(b) 3 km east of Sheriff's Port (1555)
(c) $2\frac{1}{2}$ km west of the marine station (1754)
(d) $4\frac{1}{2}$ km south-west of Clashfarland Point (1856)

C Review: angles   level 4

C1 Describe each angle below using one of these statements.

Angle is between 0° and 90°.

Angle is between 180° and 270°.

Angle is between 270° and 360°.

Angle is between 90° and 180°.

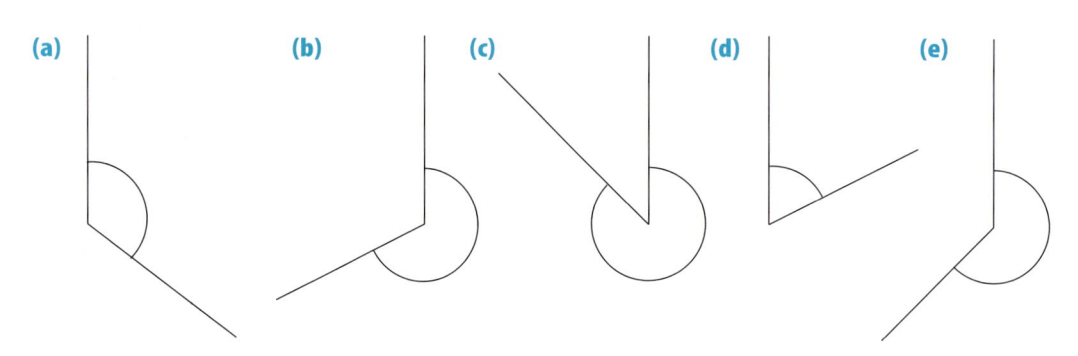

(a) (b) (c) (d) (e)

C2 What angle would you turn through clockwise **from north** to face

(a) west (b) south (c) south-east (d) north-west

C3 Which compass direction would you be facing if you turned clockwise **from north** through

(a) 90° (b) 45° (c) 225°

Ordnance Survey mapping with the permission of the Controller of Her Majesty's Stationery Office, © Crown copyright. All rights reserved. Licence No. 100001679

29 Navigation

D Bearings

T For accurate navigation, compass directions like north, south-east and so on are not enough.

A **bearing** is the angle measured clockwise from a north line to a given direction.

Bearings are always given as three digits to avoid mistakes.

*To approach the runway, turn to a bearing of **zero-three-five**.*

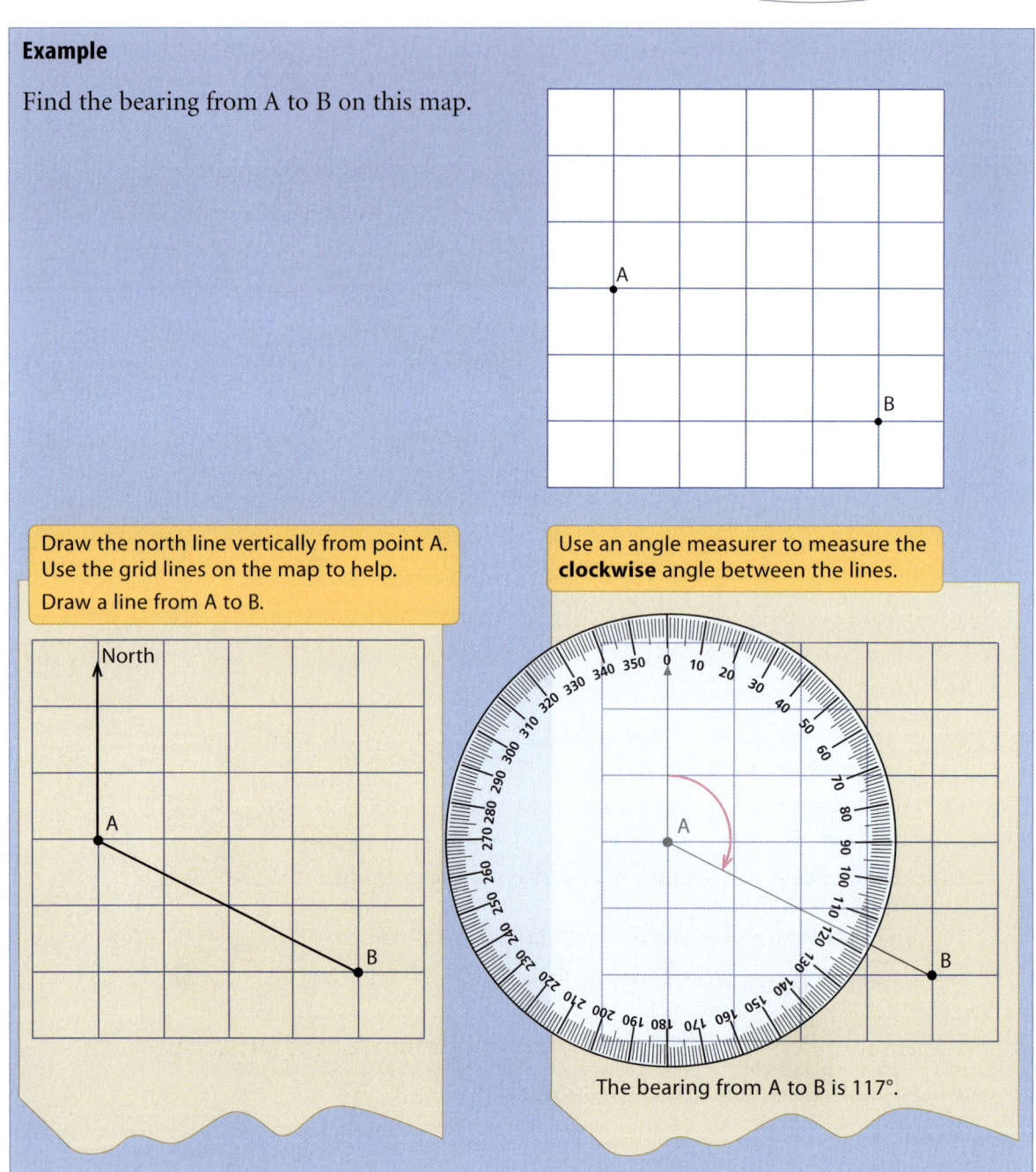

Example

Find the bearing from A to B on this map.

Draw the north line vertically from point A. Use the grid lines on the map to help.

Draw a line from A to B.

Use an angle measurer to measure the **clockwise** angle between the lines.

The bearing from A to B is 117°.

218 29 Navigation

D1 The map on sheet F1–25 shows part of central London.
The landmarks marked with letters can be seen from the top of the London Eye.

For each landmark,
- draw a straight line to its dot from the London Eye
- put your angle measurer with its centre on the London Eye's dot and its zero line along the north line
- read off the bearing of the landmark from the London Eye

The map on sheet F1–26 shows an island drawn to a scale where 1 cm represents 2 km.

D2 Find the real-life distance and bearing of
- (a) the jetty from Folly Farm
- (b) the lighthouse from Seal Point
- (c) Seal Point from Sandcombe Bay
- (d) Sandcombe Bay from the lighthouse
- (e) Folly Farm from Sandcombe Bay
- (f) Sandcombe Bay from the jetty

D3 Which feature is on a bearing of
- (a) 036° from the jetty
- (b) 275° from the jetty
- (c) 234° from Folly Farm

D4 (a) A new pier is to be placed on the coast on a bearing of 250° from Folly Farm.
Mark the position of the pier with a cross and label it P.

(b) A radio mast is to be placed 8 km from the jetty on a bearing of 025°.
On the map put a cross where the mast will be and label this R.

(c) A coastguard standing at Seal Point spots a yacht in trouble on a bearing of 295° and at a distance of 16 km.
Mark a cross where the yacht is and label it Y.

D5 (a) A boat is spotted at 1400 hours on a bearing of 193° from the lighthouse.
Draw a line at a bearing of 193° from the lighthouse.

(b) At the same time the boat is seen on a bearing of 236° from the jetty.
Mark the position of the boat with a dot and label it 1400.

(c) At 1500 hours the boat is on a bearing of 139° from the lighthouse and 198° from the jetty.
Mark the position of the boat and label it 1500.

(d) If the boat continues on exactly the same course and speed, mark where the boat will be at 1600 hours.

(e) On what bearing will someone at the jetty see the boat at 1600 hours?

(f) How far will the boat be from the jetty at 1600 hours?

Test yourself

T1 Here is an outline map of an island.
It is drawn to a scale of 1 cm to 5 km.

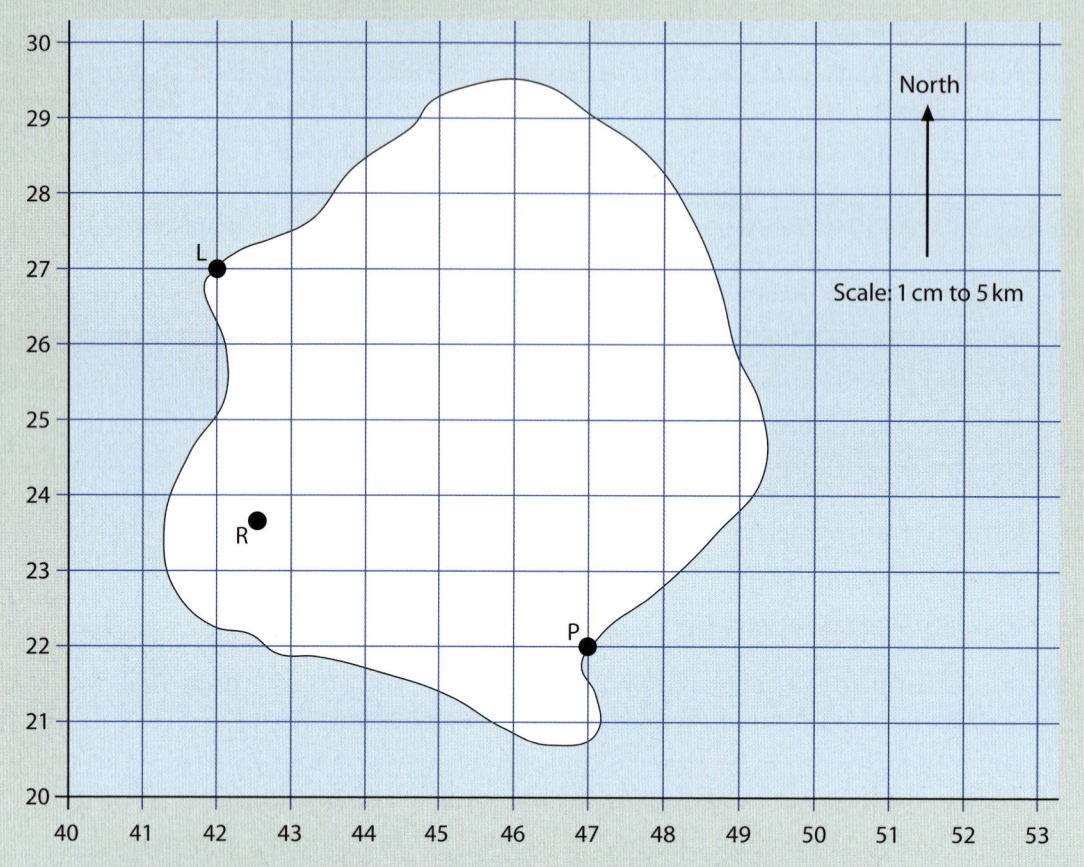

(a) Write down the four-figure grid reference of the square containing the radio mast (R).

(b) A party of visitors walks straight across the island from the port (P) to the life-boat station (L).

(i) In which direction do they walk from P to L?

(ii) How far is it from P to L?
Give your answer to the nearest kilometre.

OCR

T2 Sheet F1–27 shows the map of an island drawn to a scale where 3 cm represents 1 km.

(a) P and Q are the positions of two farmhouses.
Use the map to find the distance PQ in kilometres.

(b) There is a lighthouse 2 km from Q on a bearing of 110°.
Mark the position of the lighthouse on the map.

30 Rounding with significant figures

This work will help you
- round numbers to one significant figure
- find rough estimates by rounding
- round answers to calculations to a given number of decimal places

A Rounding a whole number to one significant figure

There were 43 576 people at a football match.

The newspaper said **40 000 see City humiliated**

The highest place value in the number 43 576 is the ten thousands figure.
The newspaper has rounded to the nearest ten thousand.
The ten thousands figure is the **most significant figure** in 43 576.

Mr Buckfast made £294 546 from the sale of his software. **£300 000 for software!** Mr Buckfast makes a fast buck …

The most significant figure in 294 546 is the hundred thousands figure.
The newspaper has rounded the number to **one significant figure**.

Rounding a number to its highest place value is called rounding to one significant figure.

A1 Round these numbers to one significant figure.
(a) 714   (b) 3831   (c) 679   (d) 2052   (e) 77
(f) 4629   (g) 356   (h) 2481   (i) 8921   (j) 509

A2 Write a headline for each of these stories.
Round each number to one significant figure.
(a) 5182 people join a protest march.
(b) 38 426 people attend an open-air concert.

A3 Work out
(a) 20 × 40   (b) 50 × 30   (c) 700 × 20   (d) 40 × 500

A4 A coach has 57 seats.
This is how Jack estimates the number of seats in 32 coaches.
Complete his estimate.

Round the numbers to one significant figure:
57 becomes 60.   32 becomes 30.
So 57 × 32 is roughly

A5 Work out a rough estimate for each of these.

(a) 37×23   (b) 216×48   (c) 59×72   (d) 32×472   (e) 51×59
(f) 196×36   (g) 42×78   (h) 61×326   (i) 56×392   (j) 271×125

A6 A concert hall has 288 seats.
Tickets for a concert cost £19. All the tickets are sold.

(a) Estimate roughly the total amount of money paid for the tickets.

(b) Is your estimate bigger or smaller than the exact amount?
How can you tell without working out the exact amount?

B Rounding a decimal to one significant figure

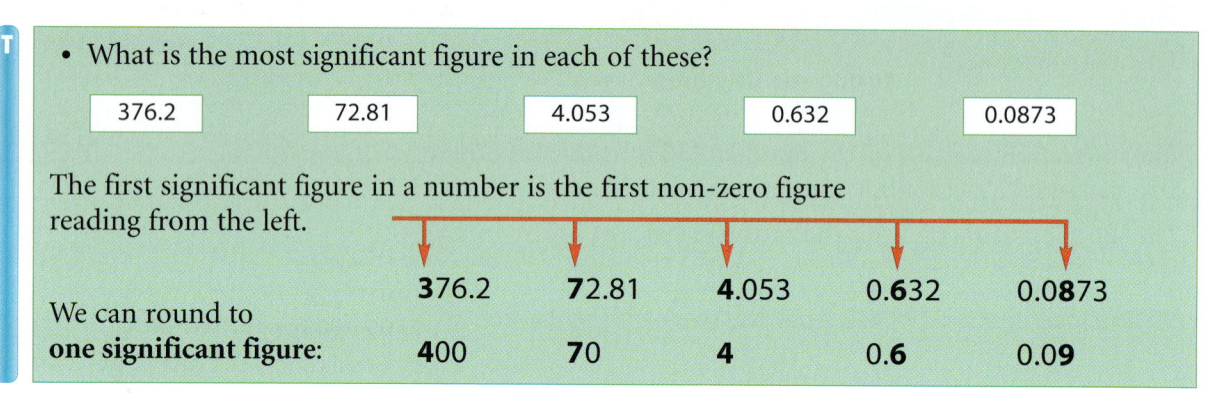

- What is the most significant figure in each of these?

  376.2   72.81   4.053   0.632   0.0873

The first significant figure in a number is the first non-zero figure reading from the left.

We can round to one significant figure:

376.2 → 400
72.81 → 70
4.053 → 4
0.**6**32 → 0.6
0.0**8**73 → 0.09

B1 Round these numbers to one significant figure.

(a) 23.4   (b) 6.754   (c) 328.7   (d) 0.513   (e) 0.762
(f) 0.00685   (g) 0.00473   (h) 74.35   (i) 0.0613   (j) 0.3865

B2 Rewrite each of these sentences, but round the number to one significant figure.
The first is done as an example.

(a) The area of the UK is 94 241 square miles.

> The area of the UK is **roughly 90 000** square miles.

(b) The area of Egypt is 386 199 square miles.
(c) An ounce is 28.2495 grams.
(d) A metre is 39.3701 inches.
(e) A cubic foot is 0.028 32 cubic metres.

B3 Round these numbers to one significant figure.

(a) 23 476   (b) 0.0607   (c) 7.0053   (d) 346.9   (e) 89.65

*B4 Round to one significant figure   (a) 983   (b) 0.096   (c) 9921

C Multiplying decimals

To find the area of a rectangle, you multiply length × width.

This picture shows a square 1 metre by 1 metre.

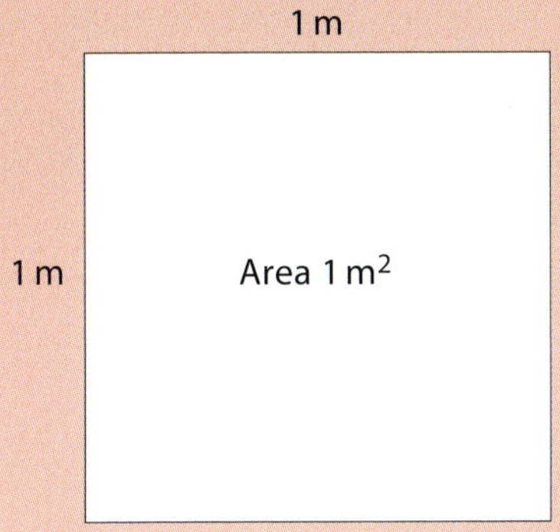

1 m

1 m   Area 1 m²

The shaded rectangle is 0.3 m by 0.2 m.
Its area is 6 hundredths of a square metre, or **0.06 m²**.

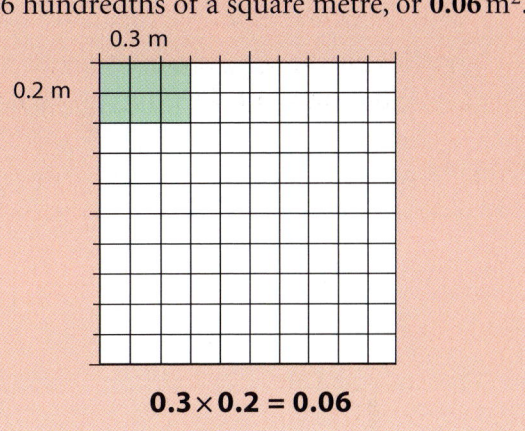

0.3 m
0.2 m

0.3 × 0.2 = 0.06

Starting with **2 × 3**, you can get to **0.2 × 0.3** like this.

2 × 3 = 6
2 × 0.3 = 0.6
0.2 × 0.3 = 0.06

C1 Rectangle A shows that **0.6 × 0.3 = 0.18**

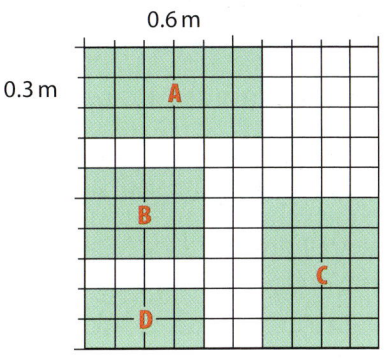

0.6 m
0.3 m

A   B   C   D

(a) What does rectangle B show?
(b) What does rectangle C show?
(c) What does rectangle D show?
(d) Work these out.
   (i) 0.6 × 0.4   (ii) 0.5 × 0.6
   (iii) 0.7 × 0.7   (iv) 0.1 × 0.9
   (v) 0.8 × 0.5   (vi) 0.3 × 0.3

C2 Copy these and fill in the missing numbers.

(a)
5 × 3 = 15
5 × 0.3 = ...
0.5 × 0.3 = ...

(b)
3 × 7 = 21
3 × 0.7 = ...
0.3 × 0.7 = ...

(c)
6 × 5 = 30
6 × 0.5 = ...
0.6 × 0.5 = ...

C3 Work these out.
(a) 0.3 × 0.8   (b) 0.7 × 0.1   (c) 0.1 × 0.1

The 'decimal places' rule for multiplication

$$0.2 \times 0.3 = 0.06$$

There are the same number of decimal places altogether here ... and here.

This rule works for other multiplications.

A Count the decimal places in the calculation.

B Ignore decimal points and multiply.

C From the right, count the same number of decimal places.

Examples

(a) 2.1×0.3

A $2.\underline{1} \times 0.\underline{3}$ (2 d.p.)
B $21 \times 3 = 63$
C 0.63

(b) 1.2×0.05

A $1.\underline{2} \times 0.\underline{05}$ (3 d.p.)
B $12 \times 5 = 60$
C 0.060

(c) 30×0.5

A $30 \times 0.\underline{5}$ (1 d.p.)
B $30 \times 5 = 150$
C 15.0

C4 **(a)** Write down the answer to 2×11.

(b) Now write down the answer to each of these.

(i) 0.2×11 (ii) 0.2×1.1 (iii) 2×0.11 (iv) 0.2×0.11 (v) 0.02×1.1

C5 **(a)** Write down the answer to 12×3.

(b) Now write down the answer to each of these.

(i) 1.2×3 (ii) 1.2×0.3 (iii) 0.12×3 (iv) 0.12×0.3 (v) 1.2×0.03

C6 **(a)** Write down the answer to 21×4.

(b) Now write down the answer to each of these.

(i) 21×0.4 (ii) 2.1×0.04 (iii) 0.21×0.4 (iv) 21×0.04 (v) 0.21×0.04

C7 You are told that $14 \times 23 = 322$.
Write down the answer to each of these.

(a) 14×0.23 (b) 1.4×2.3 (c) 0.14×2.3 (d) 1.4×0.23 (e) 0.14×0.23

C8 You are told that $216 \times 45 = 9720$.
Write down the answer to each of these.

(a) 21.6×45 (b) 2.16×4.5 (c) 216×0.45 (d) 2.16×0.45 (e) 0.216×4.5

C9 Work these out.

(a) 20×0.6 (b) 0.3×900 (c) 0.04×30 (d) 50×0.4 (e) 0.6×500
(f) 0.4×30 (g) 0.3×400 (h) 300×0.6 (i) 80×0.5 (j) 0.2×0.2

C10 This diagram shows how you can work out the area of a rectangle 2.6 m by 1.4 m by splitting it into four parts.

(a) Work out the area of each part.

(b) Work out the total area.

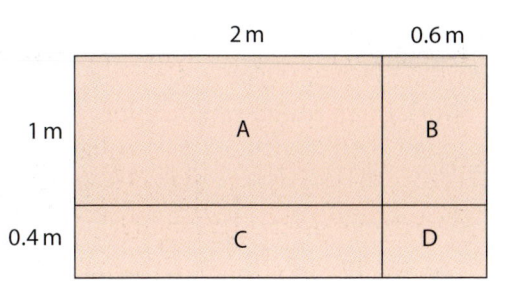

C11 Use a similar method to work out 2.3×1.2.

D Rough estimates with decimals

Example

Work out a rough estimate for 34.8×0.572.

Round the numbers to one significant figure.
Rough estimate = 30×0.6
$30 \times 6 = 180$
So $30 \times 0.6 = 18.0$ Estimate: **18**

D1 Work out a rough estimate for each of these.

(a) 21.6×0.387 (b) 0.614×48.9 (c) 3.882×0.187 (d) 48.9×0.713

D2 A group of 28 people are going to a concert. Tickets are £19.75 each.

(a) Estimate roughly the total cost of the tickets.

(b) Is your rough estimate bigger or smaller than the exact amount? How can you tell without working out the exact amount?

D3 Sadia bought 38 plants each costing £1.95.
The shop charged her £81.70.
How can you tell, without working out the exact amount, that the shop was wrong?

D4 James is packing textbooks to send to a school.
He has 62 books. Each book weighs 0.51 kg.

(a) Estimate roughly the total weight of the books.

(b) Is your estimate bigger or smaller than the exact total weight? How can you tell?

D5 Work out a rough estimate for each of these.

(a) 7.83×0.194 (b) 21.5×0.078 (c) 48.83×0.389 (d) 217.6×0.81

(e) 31.3×0.087 (f) 0.894×47.8 (g) 61.82×0.287 (h) 103.9×0.011

Example

Work out a rough estimate for $\frac{61.4 \times 0.479}{19.3}$.

Round the numbers to one significant figure.

Rough estimate = $\frac{60 \times 0.5}{20} = \frac{30}{20} = \mathbf{1.5}$

D6 Work out a rough estimate for each of these.

(a) $\frac{32.4 \times 0.212}{2.93}$ (b) $\frac{79.4 \times 0.269}{3.87}$ (c) $\frac{397 \times 0.188}{19.6}$ (d) $\frac{0.782 \times 512}{38.2}$

D7 Work out a rough estimate for each of these.

(a) $\frac{87.2 \times 0.296}{3.03}$ (b) $\frac{0.048 \times 578}{1.88}$ (c) $\frac{5879 \times 0.231}{4.12}$ (d) $\frac{0.0764 \times 582}{6.15}$

E Rounding answers

Example

Work out the area of this rectangle.
Give your answer to one decimal place.

8.65 cm

3.81 cm

Area = 8.65 × 3.81
     = 32.9|565   The digit after the first decimal place is 5 or more so round up.
     = 33.0 cm²   Leave the 0 here. It shows that the number has been rounded to one decimal place.

E1 Use a calculator to do 3.46×0.873.
Round the answer to two decimal places.

E2 Use a calculator to do these.

(a) 0.583 × 43.29, answer to 2 d.p.
(b) 10.53 × 3.275, answer to 1 d.p.
(c) 0.274 × 0.076, answer to 2 d.p.
(d) 1.483 × 0.0752, answer to 3 d.p.

E3 Daryl buys 29.5 metres of rope costing £3.87 a metre.

(a) Work out a rough estimate of the total cost.
(b) Use a calculator to find the total cost. Round it to the nearest penny.

E4 1 inch = 2.54 centimetres.
Change 36 inches to centimetres.
Give the answer to one decimal place.

E5 (a) Work out a rough estimate of the area of this floor in m².

(b) Use a calculator to find the area of the floor.
Give your result to one decimal place.

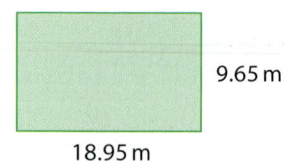

9.65 m

18.95 m

E6 The floor of a doll's house measures 1.16 m by 0.79 m.

(a) Work out a rough estimate for the area of the floor, in m².

(b) Use a calculator to find the area, giving your answer to two decimal places.

Test yourself

T1 Round these numbers to one significant figure.

(a) 276.4 (b) 8.321 (c) 46.97 (d) 0.00149 (e) 2.085

T2 Asif has a roll of film developed.
He pays for 31 reprints.
The cost of each reprint is 49 pence.

Use suitable approximations to **estimate** how much Asif pays for these reprints.
You must show all your working. *AQA*

T3 **Estimate** the value of $\dfrac{614 \times 27}{88}$.

Show clearly how you obtain your answer. *WJEC*

T4 Work these out.

(a) 50×0.4 (b) 0.4×1.3 (c) 0.2×0.4 (d) 0.03×1.2 (e) 80×0.05

T5 Work out a rough estimate for each of these.

(a) 31.4×0.488 (b) 0.423×69.6 (c) 0.282×0.184 (d) 78.9×0.493

T6 (a) The attendance at a pop concert was 65 875.
Write 65 875 correct to

(i) the nearest thousand (ii) one significant figure

(b) Safraz orders 31 tickets for another concert.
The tickets cost £21.25 each.
He wants to estimate the total cost of the tickets.

(i) Write down a calculation he could do in his head to estimate the total cost.

(ii) Is your estimate bigger or smaller than the exact cost?
Explain how you decide. *OCR*

T7 Freda buys 0.35 kg of mushrooms costing £3.97 per kilogram.

(a) Work out a rough estimate of the total cost.

(b) Use a calculator to work out the total cost. Round it to the nearest penny.

30 Rounding with significant figures 227

31 Solving equations

You should know
- that an expression such as $x + x + x$ is equivalent to $3 \times x$ or $3x$
- how to simplify an expression such as $2x + 5 + x - 4$

This work will help you
- solve equations such as $3x - 1 = x + 5$ by balancing
- form and solve equations to solve problems

A Balance puzzles

A1 The scales balance in these pictures.
Find the weight of each object.

(a)

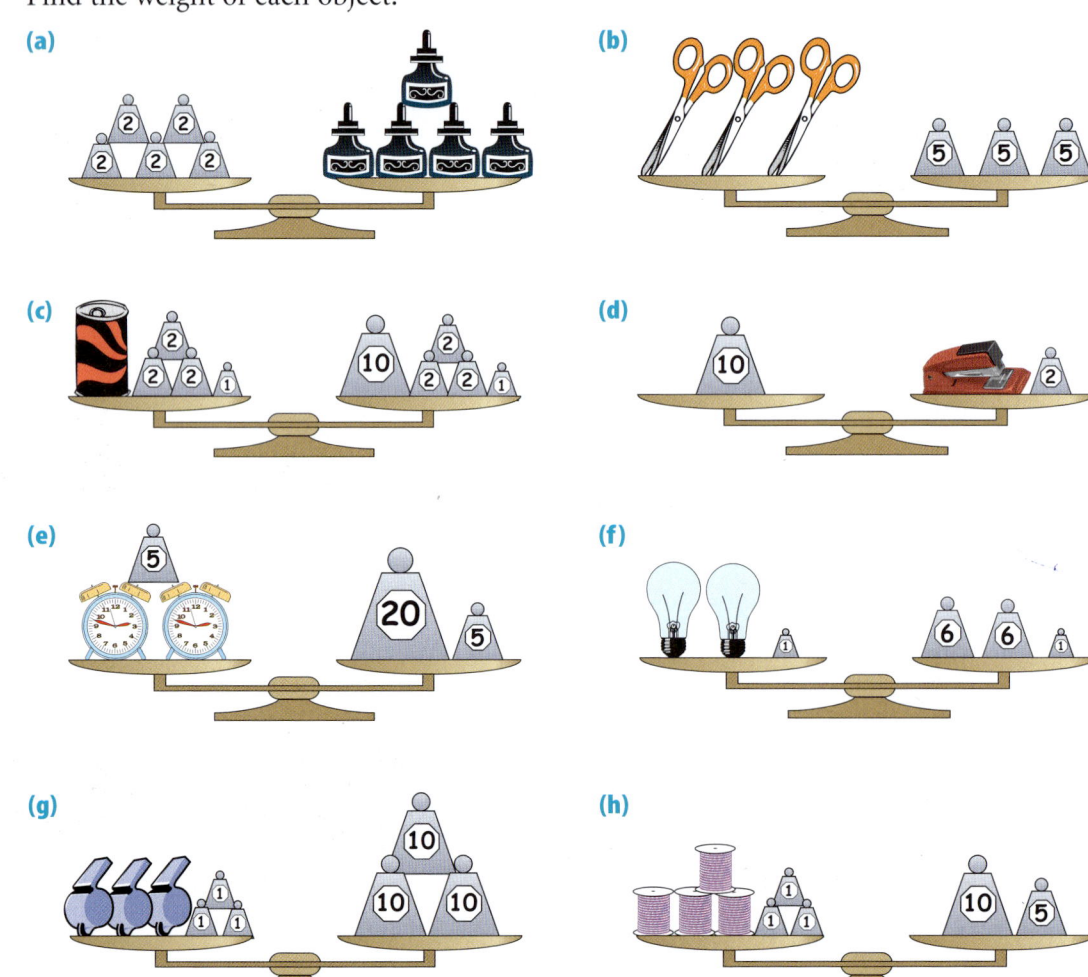

(b)

(c)

(d)

(e)

(f)

(g)

(h)

228 31 Solving equations

A2 The scales balance in these pictures.
Find the weight of each object.

(a)

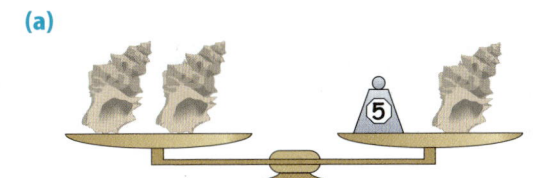

(b)

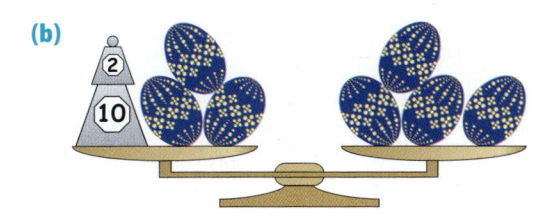

(c)

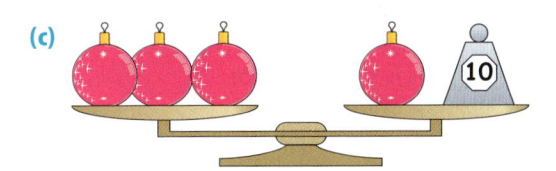

(d)

(e)

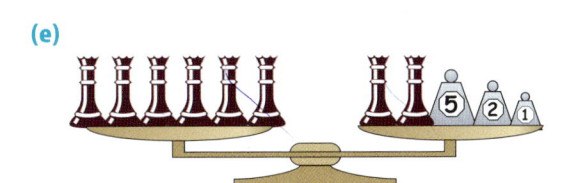

(f)

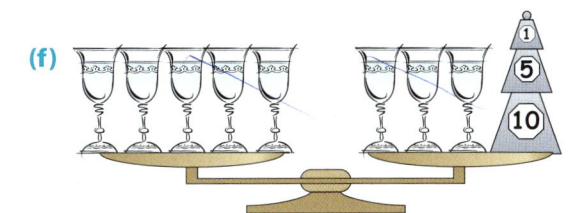

(g)

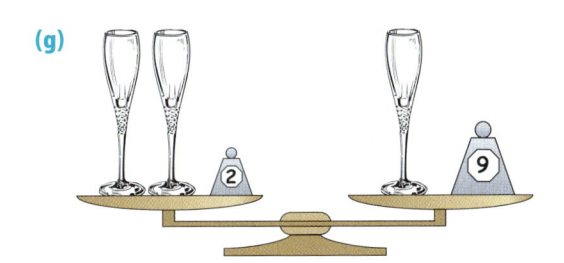

(h)

(i)

(j)

31 Solving equations

B Seeing a balance puzzle as an equation

We can write a balance puzzle as an equation using shorthand.

This puzzle can be written as $x + x + x = x + 10$
or $3x = x + 10$

The solution can be written $x = 5$

x stands for the weight of a bauble.

This is shorthand for 'The weight of a bauble is 5.'

B1 Here is a set of equations.

(a) $5x + 3 = 13$ (b) $2x + 9 = 15$ (c) $x + 16 = 3x$
(d) $6x = 4x + 12$ (e) $3x + 2 = x + 10$ (f) $5x + 1 = 2x + 13$

For each equation,
- write down the balance puzzle that matches it
- solve the puzzle and write down the solution in the form '$x = \ldots$'

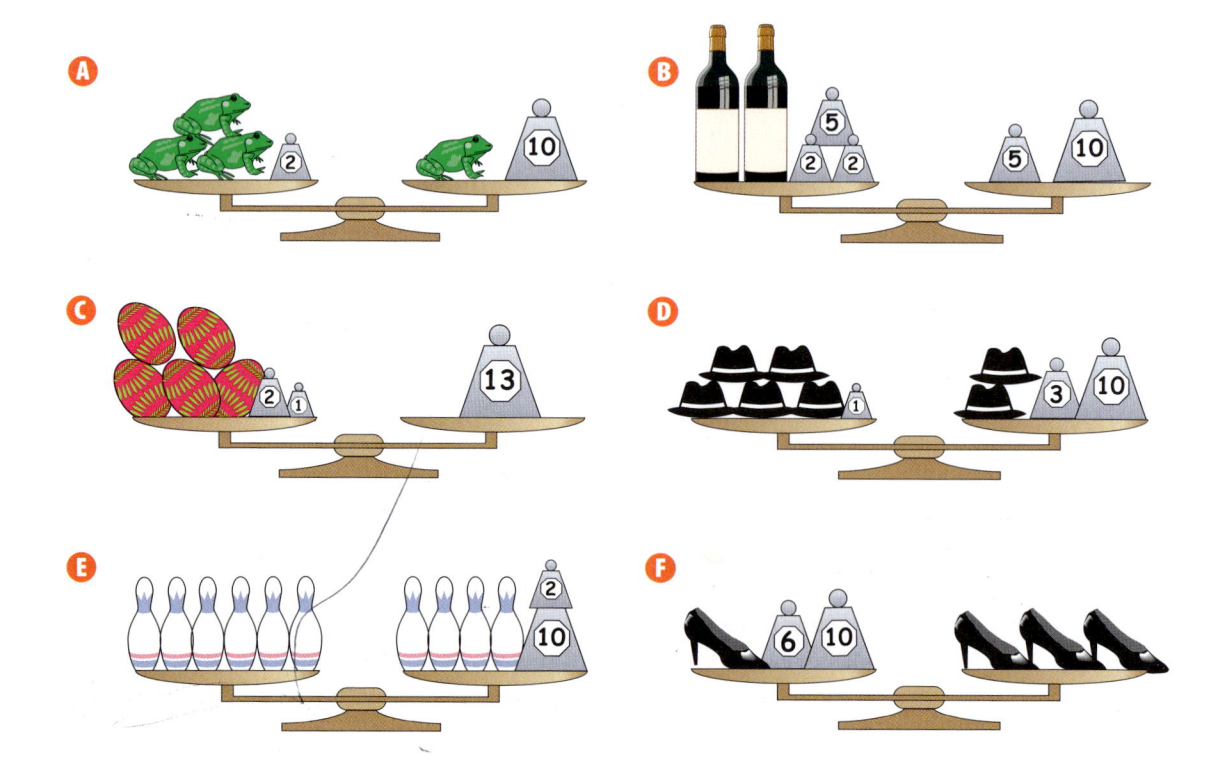

A

B

C

D

E

F

C Solving an equation using balancing

We can solve an equation by thinking of it as a balance puzzle.

Example

Use balancing to solve the equation $7x + 3 = 2x + 23$.

First we can take $2x$ away from each side.

$7x + 3 = 2x + 23$

$-2x \qquad -2x$

$5x + 3 = 23$

Now we can take 3 away from each side.

$-3 \qquad -3$

$5x = 20$

Last we can divide both sides by 5.

$\div 5 \qquad \div 5$

$x = 4$

Now we can check the solution in the original puzzle.

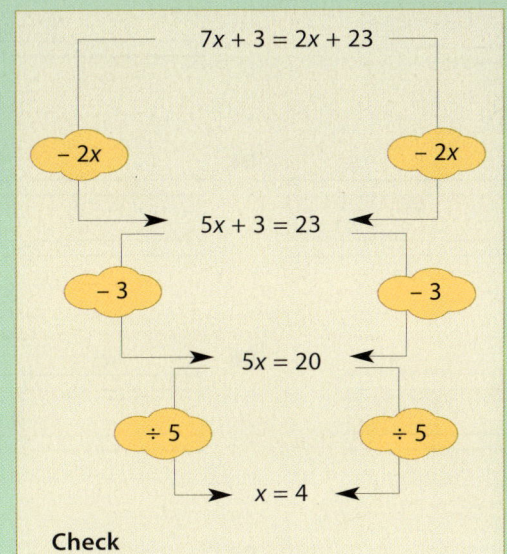

Check
left side: $(7 \times 4) + 3 = 31$
right side: $(2 \times 4) + 23 = 31$
so both sides balance.

C1 Use balancing to solve these equations.
(Show your working clearly and check each answer.)
- (a) $3x + 5 = 14$
- (b) $2x + 3 = 17$
- (c) $4x + 1 = 17$
- (d) $5x + 6 = 31$
- (e) $7x + 2 = 23$
- (f) $6x + 5 = 35$

C2 Use balancing to solve these equations.
- (a) $2x = x + 7$
- (b) $5x = 3x + 8$
- (c) $4x = 3x + 9$
- (d) $9x = 4x + 15$
- (e) $2x + 10 = 3x$
- (f) $4x + 9 = 7x$

C3 Use balancing to solve these equations.
- (a) $2x + 3 = x + 11$
- (b) $6x + 1 = 5x + 6$
- (c) $3x + 5 = x + 11$
- (d) $9x + 2 = x + 18$
- (e) $4x + 3 = 2x + 7$
- (f) $7x + 4 = 4x + 16$
- (g) $8x + 1 = 3x + 21$
- (h) $3x + 9 = 5x + 7$
- (i) $2x + 9 = 6x + 1$

C4 (a) Write down an equation for this puzzle. Use x to stand for the weight of a tin.
(b) Solve the equation to find the weight of a tin.

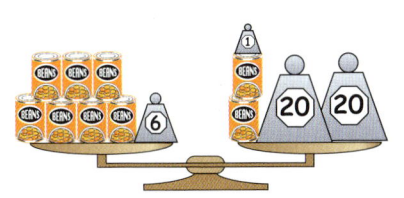

D Finding unknown lengths on strips

What does *x* stand for in each diagram?

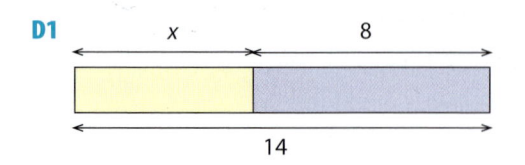

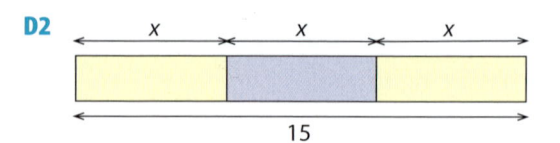

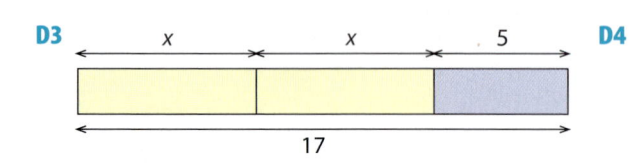

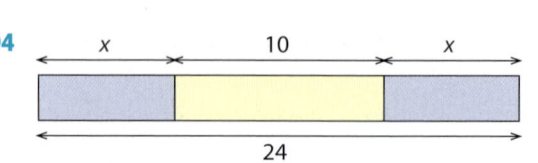

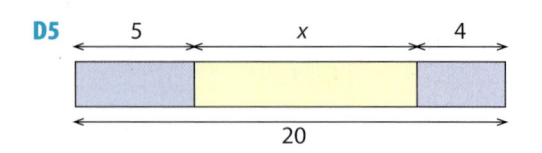

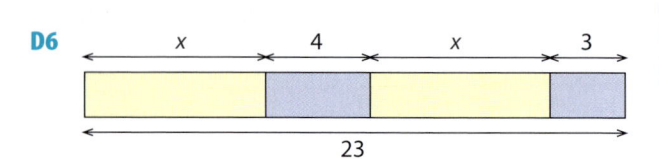

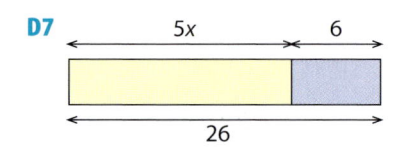

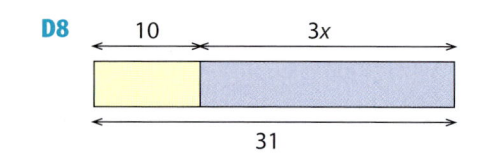

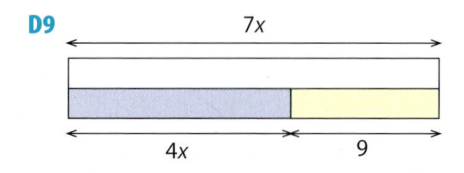

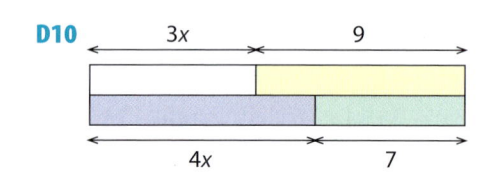

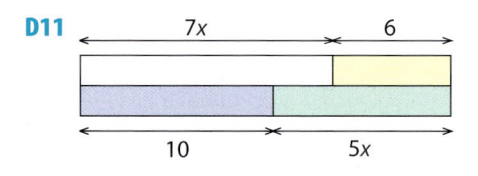

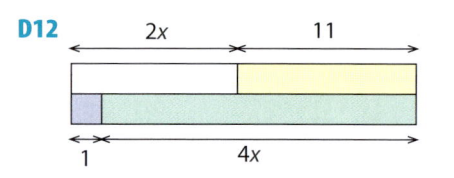

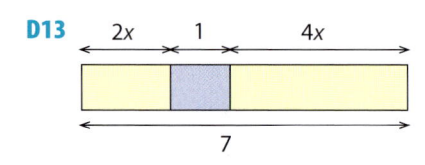

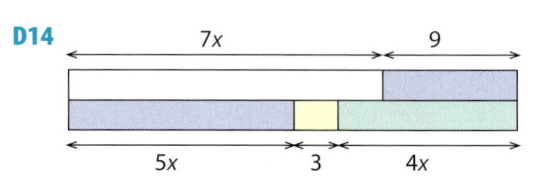

D1 x | 8 ; total 14

D2 x | x | x ; total 15

D3 x | x | 5 ; total 17

D4 x | 10 | x ; total 24

D5 5 | x | 4 ; total 20

D6 x | 4 | x | 3 ; total 23

D7 top: 5x | 6 ; bottom: 26

D8 top: 10 | 3x ; bottom: 31

D9 top: 7x ; bottom: 4x | 9

D10 top: 3x | 9 ; bottom: 4x | 7

D11 top: 7x | 6 ; bottom: 10 | 5x

D12 top: 2x | 11 ; bottom: 1 | 4x

D13 2x | 1 | 4x ; total 7

D14 top: 7x | 9 ; bottom: 5x | 3 | 4x

232 31 Solving equations

E Undoing a subtraction in an equation

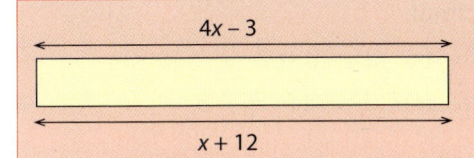

4x – 3

x + 12

To find the value of x for this strip, we can solve the equation

4x – 3 = x + 12.

First we can add 3 to each side.

Now we can take x off each side.

Last we can divide both sides by 3.

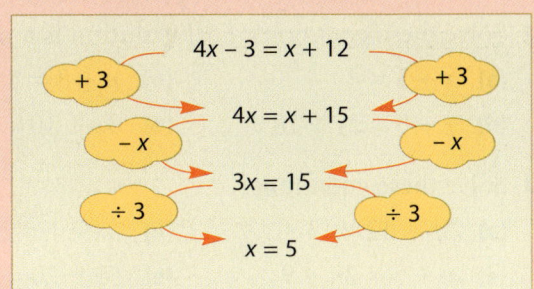

Now we can check the solution.

4x – 3 = x + 12
+ 3   + 3
4x = x + 15
– x   – x
3x = 15
÷ 3   ÷ 3
x = 5

Check
left side: (4 × 5) – 3 = 17
right side: 5 + 12 = 17
so both sides balance.

E1 Solve these equations.

(a) $x - 4 = 5$
(b) $x - 12 = 3$
(c) $2x - 1 = 11$
(d) $3x - 7 = 5$
(e) $4x - 1 = 11$
(f) $5x - 12 = 8$
(g) $2x - 3 = 15$
(h) $3x - 2 = 19$
(i) $6x - 5 = 1$

E2 Solve these equations.

(a) $5x - 1 = 4x + 3$
(b) $2x - 3 = x + 5$
(c) $5x - 2 = 3x + 4$
(d) $x + 1 = 2x - 1$
(e) $2x + 1 = 3x - 2$
(f) $4x - 9 = x + 6$
(g) $3x + 8 = 5x - 12$
(h) $x + 15 = 6x - 15$
(i) $5x - 5 = 2x + 16$

E3 Work out the value of x for each strip.

(a) 6x – 3 / 4x + 7

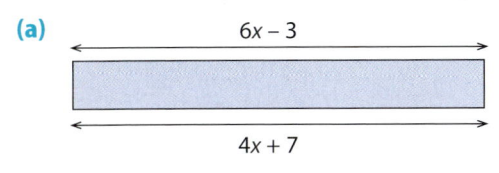

(b) 7x – 9 / 2x + 6

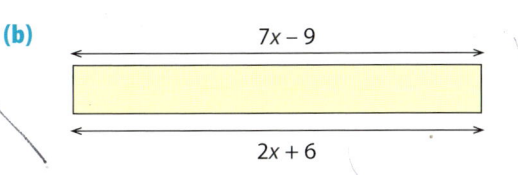

*E4 Solve these equations.

(a) $2x = 5x - 9$
(b) $6x - 12 = 4x$
(c) $x = 3x - 10$
(d) $4x - 6 = 3x - 1$
(e) $5x - 7 = 3x - 1$
(f) $4x - 25 = x - 1$

F Decimal, negative and fractional solutions

F1 Solve these equations and write each answer as a decimal.
- (a) $2x = 7$
- (b) $5n + 3 = 4$
- (c) $2x - 3 = 2$
- (d) $6p + 1 = 2p + 7$
- (e) $5x + 2 = 3x + 7$
- (f) $2y + 4 = 7y - 3$

F2 Solve these equations. Each solution is a negative number.
- (a) $x + 5 = 4$
- (b) $n + 8 = 5$
- (c) $2x + 3 = {^-}1$
- (d) $y + 8 = 2y + 10$
- (e) $3x + 10 = x + 4$
- (f) $5a + 5 = 2a - 16$

F3 Solve these equations.
- (a) $5p + 12 = {^-}3$
- (b) $4x - 1 = 2x + 5$
- (c) $2n + 5 = n + 9$
- (d) $n + 5 = 2n + 9$
- (e) $5y + 20 = 2y + 8$
- (f) $2x - 1 = 4x + 5$

F4 Solve these equations. Write each answer as a fraction.
- (a) $5x = 3$
- (b) $2p + 4 = 5$
- (c) $7y - 3 = 2$
- (d) $5x + 4 = x + 7$
- (e) $6n - 1 = 3n$
- (f) $10z - 3 = 2z + 2$

G Problem solving

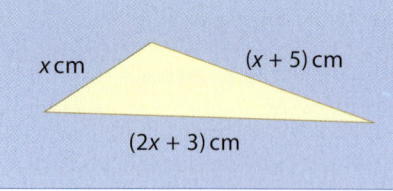

Triangle with sides x cm, $(x + 5)$ cm, $(2x + 3)$ cm.

- Find an expression, in terms of x, for the perimeter of this triangle.

The perimeter of this triangle is 40 cm.

- Find the value of x and sketch the triangle.

G1 (a) Find an expression, in terms of x, for the perimeter of this triangle.
Give your answer in its simplest form.

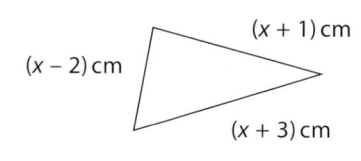

Triangle with sides $(x - 2)$ cm, $(x + 1)$ cm, $(x + 3)$ cm.

The perimeter of the triangle is 44 cm.

(b) Write down an equation and solve it to find the value of x.

G2 The width of a rectangle is x centimetres.
The length of the rectangle is $(x + 4)$ centimetres.

(a) Find an expression, in terms of x, for the perimeter of the rectangle.
Give your expression in its simplest form.

The perimeter of the rectangle is 54 centimetres.

(b) Work out the length of the rectangle.

Edexcel

G3 (a) Write an expression, in terms of x, for the sum of the angles marked in this triangle.
Give your answer in its simplest form.

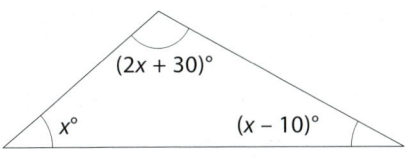

The angles of a triangle add up to 180°.

(b) Write down an equation in x and use it to find the value of x.

G4 The diagram represents a garden in the shape of a rectangle.
All measurements are given in metres.

The garden has a flower-bed in one corner.
The flower-bed is a square of side x.

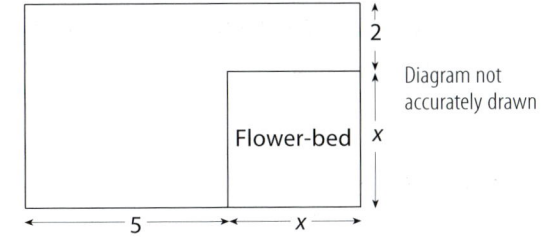

(a) Write down an expression, in terms of x, for the shortest side of the garden.

(b) Find an expression, in terms of x, for the perimeter of the garden.
Give your answer in its simplest form.

The perimeter of the garden is 20 metres.

(c) Find the value of x.

Edexcel

Test yourself

T1 Solve these.
 (a) $x + 5 = 12$ (b) $5x = 3x + 8$ *OCR*

T2 Solve these.
 (a) $x - 4 = 11$ (b) $2p + 5 = 13$ (c) $4n + 2 = 5n - 6$

T3 Solve these equations.
 (a) $3x - 5 = 7$ (b) $3x + 2 = 5x - 10$ *OCR*

T4 Solve these.
 (a) $2x = 10$ (b) $6y + 1 = 25$ (c) $8p - 3 = 3p + 13$ *Edexcel*

T5 (a) Solve $3x - 4 = x + 5$

 (b) The width of a rectangle is x cm.
 The length is 1.5 cm more than the width.
 The perimeter of the rectangle is 17 cm.

 Write down an equation satisfied by x and solve it to find x.

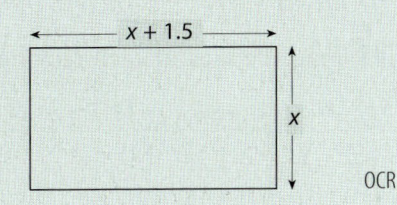

OCR

31 Solving equations

32 Written calculation 2

You should know how to
- multiply multiples of ten such as 400×70
- estimate the answer to a multiplication by rounding the numbers

This work will help you multiply and divide by a two-digit number.

You need sheets F1–28 and F1–29.

A Multiplying by a two-digit number

Here are some different ways in which people do 37×52.

Table method

	50	2
30	1500	60
7	350	14

```
  1 5 0 0
     6 0
    3 5 0
  +  1 4
  ───────
  1 9 2 4
```

Long multiplication

```
       3 7
   ×   5 2
   ───────
       7 4
   + 1 8 5 0
   ───────
     1 9 2 4
```

Lattice method

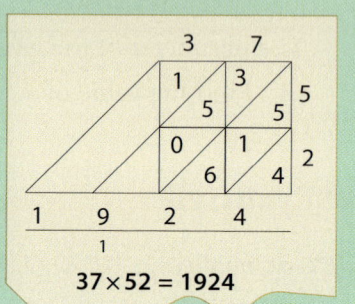

$37 \times 52 = 1924$

- Which method would you use?

A1 Work these out.
(a) 15×17 (b) 32×61 (c) 53×24 (d) 26×71

A2 Work these out.
(a) 86×73 (b) 92×87 (c) 79×65 (d) 46×99

A3 Work these out.
(a) 172×41 (b) 236×52 (c) 504×73 (d) 463×95

A4 Find the area of each rectangle below.

(a) 19 cm × 16 cm

(b) 43 m × 24 m

A5 A can of fizzy drink costs 29p.

29p

(a) (i) Which of these calculations gives the approximate cost of 41 cans in pence?

20 × 40   30 × 40   40 × 50   90 × 10

(ii) Work out the approximate cost of 41 cans.

(b) Calculate the exact cost of 41 cans.

A6 Penny arranges daffodils in bunches of 12.
She makes 57 bunches.

(a) Do an approximate calculation to estimate how many daffodils Penny used.

(b) Calculate the exact number of daffodils used.

A7 Mary has 36 cats.
Each cat eats 183 tins of cat food each year.
How many tins of cat food do Mary's cats eat altogether in a year?

A8 Do the puzzles on sheet F1–28.

B Dividing by a two-digit number

Here are two different ways in which people do 368 ÷ 23.

Chunking method

```
              3 6 8
10 × 23   − 2 3 0
              1 3 8
 5 × 23   − 1 1 5
                2 3
 1 × 23   −    2 3
                 0
```

10 + 5 + 1 = 16
so 368 ÷ 23 = 16

Long division

```
           1 6
    23)3 6 8
       − 2 3
         1 3 8
       − 1 3 8
             0
```

- Which method would you use?

B1 Work these out.

(a) 247 ÷ 13   (b) 345 ÷ 15   (c) 609 ÷ 21   (d) 891 ÷ 27

B2 Work these out.

(a) 496 ÷ 31   (b) 966 ÷ 42   (c) 972 ÷ 54   (d) 858 ÷ 39

B3 Work these out.

(a) 1116 ÷ 36   (b) 1189 ÷ 29   (c) 2352 ÷ 42   (d) 1479 ÷ 51

B4 Do the puzzles on sheet F1–29.

B5 624 biscuits are packed in boxes of 24.
How many boxes are needed?

B6 Jake has 588 tulip bulbs to plant in large pots.
He plants 21 bulbs in each pot.
How many large pots does he need?

B7 A meeting is to be held at which 442 chairs are required.
Chairs are to be set out in rows of 17 chairs.
Calculate how many rows of chairs are needed altogether.

OCR

B8 Spring rolls are sold in packets of 18.
Ky needs 300 spring rolls for a picnic.
(a) How many packets does he need to buy?
(b) How many extra spring rolls will he buy?

B9 Poonam is using beads to make bracelets.
Each bracelet needs 32 beads and she has 700 beads altogether.
(a) How many bracelets can she make?
(b) How many beads will be left over?

B10 How many 29-seater coaches are needed to carry 320 people to a hockey match?

B11 A bar of chocolate costs 26p.
How many bars could Susan buy with £6.00?

C Mixed questions

C1 Cans of cola are packed in boxes of 24.
How many cans are there altogether in 16 boxes?

C2 312 roses are arranged in bunches of 13.
How many bunches are there?

C3 A packet of crisps costs 18p.
(a) What is the total cost of 35 packets of crisps?
(b) How many packets of crisps can be bought for £4.50?

C4 A total of 400 people are going on a coach trip.
Each coach can carry 34 passengers.
Each coach costs £95 to hire.
(a) Work out how many coaches are needed.
(b) Work out the total cost of all the coaches that are needed.

C5 Bottles of mineral water cost 39p.

(a) **Estimate** the cost of 152 bottles. Show how you obtained your answer.

(b) Work out the **exact** cost of 152 bottles at 39p each.

(c) Adrian has £10.
What is the largest number of bottles of mineral water that he can buy with this?

OCR

C6 Roy is tiling a floor.
He needs to lay 28 rows of 34 tiles.
Tiles are sold in packs of 25.

How many packs of tiles would he need to buy?
Show your working clearly.

Test yourself

T1 A factory makes 28 sofas in a working week.
How many sofas will it make in the 46 working weeks in a year?

T2 A smallholder has 448 potatoes to plant.
He has 16 rows to plant them in.
How many potatoes must he put in each row?

T3 Ms Taylor buys four bars of chocolate.
Each bar costs 38p.
Work out how much change she should get from £5.

T4 The cost of a coach holiday for one person was £235.
51 people were on the coach.
Work out the total amount paid by all the coach passengers.

T5 A packet of sweets costs 22p.
How many packets could Thomas buy with £3.00?

T6 Meena types 400 words in 16 minutes.
What is her typing rate in words per minute?

OCR

T7 A theatre has 792 seats.
A pantomime is going to be performed 29 times.
All the tickets are sold. Each ticket costs £10.

(a) (i) Do an approximate calculation to estimate how much money has been taken.

(ii) Is your estimate more or less than the actual amount of money taken?
Explain your answer.

(b) Calculate the exact number of tickets sold.

OCR

32 Written calculation 2   239

Review 4

You need an angle measurer for question 10.

1 This table shows the age in years and the value of some second-hand computers.

Age (years)	5	3	1	1	5	4	4
Value (£)	80	250	450	500	100	180	200

(a) Plot these pairs of values on a scatter diagram using these scales.

(b) What type of correlation is there between the age and value of these computers?

(c) Draw a line of best fit on your scatter diagram.

(d) Use the line to estimate the value of a computer that is 2 years old.

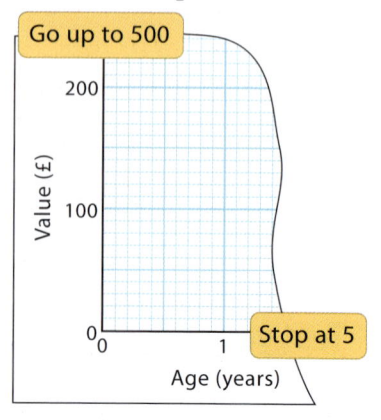

Go up to 500
Stop at 5

2 (a) Which numbers in the box are

100	4	14	36	6	24
3	49	8	9	2	27

   (i) square numbers
   (ii) cube numbers

(b) Choose one number from the box to complete each of these.
   (i) 7 squared is ...
   (ii) $\sqrt{16}$ = ...
   (iii) The cube root of 27 is ...
   (iv) 2^3 = ...

3 These questions were written for a survey on music.
Say why they are unsuitable.

(a) How many CDs have you bought in the last year?
(b) Nobody listens to classical music because it is old-fashioned. AGREE DISAGREE

4 What, roughly, are these imperial measurements in metric units?
   (a) 60 miles
   (b) 30 feet
   (c) 28 pounds
   (d) 4 pints

5 Round these to one significant figure.
   (a) 375
   (b) 409
   (c) 0.468
   (d) 0.076
   (e) 1.005

6 Work out 0.2×0.4.

7 Solve these equations.
   (a) $4x + 1 = 13$
   (b) $2x - 3 = 11$
   (c) $4x = 2x + 10$
   (d) $x + 5 = 2x + 1$
   (e) $5x + 4 = 3x + 10$
   (f) $2x + 11 = 5x + 5$

8 (a) A caretaker is laying out chairs in a hall.
       He needs to put out 27 rows with 38 chairs in each row.
       How many chairs does he need?
   (b) 816 tins of baked beans are packed in boxes of 24 tins.
       How many boxes are needed?

9 Work out a rough estimate of the total weight of each of these.
   Show your working.
   (a) 39 books that weigh 2.1 kg each
   (b) 5.9 metres of lead strip that weighs 3.06 kg per metre
   (c) 79 cars that weigh 1.075 tonnes each

10 This diagram shows the positions of a lighthouse (L) and a boat (B).

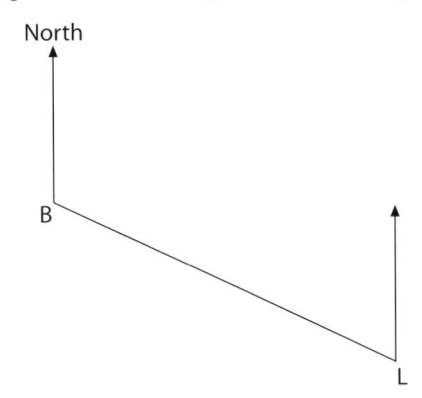

   (a) Measure the bearing of the lighthouse from the boat.
   (b) Measure the bearing of the boat from the lighthouse.
   The diagram has been drawn to scale where 1 cm represents 5 km.
   (c) How far is the boat from the lighthouse?

11 (a) Write down and simplify an expression
       for the sum of the angles of this triangle.
   (b) The angles of a triangle add up to 180°.
       Use this fact and your answer to part (a)
       to write down an equation in x.
   (c) Solve your equation, and use the solution to
       work out the size of each angle of the triangle.

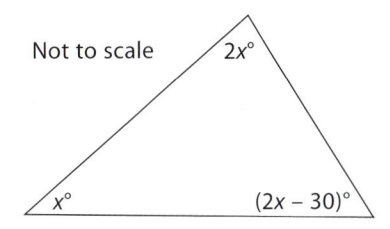

12 (a) Calculate 14×27.
   (b) Hence write down the result of the calculation 1.4×2.7.

33 Sequences

This work will help you

- find the next term in a sequence
- describe a rule you use to find the next term
- find, for example, the 10th term in a sequence and explain how you found it

A Continuing a sequence

- How do each of these sequences continue?

    | 1 | 3 | ... | Add 2 to the previous term. |
    | 1 | 3 | ... | Double the previous term and add 1. |
    | 1 | 3 | ... | Multiply the previous term by 4 and subtract 1. |
    | 1 | 3 | ... | Add the previous two terms together. |

    Each number in a sequence is called a **term**.

    These rules tell you how to get from one term to the next for each sequence.

- Make up a rule for continuing a sequence.
  Write down the first five terms of a sequence that uses your rule.
  From these terms, can someone else work out your rule and give the next two terms?

A1 Look at this sequence.

    1   4   7   10   13   ...

The rule to find the next term of this sequence is **add 3 to the previous term**.
Write down the next three terms in this sequence.

A2 For each of these sequences, the first four terms and the rule are given.
Write down the next three terms of each sequence.

(a) 2   4   6   8   ...   Add 2 to the previous term.
(b) 2   4   6   10   ...   Add the previous two terms together.
(c) 2   4   8   16   ...   Double the previous term.
(d) 2   4   10   28   ...   Multiply the previous term by 3 and subtract 2.

A3 Work out the next two terms in each of these sequences.
Write down the rule for finding the next term in the sequence.

(a) 5   7   9   11   13   15   ...
(b) 2   5   8   11   14   17   ...
(c) 5   10   20   40   80   160   ...
(d) 2   6   18   54   162   486   ...

A4 Work out the next two terms in each of these sequences.
Write down the rule for finding the next term.

(a) 20   18   16   14   12   10   ...
(b) 35   30   25   20   15   10   ...
(c) 5   3   1   ⁻1   ⁻3   ⁻5   ...
(d) 17   14   11   8   5   2   ...

A5 Write down the next two terms of the sequence

21   15   9   ...   ...

OCR

A6 Here are the first five terms of a number sequence.

192   96   48   24   12   ...

(a) Write down the next three terms in this sequence.

(b) Explain how you found your answer.

A7 (a) A sequence begins   3   4   6   10   ...
The rule for continuing the sequence is

> Double the last number and subtract 2.

What is the next number in this sequence?

(b) A different sequence begins   ⁻2   ⁻4   ⁻6   ⁻8   ...
What is the next number in this sequence?

AQA

A8 Explain how to work out the next number in the sequence: 1   5   25   125   ...

A9 (a) A sequence begins   2   3   5   8   12   ...
The rule for continuing the sequence is

> Add 1, then add 2, then add 3, then add 4 and so on.

What is the next number in this sequence?

(b) The same rule is used for a sequence that starts with the number 4.
What are the next three numbers in this sequence?

A10 Write down the next two terms of this sequence.

20   19   17   14   10   ...   ...

A11 Here are the first five terms of a number sequence.

3   8   13   18   23   ...

(a) Write down the next two terms in this sequence.

The 30th term of the number sequence is 148.

(b) Write down the 31st term of the sequence.

33 Sequences   243

A12 Barry and Kath are studying a number pattern.

The first three numbers in the number pattern are   1, 2, 4

Barry says that the next number is 8.
Kath says the next number is 7.

Explain why both Barry and Kath could be right.

Edexcel

B Describing numbers in some sequences

Look at this sequence of numbers:

   2   4   8   16   32   64   ...

The sequence begins with 2.
The rule to get from one term to the next is to multiply the previous term by 2.

The numbers in this sequence are called **powers of 2**.

B1 Here are the first four terms of a sequence of powers of 3.

   3   9   27   81   ...

What is the next term?

B2 Look at this sequence.

   1   3   5   7   9   ...

(a) Write down the next two terms in this sequence.

(b) Which of the following describes the numbers in this sequence?

| Square numbers | Multiples of 2 | Odd numbers |

B3 Here are the first five terms of a number sequence.

   2   4   6   8   10   ...

(a) Describe the numbers in this sequence.

(b) What is the 12th term in this sequence?

B4 Here is a sequence of triangle patterns.

The number of dots in each pattern
makes the sequence

   1   3   6   10   ...

1 dot   3 dots   6 dots   10 dots

Numbers in this sequence are called **triangle numbers**.

(a) (i) Draw the next triangle pattern.

   (ii) What is the 5th triangle number?

(b) Find the 7th triangle number.

244 33 Sequences

C Sequences from patterns

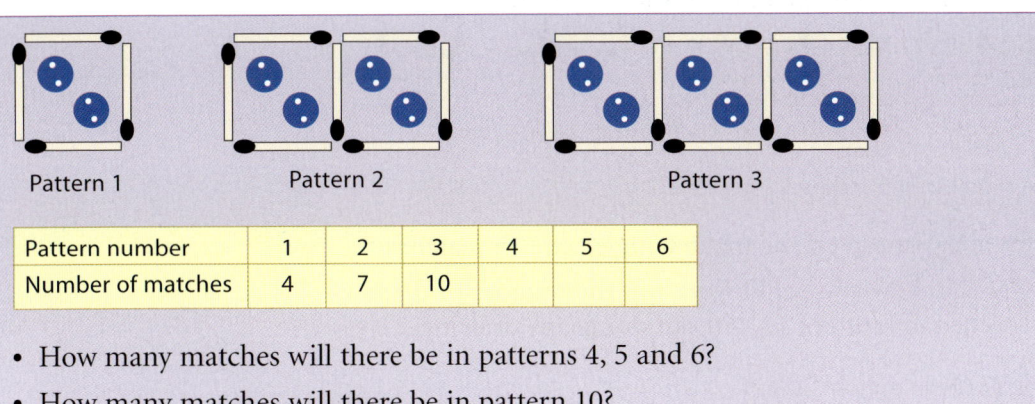

Pattern 1   Pattern 2   Pattern 3

Pattern number	1	2	3	4	5	6
Number of matches	4	7	10			

- How many matches will there be in patterns 4, 5 and 6?
- How many matches will there be in pattern 10? Explain how you worked this out.
- Which pattern has 37 matches in it?

C1 Look at the number of buttons in the patterns above.

(a) How many buttons will there be in pattern 4?

(b) How many will there be in pattern 5?

(c) Copy and complete this table.

Pattern number	1	2	3	4	5	6
Number of buttons	2	4	6			

(d) How many buttons will there be in the 10th pattern?

(e) One pattern has 42 buttons in it. Which pattern is it?

C2 Here are some patterns made from sticks.

Pattern 1   Pattern 2   Pattern 3

(a) Draw pattern 4.

(b) Copy and complete the table.

Pattern number	Number of sticks
1	6
2	10
3	14
4	
5	

Edexcel

C3 The diagram shows some patterns made with matches.

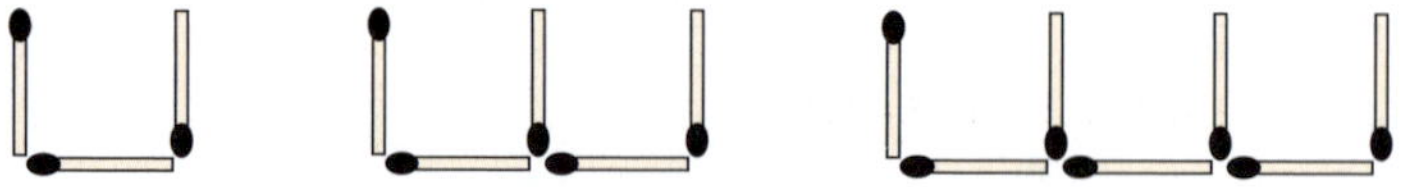

(a) Copy and complete the table.

Pattern number	1	2	3	4	5
Number of matches	3	5			

(b) Which pattern can be made with exactly 15 matches?

(c) Explain how you could work out the number of matches needed for pattern 12 without doing any drawing.

OCR

C4 Look at these match shapes.

Shape 1   Shape 2   Shape 3

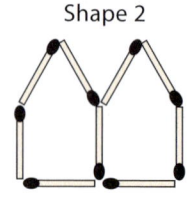

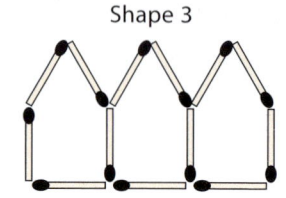

5 matches   9 matches

(a) Copy and complete this table.

Shape number	1	2	3	4	5
Number of matches	5	9			

(b) How many matches are there in shape 12?
Explain how you can work this out without drawing a diagram.

OCR

C5 Shape 1   Shape 2   Shape 3

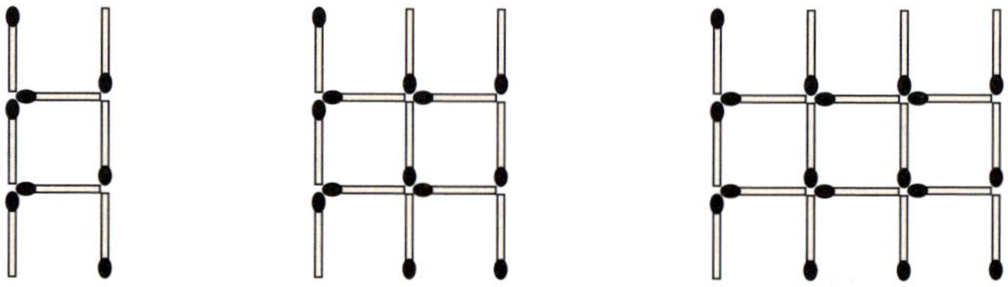

(a) Copy and complete this table for the shapes above.

Shape number	1	2	3	4	5
Number of matches	8				

(b) How many matches would there be in shape 8?
Explain carefully how you got your answer.

(c) One shape is made from 63 matches.
Which shape is this?

Test yourself

T1 Here are the first five terms of a number sequence.

126   122   118   114   110

(a) Write down the next two terms of the number sequence.

(b) Explain how you found your answer.

The 20th term of the number sequence is 50.

(c) Write down the 21st term of the number sequence

Edexcel

T2 Here is the rule for finding a term in a sequence.

> Multiply the previous term by 3 and add 2.

The first three terms in the sequence are 2, 8 and 26.
Work out the next two terms.

Edexcel

T3 (a) These are the first four terms of a sequence.

5   9   13   17

  (i) Write down the tenth term.

  (ii) Explain how you worked out your answer.

(b) The rule for another sequence is 'multiply the previous term by 2 and add 1'.
The first term of the sequence is 3.

  (i) Write down the second term.   (ii) Work out the sixth term.

OCR

T4 (a) Write down the next two terms in the sequence: 1   3   5   7

(b) What type of number are the terms in the sequence?

T5 Here are some patterns made up of dots.

Pattern 1   Pattern 2   Pattern 3

(a) Draw pattern 4.

(b) Copy and complete this table.

Pattern number	1	2	3	4	5
Number of dots	10	14	18		

(c) How many dots are used in pattern 10?

T6 Write down the next term in the sequence: 2   6   12   20   30   …

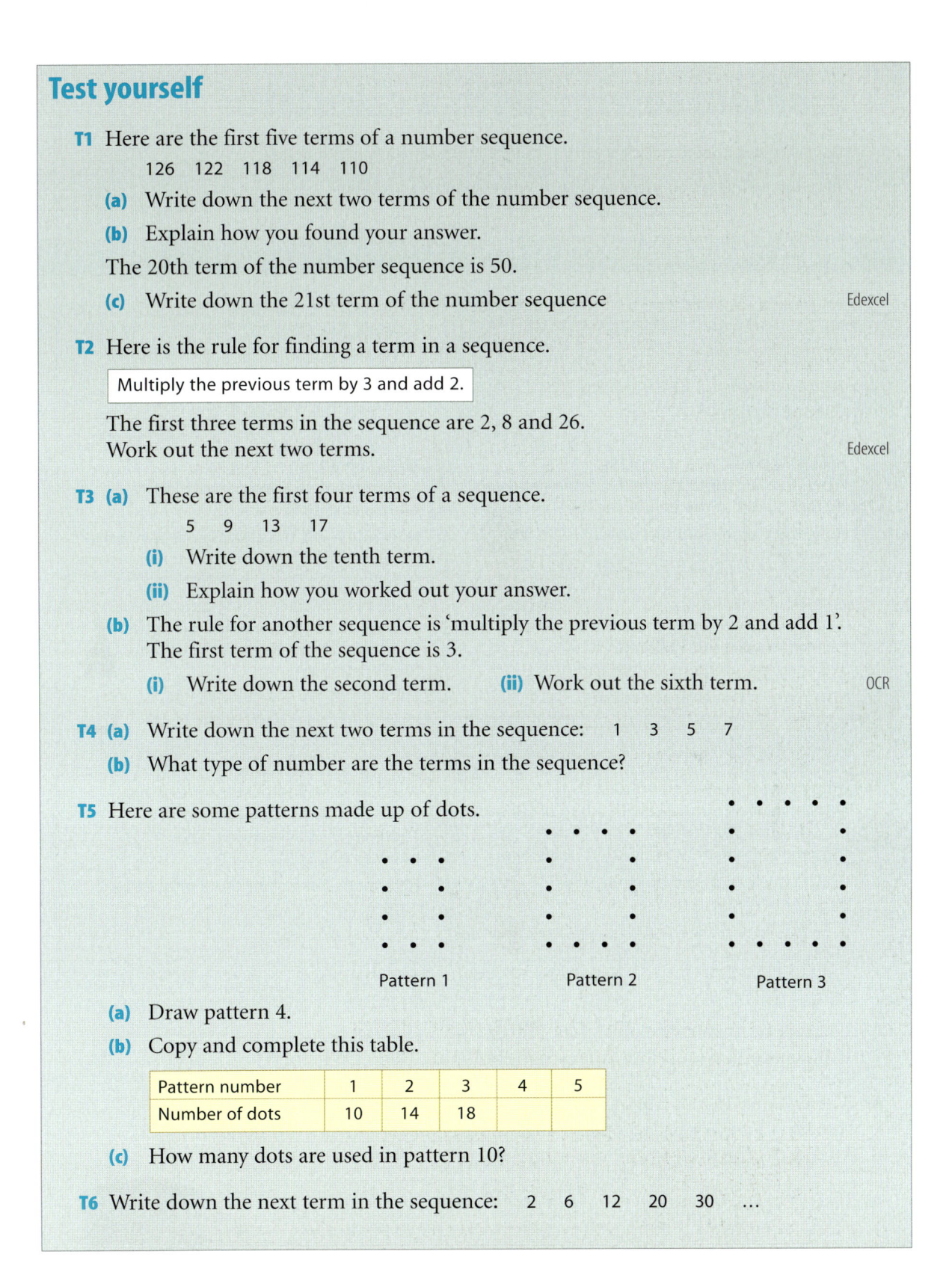

34 Problem solving with a calculator

You will revise how to decide whether to add, subtract, multiply or divide.

This work will help you use a calculator when solving a problem.

A Which calculation?

- Which of these calculations goes with each problem below?

  (Some calculations may be used twice and some not at all.)

  | 312 + 39 | 39 − 312 | 312 − 39 |
  | 312 × 39 | 39 ÷ 312 | 312 ÷ 39 |

  A Josh sold plants at a school fair.
  When the fair started he had 312 plants to sell.
  He had 39 left at the end of the fair.
  How many plants did Josh sell?

  B There are 39 rooms in a school.
  Each room is to have a smoke alarm.
  Alarms cost £312 each.
  How much will the alarms cost altogether?

  C A school hires coaches to take children on a trip.
  Each coach takes 39 children.
  312 children are going on the trip.
  How many coaches are needed?

  D Sheila has 39 people working for her.
  She buys them each a bottle of wine for Christmas.
  The wine costs £312 altogether.
  How much does each bottle cost?

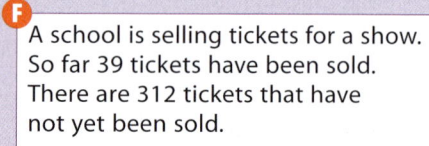

  E Dilip delivers leaflets to houses.
  He went out on Saturday with a bag of leaflets.
  He delivered 312 leaflets.
  Afterwards he had 39 leaflets left in his bag.
  How many leaflets did he have in his bag when he started?

  F A school is selling tickets for a show.
  So far 39 tickets have been sold.
  There are 312 tickets that have not yet been sold.
  How many tickets are there altogether?

A1 Each room in an office block has 48 light bulbs.
If there are 27 rooms, how many light bulbs are there altogether?

A2 The distance by rail from London to Edinburgh is 405 miles.
A train on its way from London to Edinburgh is 188 miles from London.
How far is the train from Edinburgh?

A3 Paul's truck can hold 28 tonnes of coal.
He has to move 420 tonnes of coal from one place to another.
How many journeys does he need to make?

A4 Errol buys a carpet whose area is 14.6 square metres.
The carpet costs £13.45 per square metre.
How much does Errol pay?

A5 A group of 48 people hire a coach and agree to share the cost equally.
The coach hire costs £600. How much does each person pay?

A6 Ronnie bought some 32p stamps.
He paid £11.20 altogether.
How many stamps did he buy?

A7 Karen is arranging a picnic lunch for 8 people.
She spends £12.45 on sandwiches, £1.89 on crisps and £3.26 on drinks.

(a) What is the total cost of the picnic?

(b) The 8 people agree to share the total cost equally.
How much does each person pay?

A8 Hayley buys 6 ices and 4 lollies.
She pays £6.70 altogether.
The ices cost 75p each.

(a) How much did the 6 ices cost altogether?

(b) What was the cost of the 4 lollies?

(c) How much did each lolly cost?

A9 Here is the menu at Lou's café.

Burger	£1.29
Cheeseburger	£1.59
Doughnut	69p

Jack bought 3 burgers, 2 cheeseburgers and some doughnuts.
He paid £9.81 altogether.

(a) How much did the burgers and cheeseburgers cost altogether?

(b) How much did the doughnuts cost altogether?

(c) How many doughnuts did Jack buy?

A10 Here are the ticket prices for Fab Funfair.

Mr Blake and his two children are going to the Funfair.
So are Mr Patel and his two children.

Adult £16.55
Child £12.85
Group ticket
(2 adults and up to 4 children)
£70

(a) How much will the Blakes and the Patels pay altogether if they go in separately?

(b) How much will each family save if the two families go in together as a group?

B Showing working

Example

Paul sends his daughter to post 6 identical parcels.
He gives her a £20 note and she comes back with £4.52 change.
How much did each parcel cost to post?

Cost of posting 6 parcels = £20 − £4.52 = £15.48
Cost of posting each parcel = £15.48 ÷ 6 = **£2.58**

B1

Scary Park	
Adult	£19
Child	£13

Here are the ticket prices for entry to Scary Park.
A group of 7 adults and 15 children visit the park.
How much do they pay altogether?

B2 Sandra buys a desk, a chair and a lamp.
The desk costs £57.95. The chair costs £24.75.
The total cost of all three things is £101.25.

How much does the lamp cost?

B3 When Sarah goes on a business trip she claims 34p for every mile she drives.

She drives on business from her home to Birmingham (73 miles), then from Birmingham to Manchester (89 miles) and finally back home (112 miles).

(a) How far did she travel altogether?

(b) How much can she claim for this journey?

B4 Here is part of the menu at a Chinese restaurant.

8 people have a meal.

They order 3 crispy seaweed, 3 sesame prawn toast, 2 sweet and sour pork, 3 beef chow mein, 2 Peking duck and 5 fried rice.

They share the total cost of the meal equally.
How much does each person pay?

Crispy seaweed	£3.25
Sesame prawn toast	£3.95
Sweet and sour pork	£4.50
Beef chow mein	£4.95
Peking duck	£8.85
Fried rice	£1.85

B5 Kylie bought 12 tins of blue paint and 9 rolls of wallpaper.
She remembered that each tin of paint cost £4.89 and the total bill came to £93.60.
How much did each roll of wallpaper cost?

B6 Gail is going to make fruit cakes to sell at a fair.
She spends the following amounts on the ingredients.

Flour £5.40   Sugar £3.75   Butter £4.90   Eggs £11.80   Dried fruit £13.20

Gail makes 24 cakes from these ingredients.
She sells them at £3.75 each. All the cakes are sold.

(a) How much profit does Gail make?

(b) How much does the dried fruit for one cake cost?

B7 Rachel bought a ringbinder, paper and some felt-tips.
The ringbinder cost £3.49, the paper cost £2.75 and the felt-tips were 37p each.
The total cost was £11.42.

How many felt-tips did Rachel buy?

B8 A family of 2 adults and 3 children are going to London by train.
The normal fares are

    Adult   £14.80   Child   £8.20

If the family buy a Family Railcard, costing £20, they get these reduced fares.

    Adult   £9.90   Child   £2.00

If they only use the Railcard this one time, how much do they save by buying it and getting the reduced fares?

C Changing money to a different currency

If you go abroad, you may need to change your money into a different currency.
Suppose the exchange rate between the pound and the US dollar is **£1 = US$1.84**.
To change pounds to dollars you **multiply** by 1.84.

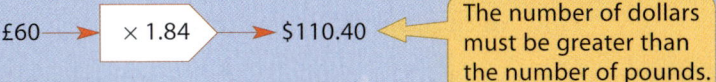

£60 → × 1.84 → $110.40

The number of dollars must be greater than the number of pounds.

To change dollars to pounds you **divide** by 1.84.

The number of pounds must be less than the number of dollars.

£60 ← ÷ 1.84 ← $110.40

When you are working with money, give your answers to two decimal places.

C1 Bharat goes to Canada. The exchange rate is £1 = 2.07 Canadian dollars.

(a) He changes £120 into Canadian dollars. How many dollars does he get?

(b) When he leaves Canada, he changes 73.50 dollars into pounds.
The exchange rate is the same.
How much does he get, to the nearest penny?

C2 The exchange rate between the pound and the Swiss franc is £1 = 2.38 Swiss francs.

Change (a) £33.60 to Swiss francs (b) 88.70 Swiss francs to £, to the nearest penny

C3 The exchange rate between the pound and the Japanese yen is £1 = 214 yen.

Change (a) £64 to yen   (b) 850 yen to £, to the nearest penny

C4 The exchange rate between the pound and the Australian dollar is £1 = 2.44 dollars.

Change (a) £240 to dollars   (b) 850 dollars to £, to the nearest penny

C5 Erik had a mixture of English and Norwegian money.
He had £8.50 and 86 Norwegian kroner.
£1 was worth 11.52 Norwegian kroner.

What was Erik's money worth

(a) in Norwegian kroner (b) in pounds

Test yourself

T1 Venus chocolate bars cost 28p each.
A special Christmas tin contains 16 bars and costs £4.99.

If you buy the tin instead of 16 separate bars, how much are you paying for the tin itself?

T2 (a) Rides at a fairground cost £1.50 each.
How many rides can Chris have if he has £5 to spend?

(b) Sam buys an ice cream for £1.25 and some candy floss for 99p.
How much change should he get from £10?

(c) A stall holder paid £25.50 to rent his stall.
He paid £43.20 for his stock.
His takings were £113.10.

How much profit did he make?

OCR

T3 This is part of Sari's electricity bill.

How much does she pay?

> **OHM Electricity Company**
> Present reading   7466 units
> Last reading   6942 units
> Each unit costs 4.5p

AQA

T4 A computer magazine is published every month and costs £2.99 per copy.
If you place a regular order you can get the magazine for three months for a cost of £5.49.

Chris buys the magazine for a year by paying for three months at a time. During the year, how much would be saved using this method rather than buying a copy every month?

WJEC

T5 The table shows the exchange rates between different currencies.

> £1 (pound) is worth 1.64 euros
> $1 (dollar) is worth 1.05 euros

(a) Jane changes £400 into euros.
How many euros does she receive?

(b) Sonia changes 672 euros into dollars.
How many dollars does she receive?

AQA

35 Working with expressions 2

This work will help you
- substitute into expressions such as $2a - b$
- simplify expressions such as $3a + 2b + 5a - 3b$

A Substituting into expressions such as $2a - b$

Examples

Find the value of $a + b$ when $a = 3$ and $b = 5$.

$a + b = 3 + 5$
$ = 8$

Find the value of $a - b + 5$ when $a = 7$ and $b = 3$.

$a - b + 5 = 7 - 3 + 5$
$ = 9$

Find the value of $2a + 5b$ when $a = 4$ and $b = 6$.

$2a + 5b = (2 \times 4) + (5 \times 6)$
$ = 8 + 30$
$ = 38$

You can use brackets to remind you to do the multiplications first.

A1 What is the value of each expression when $a = 5$ and $b = 2$?
  (a) $a + b$ (b) $a + b + 3$ (c) $a - b$ (d) $a - b - 1$

A2 Evaluate each expression when $m = 2$ and $n = 3$.
  (a) $n + m$ (b) $m + n - 4$ (c) $10 + m - n$ (d) $n - 1 + m$

A3 What is the value of each expression when $x = 3$ and $y = 4$?
  (a) $2x + y$ (b) $x + 3y$ (c) $2x + 5y$ (d) $2y + 5x$

A4 Evaluate each expression when $p = 2$ and $q = 7$.
  (a) $p + 2q$ (b) $5p + q$ (c) $3p + 2q$ (d) $10p + 4q$

A5 Evaluate each expression when $a = 8$ and $b = 3$.
  (a) $a - b$ (b) $2a - b$ (c) $3a - 2b$ (d) $5b - a$

A6 Evaluate each expression when $x = 7$ and $y = 4$.
  (a) $2x - 3y$ (b) $5y + 3x$ (c) $3x - 4y$ (d) $2y - x$

A7 What is the value of each expression when $c = 4$ and $d = 5$?
  (a) $4c + d + 3$ (b) $c + 5d - 1$ (c) $2c + 3d + 6$ (d) $2c - d - 3$

A8 What is the value of each expression when $a = 3$, $b = 2$ and $c = 1$?
  (a) $a + b + c$ (b) $2a + b + 3c$ (c) $a + b - c$ (d) $4a - 3b + c$

B Simplifying expressions such as $3a + 2b + a + 5b$

• Find an expression for the perimeter of each shape.

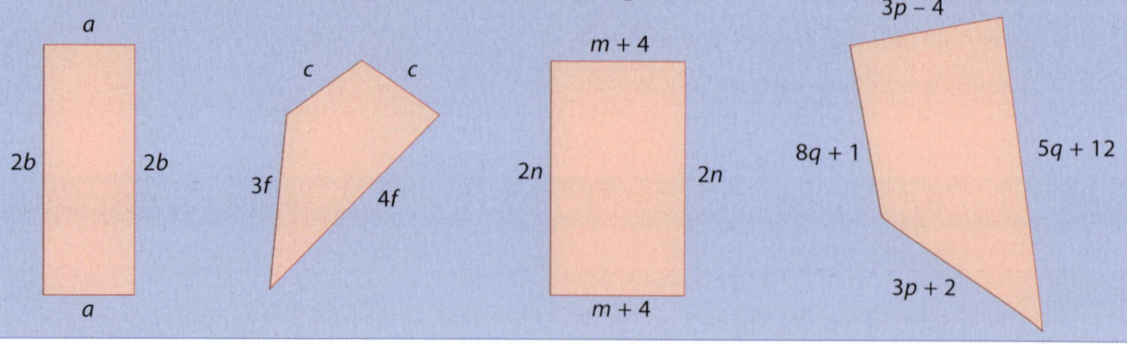

B1 Simplify each of these expressions.

(a) $5p + 2q + 3p + 3q$
(b) $6a + 8b + 2b + 5a$
(c) $x + 5y + x + 2y$
(d) $3a + 4b + a + 2b$
(e) $3x + 3y + y + x$
(f) $p + 5q + 3p + q$

B2 Simplify each of these expressions.

(a) $e + 5 + 4f - 2 + e + 3f$
(b) $6j + 10k - 6 + j + 5k$
(c) $4h + 6m - 3 + h - 4 + 2m$

B3 Work out and simplify an expression for the perimeter of each of these shapes.

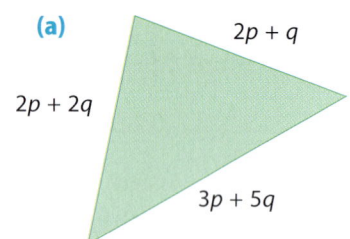

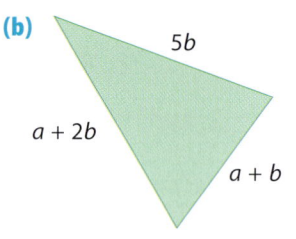

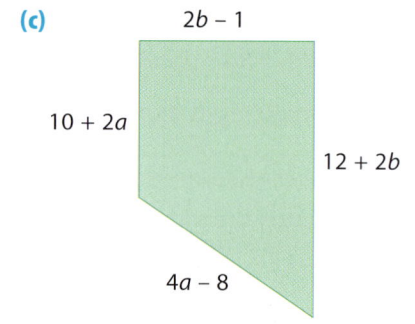

B4 Find an expression for each length marked **?**.

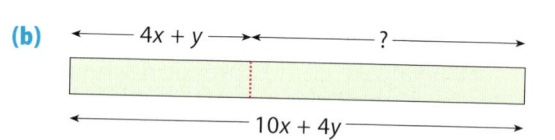

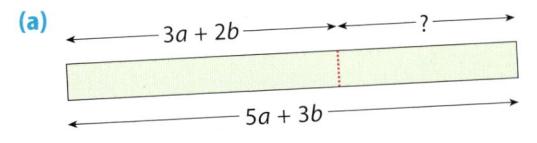

B5 The perimeter of this shape is $8p + 5q$.
Write an expression for the missing length.

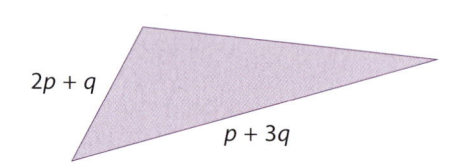

C Simplifying expressions such as $3a + 2b + a - 5b$

When simplifying an expression that involves subtraction it can help to reorder the expression first.

Examples

$2x + 6y + 5x - 3y = 2x + 5x + 6y - 3y$
$= 7x + 3y$

$7a + 2b - 3a - 5b = 7a - 3a + 2b - 5b$
$= 4a - 3b$

C1 Simplify each of these expressions.
(a) $6a + 4b + 3a - 2b$
(b) $7x + 5y - 3y + 2x$
(c) $8x + y - 5x + 2y$
(d) $2h + 4k + h - 3k$
(e) $5f + 2g + 3f - 6g$
(f) $4c + 5d - c - d$
(g) $4p + q + p - 5q$
(h) $7m - n + 2m + 5n$
(i) $5h - g + h - 2g$

C2 Simplify each of these expressions.
(a) $2a + 5b - a + 1$
(b) $4a + 3b + 5 - b$
(c) $6j + 10k - 6 + j - 5k$
(d) $4h + 6m + 3 - h - 4 + 2m$

C3 Work out and simplify an expression for the perimeter of each of these shapes.

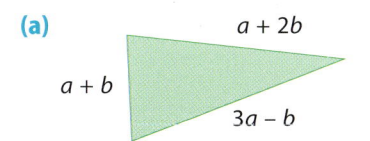

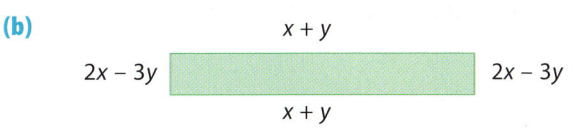

(a) Triangle with sides $a + b$, $a + 2b$, $3a - b$

(b) Rectangle with sides $x + y$, $2x - 3y$, $x + y$, $2x - 3y$

Test yourself

T1 When $a = 5$ and $b = 2$, find the value of $3a + b$.

T2 Simplify (a) $3g + 5h + g + 2h$ (b) $2p - q + 7p - 4q$

T3 Simplify (a) $a + a + a + a$ (b) $4b + 2c + 3b - 6c$ *Edexcel*

T4 Simplify $6x + 2y - x + 5y$. *OCR*

T5 This cuboid is a framework made from rods.

There are four rods of length c, four of length $2c$ and four of length d.

Write down an expression for the total length of the twelve rods.
Give your answer in its simplest form. *OCR*

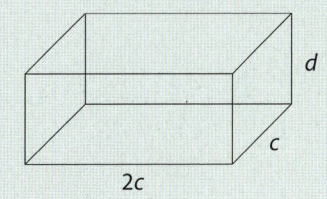

36 Calculating with negative numbers

You will revise adding and subtracting negative numbers.
This work will help you multiply and divide negative numbers.
You need sheets F1–30 and F1–31.

A Adding and subtracting

A1 Work these out.
(a) 2 – 7   (b) ⁻2 + 5   (c) 1 – 5   (d) ⁻3 + 9   (e) ⁻3 + 3
(f) ⁻1 – 3   (g) ⁻2 – 8   (h) 0 – 4   (i) ⁻3 – 10   (j) ⁻5 – 4

Adding a negative number 2 + ⁻6 is the same as subtracting a positive number 2 – 6

Subtracting a negative number 2 – ⁻6 is the same as adding a positive number 2 + 6

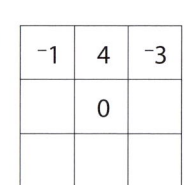

A2 Work these out.
(a) 5 + ⁻2   (b) 2 + ⁻5   (c) 6 + ⁻6   (d) ⁻7 + ⁻3
(e) ⁻1 + ⁻9   (f) ⁻2 + ⁻1 + ⁻3   (g) ⁻3 + ⁻3 + ⁻3   (h) ⁻7 + 3 + ⁻1

A3 Find the missing number in each calculation.
(a) 5 + ■ = 4   (b) 3 + ■ = ⁻4   (c) ⁻6 + ■ = 2
(d) ■ + ⁻2 = ⁻5   (e) 6 + ■ = ⁻3   (f) ■ + ⁻8 = ⁻9

A4 In a magic square the numbers in each row, each column and each diagonal add to the same total.

Copy and complete these magic squares.

(a)
4		
	1	
	5	⁻2

(b)
1	0	
	6	
	⁻1	

(c)
⁻1	4	⁻3
	0	

(d)
1	⁻6	
	⁻2	
		⁻5

A5 Work these out.
(a) 3 – ⁻2   (b) 1 – ⁻9   (c) 6 – ⁻4   (d) 1 – ⁻6   (e) ⁻1 – ⁻6
(f) ⁻2 – ⁻5   (g) ⁻3 – ⁻3   (h) ⁻10 – ⁻4   (i) ⁻8 – ⁻1   (j) ⁻7 – ⁻4

A6 Work these out.
(a) 2 – 5   (b) ⁻3 + 8   (c) ⁻6 – 3   (d) ⁻4 + ⁻7   (e) 1 – ⁻3
(f) 4 – ⁻5   (g) ⁻2 + ⁻6   (h) ⁻1 – ⁻7   (i) 0 – ⁻5   (j) ⁻9 – ⁻7

A7 Choose pairs of numbers from the loop to make these calculations correct.

(a) ■ − ■ = ⁻4 (b) ■ + ■ = ⁻5
(c) ■ + ■ = ⁻4 (d) ■ − ■ = ⁻6
(e) ■ − ■ = 8   (f) ■ + ■ = ⁻10

Loop: ⁻3, 6, ⁻5, 2, 1, 4, ⁻7

*A8 Use two numbers from 7, 2, ⁻5, ⁻8 and + or − to get the following results.

(a) ⁻13 (b) ⁻6 (c) ⁻5 (d) ⁻10 (e) 12

B Multiplying

- Match the expressions on the left with the expressions on the right.
- Can you work out the answer to each multiplication?

A ⁻2 + ⁻2
B 0 + 0
C ⁻4 + ⁻4 + ⁻4
D ⁻2 + ⁻2 + ⁻2 + ⁻2 + ⁻2

P ⁻2 × 5
Q 2 × ⁻2
R 3 × ⁻4
S 2 × 0

- Can you continue these patterns?

4 × 3 = 12
4 × 2 = 8
4 × 1 =
4 × 0 =
4 × ⁻1 =
4 × ⁻2 =
4 × ⁻3 =

⁻2 × 3 = ⁻6
⁻2 × 2 = ⁻4
⁻2 × 1 =
⁻2 × 0 =
⁻2 × ⁻1 =
⁻2 × ⁻2 =
⁻2 × ⁻3 =

- Can you complete this multiplication grid, supplied on sheet F1–30?

×	4	3	2	1	0	⁻1	⁻2	⁻3	⁻4
4	16	12	8						
3									
2									
1									
0									
⁻1									
⁻2									
⁻3									
⁻4									

- Can you find rules for multiplying positive and negative numbers?

B1 Write down the answers to these.

(a) 4 × ⁻3 (b) ⁻3 × 2 (c) 3 × ⁻3 (d) ⁻4 × 0 (e) 4 × ⁻1
(f) ⁻2 × ⁻3 (g) ⁻4 × ⁻3 (h) 1 × 4 (i) ⁻3 × ⁻3 (j) ⁻2 × ⁻4

36 Calculating with negative numbers 257

Rules for multiplying positive and negative numbers

negative × positive   ⁻5 × 4 = ⁻20

positive × positive   5 × 4 = 20

→ negative

positive × negative   5 × ⁻4 = ⁻20

negative × negative   ⁻5 × ⁻4 = 20

→ positive

B2 Calculate these.

(a) 6 × ⁻4   (b) ⁻5 × ⁻3   (c) ⁻2 × 5   (d) 3 × 7   (e) ⁻3 × 7

(f) ⁻3 × ⁻7   (g) 3 × ⁻7   (h) 2 × 6 × ⁻3   (i) ⁻5 × ⁻7 × 2   (j) ⁻4 × ⁻1 × ⁻2

B3 Copy and complete these multiplication grids.

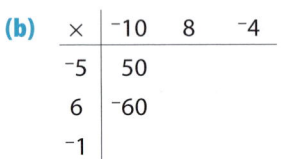

(a)
×	4	⁻3	2
5	20	⁻15	
⁻2			
⁻4			

(b)
×	⁻10	8	⁻4
⁻5	50		
6	⁻60		
⁻1			

B4 This is a 'multiplication wall'.

The number on each brick is found by multiplying the two numbers on the bricks below.

What will be the number on the top brick of this wall?

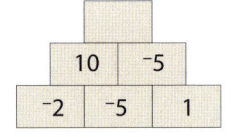

          [ ]
       [10][⁻5]
     [⁻2][⁻5][1]

B5 Copy and complete these multiplication walls.

(a)
        [ ]
      [ ][ ]
    [⁻2][3][⁻1]

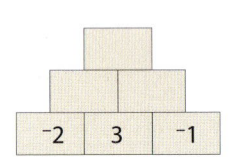

(b)
        [ ]
      [ ][ ]
    [⁻3][⁻4][2]

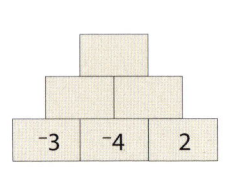

(c)
          [ ]
        [ ][ ]
      [ ][ ][ ]
    [⁻2][2][⁻1][3]

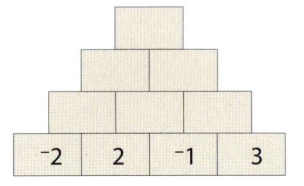

B6 Find the missing number in each calculation.

(a) 5 × ■ = ⁻30   (b) ⁻4 × ■ = ⁻28   (c) ■ × ⁻3 = 15   (d) ■ × ⁻4 = 24

B7 Copy and complete these multiplication walls.

(a)
       [⁻80]
     [ ][8]
   [ ][ ][⁻4]

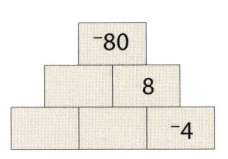

(b)
        [72]
      [ ][⁻6]
    [⁻4][ ][ ]

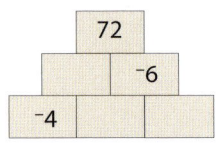

(c)
          [⁻120]
        [⁻6][ ]
      [ ][ ][⁻10]
    [ ][⁻1][ ][ ]

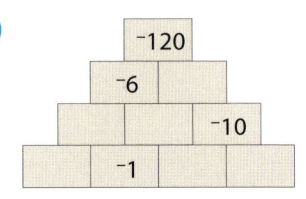

B8 Copy and complete these multiplication grids.

(a)
×	5	⁻3
	10	
⁻3	⁻15	

(b)
×		5	
		⁻15	
⁻1	5		⁻6
	⁻20	20	

(c)
×			⁻2
	1		
⁻4	12	0	
			⁻10

*__B9__ In this grid each letter corresponds to a number.
For example, K corresponds to 20 because 5 × 4 = 20.

×	2	⁻3	4	⁻6
⁻2	A	B	C	D
⁻3	E	F	G	H
5	I	J	K	L
⁻5	M	N	O	P

(a) What number corresponds to the letter J?
(b) What letter corresponds to the number ⁻10?
(c) For each set of numbers, work out the corresponding letters to spell a word.
    (i) 30, ⁻4, ⁻8, 20   (ii) 9, 10, 15, 12   (iii) ⁻12, ⁻30, ⁻20, 6, ⁻6

*__B10__ Do the multiplication wall puzzles on sheet F1–31.

C Dividing

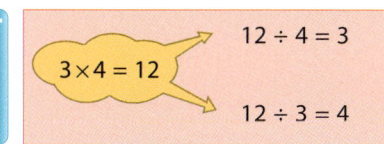

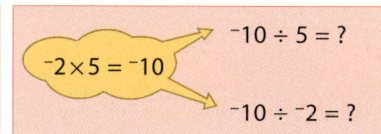

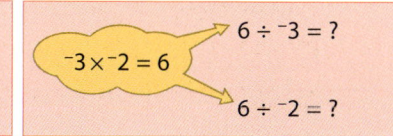

3 × 4 = 12 → 12 ÷ 4 = 3 ; 12 ÷ 3 = 4

⁻2 × 5 = ⁻10 → ⁻10 ÷ 5 = ? ; ⁻10 ÷ ⁻2 = ?

⁻3 × ⁻2 = 6 → 6 ÷ ⁻3 = ? ; 6 ÷ ⁻2 = ?

C1 Work these out.
(a) 12 ÷ ⁻2   (b) ⁻8 ÷ 4   (c) ⁻6 ÷ ⁻3   (d) ⁻14 ÷ ⁻2
(e) 20 ÷ ⁻5   (f) ⁻30 ÷ 10   (g) ⁻15 ÷ ⁻5   (h) ⁻16 ÷ ⁻8

C2 Find the missing number in each calculation.
(a) 30 ÷ ■ = ⁻15   (b) ⁻20 ÷ ■ = ⁻4   (c) ■ ÷ ⁻3 = 4
(d) ■ ÷ ⁻4 = 6   (e) ⁻25 ÷ ■ = 5   (f) ■ ÷ ⁻6 = ⁻3

C3 Choose pairs of numbers from the loop to make these calculations correct.
(a) ■ ÷ ■ = ⁻3   (b) ■ ÷ ■ = 2
(c) ■ ÷ ■ = 4   (d) ■ ÷ ■ = ⁻5

(⁻10, ⁻12, 3, 5, ⁻5, ⁻3, ⁻15, ⁻4)

36 Calculating with negative numbers

Rules for dividing positive and negative numbers

negative ÷ positive → ⁻20 ÷ 4 = ⁻5 → negative

positive ÷ negative → 20 ÷ ⁻4 = ⁻5 → negative

positive ÷ positive → 20 ÷ 4 = 5 → positive

negative ÷ negative → ⁻20 ÷ ⁻4 = 5 → positive

C4 Calculate these.
(a) 5 × ⁻2
(b) ⁻20 ÷ ⁻10
(c) ⁻30 ÷ 6
(d) ⁻4 × ⁻8
(e) ⁻5 × 8
(f) ⁻35 ÷ ⁻5
(g) 6 × ⁻4
(h) 18 ÷ ⁻9
(i) ⁻25 ÷ ⁻5
(j) ⁻7 × ⁻9

C5 Find the missing number in each calculation.
(a) 7 × ■ = ⁻28
(b) ⁻5 × ■ = 30
(c) ■ ÷ 2 = ⁻6
(d) ■ × 4 = ⁻16
(e) ■ ÷ ⁻7 = ⁻2
(f) ■ × ⁻4 = ⁻40
(g) ■ × ⁻9 = ⁻27
(h) ⁻45 ÷ ■ = 9
(i) 24 ÷ ■ = ⁻3

C6 Here is a number machine chain.

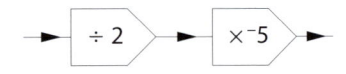

→ ÷ 2 → × ⁻5 →

Find the output for each of these inputs.
(a) 10
(b) ⁻8
(c) ⁻2

C7 Choose pairs of numbers from the loop to make these calculations correct.
(a) ■ ÷ ■ = ⁻3
(b) ■ × ■ = 14
(c) ■ × ■ = ⁻6
(d) ■ ÷ ■ = ⁻5
(e) ■ ÷ ■ = 5
(f) ■ × ■ = ⁻63

⁻7   ⁻3   3   10
  7   ⁻2   21   ⁻10

C8 Use two numbers from 6, ⁻15, 3, ⁻3 and × or ÷ to get the following results.
(a) 2
(b) ⁻2
(c) ⁻9
(d) 45
(e) 5

C9 Use two numbers from 12, ⁻12, 3, ⁻6 and × or ÷ to get the following results.
(a) 2
(b) 72
(c) ⁻4
(d) ⁻2
(e) ⁻36

*C10 Here is a number machine chain.

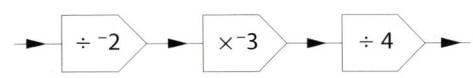

→ ÷ ⁻2 → × ⁻3 → ÷ 4 →

(a) Find the output for an input of ⁻16.
(b) Which input gives an output of 9?

260　36 Calculating with negative numbers

D Negative square roots and cube roots

D1 (a) Copy and complete $(^-5)^2 = {}^-5 \times {}^-5 = \ldots$

(b) Work out (i) $(^-3)^2$ (ii) $(^-4)^2$ (iii) $(^-8)^2$

---

6 squared is $6^2 = 6 \times 6 = 36$ so the **positive square root** of 36 is 6.

$(^-6)$ squared is $(^-6)^2 = {}^-6 \times {}^-6 = 36$ so the **negative square root** of 36 is $^-6$.

D2 (a) Write down the positive square root of 100.

(b) Write down the negative square root of 100.

D3 What is the negative square root of 81?

D4 Find two numbers that fit each statement.

(a) ■² = 49   (b) ■² = 4   (c) ■² = 1   (d) ■² = 64

D5 Write down

(a) the negative square root of 144

(b) the negative square root of 196

D6 (a) Copy and complete $(^-2)^3 = {}^-2 \times {}^-2 \times {}^-2 = \ldots$

(b) Work out (i) $(^-1)^3$ (ii) $(^-5)^3$ (iii) $(^-6)^3$

---

4 cubed is $4^3 = 4 \times 4 \times 4 = 64$ so the **cube root** of 64 is 4.

$(^-4)$ cubed is $(^-4)^3 = {}^-4 \times {}^-4 \times {}^-4 = {}^-64$ so the **cube root** of $^-64$ is $^-4$.

D7 Find the cube root of each of these.

(a) 8   (b) 27   (c) $^-8$ (d) $^-27$ (e) 125

D8 (a) A cube has a volume of 1000 cm³.
What is the length of one edge?

(b) What is the cube root of 1000?

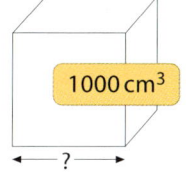

1000 cm³

?

D9 Copy and complete these.

(a) $2^■ = 8$ (b) $(^-■)^2 = 121$ (c) $(^-5)^3 = ■$ (d) $(■)^3 = {}^-1$

(e) $(^-13)^2 = ■$ (f) $4^■ = 64$ (g) $(^-■)^2 = 225$ (h) $(■)^3 = {}^-1000$

36 Calculating with negative numbers

E Mixed questions

E1 Work these out.

(a) $3 + {}^-10$
(b) $5 \times {}^-6$
(c) $5 - 9$
(d) $10 \div {}^-2$
(e) ${}^-7 + {}^-2$
(f) ${}^-4 \times {}^-5$
(g) ${}^-16 \div 8$
(h) $({}^-10)^2$
(i) ${}^-12 \div {}^-6$
(j) $6 - {}^-1$

E2 Work these out.

(a) $2 + {}^-6 + {}^-3$
(b) $2 - 3 - 4$
(c) $3 \times {}^-2 \times {}^-4$
(d) ${}^-3 \times {}^-2 \times {}^-7$

E3 Calculate these.

(a) $(2 + {}^-3) \times 5$
(b) $4 \times (2 - 9)$
(c) $(1 - 4)^2$
(d) $({}^-1 + {}^-4) \times {}^-3$
(e) $\dfrac{{}^-1 + {}^-5}{2}$
(f) $\dfrac{3 \times {}^-6}{9}$
(g) $\dfrac{2 - 11}{{}^-3}$
(h) $\dfrac{({}^-6)^2}{{}^-9}$

E4 Find the missing number in each calculation.

(a) $6 - \blacksquare = {}^-4$
(b) $\blacksquare \times {}^-3 = 27$
(c) $\blacksquare \div 5 = {}^-4$
(d) $2 + \blacksquare + {}^-4 = {}^-3$
(e) ${}^-2 \times \blacksquare = {}^-18$
(f) ${}^-24 \div \blacksquare = 3$

E5 This table shows the lowest temperatures each day for a week in Glasgow in winter.

Day	Mon	Tue	Wed	Thur	Fri	Sat	Sun
Temperature (°C)	${}^-7$	3	${}^-6$	2	${}^-3$	${}^-7$	${}^-3$

(a) Which days of the week were coldest?
(b) What was the difference between the highest and lowest temperatures in the table?
(c) Calculate the mean of the temperatures in the table.

E6 A sequence begins $2, {}^-6, 10, {}^-22, \ldots$

A rule to continue this sequence is

> Add 1 to the last number and then multiply by ${}^-2$.

What are the next two numbers in this sequence?

E7 Here is a number machine chain.
Find the output for each of these inputs.

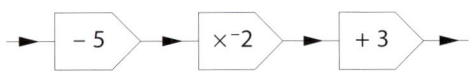

$\rightarrow \boxed{-5} \rightarrow \boxed{\times {}^-2} \rightarrow \boxed{+3} \rightarrow$

(a) 8
(b) 1
(c) ${}^-5$

E8 Choose numbers from the loop to make these calculations correct.

(a) $\blacksquare \div \blacksquare = {}^-3$
(b) $\blacksquare \times \blacksquare = {}^-16$
(c) $\blacksquare \times \blacksquare \times \blacksquare = 24$
(d) $(\blacksquare)^3 = {}^-27$
(e) $3 \times (\blacksquare)^2 = 48$
(f) $(\blacksquare)^3 \div 8 = {}^-8$

Loop: $2, {}^-2, 3, {}^-3, {}^-4, 8, 9$

E9 Work out the value of each of these expressions when $x = {}^-6$.

(a) $12 - x$
(b) $2x + 3$
(c) x^2
(d) $10 + 3x$

E10 A rough formula for conversion of temperatures is

$$F = 2C + 30$$

where C is the temperature in °C
and F is the temperature is °F.

What is the value of F when

(a) $C = 10$
(b) $C = {}^-11$
(c) $C = {}^-15$
(d) $C = {}^-18$

E11 Use two numbers from 6, 9, $^-2$, $^-10$ and $+$, $-$, $\times$ or $\div$ to get the following results.

(a) $^-4$
(b) $^-11$
(c) 16
(d) $^-18$
(e) 5

Test yourself

T1 Calculate these.

(a) $3 \times {}^-4$
(b) $^-5 \times 5$
(c) $^-6 \times {}^-3$
(d) $(^-5)^2$
(e) $^-3 \times {}^-2 \times 4$

T2 Calculate these.

(a) $^-12 \div 4$
(b) $^-8 \div {}^-4$
(c) $14 \div {}^-7$
(d) $^-18 \div {}^-2$
(e) $^-36 \div 9$

T3 Calculate these.

(a) $^-6 \times {}^-3$
(b) $^-6 \div {}^-3$
(c) $^-12 \times 2$
(d) $^-12 \div 2$
(e) $^-2 \times {}^-3 \times {}^-1$

T4 Find the missing number in each calculation.

(a) $3 \times \square = {}^-24$
(b) $^-2 \times \square = 12$
(c) $\square \div 3 = {}^-4$
(d) $\square \div {}^-3 = 5$
(e) $15 \div \square = {}^-5$
(f) $\square \times {}^-6 = {}^-18$

T5 Write down

(a) the negative square root of 121
(b) the cube root of $^-125$

T6 Choose pairs of numbers from the loop to make these calculations correct.

(a) $\square + \square = {}^-6$
(b) $\square \times \square = {}^-15$
(c) $\square - \square = {}^-8$
(d) $\square \div \square = {}^-4$
(e) $\square + \square = {}^-13$
(f) $\square \times \square = 40$

$^-5 \quad ^-7 \quad 3 \quad ^-8 \quad 2 \quad 5$

T7 Calculate these.

(a) $(1 - 4) \times {}^-2$
(b) $\dfrac{^-2 + {}^-7}{^-3}$
(c) $^-4 \times (1 - {}^-3)$
(d) $\dfrac{^-1 \times {}^-5 \times 6}{2}$

37 Brackets

You need to know how to simplify expressions like $2a + 3 - a + 5$ and $4s \times 2$.

This work will help you
- simplify simple divisions
- multiply out brackets
- factorise expressions using brackets

You need sheets F1–32 and F1–33.

A Dividing an expression by a number

So $2n \times 4 = 8n$

So $8n \div 4 = 2n$ or $\dfrac{8n}{4} = 2n$

A1 Find the missing number or expression in each statement.

(a) ■ $\times 5n = 10n$ (b) $2y \times$ ■ $= 6y$ (c) ■ $\times 5 = 30a$ (d) $4 \times$ ■ $= 28b$

A2 Simplify each division.

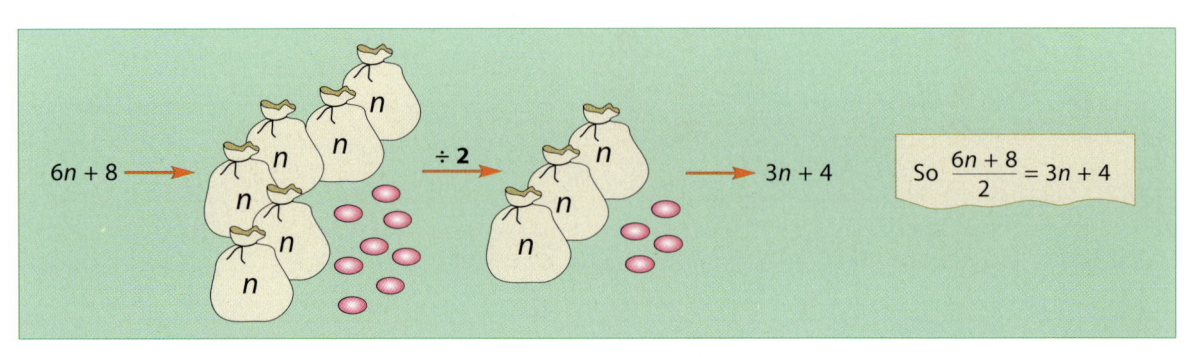

(a) $\dfrac{4n}{2}$ (b) $\dfrac{6a}{3}$ (c) $\dfrac{15y}{5}$ (d) $\dfrac{20x}{4}$ (e) $\dfrac{36b}{9}$

So $\dfrac{6n + 8}{2} = 3n + 4$

A3 Simplify these.

(a) $\dfrac{4n + 6}{2}$ (b) $\dfrac{15n + 10}{5}$ (c) $\dfrac{5p + 10}{5}$ (d) $\dfrac{18 + 12w}{3}$

B Expressions with brackets

Here is a box of crisps.
We don't know how many packets are in one box.
So let n stand for the number of packets in a box.

n

Here is one box and 2 more packets.
So here we have $n + 2$ packets.

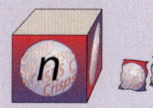

$n + 2$

Here are 3 lots of 'a box and 2 packets'.   It is the same as 3 boxes and 6 packets.

$3(n + 2)$

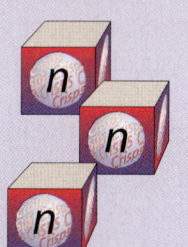

$3n + 6$

$3(n + 2)$ and $3n + 6$ are called **equivalent expressions**.

B1 There are three pairs of equivalent expressions here.
Pair them up and find the odd one left over.

| $2(x + 4)$ | $2(x + 16)$ | $2x + 4$ | $2(x + 8)$ | $2x + 16$ | $2(x + 2)$ | $2x + 8$ |

B2 There are three pairs of equivalent expressions here.
Pair them up and find the odd one left over.

| $3a + 18$ | $3(a - 2)$ | $3a - 6$ | $3(a + 6)$ | $3a - 18$ | $3(a - 6)$ | $3a - 2$ |

B3 Multiply out the brackets in each of these expressions.

(a) $2(x + 5)$ (b) $3(y + 3)$ (c) $5(p - 6)$ (d) $10(7 + q)$ (e) $4(v - 5)$

Each term inside the brackets
is multiplied by the number outside. $5(3x + 4) = 5 \times 3x + 5 \times 4 = 15x + 20$

B4 Multiply out the brackets in each of these expressions.

(a) $3(2x + 4)$ (b) $2(4y - 3)$ (c) $6(1 + 3p)$ (d) $6(1 - 3p)$ (e) $8(5 - 3v)$

B5 Find what is missing in each of these.

(a) $2(a + 6) = 2a + \blacksquare$ (b) $\blacksquare(b + 2) = 3b + 6$ (c) $4(c + \blacksquare) = 4c + 20$

C Factorising an expression

The reverse of multiplying out an expression is called **factorising** an expression.
To **factorise completely**, you should make the factor outside the brackets as big as you can.

Examples

Factorise $6a + 18$.

$6a + 18$
$= 6(a + 3)$

Factorise $12a - 16$.

$12a - 16$
$= 4(3a - 4)$

We could write this as $2(6a - 8)$ but we would not have factorised it completely.

C1 What is the largest whole number that divides exactly into

(a) 12 and 16   (b) 20 and 18   (c) 12 and 24   (d) 14 and 21

C2 Copy each of these, filling in the missing numbers.

(a) $6a + 8 = \blacksquare(3a + 4)$ (b) $10b - 15 = \blacksquare(2b - 3)$ (c) $14c + 6 = \blacksquare(7c + 3)$

C3 Factorise each of these expressions.

(a) $2x + 8$ (b) $3y + 9$ (c) $5p - 15$ (d) $20 + 4q$ (e) $12v - 24$

C4 Factorise each of these completely.

(a) $6x + 9$ (b) $8x + 12$ (c) $25 - 15x$ (d) $9x + 12$ (e) $8x - 28$

C5

E	G	H	O	N	A	T	R	S
2	3	4	5	$x+3$	$2x+3$	$x+15$	$3x+2$	$3x+6$

Factorise each of the expressions below into two factors.
Use the code above to find the letter for each factor.

$4x + 6$ $5x + 15$ $9x + 6$

For example, $4x + 6 = 2(2x + 3)$.
The two factors are 2 and $2x + 3$. So your first two letters are E and A.

Rearrange your letters to make the name of a fruit.

C6

S	C	D	E	P	N	W	R	U	O
2	3	4	5	6	7	$x+1$	$2x+1$	$2x+3$	$3x+4$

Factorise completely the expressions in each part.
Use the letters in the code above to find three flowers.

(a) $6x + 8$ $10x + 5$

(b) $4x + 6$ $6x + 3$ $9x + 12$

(c) $7x + 7$ $4x + 2$ $18x + 24$ $12x + 16$

D Factorising more complex expressions

Sometimes a **letter** may be the factor outside a bracket.

Examples

'Expand' means 'multiply out'.

Multiply out $w(w + 3)$.   Expand $a(2a - 3)$.   Factorise $n^2 + 4n$.   Factorise $3m^2 - 5m$.

$w(w + 3)$
$= w \times w + w \times 3$
$= w^2 + 3w$

$a(2a - 3)$
$= a \times 2a - a \times 3$
$= 2a^2 - 3a$

$n^2 + 4n$
$= n \times n + n \times 4$
$= n(n + 4)$

$3m^2 - 5m$
$= m \times 3m - m \times 5$
$= m(3m - 5)$

D1 Copy each of these, filling in what is missing.
   (a) $a(a + 4) = a^2 + \blacksquare$
   (b) $b(2b - 3) = 2b^2 - \blacksquare$
   (c) $c(1 + c) = c + \blacksquare$

D2 Multiply out each of these expressions.
   (a) $n(n + 3)$
   (b) $m(m - 4)$
   (c) $r(1 + 2r)$
   (d) $s(4s - 3)$
   (e) $x(3x + 4)$
   (f) $y(3 - 5y)$

D3 Multiply out these expressions.
   (a) $4v(v + 5)$
   (b) $2w(w - 4)$
   (c) $2x(x + 1)$
   (d) $3y(2 - y)$

D4 There are three pairs of equivalent expressions here, and one left over.
Find the three pairs, and multiply out the one left over.

| $n(2n + 3)$ | $n^2 + n$ | $n(3n + 2)$ | $2n^2 + 3n$ | $n(n + 1)$ | $3n^2 + 2n$ | $n(2n + 1)$ |

D5 Copy each of these, filling in what is missing.
   (a) $n(\blacksquare + 2) = n^2 + 2n$
   (b) $\blacksquare(n + 3) = n^2 + 3n$
   (c) $n(n + \blacksquare) = n^2 + 4n$

D6 Factorise each of these expressions.
   (a) $m^2 + 9m$
   (b) $n^2 - 5n$
   (c) $2x^2 + x$
   (d) $3y^2 - 5y$
   (e) $3p + 4p^2$
   (f) $2q - 5q^2$
   (g) $v^2 + 4v$
   (h) $4w^2 - w$

Sometimes when you multiply out a bracket there may be more than one letter inside. Just multiply each term inside by whatever is outside.

Expand $3(a + 2b)$.   Expand $4(2x - 3y)$.

$3(a + 2b)$
$= 3 \times a + 3 \times 2b$
$= 3a + 6b$

$4(2x - 3y)$
$= 4 \times 2x - 4 \times 3y$
$= 8x - 12y$

D7 Expand these expressions.
   (a) $2(a + b)$
   (b) $3(f - e)$
   (c) $4(2g + h)$
   (d) $3(k - 3g)$
   (e) $4(2h + 3j)$
   (f) $5(2w + u)$

D8 Factorise these expressions.
   (a) $3a + 3b$
   (b) $3g - 6h$
   (c) $7k + 14l$
   (d) $5w + 15z$

E Adding an expression containing brackets

To add an expression containing brackets, first multiply out the brackets.

Examples

Simplify
$4 + 2(a + 3)$.

$4 + 2(a + 3)$
$= 4 + 2a + 6$
$= 2a + 10$

Simplify
$2a + 3(a - 4)$.

$2a + 3(a - 4)$
$= 2a + 3a - 12$
$= 5a - 12$

Simplify
$4(2a + 3) + 5a$.

$4(2a + 3) + 5a$
$= 8a + 12 + 5a$
$= 13a + 12$

Simplify
$2(a - 3) + 5(2a + 1)$.

$2(a - 3) + 5(2a + 1)$
$= 2a - 6 + 10a + 5$
$= 12a - 1$

E1 Simplify the following expressions.

(a) $3(z + 5) + 4$
(b) $5 + 10(b + 2)$
(c) $2(x + 8) + 3x$
(d) $2y + 3(4 + y)$
(e) $6(a - 3) + 2a$
(f) $2(4 - c) + 4c$

E2 Simplify the following expressions.

(a) $3x + 2(2x + 4)$
(b) $4(3w + 2) + 3w$
(c) $15 + 2(5 + 3z)$
(d) $4u + 2(2u - 3)$
(e) $4(3 - 5v) - 10$
(f) $50 + 12(3w - 4)$

E3 There are three pairs of equivalent expressions here. Can you find them?

P $2x + 3(2x + 3)$ **Q** $4(2x + 3) - 6$ **R** $2(4x + 3) + 3$ **S** $2x + 5(2x - 1)$ **T** $3(4x - 1) - 2$ **U** $4x + 2(2x + 3)$

E4 Simplify these.

(a) $2(a + 3) + 3(a + 2)$
(b) $4(b - 1) + 2(b + 3)$
(c) $2(5 + c) + 4(2c - 2)$

E5 This puzzle is on sheet F1–32.

F Subtracting an expression containing brackets

When subtracting an expression with brackets, you need to be careful about the signs.

Examples

Simplify $8 - (a + 3)$.

$8 - (a + 3)$
$= 8 - a - 3$
$= 5 - a$

Simplify $8 - (a - 3)$.

$8 - (a - 3)$
$= 8 - a + 3$
$= 11 - a$

Simplify $5a - 2(a + 4)$.

$5a - 2(a + 4)$
$= 5a - 2a - 8$
$= 3a - 8$

Simplify $5a - 2(a - 4)$.

$5a - 2(a - 4)$
$= 5a - 2a + 8$
$= 3a + 8$

F1 Simplify each of these expressions.

(a) $15 - (a + 2)$
(b) $8b - (2b + 5)$
(c) $12 - (c - 4)$
(d) $6d - (3d - 2)$
(e) $12 - (1 + 3e)$
(f) $6f - (8 - 2f)$

F2 Simplify each of these.
- (a) $12 - 2(n + 3)$
- (b) $7n - 3(n - 2)$
- (c) $10 - 5(n - 2)$
- (d) $8n - 3(2 + n)$
- (e) $8n - 3(2 - n)$
- (f) $15 - 3(5 - n)$

F3 Simplify these expressions.
- (a) $2x + 5 - (x + 2)$
- (b) $4(h + 2) - (3h - 1)$
- (c) $3(j - 1) - 2(1 + j)$
- (d) $5(x + 3) - 3(x + 2)$
- (e) $3(y + 4) - 2(y - 5)$
- (f) $6(z + 4) - 4(z + 5)$

F4 There are three pairs of equivalent expressions here, and an odd one out. Which is the odd one out?

$(4x + 3) - (2x + 1)$ $\quad$ $3(x + 3) - 2(x + 1)$ $\quad$ $3(2x + 1) - (4x + 1)$ $\quad$ $2(3x + 1) - 5(x - 1)$

$(2x - 3) - (x + 1)$ $\quad$ $3(x + 2) - 2(x + 1)$ $\quad$ $3(x - 2) - 2(x - 1)$

*F5 This puzzle is on sheet F1–33.

Test yourself

T1 Expand these.
- (a) $3(d + 4)$
- (b) $5(u - 2)$
- (c) $4(2 + s)$
- (d) $2(3 - y)$

T2 Multiply these out.
- (a) $2(3e + 2)$
- (b) $6(3p - 2)$
- (c) $3(1 + 2w)$
- (d) $3(1 - 2w)$

T3 Factorise these.
- (a) $3x + 6$
- (b) $7a - 14$
- (c) $8 + 12b$
- (d) $10n - 15$

T4 Expand these.
- (a) $d(d + 2)$
- (b) $u(u - 4)$
- (c) $h(2h + 3)$
- (d) $j(3j - 7)$

T5 (a) Expand $5(x - 4)$. $\quad$ (b) Expand $x(3 - x)$. $\hfill$ *Edexcel*

T6 Factorise $\quad$ (a) $x^2 + 6x$ $\quad$ (b) $a^2 - 14a$ $\quad$ (c) $2n^2 + n$ $\quad$ (d) $2n^2 - 3n$

T7 Expand these.
- (a) $3(s + 2t)$
- (b) $4(d - 3w)$
- (c) $3(2e - 2f)$
- (d) $5(3k + 2g)$

T8 Factorise these. $\quad$ (a) $4x + 4y$ $\quad$ (b) $6a + 12b$ $\quad$ (c) $5s - 10t$

T9 Simplify these.
- (a) $12 + 2(a + 1)$
- (b) $8a + 2(3 - a)$
- (c) $3a + 2(3a - 3)$
- (d) $12 + 3(4a + 2)$

T10 Simplify these.
- (a) $10 - (2 + t)$
- (b) $6x - (2x - 3)$
- (c) $8v - 2(3v + 4)$
- (d) $15 - 3(1 - 2h)$

38 Pie charts

You should know
- how to work with fractions and percentages
- how to measure angles
- that the angles at the centre of a circle add up to 360°

This work will help you draw and interpret pie charts.

You need a pie chart scale or an angle measurer.

A Review: fractions, percentages and angles

A1 In a class of 24 students there are 12 who have been to Spain on holiday.
  (a) What fraction of the students have been to Spain?
  (b) What percentage of the students is this?

A2 In a group of 40 college students only 10 of them eat breakfast.
  (a) What fraction of these students eat breakfast?
  (b) Write this fraction as a percentage.

A3 In a primary school 60 children are met by a grandparent at the end of the day. The school has 360 pupils.
What fraction of the pupils are met by a grandparent?

A4 (a) What fraction of this circle is shaded grey?
  (b) Calculate the size of the angle in the black sector.
  (c) What percentage of the circle is white?

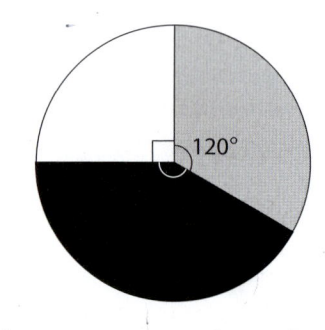

A5 Calculate (a) $\frac{1}{3}$ of 360 (b) $\frac{1}{4}$ of 360 (c) $\frac{1}{5}$ of 200 (d) $\frac{1}{8}$ of 160

A6 In a secondary school, $\frac{1}{4}$ of the students like swimming.
200 students like swimming.
How many students in total go to this school?

A7 Calculate (a) 25% of 180 (b) 20% of 300 (c) 40% of 300

A8 Use a calculator to find these.
  (a) 13% of 400 (b) 56% of 250 (c) 28% of 1400 (d) 7% of 2500

B Reading a pie chart: simple fractions and percentages

B1 This chart shows sales of ice creams at a school fête.
The total number of ice creams sold was 600.

(a) What flavour of ice cream sold the worst?
(b) What fraction of the ice creams sold were chocolate?
(c) How many ice creams sold were chocolate?
(d) What fraction of the ice creams were vanilla?
(e) How many vanilla ice creams were sold?
(f) Calculate the size of the angle for the strawberry ice creams.
(g) How many strawberry ice creams were sold?
(h) How many mint ice creams were sold?

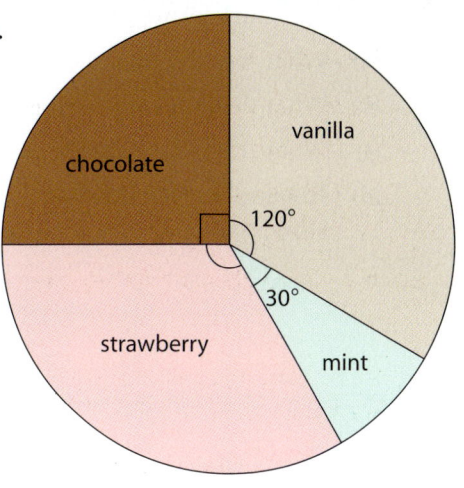

B2 This pie chart shows how Heather spent a typical Monday.

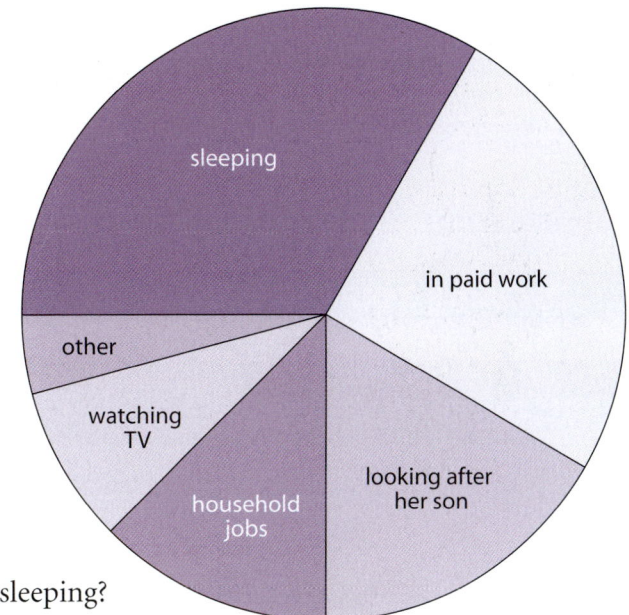

(a) Measure the angle for the time she spent sleeping.
(b) What fraction of the day did she spend sleeping?
(c) How many hours did she spend sleeping?
(d) (i) Copy and complete this table for Heather's day.

Activity	Angle	Number of hours
Sleeping		
In paid work		

(ii) Check that the total number of hours is 24.

38 Pie charts   271

B3 Leon did a survey to find out how people kept up-to-date with the news. The pie chart shows his results.

(a) What was the most common reply?
(b) What percentage of people said 'internet'?
(c) What fraction of people said 'newspaper'?
(d) 40 people said 'radio'. How many people did Leon ask altogether?

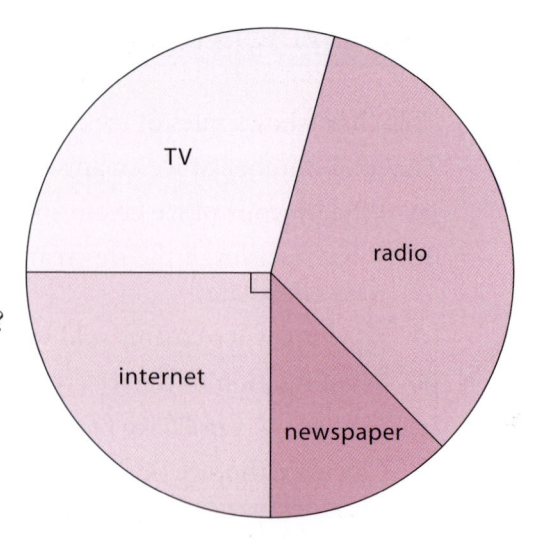

B4 24 students were asked to name their favourite chocolates. The pie chart shows the results.

(a) What fraction of the students chose truffle?
(b) Work out the size of the angle for cream.
(c) How many of the 24 students chose toffee?

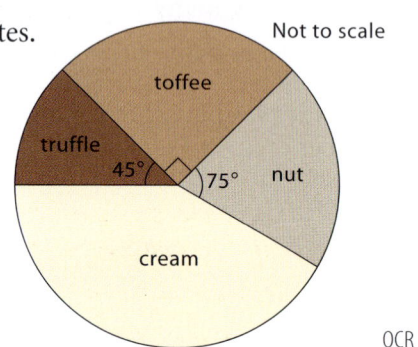

OCR

C Reading a pie chart: the unitary method

900 school students were asked:

'What is the first thing you usually do when you get home from school?'

Their replies are shown in the pie chart below.

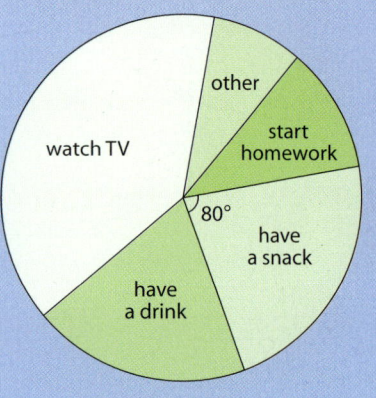

How many students usually have a snack?

Angle		Number of students
360°	shows	900
1°	shows	2.5
80°	shows	200

÷ 360, × 80

First find out what 1° shows.
Then find out what 80° shows.

So 200 students usually have a snack.

- How many students usually watch TV?

272 38 Pie charts

C1 720 cars were sold at an auction.
The pie chart shows the countries where they were made.

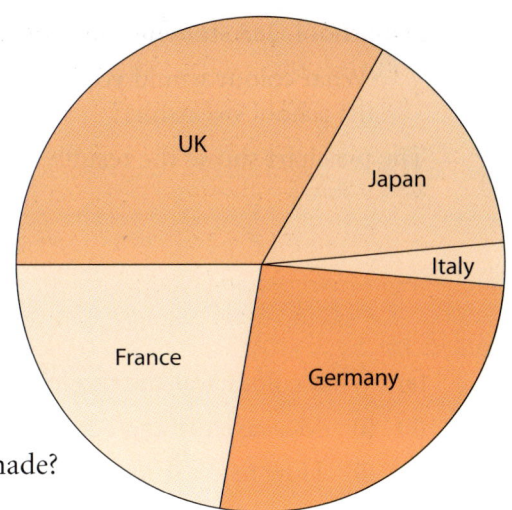

(a) In which country were most of these cars made?
(b) How many cars are represented by 1°?
(c) (i) Measure the angle for the cars made in France.
   (ii) How many of the cars sold were made in France?
(d) Work out the number of cars made in
   (i) Germany   (ii) Japan   (iii) UK   (iv) Italy

C2 Sue recorded the ducks she saw on a pond one afternoon.
The pie chart shows her results.

(a) What fraction of these ducks were Mallards?

She saw 36 Mallards.

(b) How many ducks did Sue see altogether?
(c) How many Teals did she see?
Show your working clearly.
(d) (i) Calculate the angle for Shovelers.
   (ii) How many Shovelers did she see?

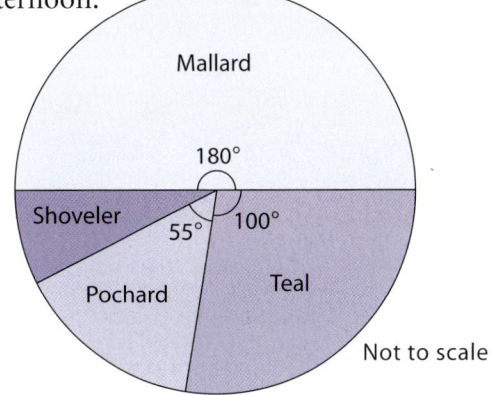

C3 This pie chart gives information about the types of DVD rented from a shop one day.

(a) What fraction of the DVDs were children's?

There were 80 action DVDs rented.

(b) How many DVDs were rented altogether?
(c) How many comedy DVDs were rented?

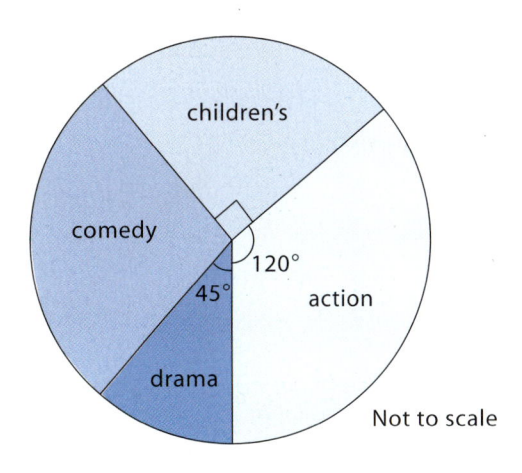

C4 In a school, 288 students were asked:

'What colour would you like for the school sweatshirt?'

The pie chart shows the results.

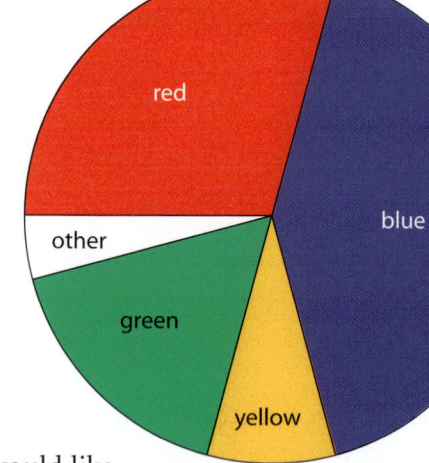

(a) What colour was the mode?
(b) (i) Measure the angle for red.
   (ii) How many students would like red?
(c) Work out the number of students who would like
   (i) blue   (ii) green   (iii) yellow

D Drawing a pie chart: angles

This table shows how Tom spent his weekly allowance of £20 last week.

Item	Amount
Clothes	£8
Savings	£5
Music	£4
Magazines and sweets	£3

We can use an angle measurer to show this information on a pie chart.

First, work out the angles to use.

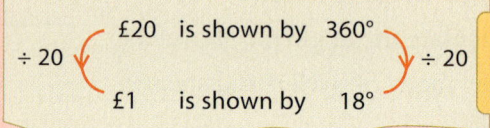

£20 is shown by 360°
÷ 20 ↓   ↓ ÷ 20
£1 is shown by 18°

Divide 360° by 20 to work out the angle for £1.

Item	Amount	Angle
Clothes	£8	8 × 18° = 144°
Savings	£5	5 × 18° = 90°
Music	£4	4 × 18° = 72°
Magazines and sweets	£3	3 × 18° = 54°
Totals	£20	360°

Work out the total as a check.

274   38 Pie charts

D1 Kerry records the eye colour of the people in her class.

(a) How many people are there in her class?

(b) In a pie chart, what angle will represent 1 person?

(c) What will be the angle for people with blue eyes?

(d) Work out all the angles and draw the pie chart. Label each sector.

Colour	Frequency
Brown	10
Blue	4
Green	3
Grey	1

D2 Sam is a car salesman.
He records the number of cars of each make that he sells in a month.

Draw and label a pie chart to represent this information.

Make	Frequency
Ford	16
Rover	10
Vauxhall	6
BMW	4

AQA

D3 In an English lesson, the 24 pupils in a class were each asked to write down the first vowel in their name.

The table shows the information.

The information can be shown in a pie chart.
Construct the pie chart.

First vowel in a pupil's name	Number of pupils
A	6
E	3
I	5
O	8
U	2

Edexcel

D4 One evening, 30 people used a sports centre.
The activities they took part in are shown in the table.

Activity	Gym	Swimming	Squash	Aerobics
Frequency	12	3	6	9

Draw a pie chart to show this information.

D5 Pali asked 180 boys what was their favourite sport.
Here are his results.

Sport	Soccer	Rugby	Cricket	Basketball	Other
Number of boys	74	25	18	37	26

(a) Draw a pie chart to show these results.

Pali also asked 90 girls about their favourite sport.
In a pie chart showing the results, the angle for tennis was 84°.

(b) How many of these girls said that tennis was their favourite sport?

OCR

38 Pie charts 275

E Drawing a pie chart: percentages

This table shows how Tom spent his weekly allowance of £20 last week.

Item	Amount
Clothes	£8
Savings	£5
Music	£4
Magazines and sweets	£3

We can use a pie chart scale to show this information on a pie chart.

First, work out the percentages to use.

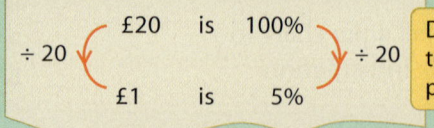

£20 is 100%
÷ 20 ↓   ↓ ÷ 20
£1 is 5%

Divide 100% by 20 to work out the percentage for £1.

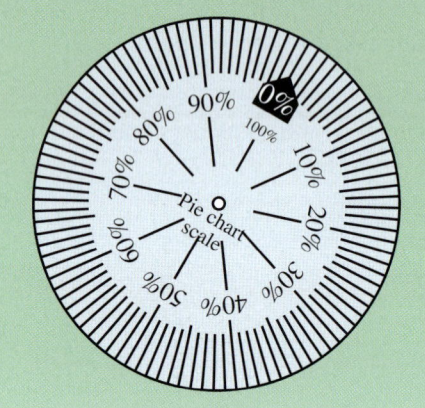

Item	Amount	Angle
Clothes	£8	8 × 5% = 40%
Savings	£5	5 × 5% = 25%
Music	£4	4 × 5% = 20%
Magazines and sweets	£3	3 × 5% = 15%
Totals	£20	100%

Work out the total as a check.

E1 This table shows the percentage of plain chocolate which is water, protein, fat or carbohydrate.

Water	Protein	Fat	Carbohydrate
1%	5%	29%	65%

Draw and label a pie chart to show this information.

OCR

E2 Karen records the eye colour of the people in her class.

(a) How many people are there in her class?
(b) What percentage of the class is 1 person?
(c) What percentage of the class have blue eyes?
(d) Work out all the percentages and draw the pie chart. Label each sector.

Colour	Frequency
Brown	13
Blue	8
Green	3
Grey	1

276 38 Pie charts

E3 Paul asked 50 boys what was their favourite fruit.
Here are his results.

Fruit	Apple	Orange	Banana	Grapes	Other
Number of boys	8	6	20	9	7

(a) Draw a pie chart to show these results.

Paul also asked some girls about their favourite fruit.
This pie chart shows the results.

(b) State one way in which the girls' and boys' results are similar.

(c) State one way in which the girls' results are different from the boys' results.

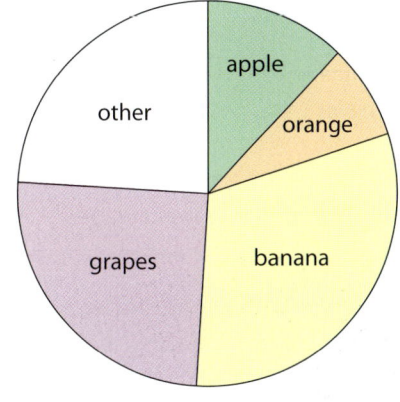

OCR

E4 This table shows the percentage of people of different categories injured in road accidents in one English county.

Category	Percentage of people injured in road accidents
Car occupants	62
Pedestrians	11
Cyclists	12
Motorcyclists	10
Occupants of heavy vehicles	5

(a) Altogether 8859 people were injured.
How many car occupants were injured?

(b) This table shows the **number** of people of different categories injured in one town.

Draw and label a pie chart to represent this information.
Show your working.

Category	Number
Vehicle occupants	72
Pedestrians	45
Cyclists	18
Motorcyclists	15

OCR

38 Pie charts 277

F Handling real data

Beth and Geeta are working on a project on eating habits.

Beth investigates ready meals … … and Geeta looks at vegetarian meals.

I eat ready meals …	Number of people
… always	8
… usually	10
… sometimes	23
… never	5

I eat vegetarian meals …	Number of people
… always	5
… usually	11
… sometimes	43
… never	2

- Can you show each of these sets of information in a pie chart?

  Use either angles or percentages.
  Don't round until the end of each calculation.

- Try one of these surveys in your class.
  Compare the results for your class with Beth's or Geeta's.

When you work with real data, the percentages or angles will often need to be rounded to the nearest whole number.

This may mean the sum of percentages is not 100%, or the sum of angles is not 360°. The simplest solution is to adjust the largest sector by 1% or 1° to give the correct total.

F1 Julia asked 150 people what was their favourite crisp flavour.

Flavour	Ready salted	Salt and vinegar	Cheese and onion	Other
Number of people	21	50	64	15

(a) Draw a pie chart to show this information.

(b) Try Julia's survey on your class and draw a pie chart to show the information. How do the results of your survey compare with Julia's?

F2 Ken asked his classmates what was their favourite fruit.

Fruit	Apple	Banana	Orange	Grape	Other
Number of people	5	10	3	6	3

(a) How many people are there in Ken's class?

(b) Draw a pie chart to illustrate this information.

F3 In a 1996 survey, a total of 2975 families with dependent children were asked who looked after the children.

The results are shown in the table.

Draw a pie chart to show these results.

Main carer	Number of families
Couple	2352
Widowed, divorced or separated mother	357
Single mother	208
Lone father	58

F4 In a 1996 survey, a total of 9128 people were asked what type of home they lived in.

Here are the results.

Draw a pie chart to show these results.

Type of home	Frequency
Detached house	1917
Semi-detached house	2921
Terraced house	2465
Flat or maisonette	1825

Test yourself

T1 The pie chart shows the proportions of complaints made about different parts of the Health Service last year.

(a) What fraction of the complaints were made about doctors?

(b) There were 400 complaints made about hospitals. How many complaints were made altogether?

(c) Work out the number of complaints made about dentists.

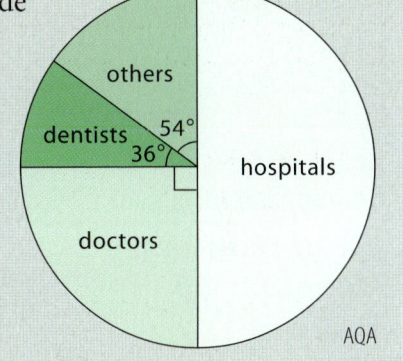

AQA

T2 The table gives information about the medals won by Austria in the 2002 Winter Olympic Games.

Draw an accurate pie chart to show this information.

Medal	Frequency
Gold	3
Silver	4
Bronze	11

Edexcel

T3 There are 240 houses on a housing estate. The table shows the total number of each type of house.

Draw and label a pie chart to represent the information in the table.

Type of house	Frequency
Semi-detached	30
3 bedroom detached	60
4 bedroom detached	68
Terraced	82

AQA

39 Working with expressions 3

This work will help you

- substitute positive and negative numbers into expressions
- simplify expressions such as $2a \times 3b$ and $2y \times y$
- simplify expressions such as $2ab + 3ab$

You need sheets F1–34, F1–35 and F1–36.

A Substituting into linear expressions

Brackets are worked out first.
Multiplications and divisions are worked out before additions and subtractions.

Examples

Find the value of
$3n - 1$ when $n = 2$.

$3n - 1 = 3 \times 2 - 1$
$ = 6 - 1$
$ = 5$

Find the value of
$3(n - 1)$ when $n = 5$.

$3(n - 1) = 3 \times (5 - 1)$
$ = 3 \times 4$
$ = 12$

Find the value of
$\dfrac{x - 5}{2}$ when $x = 11$.

$\dfrac{x - 5}{2} = \dfrac{11 - 5}{2}$
$\phantom{\dfrac{x - 5}{2}} = \dfrac{6}{2}$
$\phantom{\dfrac{x - 5}{2}} = 3$

Be expressive! a game for two players

You need sheet F1–34.
Players take turns.

Player 1
Pick any expression from the expression box.
Put the substitution value into the expression, and work out the result.
Put a cross on the square with that result in it.
Then cross out the expression you used.

Player 2
Do the same, but draw a circle on the square with the result in.

Winner
The first player with three in a line is the winner.

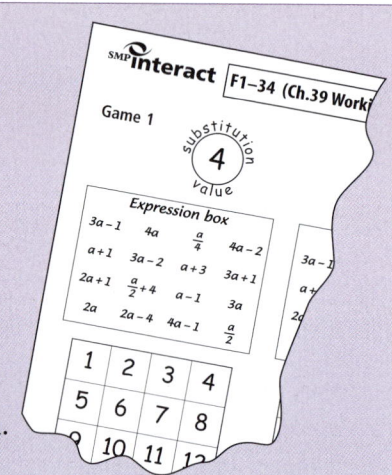

A1 For each pair of expressions, say which is larger when $n = 6$.

(a) $3n$ and $n + 8$ (b) $\dfrac{n}{2}$ and $n - 4$ (c) $2n$ and $n + 5$

A2 Find the value of each of these expressions when $x = 8$.
(a) $3x + 1$
(b) $4x - 5$
(c) $\dfrac{x}{2} + 3$
(d) $2x - 16$
(e) $\dfrac{x}{2} - 1$
(f) $2(x + 7)$
(g) $\dfrac{x + 4}{2}$
(h) $\dfrac{x - 4}{4}$

A3 In each part, work out which expression is biggest when $a = 5$.
(a) $3a - 12$ $\dfrac{a + 9}{2}$ $5a - 20$ $2a + 1$
(b) $\dfrac{a}{5} + 10$ $4a - 10$ $2(a + 1)$ $\dfrac{a + 13}{2}$

A4 Copy and complete this working to evaluate $3a + 8$ when $a = {}^-2$.

When $a = {}^-2$, $3a + 8$
$= 3 \times {}^-2 + 8$
$= \blacklozenge + 8$
$= \blacklozenge$

A5 Evaluate each of these expressions when $x = {}^-2$.
(a) $2x$
(b) $4x$
(c) $2x + 5$
(d) $2(x + 5)$
(e) $3x + 1$

A6 Evaluate each of these expressions when $x = {}^-10$.
(a) $\dfrac{x}{2}$
(b) $\dfrac{x}{5}$
(c) $\dfrac{x}{2} - 6$
(d) $\dfrac{x + 16}{3}$
(e) $\dfrac{x + 2}{4}$

B Squares and cubes

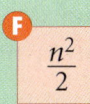

A n^2 **B** n^3 **C** $n^2 + 5$ **D** $n^3 - 1$ **E** $2n^2$ **F** $\dfrac{n^2}{2}$

- Find the value of each expression when $n = 5$.
- Which expression has the highest value when $n = 2$?
- Which expression has the lowest value when $n = 6$?

B1 Find the value of each of these expressions when $n = 4$.
(a) n^2
(b) n^3
(c) $n^2 - 5$
(d) $n^3 + 6$

B2 Evaluate each of these when $x = 3$.
(a) x^2
(b) x^3
(c) $x^2 + 10$
(d) $x^3 - 7$
(e) $3x^2$
(f) $2x^3$
(g) $5x^2$
(h) $\dfrac{x^3}{9}$

B3 Copy and complete this working to find the value of $20 - n^2$ when $n = 4$.

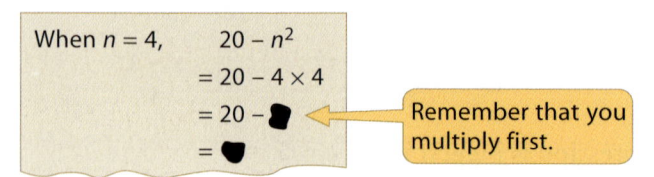

When $n = 4$, $\quad 20 - n^2$
$= 20 - 4 \times 4$
$= 20 - \blacksquare$
$= \blacksquare$

Remember that you multiply first.

B4 Find the value of each of these expressions when $n = 2$.
 (a) $3 + n^2$ (b) $5 - n^2$ (c) $9 + n^3$ (d) $10 - n^3$

B5 Find the value of a^2 when $a = 1$.

B6 Use a calculator to find the value each of these when $x = 15$.
 (a) x^2 (b) x^3 (c) $x^2 + 16$ (d) $x^3 - 25$
 (e) $7x^2$ (f) $3x^3$ (g) $\dfrac{x^2}{25}$ (h) $\dfrac{x^3}{45}$

B7 When a car brakes it leaves skid marks on the road.
This rule tells you roughly how long a skid will be in metres.
$$L = \dfrac{s^2}{75}$$
L is the length of the skid in metres; s is the speed in miles per hour (m.p.h.).
 (a) Work out L when $s = 30$.
 (b) A car is moving at 15 m.p.h. and then skids to a stop.
     Roughly how long will the skid marks be?
 (c) Roughly how long will the skid marks be for a car moving at 45 m.p.h?
 (d) How long will the skid marks be for a car moving at 70 m.p.h?
     Give your answer correct to the nearest metre.
 (e) A car is travelling straight towards a wall at 90 m.p.h.
     The wall is 80 metres away when the driver begins braking.
     Will the car hit the wall?

B8 (a) Copy and complete:
 $(^-3)^2 = {^-3} \times {^-3} = \ldots\ldots$
 (b) What is the value of n^2 when $n = {^-5}$?

B9 Find the value of each of these expressions when $k = {^-2}$.
 (a) k^2 (b) $k^2 + 3$ (c) $k^2 - 1$ (d) $k^2 - 5$

B10 Find the value of each of these expressions when $k = {^-4}$.
 (a) $2k^2$ (b) $3k^2$ (c) $\dfrac{k^2}{2}$ (d) $\dfrac{k^2}{8}$

C Using more than one letter

Examples

Find the value of $5(x + y)$ when $x = 6$ and $y = 2$.

$5(x + y) = 5 \times (x + y)$
$= 5 \times (6 + 2)$
$= 5 \times 8$
$= 40$

Find the value of $5ab$ when $a = 6$ and $b = 2$.

$5ab = 5 \times a \times b$
$= 5 \times 6 \times 2$
$= 60$

Find the value of $m^2 + n^2$ when $m = 4$ and $n = 7$.

$m^2 + n^2 = 4^2 + 7^2$
$= (4 \times 4) + (7 \times 7)$
$= 16 + 49$
$= 65$

C1 If $a = 3$ and $b = 5$, find the value of each of these expressions.
(a) $a + b$ (b) $3(a + b)$ (c) $3a + 4b$ (d) $10(b - a)$ (e) $5a - 3b$

C2 What is the value of each expression when $p = 2$ and $q = 3$?
(a) pq (b) $pq + 5$ (c) $pq - 4$ (d) $4pq$ (e) $3pq + 10$

C3 When $u = 5$ and $v = 4$, evaluate these.
(a) $u^2 + v^2$ (b) $u^2 - v^2$ (c) $u^2 + v$ (d) $u^2 - v$ (e) $u^2 + v^2 + 3$

C4 When $a = 2$, $b = 5$ and $c = 10$, evaluate these.
(a) $a + b + c$ (b) ab (c) bc (d) $3ac$ (e) $b^2 + c$

C5 Find the value of each of these when $u = 4$, $v = 8$ and $w = 24$.
(a) $\dfrac{v}{u}$ (b) $\dfrac{v}{u} + 3$ (c) $\dfrac{w}{u} + 10$ (d) $\dfrac{u + v}{2}$ (e) $\dfrac{w}{v} - 2$

C6

N	G	H	A	E	L	U	R	F	B	T	W
1	2	3	6	8	9	10	12	13	18	24	36

Evaluate each expression below when $a = 2$, $b = 3$ and $c = 6$.
Then find the letter in the box above and rearrange the letters in each part to make a word.

(a) ab $\dfrac{c}{a}$ $3(a + c)$ c^2

(b) $2(a + b)$ $a^2 + 9$ $2ab - 11$

(c) bc $\dfrac{c}{b}$ b^2 $2b + c$ ba $\dfrac{c}{a} + 3$ $2a^2$

C7 With a partner, play the games on sheet F1–35.

C8 What is the value of each expression when $x = 6$ and $y = {}^-2$?
(a) $x + y$ (b) xy (c) $y - x$ (d) $2xy$ (e) $x^2 + y^2$

C9 Do the puzzles on sheet F1–36.

D Area and simplifying

- Find an expression for the area of each rectangle.

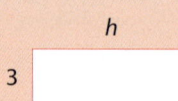

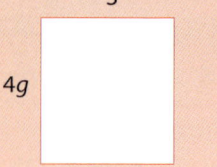

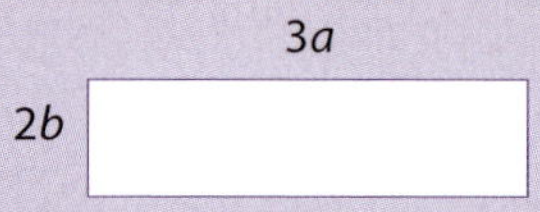

  Rectangle 1: 3 by h
  Rectangle 2: 5 by 2k, with 4g below
  Rectangle 3: 3 by (square)

Rectangle: 2b by 3a

Area of this rectangle = $3a \times 2b$
$= 3 \times a \times 2 \times b$
$= 3 \times 2 \times a \times b$
$= 6ab$

- Find an expression for the area of each square and rectangle. Write each expression in its simplest form.

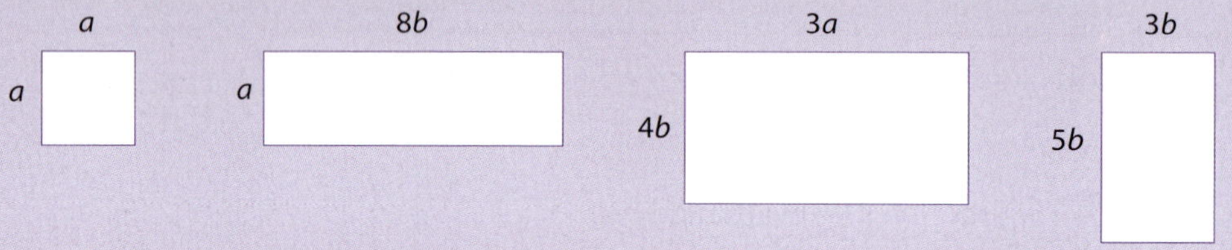

  Square: a by a
  Rectangle: a by 8b
  Rectangle: 4b by 3a
  Rectangle: 5b by 3b

- What is the area of each shape when $a = 5$ and $b = 2$?

D1 Write down and simplify expressions for the areas of these shapes.

(a) 2 by 6g   (b) 3h by 5   (c) 6 by 4k

D2 Simplify each of these expressions.

(a) $2 \times 3x$ (b) $4 \times 5y$ (c) $8 \times 4a$ (d) $3b \times 9$ (e) $7n \times 5$

D3 (a) Write down and simplify an expression for the area of this rectangle.

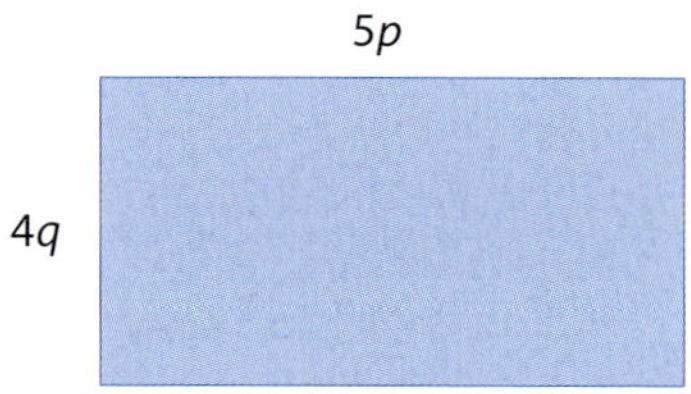

4q by 5p

(b) What is the area when $p = 3$ and $q = 2$?

284 39 Working with expressions 3

D4 Write down and simplify expressions for the areas of these shapes.

(a) 4b, 2a

(b) 3x, 3y

(c) 7k, 4h

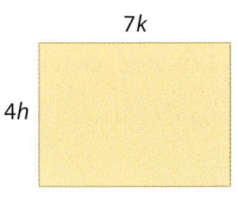

D5 Simplify each of these expressions.

(a) $5a \times b$ (b) $6m \times n$ (c) $3a \times 5b$ (d) $2x \times 3y$ (e) $2m \times 2n$

(f) $6j \times 5k$ (g) $y \times 5x$ (h) $7p \times 3q$ (i) $8x \times 4y$ (j) $5a \times 5b$

D6 (a) Write down and simplify an expression for the area of this rectangle.

(b) What is the area of the shape when $k = 3$?

(3k by 2k rectangle)

D7 Simplify each of these expressions.

(a) $3a \times 5a$ (b) $2b \times 4b$ (c) $6c \times c$ (d) $5d \times 5d$ (e) $e \times 10e$

You can think of an expression like $2ab + ab$ as adding the areas of two rectangles.

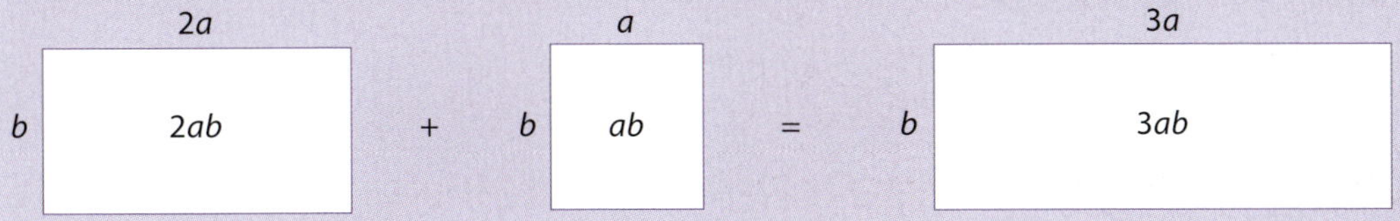

2a		a		3a
b 2ab	+	b ab	=	b 3ab

$2ab + ab = 3ab$

D8 Write each of these in its simplest form.

(a) $ab + ab + ab$ (b) $3ab + ab$ (c) $5ab + 2ab$

(d) $2a^2 + 3a^2$ (e) $5b^2 + b^2$ (f) $c^2 + 5c^2$

D9 Write each of these in its simplest form.

(a) $5xy - 2xy$ (b) $4xy - xy$ (c) $6xy - 5xy$

(d) $9x^2 - 4x^2$ (e) $4y^2 - 3y^2$ (f) $9z^2 - z^2$

D10 Write each of these in its simplest form.

(a) $4mn + 3mn - 2mn$ (b) $5pq + 2pq - pq$ (c) $7gh - 6gh + gh$

(d) $6k^2 + 3k^2 - 2k^2$ (e) $5y^2 + 2y^2 - 6y^2$ (f) $8a^2 - 2a^2 + 4a^2$

Test yourself

T1 Evaluate each of these expressions when $x = 8$.

(a) $5x$ (b) $x + 12$ (c) $\dfrac{x}{4}$ (d) $x - 3$ (e) x^2

(f) $2x - 4$ (g) $3x + 12$ (h) $\dfrac{x}{2} + 3$ (i) $\dfrac{x+2}{5}$ (j) $3 + 2x$

T2 Work out the value of each of these.

(a) $3(a + 2)$ when $a = 6$ (b) $2(b - 3)$ when $b = 8$

(c) $4(c - 1)$ when $c = 7$ (d) $4(1 + d)$ when $d = 9$

T3 Find the value of each of these when $e = 2$, $f = 5$ and $g = 6$.

(a) ef (b) $fg + 4$ (c) $e + g$ (d) $3(f + g)$

(e) $10(g - f)$ (f) $2eg$ (g) f^2 (h) $2f^2$

(i) $g^2 + 4$ (j) $g^2 + f^2$ (k) $\dfrac{g}{e} - 3$ (l) $\dfrac{g^2}{9}$

T4 Evaluate each of these when $k = {}^-3$.

(a) $k + 7$ (b) $2k$ (c) $k + 1$ (d) k^2 (e) $k - 2$

T5 Evaluate these when $a = 5$ and $b = {}^-2$.

(a) $a + b$ (b) $a^2 + b^2$ (c) $2(a - b)$ (d) $\dfrac{a+b}{3}$ (e) ab

T6 Work out the value of $2k^2$ when $k = {}^-5$.

T7 (a) Find the value of $3x + 4y$

  (i) when $x = 2$ and $y = 5$

  (ii) when $x = 6$ and $y = {}^-3$

(b) Find the value of $a^3 + b^2$ when $a = 2$ and $b = 5$.

AQA

T8 Look at these shapes.

Write as simply as possible an expression for

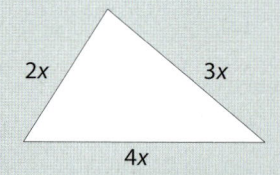

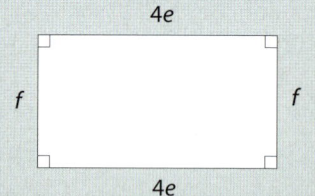

(a) the perimeter of the triangle

(b) the perimeter of the rectangle

(c) the area of the rectangle

Triangle sides: $2x$, $3x$, $4x$

Rectangle sides: $4e$, f

OCR

T9 Simplify each of these.

(a) $4m \times 2n$ (b) $3c \times 5c$ (c) $pq + pq + pq$

(d) $4xy + 5xy - xy$ (e) $5k^2 - k^2$ (f) $3w^2 + 4w^2$

40 Multiplying and dividing fractions

You should know how to
- multiply a fraction by a whole number
- work with mixed numbers
- find a fraction of a quantity when the result is a whole number

This work will help you
- divide a fraction by a whole number
- find a fraction of a quantity when the result is a fraction or mixed number
- multiply a fraction by a unit fraction

A Finding a fraction of a quantity: fractional results 1

$\frac{1}{3}$ of $4 = 4 \div 3$

Share 4 cakes equally between 3 people.

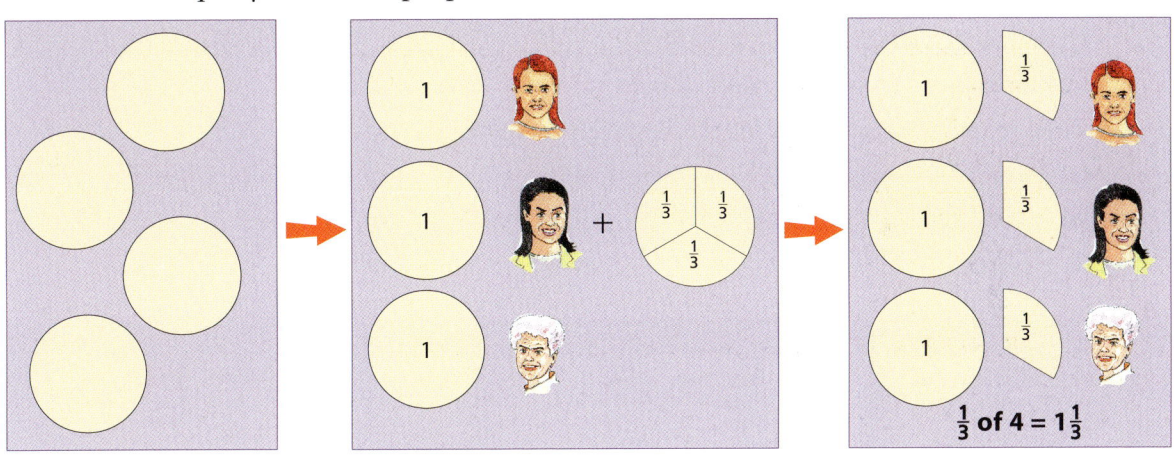

$\frac{1}{3}$ of $4 = 1\frac{1}{3}$

A1 Three buns are shared equally between two people. How many buns does each person get?

A2 Find four pairs of matching calculations.

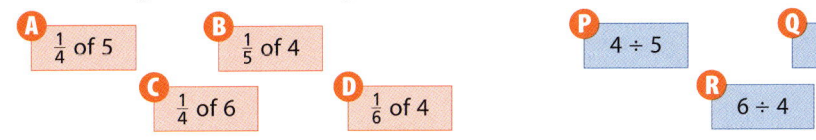

- **A** $\frac{1}{4}$ of 5
- **B** $\frac{1}{5}$ of 4
- **C** $\frac{1}{4}$ of 6
- **D** $\frac{1}{6}$ of 4
- **P** $4 \div 5$
- **Q** $4 \div 6$
- **R** $6 \div 4$
- **S** $5 \div 4$

A3 Work these out. Write your answers as mixed numbers.

(a) $\frac{1}{2}$ of 7　　(b) $\frac{1}{4}$ of 5　　(c) $\frac{1}{3}$ of 10　　(d) $\frac{1}{4}$ of 14

(e) $\frac{1}{5}$ of 6　　(f) $\frac{1}{3}$ of 16　　(g) $\frac{1}{4}$ of 21　　(h) $\frac{1}{8}$ of 12

B Finding a fraction of a quantity: fractional results 2

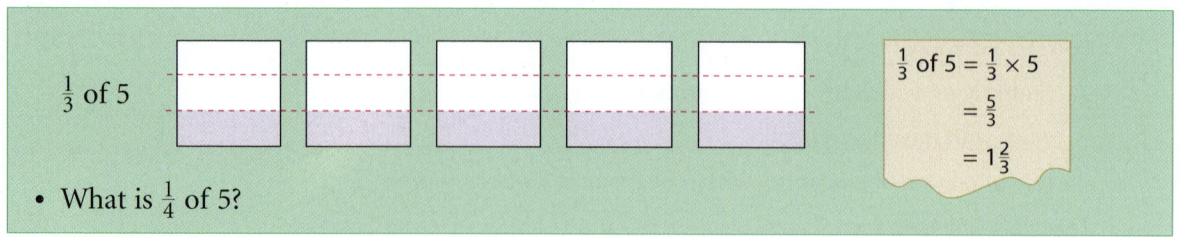

$\frac{1}{3}$ of 5

$\frac{1}{3}$ of $5 = \frac{1}{3} \times 5$
$= \frac{5}{3}$
$= 1\frac{2}{3}$

- What is $\frac{1}{4}$ of 5?

B1 (a) Which calculation below is equivalent to $\frac{1}{4}$ of 7?

A $\frac{1}{4} + 7$ **B** $\frac{1}{4} \times 7$ **C** $\frac{1}{4} \div 7$ **D** $7 - \frac{1}{4}$

(b) Use your answer to (a) to work out $\frac{1}{4}$ of 7 and write the result as a mixed number.

B2 Work these out. Give your answers as mixed numbers in their simplest form.

(a) $\frac{1}{4}$ of 15   (b) $\frac{1}{3}$ of 5   (c) $\frac{1}{5}$ of 12   (d) $\frac{1}{4}$ of 18   (e) $\frac{1}{8}$ of 14

B3 Work out each answer and use the code to change it to a letter.

S	O	B	H	K	L	T	E	A	C	N	D
$\frac{2}{3}$	$\frac{3}{4}$	$1\frac{1}{2}$	$1\frac{2}{5}$	$1\frac{3}{5}$	$1\frac{4}{5}$	$2\frac{1}{3}$	$2\frac{1}{2}$	$2\frac{2}{3}$	$2\frac{3}{4}$	$3\frac{3}{4}$	$4\frac{3}{4}$

(You may need to simplify your answer.)

Then rearrange each set of letters to spell a piece of furniture.

(a) $\frac{1}{2}$ of 3 $\frac{1}{4}$ of 11 $\frac{1}{5}$ of 7 $\frac{1}{4}$ of 15 $\frac{1}{2}$ of 5

(b) $\frac{1}{4}$ of 19 $\frac{1}{5}$ of 8 $\frac{1}{3}$ of 2 $\frac{1}{4}$ of 10

(c) $\frac{1}{4}$ of 3 $\frac{1}{3}$ of 7 $\frac{1}{5}$ of 9 $\frac{1}{8}$ of 6 $\frac{1}{6}$ of 4

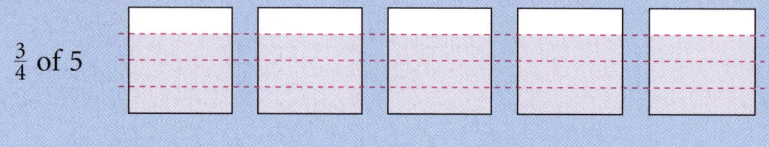

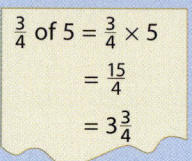

$\frac{3}{4}$ of 5

$\frac{3}{4}$ of $5 = \frac{3}{4} \times 5$
$= \frac{15}{4}$
$= 3\frac{3}{4}$

- What is $\frac{2}{5}$ of 8?

B4 (a) Which calculation below is equivalent to $\frac{3}{4}$ of 3?

A $\frac{3}{4} \div 3$ **B** $3 + \frac{3}{4}$ **C** $3 \div \frac{3}{4}$ **D** $\frac{3}{4} \times 3$

(b) Use your answer to (a) to work out $\frac{3}{4}$ of 3 and write it as a mixed number.

B5 Work these out. Give your answers as mixed numbers.

(a) $\frac{2}{3}$ of 4   (b) $\frac{3}{4}$ of 7   (c) $\frac{2}{5}$ of 4   (d) $\frac{3}{4}$ of 6   (e) $\frac{2}{3}$ of 10

B6 Work out each answer and use the code to change it to a letter.

R	A	D	S	C	B	E	H	I	F	T	P
$\frac{6}{7}$	$1\frac{1}{5}$	$1\frac{1}{3}$	$1\frac{1}{2}$	$1\frac{2}{3}$	$2\frac{1}{4}$	$2\frac{2}{5}$	$2\frac{4}{5}$	$3\frac{1}{5}$	$3\frac{1}{3}$	$3\frac{3}{4}$	$6\frac{3}{4}$

Then rearrange each set of letters to spell an item of food.

(a) $\frac{2}{3}$ of 2 $\frac{2}{5}$ of 3 $\frac{3}{4}$ of 3 $\frac{2}{5}$ of 6 $\frac{3}{7}$ of 2

(b) $\frac{3}{4}$ of 2 $\frac{2}{5}$ of 8 $\frac{2}{3}$ of 5 $\frac{2}{5}$ of 7

(c) $\frac{3}{4}$ of 9 $\frac{5}{8}$ of 6 $\frac{3}{8}$ of 4 $\frac{3}{5}$ of 2 $\frac{3}{10}$ of 4

C Dividing a unit fraction by a whole number

This is $\frac{1}{2}$ ...   ... and this is $\frac{1}{2} \div 3$ 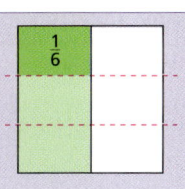 ...   ... so $\frac{1}{2} \div 3 = \frac{1}{6}$.

C1 (a) Which diagram below matches $\frac{1}{4} \div 2$?

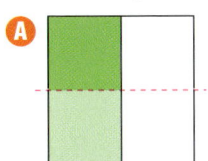

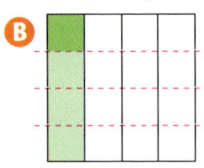

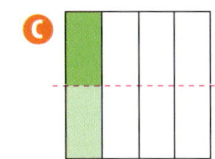

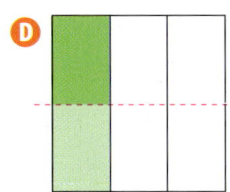

A   B   C   D

(b) Work out $\frac{1}{4} \div 2$.

C2 (a) Match each calculation to a diagram.

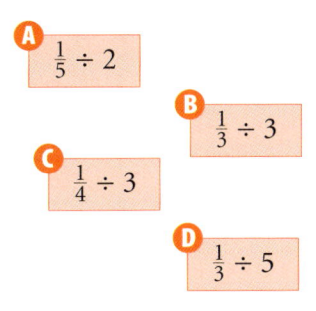

A $\frac{1}{5} \div 2$

B $\frac{1}{3} \div 3$

C $\frac{1}{4} \div 3$

D $\frac{1}{3} \div 5$

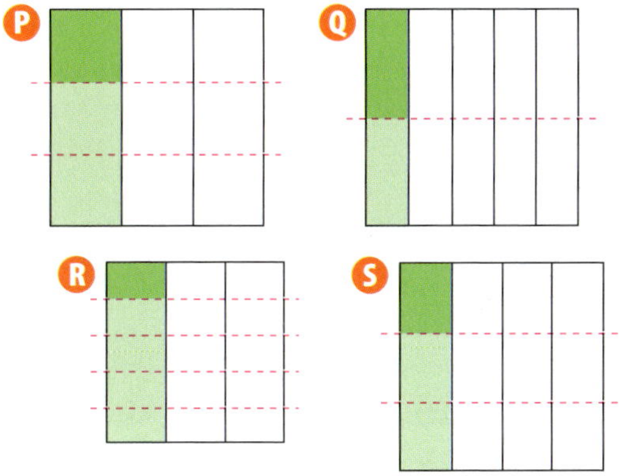

P   Q   R   S

(b) Work out the result of each calculation.

C3 Work these out.

(a) $\frac{1}{2} \div 2$ (b) $\frac{1}{5} \div 3$ (c) $\frac{1}{6} \div 2$ (d) $\frac{1}{3} \div 4$ (e) $\frac{1}{2} \div 4$

C4 Moira has a quarter of a bar of chocolate. She shares it equally with her friend Iain. What fraction of the bar do they each get?

40 Multiplying and dividing fractions

This is $\frac{1}{5}$ ...   ... and this is $\frac{1}{2}$ of $\frac{1}{5}$ 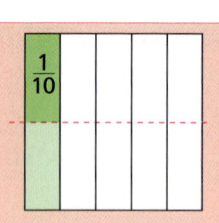 ...   ... $\frac{1}{2}$ of $\frac{1}{5}$ = $\frac{1}{5}$ ÷ 2
                                                                = $\frac{1}{10}$

C5 (a) Which diagram below matches $\frac{1}{2}$ of $\frac{1}{3}$?

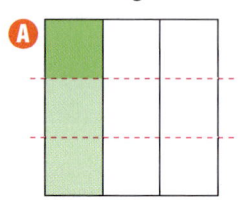

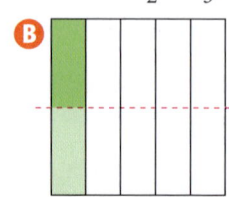

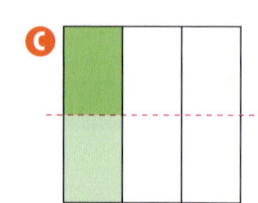

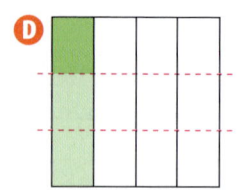

   A   B   C   D

(b) Work out $\frac{1}{2}$ of $\frac{1}{3}$.

C6 Work these out.

(a) $\frac{1}{2}$ of $\frac{1}{4}$ (b) $\frac{1}{2}$ of $\frac{1}{8}$ (c) $\frac{1}{2}$ of $\frac{1}{6}$ (d) $\frac{1}{3}$ of $\frac{1}{2}$ (e) $\frac{1}{4}$ of $\frac{1}{2}$

D Dividing a fraction by a whole number

This is $\frac{3}{4}$ ...   ... and this is $\frac{3}{4}$ ÷ 2 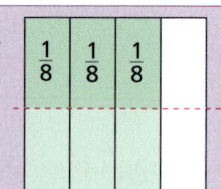 ...   ... so $\frac{3}{4}$ ÷ 2 = $\frac{3}{8}$.

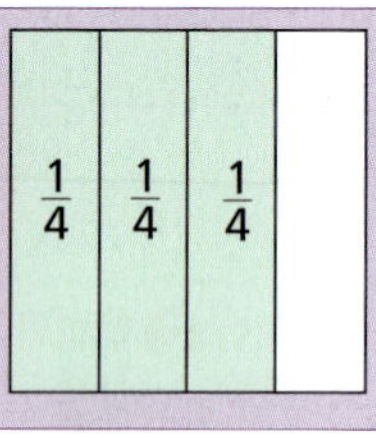

This is $\frac{2}{3}$ ...   ... and this is $\frac{1}{5}$ of $\frac{2}{3}$ 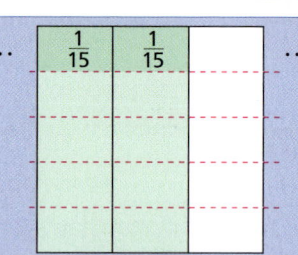 ...   ... $\frac{1}{5}$ of $\frac{2}{3}$ = $\frac{2}{3}$ ÷ 5
                                                                                 = $\frac{2}{15}$

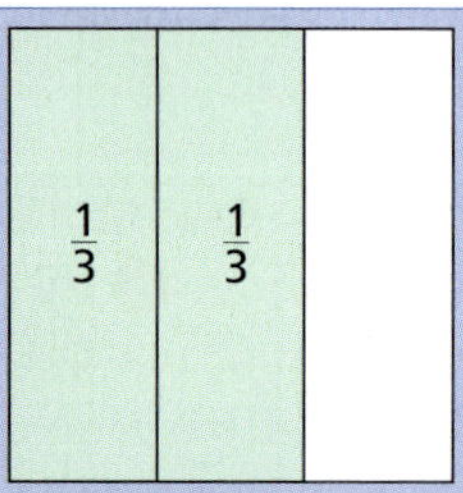

D1 (a) Which diagram below matches $\frac{2}{3}$ ÷ 3?

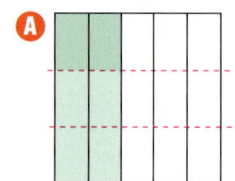

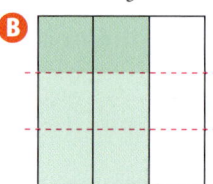

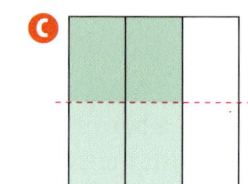

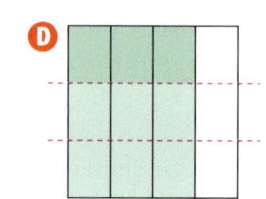

   A   B   C   D

(b) Work out $\frac{2}{3}$ ÷ 3.

290 40 Multiplying and dividing fractions

D2 (a) Match each calculation to a diagram.

- A: $\frac{3}{5} \div 2$
- B: $\frac{5}{6} \div 2$
- C: $\frac{2}{5} \div 3$

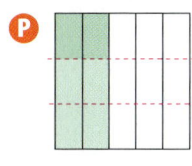

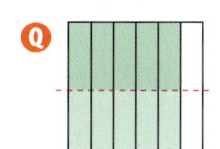

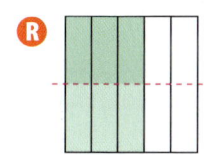

P, Q, R (diagrams)

(b) Work out the result of each calculation.

D3 Cath has $\frac{4}{5}$ of a cake and has to share it equally between two people. What fraction of the cake do they each get?

D4 Work these out.

(a) $\frac{2}{3} \div 2$ (b) $\frac{2}{3} \div 4$ (c) $\frac{3}{4} \div 3$ (d) $\frac{3}{4} \div 4$

D5 Work these out.

(a) $\frac{1}{2}$ of $\frac{2}{5}$ (b) $\frac{1}{2}$ of $\frac{3}{5}$ (c) $\frac{1}{2}$ of $\frac{5}{8}$ (d) $\frac{1}{4}$ of $\frac{2}{3}$

E Multiplying fractions

Here is John's working for $\frac{1}{2} \times \frac{1}{3}$.

$\frac{1}{2} \times \frac{1}{3} = \frac{1}{2}$ of $\frac{1}{3}$
$= \frac{1}{3} \div 2$
$= \frac{1}{6}$

Can you calculate these?

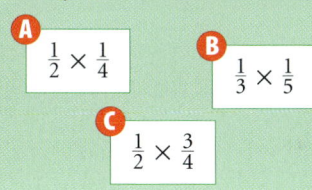

- A: $\frac{1}{2} \times \frac{1}{4}$
- B: $\frac{1}{3} \times \frac{1}{5}$
- C: $\frac{1}{2} \times \frac{3}{4}$

E1 Work these out.

(a) $\frac{1}{2} \times \frac{1}{5}$ (b) $\frac{1}{2} \times \frac{1}{8}$ (c) $\frac{1}{3} \times \frac{1}{4}$ (d) $\frac{1}{3} \times \frac{2}{5}$

E2 Work out each answer and use the code to change it to a letter.

S	G	R	I	O	A	D	P	W	L	E	M
$\frac{1}{12}$	$\frac{1}{10}$	$\frac{1}{9}$	$\frac{1}{8}$	$\frac{1}{6}$	$\frac{3}{16}$	$\frac{1}{5}$	$\frac{1}{4}$	$\frac{3}{8}$	$\frac{1}{2}$	$\frac{2}{5}$	$\frac{3}{4}$

Then rearrange each set of letters to spell a city.

(a) $\frac{4}{5} \div 2$ $\frac{1}{2}$ of $\frac{2}{9}$ $\frac{1}{2}$ of $1\frac{1}{2}$ $\frac{5}{6} \div 5$

(b) $\frac{1}{10} \times \frac{5}{6}$ $\frac{1}{3}$ of $\frac{3}{4}$ $\frac{1}{16}$ of 3 $\frac{3}{8} \div 3$ $2 \times \frac{1}{18}$

(c) $\frac{3}{5} \div 3$ $\frac{1}{2} \times \frac{2}{5}$ $\frac{1}{4}$ of 3 $\frac{1}{3} \times \frac{1}{3}$ $\frac{3}{8} \div 2$ $\frac{1}{4} \times \frac{1}{2}$

(d) $\frac{1}{2}$ of $\frac{3}{4}$ $\frac{1}{2}$ of $\frac{1}{5}$ $\frac{1}{3}$ of $1\frac{1}{2}$ $\frac{1}{8}$ of $\frac{2}{3}$ $\frac{1}{4} \times \frac{2}{3}$ $\frac{1}{4} \times \frac{3}{4}$ $\frac{1}{5} \times \frac{1}{2}$

40 Multiplying and dividing fractions

Test yourself

T1 On a school trip, each child is given $\frac{1}{4}$ of a bar of chocolate.
How many bars of chocolate are needed for 20 children?

T2 Fiona's dog eats $\frac{2}{3}$ of a tin of dog food each day.
How many tins does she need to feed her dog for 9 days?

T3 Three apples are shared equally between six people.
What fraction of an apple does each person get?

T4 Three sausages are shared equally between four people.
How much does each person get?

T5 Work these out. Write your answers as mixed numbers.

(a) $\frac{1}{3}$ of 7 (b) $\frac{1}{5}$ of 7

T6 Work out $\frac{3}{4}$ of 9 and write your answer as a mixed number.

T7 Helen shares $\frac{1}{2}$ of a cake equally between her two sons.
What fraction does each son get?

T8 Work out $\frac{1}{5} \div 4$.

T9 What is $\frac{1}{2}$ of $\frac{1}{6}$?

T10 Calculate $\frac{1}{3} \times \frac{3}{4}$.

T11 Calculate these.

(a) $\frac{3}{8} \times \frac{1}{2}$ (b) $\frac{3}{8} \div 6$

OCR

41 Working with formulas 2

This work will help you
- draw and interpret graphs from formulas
- form and simplify expressions and formulas
- form and solve equations from expressions and formulas

A Formulas and graphs

Sara decorates cakes.
She uses this formula to work out how much ribbon to cut to wrap round a cake.

$L = 3d + 40$

L is the length of ribbon and d is the diameter of the cake.

She bakes a cake that has a diameter of 25 cm.

Using the formula gives $L = 3 \times 25 + 40$
$= 75 + 40$
$= 115$

So she cuts 115 cm of ribbon for this cake.

- Copy and complete the table for different sizes of cake.

Diameter of cake in cm (d)	5	10	15	20	25	30
Length of ribbon in cm (L)					115	

- Draw axes like the ones on the right.
  Plot the points from your table.
  Join them with a line.

- Sara cuts a 94 cm length of ribbon for a cake.
  What is the diameter of the cake?

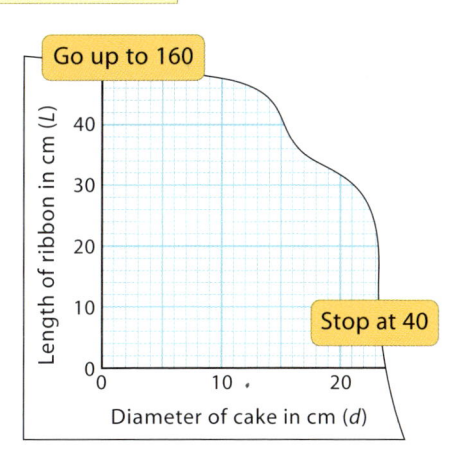

Go up to 160

Stop at 40

A1 A rough rule for working out a person's height is

| height in centimetres = 3 × distance round head in centimetres |

(a) Copy and complete this table using the rule.

Distance round head in cm	40	45	50	55	60	65
Height in cm	120	135				

(b) Draw axes like the ones on the right.
Plot the points from your table.
Join them with a line.

Use your graph to answer these.

(c) The distance round Harry's head is 58 cm.
How tall does the graph say he is?

(d) Aifa's height is 140 centimetres.
What is the distance round her head?

(e) Chloë is 165 cm tall.
Would a bandage 120 cm long
go round her head twice?

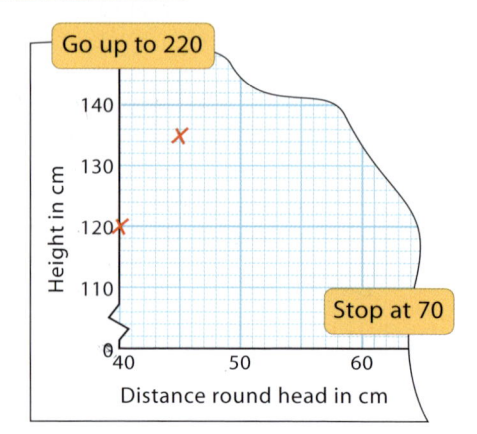

A2 When a lorry dumps waste at a tip, it has to pay.
A computer works out the charge.

At Waterdale tip, the formula the computer uses is $c = 35 + 10w$.
c is the charge in £.
w is the weight of rubbish tipped in tonnes.

(a) A lorry tips 12 tonnes. How much will it cost?

(b) Copy and complete this table.

Weight of rubbish (w)	2	4	6	8	10	12
Charge in pounds (c)	55					

(c) Draw and label axes like the ones on the right.
Plot the points from your table.
Join them with a line.

Use your graph to answer these.

(d) How much will it cost to tip 7 tonnes of rubbish?

(e) How much will it cost to tip 5 tonnes?

(f) Bob paid £130 to tip rubbish.
How much did his rubbish weigh?

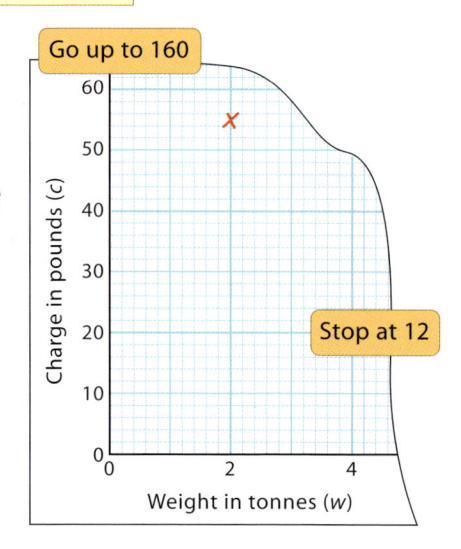

A3 Mendip Mushrooms supply mushroom compost to gardeners.
The formula they use for working out the cost of a delivery is $c = 6w + 40$.
c is the cost in £, w is the weight in tonnes.

(a) How much would 4 tonnes of compost cost delivered to your door?

(b) How much would 1 tonne cost?

(c) Copy and complete this table for the cost of deliveries of Mendip Mushrooms compost.

Weight (w)	1	4	6
Cost in £(c)			

(d) Draw axes like these with w going across from 0 to 8 and c going up from 0 to 90. Plot the points from your table and draw the graph for weights up to 8 tonnes.

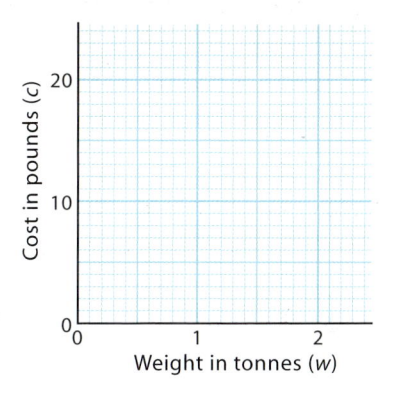

(e) Dave asks for £55 worth of compost to be delivered. How much compost will he get in tonnes?

(f) About how much compost can you buy for £60?

A4 Fuming Fertilisers also supply mushroom compost.
The formula they use for working out the cost of a delivery is $c = 10w + 10$.
c is the cost in £, w is the weight in tonnes.

(a) Copy and complete the table below for Fuming Fertilisers' prices.

Weight (w)	1	4	7
Cost in £ (c)			

(b) On the same axes you used for A3, draw the graph of $c = 10w + 10$.

(c) What do Fuming Fertilisers charge for a delivery of 5.5 tonnes of compost?

(d) How much compost can you buy from Fuming Fertilisers for £48?

(e) Use the graphs to say which company would be cheaper for 10 tonnes of compost. Explain your answer carefully.

(f) Explain carefully how you can tell that both companies will charge the same to deliver 7.5 tonnes of compost.

41 Working with formulas 2

B Forming and using formulas

A company uses this arrow diagram to work out the cost in pounds to hire a car.

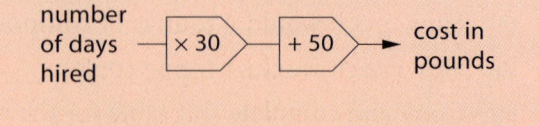

number of days hired → ×30 → +50 → cost in pounds

You could write this as a formula in words.

cost = 30 × number of days hired + 50

You could write the formula in shorthand using C for the cost in pounds and d for the number of days hired.

$C = 30d + 50$

Jane hires a car for 5 days.
How much will she pay?

$d = 5$ so $C = 30 \times 5 + 50$
$= 150 + 50$
$= 200$

So the cost is £200.

Arnie pays the company £140.
Form and solve an equation to find how many days he hired the car for.

$C = 140$ so $140 = 30d + 50$ ← Take 50 from both sides.
$90 = 30d$ ← Divide both sides by 30.
$3 = d$

So he hired the car for 3 days.

B1 A formula to work out the perimeter of a square is

$P = 4s$

P is the perimeter of the square and s is the length of one side.

(a) Calculate the perimeter of a square where one side measures 15 cm.

(b) A square has a perimeter of 100 m.
What is the length of one side?

B2 A shoe shop uses this arrow diagram to change adult UK shoe sizes to continental ones.

UK shoe size → +33 → continental shoe size

(a) Change a UK shoe size of 1 to continental shoe size.

(b) Write down a formula that links UK shoe size (U) to continental shoe size (C).

(c) Helen takes a UK size 5 shoe.
What is her continental shoe size?

(d) Veronique takes a continental size 40 shoe. What is her UK shoe size?

(e) What is the value of C when $U = 3$?

B3 The Beeches Hotel caters for wedding parties.
The hotel uses this formula to work out the cost.

$$C = 10n + 50$$

C is the cost in pounds, n is the number of people in the party.

(a) What will it cost for a party of 30 people?

(b) Another hotel, The Oaks, uses this formula.

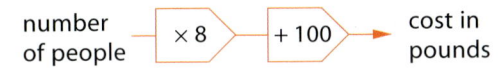

number of people → ×8 → +100 → cost in pounds

Write this as a formula connecting C and n.
C is the cost in pounds,
n is the number of people in the party.

OCR

B4 Mila is having a party.
She uses this rule to work out how many litre bottles of drink to buy.

| number of bottles = number of people ÷ 2, plus another 10 bottles |

(a) How many bottles will she buy if she expects 100 people?

(b) Write the rule as a formula connecting N and p using N to stand for the number of bottles and p to stand for the number of people.

(c) What is the value of N when $p = 50$?

B5 The cost of tipping waste at my local tip is worked out using this rule.

Cost in £ = 15 × weight in tonnes + 30

(a) How much will it cost to tip 5 tonnes of waste?

(b) Write this as a formula connecting C and w.
C is the cost in pounds and w is the weight in tonnes.

(c) On one trip to this tip Ron is charged £60 to tip some waste.
Form and solve an equation to find the weight of this waste.

B6 Each year the Tallis School has a leaving barbecue for year 11.
A teacher uses this rule to work out how many sausages to buy.

| 2 sausages for each ticket sold, plus 50 extra |

(a) This year, 120 tickets have been sold for the barbecue.
How many sausages will the teacher buy?

(b) Using S for the number of sausages and T for the number of tickets, write down the teacher's formula for S in terms of T.

(c) Work out the value of S when $T = 60$.

(d) Last year the teacher bought 350 sausages.
Form and solve an equation to find the number of tickets sold last year.

C Forming and using expressions and formulas

Jan has some pencils.
Mary has 2 more pencils than Jan.

| Let **n** stand for the number of pencils that Jan has. | Then an expression for the number of pencils that Mary has is **n + 2**. | Altogether they have **2n + 2** pencils. |

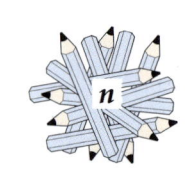

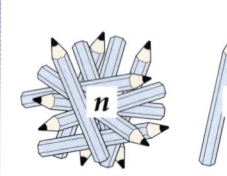

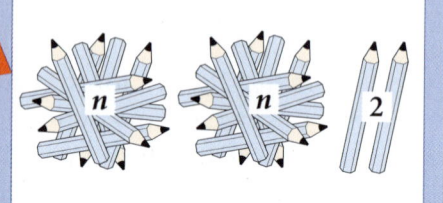

- Jan and Mary have 40 pencils in total.
  Form and solve an equation to find the number of pencils that Jan has.

C1 Fiona has m sweets.
Hamish has 2 sweets fewer than Fiona.
Write down an expression for the number of sweets Hamish has.

C2 A bun costs 40p.
Write down an expression for the cost in pence of x buns.

C3 (a) A shop has 100 computer games.
Then they sell n games.
Which of these expressions tells you the number of the games left in the shop?

| $n - 100$ | $100 + n$ | $100 - n$ | $n + 100$ |

(b) One Monday, the shop starts with m games.
During the day it sells p games.
Which of these expressions tells you the number of the games left in the shop?

| $m + p$ | $m - p$ | $p - m$ | $p + m$ |

C4 Calculators cost £6 each.
Chloë buys n calculators and she pays with a £50 note.
Which of the formulas below tells you the change, £C, that she gets?

| $C = 50 + n$ | $C = 6n$ | $C = 50 - n$ | $C = 50 - 6n$ | $C = 6n - 50$ |

C5 A pie costs 65 pence.
Pam buys n pies.
The total cost is C pence.
Write down a formula connecting C and n.

Edexcel

C6 Chris is a trainee programmer.
His wages each month, £W, are calculated with this formula.

$W = 7h - 5n$

h is the number of hours he works.
n is the number of mistakes he makes.

(a) Work out W when $h = 100$ and $n = 10$.

(b) In April he works for 200 hours and makes 40 mistakes.
What will his wages be?

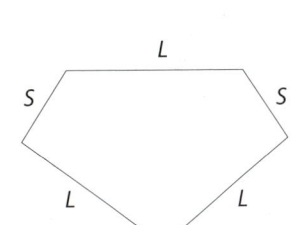

C7 Some frameworks are made from long and short struts.
The length of a long strut is L cm.
The length of a short strut is S cm.

(a) Write down a formula for the perimeter,
R cm, of this framework.
Write the formula as simply as possible.
Start it with $R = \ldots$

(b) The formula for the perimeter, P cm, of a different framework is $P = 6L + 3S$.
If $L = 5$ and $S = 2$, work out the perimeter of this framework.

OCR

C8 (a) Cream doughnuts cost 35 pence each.
What is the cost of d doughnuts?

(b) Mince pies cost 40 pence each.
How much will m mince pies cost?

(c) Write an expression for the total cost in pence of d doughnuts and m mince pies.

C9 Biscuits cost p pence each. Teas cost q pence each.
Use the letters p and q to write down the total cost of 3 biscuits and 2 teas.

C10 In a computer game you score 1 point for hitting a gnome,
2 points for hitting a hairy monster and 5 points for hitting an imp.

Write down a formula for the total score, T, if you hit
g gnomes, h hairy monsters and i imps.

C11 Simon, Stephen and Greg collect stickers.

(a) Simon has n stickers.
Stephen has three times as many stickers as Simon.
Write down an expression for the number of stickers that Stephen has.

(b) Greg has 10 more stickers than Simon.
Write down an expression for the number of stickers that Greg has.

(c) Find and simplify an expression for the number of stickers they have altogether.

(d) They have 100 stickers altogether.
Form and solve an equation to find the number of stickers Simon has.

41 Working with formulas 2

C12 Audrey sells packets of sweets.
There are three sizes of packets.

small   medium   large

There are n sweets in the small packet.

There are twice as many sweets in the medium packet as there are in the small packet.

(a) Write down an expression, in terms of n, for the number of sweets in the medium packet.

There are 15 more sweets in the large packet than in the medium packet.

(b) Write down an expression, in terms of n, for the number of sweets in the large packet.

A small packet of sweets costs 20p.
Sebastian buys q small packets of sweets.

(c) Write down an expression, in terms of q, for the cost in pence of the sweets.   *Edexcel*

C13 A box contains 6 bottles of wine.

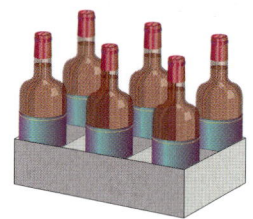

(a) One bottle of wine weighs w kg.
The box weighs 1 kg less than one bottle of wine.
Show that the total weight in kilograms of **two** boxes, each with six bottles of wine, is $14w - 2$.

(b) The total weight of the two boxes and their bottles is 19 kg.
Write down an equation in w and solve it to find the weight of one bottle of wine.

OCR

C14 Eggs are sold in boxes.
A small box holds 6 eggs.

Hina buys x small boxes of eggs.

(a) Write down, in terms of x, the total number of eggs in these small boxes.

A large box holds 12 eggs.
Hina buys 4 less of the large boxes of eggs than the small boxes.

(b) Write down, in terms of x, the number of large boxes she buys.

(c) Find, in terms of x, the total number of eggs in the **large** boxes that Hina buys.

(d) Find, in terms of x, the total number of eggs that Hina buys.
Give your answer in its simplest form.   *Edexcel*

Test yourself

T1 A builder calculates the cost of his work, in pounds, using this formula.

> Multiply the number of hours worked by 8, then add 12.

(a) What is the cost of his work for a job which takes 6 hours?

(b) What is the cost of his work for a job which takes $\frac{1}{2}$ hour?

(c) Write a formula connecting C and n
where C is the cost in pounds,
n is the number of hours worked.

OCR

T2 A spring stretches when objects are hung from it.
The formula for its length is

$l = 2w + 16$

w is the weight in kg.
l is the length of the spring in cm.

(a) Copy and complete this table.

w	0	2	4	6	8	10
l	16			28		36

(b) Draw the graph on a copy of the grid on the right.

(c) Jane hangs an object on the spring.
She measures the length of the spring.
It is 29 cm.

Use your graph to find the weight of the object.

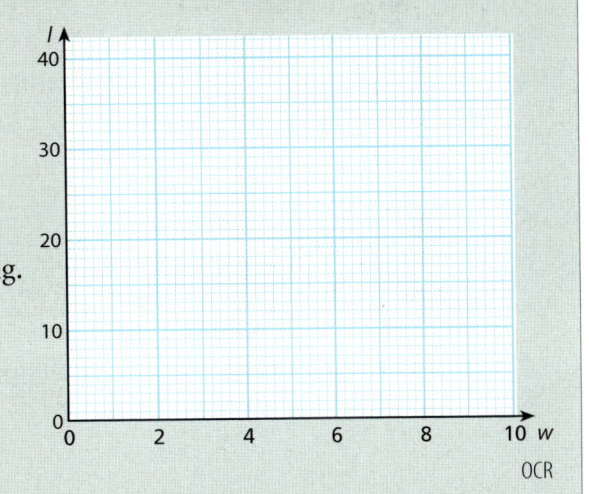

OCR

T3 Daniel buys n books at £4 each. He pays for them with a £20 note.
He receives C pounds in change. Write down a formula for C in terms of n.

Edexcel

T4 (a) Brooke, Stephanie and Eve have some sweets. Brooke has p sweets.
Stephanie has 5 more sweets than Brooke.
Write down an expression for the number of sweets that Stephanie has.

(b) Eve has twice as many sweets as Brooke.
Write down an expression for the number of sweets that Eve has.

(c) Find and simplify an expression for the number of sweets they have altogether.

(d) They have 61 sweets altogether.
Form and solve an equation to find the number of sweets Brooke has.

Review 5

You need an angle measurer or pie chart scale for question 16.

1 Here are the first five terms of a number sequence.

1   8   15   22   29   ...

(a) Write down the next two terms in this sequence.

(b) Explain how you found your answer.

2 Simplify each of these expressions.

(a) $2a + 3b + a + b$ (b) $3a + 2b + a - 5b$ (c) $3a \times 2b$

3 Work these out.

(a) $3 + {}^-2$ (b) ${}^-3 - {}^-2$ (c) ${}^-3 \times 2$ (d) ${}^-3 \times {}^-2$

(e) $4 \times {}^-3$ (f) $20 \div {}^-2$ (g) ${}^-20 \div {}^-2$ (h) $({}^-10)^2$

4 Expand these.

(a) $3(x + 2)$ (b) $5(2m - 1)$ (c) $a(a + 2)$ (d) $x(x - 8)$

5 This shape is made with rods of two different lengths. Some have length a cm, the others have length b cm.

Write down a formula for the perimeter, P cm, of the shape. Write the formula as simply as possible.

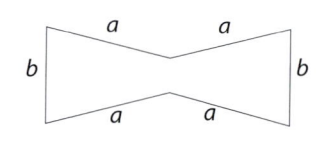

6 Given that $k = {}^-5$, work these out.

(a) $2k$ (b) $2k - 1$ (c) $2k + 1$ (d) k^2 (e) $3k^2$

7 Find and simplify an expression for the perimeter of this kite.

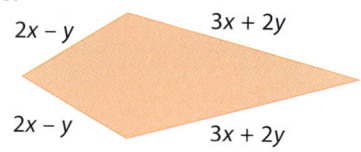

8 Here is the rule for finding a term in a sequence.

> Multiply the previous term by 2 and subtract 3.

The first three terms in the sequence are 6, 9 and 15. Work out the next two terms.

9 Factorise each of these fully.

(a) $3a + 12$ (b) $4b + 6$ (c) $6c - 18$ (d) $d^2 + 5d$

10 What is the value of $ab + c$ when $a = {}^-5$, $b = {}^-2$ and $c = 3$?

11 To cook a joint of beef, May allows 30 minutes per kilogram plus another 20 minutes.

    (a) How many minutes will May cook a 2 kg joint of beef for?

    (b) How many minutes will she allow for a 3 kg joint?

    (c) Write May's rule as a formula.
Use w to stand for the weight of the beef in kg
and t to stand for the time it takes to cook in minutes.

12 Work these out.

    (a) $\frac{1}{4} \times \frac{1}{8}$ **(b)** $\frac{1}{2} \times \frac{3}{4}$ **(c)** $\frac{1}{4} \div 2$ **(d)** $\frac{1}{3} \div 3$

13 This diagram shows some patterns made from tiles.

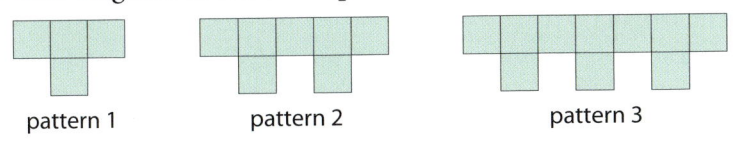

pattern 1   pattern 2   pattern 3

    (a) Draw pattern 4.

    (b) Copy and complete the table.

Pattern number	1	2	3	4	5	6
Number of tiles	4	7	10			

    (c) Which pattern can be made with exactly 25 tiles?

    (d) (i) How many tiles are there in pattern 10?

         (ii) Explain how you can work this out without drawing a diagram.

14 Harry has n bananas.
Harriet has twice as many.

    (a) Write an expression for the number of bananas Harriet has.

Henrietta has 5 more bananas than Harry.

    (b) Write an expression for the number of bananas Henrietta has.

    (c) Find and simplify an expression for the number of bananas Harry, Harriet and Henrietta have altogether.

15 Find out how much people in these jobs are paid in a week.

    (a) **Mechanic** — £7.35 an hour, 38 hours a week

    (b) **Chef** — £8.32 an hour, 37.5 hours a week

    (c) **Part-time care assistant** — 18 hours a week, £6.85 an hour

16 This table shows how a group of people get to work.

Method	Car	Bike	Bus	Train	Walk
Number of people	9	5	2	3	1

Draw a clearly labelled pie chart to show this information.

Review 5   303

42 Travel

This work will help you

- read a distance–time graph
- carry out calculations involving speed

A Calculating speed

A speedboat travels at a constant speed.
It travels 24 metres in 4 seconds.
What is its speed?

24 metres
4 seconds

6 metres / 1 second   6 metres / 1 second   6 metres / 1 second   6 metres / 1 second

The boat travels 24 m in 4 seconds so it travels 6 m in 1 second.

The speed is 6 metres per second or 6 m/s.

Speed usually changes during a journey.
If we know the time taken and the distance travelled, we can work out the **average speed** for the journey.

These children are running away from Fang the dog.
The distances show how far they have run in 10 seconds.

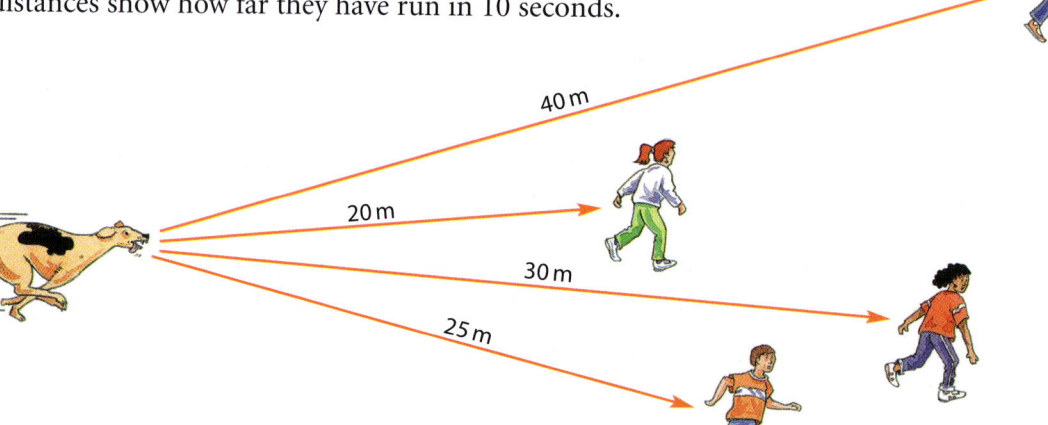

40 m
20 m
30 m
25 m

- Who is fastest?
- What are their average speeds?
- How would their speeds change if they carried on running for 1 minute?

A1 A cyclist takes 6 seconds to travel 48 metres at constant speed.
What is her speed in metres per second (m/s)?

A2 Find the speed, in metres per second, of
- (a) a horse running 200 m in 20 seconds
- (b) a boy running 50 m in 10 seconds
- (c) a train travelling 600 m in 15 seconds
- (d) a car travelling 150 m in 5 seconds

A3 Work out the average speed of these in km/h (kilometres per hour).
- (a) A train that goes 140 km in 2 hours
- (b) A ship that takes 5 hours to sail 75 km
- (c) A plane that flies 630 km in 3 hours
- (d) A coach that travels 160 km in 4 hours

A4 Four pigeons were released together.
These are the distances they flew and the times taken.

Pigeon	Flatford Flyer	Walter	Bolton Queen	Caeredwen
Distance flown (km)	100	90	174	144
Time taken (hours)	4	3	6	6

- (a) Calculate the average speed in kilometres per hour (km/h) of each pigeon.
- (b) Which pigeon flew (i) the fastest (ii) the slowest

A5 Calculate the average speed of these. State the units clearly in your answer.
- (a) A man who runs 150 m in 15 seconds
- (b) An aircraft that takes 3 hours to fly 840 miles
- (c) A space shuttle that travels 54 000 miles in 3 hours
- (d) A car that goes 75 miles in 2 hours

A6 A car travels 12 kilometres in 15 minutes.
- (a) At the same average speed, how far would it travel in one hour?
- (b) What is the speed of the car in km/h?

A7 For each of these find
- the distance it would travel in one hour
- the speed in km/h

- (a) A plane that travels 150 km in half an hour
- (b) A horse that travels 5 km in 15 minutes
- (c) A ship that travels 8 km in 20 minutes

A8 Christine leaves home at 8:00 a.m. and drives 150 miles to Cambridge.
She arrives in Cambridge at 11:00 a.m.
- (a) How long does it take her to get to Cambridge?
- (b) What is the average speed for her journey in m.p.h. (miles per hour)?

B Distance–time graphs

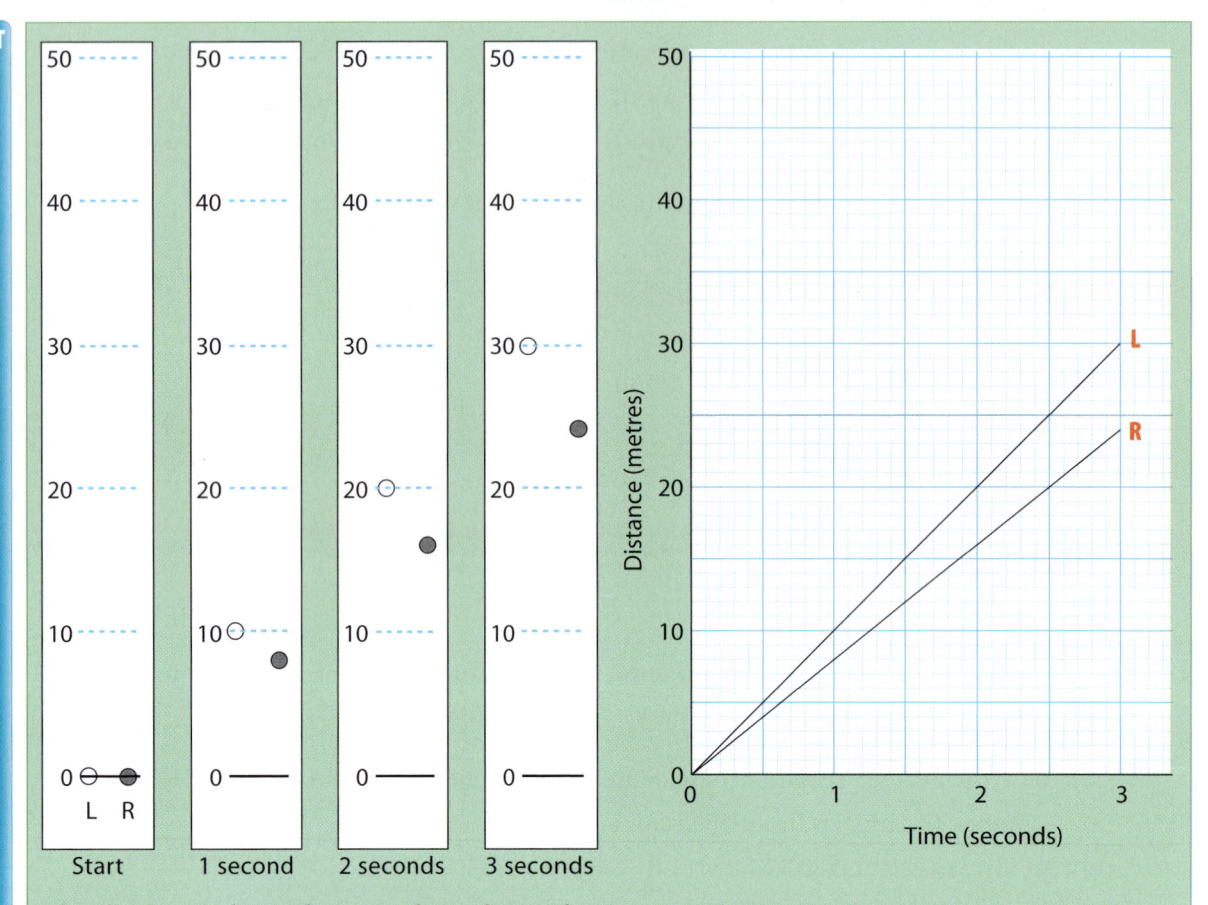

The diagrams above shows Lazlo and Rani having a race over 50 metres.

- How fast is Lazlo going?
- How fast is Rani going?
- How far apart are they after 3 seconds?
- If their speeds do not change, where will each of them be after 4 seconds?

This graph shows the journey of some friends who go out walking one day.

- What was their furthest distance from home?
- How fast were they walking for the first two hours?
- What did they do after they had been walking for two hours?
- Describe what is happening in each part of the journey.

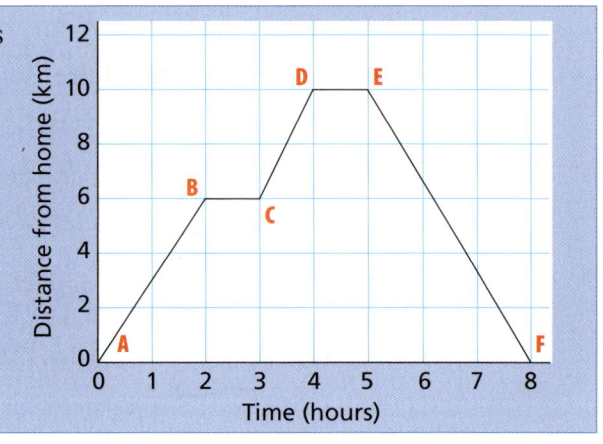

306 42 Travel

B1 These are graphs of six people going along a path.
   (a) How far did person A go in 1 second?
   (b) How long did it take person C to go 15 m?
   (c) Who was going faster, B or D?
       How can you tell?
   (d) Work out the speed of each person in m/s.
   (e) One of these people was a man on a bike.
       Which of these is this most likely to be?
   (f) One of these was an old lady with a stick.
       Which of these is this most likely to be?

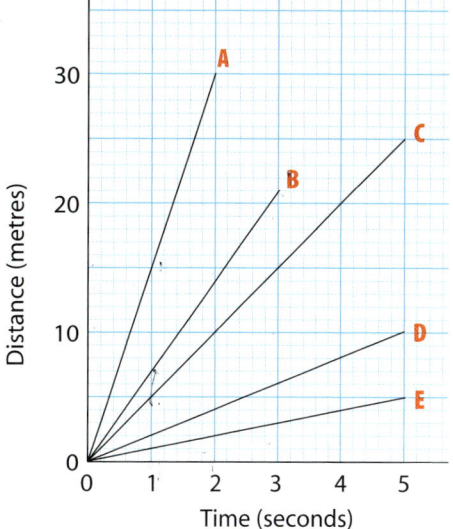

B2 These three graphs represent journeys.

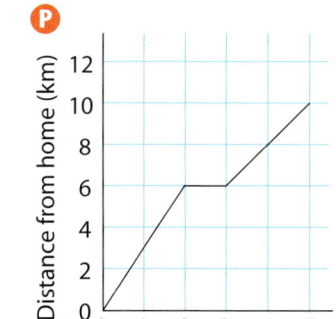

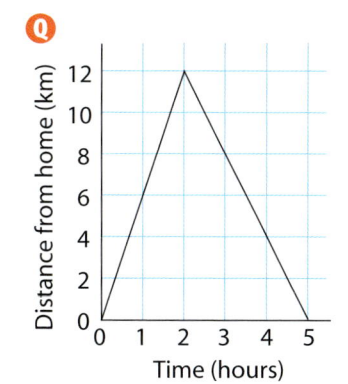

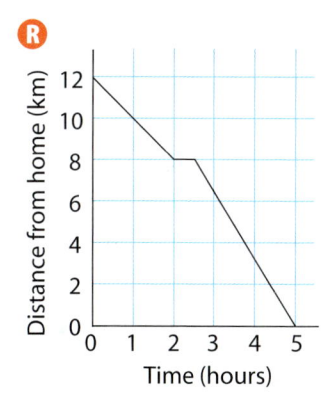

Match each of these statements to one of the graphs above.
   (a) We stopped for a break for an hour.
   (b) We headed home and it took five hours to get there.
   (c) We walked a total of 10 km.
   (d) We only stopped for half an hour.
   (e) It took two hours to get there but three hours to get back.
   (f) For the first two hours we went at 6 km/h.
   (g) Coming home we went at 4 km/h.

B3 (a) In journey P did they go faster before their break or after it?
   (b) In journey Q did they go faster going away from home or coming back?
   (c) What was the speed for the first two hours of journey P?
   (d) What was the speed for the first two hours of journey R?

B4 Barry goes on a hike with his Duke of Edinburgh group.
This graph shows their journey.

(a) What was their speed for the first two hours?

(b) What was their speed between 12 noon and 2 p.m.?

(c) What happened between 2 p.m. and 3 p.m.?

(d) How far did they walk between 3 p.m. and 5 p.m.?

(e) What was their speed between 3 p.m. and 5 p.m.?

(f) What was their speed between 5 p.m. and 7 p.m.?

(g) Between which times were they walking fastest?

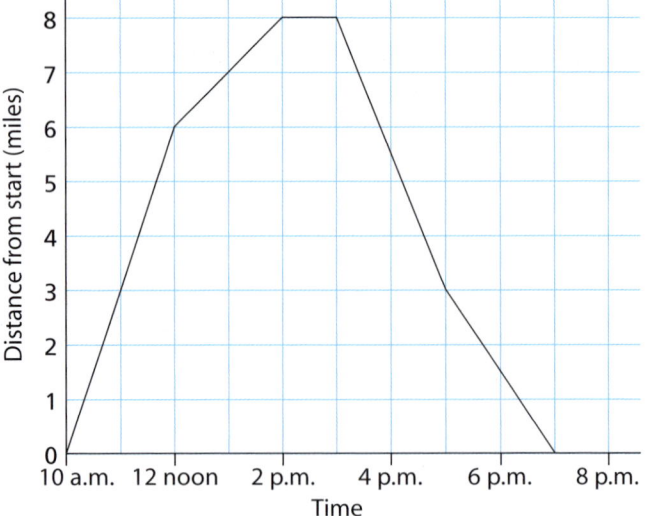

B5 Draw axes as in B4, but go up to 10 miles.

(a) Draw the graph to show this journey.

- We left home at 10 a.m. and for the first 3 hours our speed was 3 m.p.h.
- After that we stopped for lunch for an hour.
- After lunch we started to head back and went for 2 hours at 2 m.p.h.
- Then we found this brilliant stream and messed about there for a whole hour.
- Although we were tired we got back home by walking steadily for another 2 hours.

(b) What was the speed for the last part of the walk?

B6 Elaine went for a walk.
Her walk is represented by the graph below.

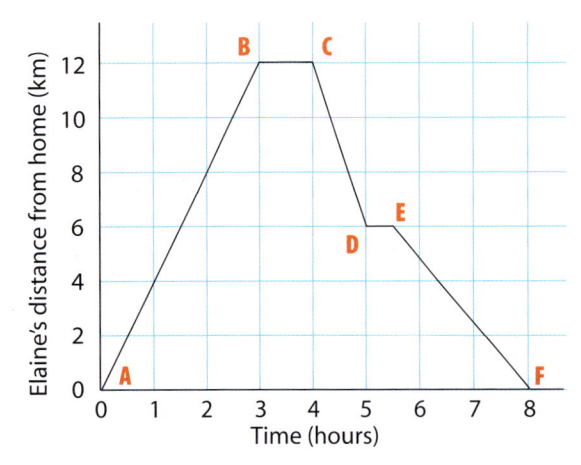

(a) Describe the part of her walk represented by sections CD, DE and EF.

(b) On which section of her walk did she walk fastest?

(c) What was her average speed for the first 2 hours?

OCR

308 42 Travel

C Calculating distance and time

A greyhound runs at a speed of roughly 16 m/s.
How far will it run in 5 seconds?

In 1 second it goes 16 m.

In 5 seconds it goes
5 × 16 m = 80 m.

C1 How far will these animals travel in 5 seconds?
  (a) A chicken at 4 m/s
  (b) A black mamba snake at 9 m/s
  (c) A warthog at 13 m/s
  (d) A wildebeest at 25 m/s

C2 How far will these animals go?
  (a) A pig going at 5 m/s for 10 seconds
  (b) An elephant going at 10 m/s for 8 seconds
  (c) A grizzly bear going at 13 m/s for 20 seconds
  (d) A horse going at 20 m/s for 15 seconds

C3 How far are these journeys?
  (a) A car travelling at 50 m.p.h. for 3 hours
  (b) A plane travelling at 600 km/h for 4 hours
  (c) A train travelling at 120 km/h for 2 hours
  (d) A ship going at 40 km/h for 12 hours
  (e) A cyclist going at 25 km/h for 5 hours

C4 A car driver estimates he drives long distances at an average speed of 60 m.p.h. How far should he have travelled after
  (a) half an hour
  (b) $3\frac{1}{2}$ hours
  (c) $2\frac{1}{4}$ hours
  (d) $6\frac{1}{4}$ hours

A car can travel long distances at an average speed of 50 m.p.h.
How long will it take to go 250 miles?

50 miles
1 hour

So find out how many 50 miles there are in 250 miles.
250 ÷ 50 = 5   So it takes 5 hours.

C5 Pam walks at a steady speed of 4 km/h.
How long does she take to walk 12 km?

C6 Alvin's speedboat travels at 20 m.p.h.
How long does it take to travel 80 miles?

42 Travel 309

C7 Yves cycles at a steady speed of 25 km/h.
How long does it take him to cycle 150 km?

C8 How long would each of these animals take to cover 120 metres?

(a) An elk running at 20 m/s

(b) An elephant running at 12 m/s

(c) A cat running at 15 m/s

(d) A cheetah running at 30 m/s

C9 In a tall office block the distance between the top and bottom floors is 90 m.
The lift goes up at an average speed of 5 m/s.
How long does it take to go from the bottom to the top floor?

C10 A boat travels at a speed of 8 km/h.
How long will it take to travel 20 km?

C11 A car travels at a steady speed of 50 m.p.h.
How long does it take to travel 175 miles?

Using a calculator

A plane travels 400 km in $2\frac{1}{2}$ hours. What is its average speed?

$2\frac{1}{2}$ hours = 2.5 hours, so on a calculator $\boxed{400 \div 2.5 = 160}$

C12 How would you enter these into a calculator?

(a) $1\frac{1}{2}$ hours

(b) $3\frac{1}{4}$ hours

(c) 5 hours and 30 minutes

C13 Work out the average speeds of these.

(a) A coach that takes $3\frac{1}{2}$ hours to travel 140 miles.

(b) A plane that flies a distance of 225 miles in 1 hour 15 minutes.

(c) A non-stop flight of 5625 miles that takes twelve-and-a-half hours.

C14 A French high-speed train can travel at 180 m.p.h.

(a) How far can it travel at this speed in 3 hours?

(b) The distance from Marseilles to Paris is about 450 miles.
How long would the journey take at 180 m.p.h.?

A tricky problem

You are in a game reserve and 100 m away from your safe truck.
A wildebeest 100 m in the other direction starts to chase you.

A human being can run at 8 m/s, a wildebeest at 25 m/s.
Will you make it back to the truck before it catches you?

A lion can run at 22 m/s. Would it catch you in the same situation?

Find out the speeds of some other animals. Would they catch you?

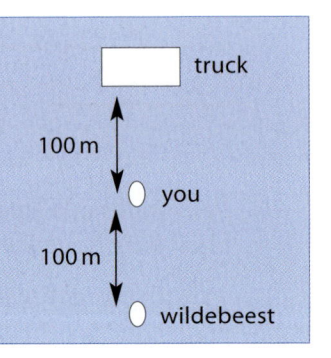

Test yourself

T1 Sharon travels from Leeds to London in her car.
The distance she travels is 200 miles.
The journey takes her 4 hours.
Find Sharon's average speed. *AQA*

T2 Alan drove 12 miles.
The journey took 15 minutes.
What was Alan's average speed? *AQA*

T3 Elizabeth went for a cycle ride.
The distance–time graph shows her ride.

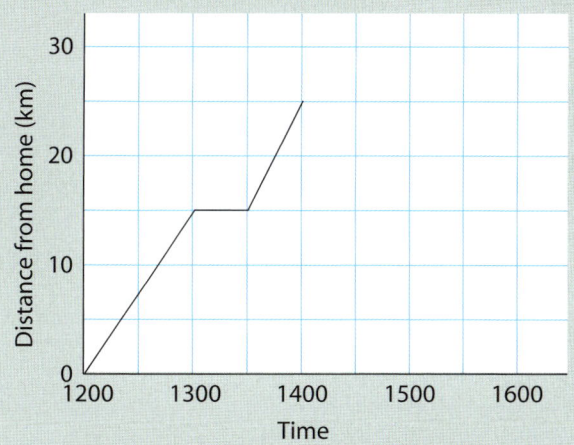

She set off from home at 1200 and had a flat tyre at 1400.
During her ride she stopped for a rest.

(a) (i) At what time did she stop for a rest?

(ii) At what speed did she travel after her rest?

It took Elizabeth 15 minutes to repair the flat tyre.
She then cycled home at 25 kilometres per hour.

(b) Copy the graph on to squared paper.
Complete the distance–time graph to show this information. *Edexcel*

T4 Mr Nagra left home in his van at 07:30.
He arrived at the motorway at 08:10.

(a) How long did this part of the journey take him?

He then drove along the motorway at a steady speed of 60 miles per hour.

(b) How far did he travel along the motorway in $1\frac{1}{2}$ hours? *OCR*

T5 Simon cycles at a steady speed of 20 km/h.
How long does it take him to travel 30 km?

43 Graphs from rules

This work will help you
- plot points and draw the graph of a straight line, given its equation
- read off the coordinates of points on a straight line

You need sheets F1–37, F1–38, F1–39, F1–40 and F1–41.

A Patterns in coordinates

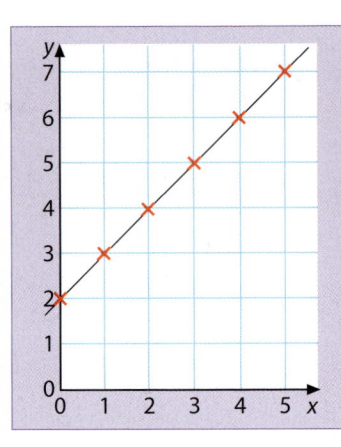

This table shows the coordinates of some points on the straight line drawn on the grid.

x-coordinate (x)	0	1	2	3	4	5
y-coordinate (y)	2	3	4	5	6	7

- Which of these rules fits the coordinates in the table?

$y = x + 1$ $y = 2x$ $y = x + 2$

$y = 2$ $y + x = 2$

A1 Look at the numbers in this table. Which of the rules below is true?

Remember it must work for all the pairs of numbers in the table.

x	0	1	2	3	4	5
y	0	5	10	15	20	25

$y = 5$ $x + y = 5$ $y = 5x$ $y = x + 5$

A2 Which of the rules below is true for this table?

x	0	1	2	3	4	5
y	3	4	5	6	7	8

$y = x + 3$ $y = 3x + 3$ $y + x = 3$

A3 Which of the rules below is true for this table?

x	0	1	2	3	4	5
y	0	3	6	9	12	15

$y = x + 3$ $y = 3x$ $y + x = 3$

A4 Which of the rules below is true for this table?

x	0	1	2	3	4	5
y	5	7	9	11	13	15

$y = x + 2$ $y = 2x$

$y = 2x + 5$ $y = x + 5$

A5 Here are four rules and four tables.
Which rule goes with which table?

$y = 4x$ $y = 4x + 1$
$y = 2x + 4$ $y = 2x + 3$

A

x	-1	0	1	2	3	4
y	2	3	5	7	9	11

B

x	-1	0	1	2	3	4
y	2	4	6	8	10	12

C

x	-1	0	1	2	3	4
y	-4	0	4	8	12	16

D

x	-1	0	1	2	3	4
y	-3	1	5	9	13	17

B Drawing a straight-line graph

Rules such as $y = 2x + 3$ that link a number of ys with a number of xs always give a straight-line graph.

- Copy and complete the table for $y = 2x + 3$.

x	0	1	2	3	4	5
y		5				

- Plot the points on a grid like this and join the points with a straight line.

- Label your line with the rule $y = 2x + 3$.
It is called the **equation** of the graph.

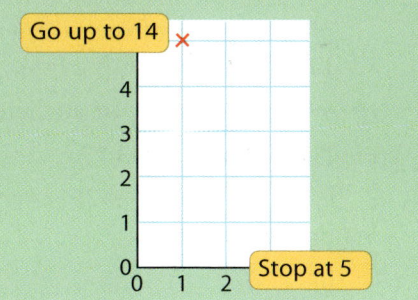

Go up to 14
Stop at 5

- Use your graph to find the value of y when $x = 1.5$.

B1 (a) Copy and complete this table for the rule $y = x + 1$.

x	0	1	2	3	4	5
y	1					

(b) On axes like the ones on the right, plot the points from your table. Join the points with a line.

(c) What is the value of y when $x = 6$?

(d) Find y when $x = 2.5$.

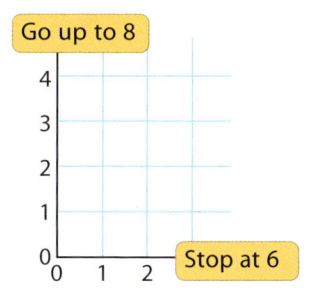

Go up to 8
Stop at 6

43 Graphs from rules

B2 (a) Copy and complete this table for the rule $y = 2x$.

x	0	1	2	3	4	5
y					8	

Go up to 10
Stop at 5

(b) On axes like the ones on the right, plot the points from your table. Join the points with a line.

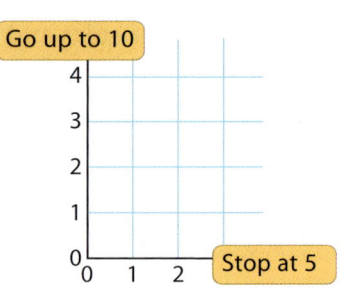

(c) (i) Copy and complete the table for the rule $y = x + 2$.

x	0	1	2	3	4	5
y					6	

(ii) On the same grid as you used in (b), plot the points from this table. Join the points with a line.

(d) What are the coordinates of the point where the lines cross?

B3 (a) Copy and complete this table for the equation $y = 2x + 1$.

x	0	1	2	3	4	5
y					9	

(b) On axes like the ones on the right, plot the points from your table. Join the points with a line.

Go up to 12
Stop at 5

(c) What is the value of y when $x = 1.5$?

(d) Find y when $x = 3.7$.

(e) Copy and complete these coordinates for points on the line.
  (i) (2.5, ___)   (ii) (___ , 10)   (iii) (___ , 6.6)

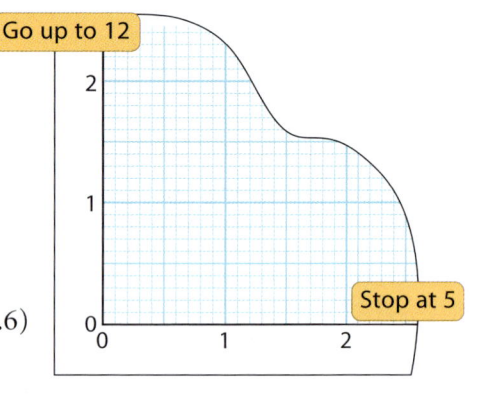

B4 (a) Copy and complete this table for the equation $y = 4x + 3$.

x	0	1	2	3	4	5
y					19	

Go up to 25
Stop at 5

(b) On axes like the ones on the right, plot the points from your table. Join the points with a line.

(c) What is the value of y when $x = 2.5$?

(d) Copy and complete these coordinates for points on the line.
  (i) (3.5, ___)   (ii) (___ , 9)   (iii) (___ , 21)

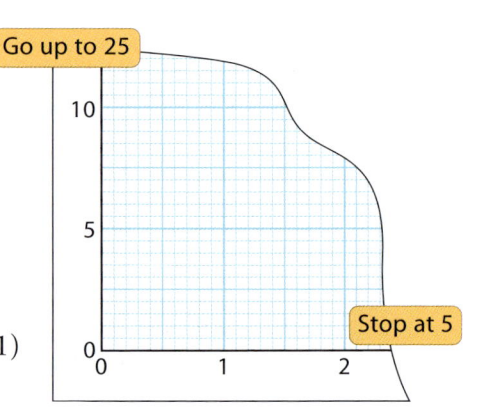

43 Graphs from rules

C Including negative coordinates

- Copy and complete the table for $y = 2x - 1$.

x	-2	-1	0	1	2	3
y		-3				

- Plot the points on the axes on sheet F1–37 and join them up.
- Use your graph to find the value of y when $x = {}^-1.8$.
- What is the value of x when $y = 4$?

- Copy and complete the table for $y = 3x + 2$.

x	-2	-1	0	1	2	3
y		-1				

- Plot the points on the axes on sheet F1–38 and join them up.
- Use your graph to find the value of y when $x = 2.4$.
- Use your graph to find the value of y when $x = {}^-1.2$.
- What is the value of x when $y = 3.2$?

C1 (a) Copy and complete this table for $y = 3x - 1$.

x	-1	0	1	2
y	-4			

(b) Draw the graph of $y = 3x - 1$ on sheet F1–39.
(c) Find the value of y when $x = 1.7$.
(d) Find the value of x when $y = 0.2$.

C2 (a) Copy and complete this table for $y = 4x + 2$.

x	-2	-1	0	1	2	3
y		-2				

(b) Draw the graph of $y = 4x + 2$ on sheet F1–40.
(c) Find the value of y when $x = {}^-1.5$.
(d) Find the value of x when $y = 8.4$.

C3 (a) Copy and complete this table of values for $y = 2x + 3$.

x	-4	-2	0	2
y	-5			

(b) Draw the graph of $y = 2x + 3$ on grid A on sheet F1–41.
(c) Use your graph to find
  (i) the value of y when $x = 0.5$
  (ii) the value of x when $y = {}^-3.6$

43 Graphs from rules

C4 (a) Copy and complete this table for $y = 4x - 2$.

x	-1	0	1	2
y		-2		

(b) Draw the graph of $y = 4x - 2$ on grid B on sheet F1–41.
(c) Find the value of y when $x = -0.5$.
(d) Find the value of x when $y = 4$.

*C5 (a) Copy and complete this table for $y = 1 - 2x$.

x	-2	-1	0	1	2	3
y		3				

(b) Draw the graph of $y = 1 - 2x$ on grid C on sheet F1–41.
(c) Find the value of x when $y = 2$.

D Equations of horizontal and vertical lines

- List the coordinates of all the points marked on the line.
- What do you notice about the y-coordinates of all the points on the line?
- Which of these equations could be the equation of the line?

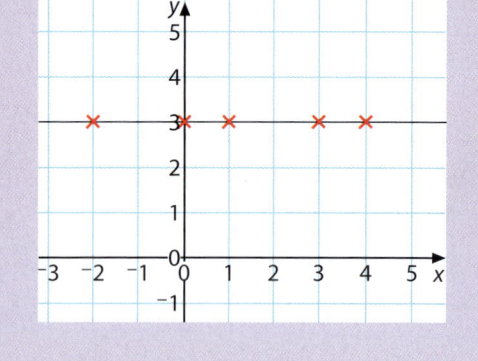

    $y = 3$ $x = 3$ $y = x + 3$

D1 (a) Copy and complete this table for points marked on the line on this grid.

x	2			
y	-1			

(b) What do you notice about the coordinates of the points on this line?
(c) Which of these equations could be the equation of this line?

    $y = x + 2$ $y = 2$ $x = 2$

D2 Copy this diagram on to squared paper.
  (a) Label each of the lines with its equation.
      (One line is labelled for you.)
  (b) On the same diagram, draw and label the line $y = x$.
  (c) What are the coordinates of the point where
      the line $y = x$ crosses the line $y = -2$?

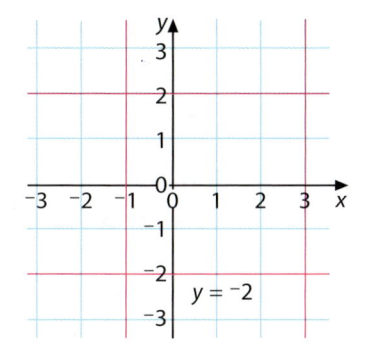

D3 On squared paper, draw x- and y-axes both going from -5 to 5.
On your axes, draw and label lines with these equations.
  $y = 4$ $x = -3$ $y = -1$ $x = 5$ $y = -4$

E Implicit equations

To draw the graph of $x + y = 4$ you need to find points that fit the equation.
- Copy and complete this table for $x + y = 4$.

x	-1	0	1	2	3	4	5
y			3				

- On graph paper draw axes with both x and y going from -1 to 5.
Plot your points and draw the line $x + y = 4$.

E1 (a) Copy and complete the table for $x + y = 7$.

x	0	1	2	3	4	5	6	7
y	7							0

  (b) On graph paper, draw axes with both x and y going from 0 to 8.
      Plot the points from the table.
      Draw and label the line $x + y = 7$.
  (c) Copy and complete these coordinates for points on the line.
      (i) $(2.5, ...)$ (ii) $(..., 5.5)$
  (d) Which of these points are on the line $x + y = 7$?
      $(1.2, 7)$ $(3.2, 3.8)$ $(0.1, 7.1)$ $(0.9, 6.1)$

E2 (a) Copy and complete the table for $x + y = 3$.

x	-2	-1	0	1	2	3	4	5
y		4						

(b) On graph paper, draw axes with both x and y going from -2 to 5.
Plot the points from the table.
Draw and label the line $x + y = 3$.

(c) (i) What is the value of y when $x = 1.7$?

(ii) What is the value of x when $y = -0.5$?

E3 (a) Which of these points are on the line $x + y = 8$?
(1, 10) (2, 6) (3, 5) (4, 1) (-1, 9) (1.5, 6.5)

(b) Copy and complete these coordinates so that they are points on the line $x + y = 8$.
(i) (1, …)   (ii) (6, …)   (iii) (-2, …)   (iv) (…, 0)   (v) (…, 0.5)

E4 Which of these points are on the line $x + 5y = 12$?
(5, 4) (7, 1) (7, 5) (2, 2) (-3, 3) (12, 0) (6, 1)

E5 Follow these steps to draw the graph of $2x + y = 10$.

(a) First copy this table of values.

x	0	1	2	3	4	5
y						

(b) When x is 0, you get
$$2 \times 0 + y = 10$$
What is y?
Put it in your table.

(c) When x is 1, you get
$$2 \times 1 + y = 10$$
Find the value of y and put it in the table.

(d) In the same way find values of y for the other values of x and put them in the table.

(e) On graph paper, draw axes with both x and y going from 0 to 10.
Plot the points from the table. Draw and label the line $2x + y = 10$.

(f) Find the value of y when $x = 3.5$.

(g) What is x when $y = 7$?

*E6 (a) Copy and complete this table of values for the equation $3x + 2y = 12$.

x	-2	-1	0	1	2	3	4	5
y								

(b) Draw the graph of $3x + 2y = 12$ for values of x from -2 to 5.

Test yourself

T1 Write down the equation of each of the lines in this diagram.

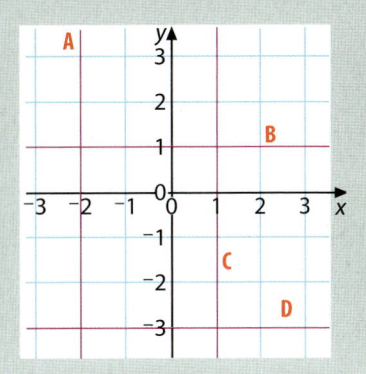

T2 (a) Copy and complete the table of values for $y = 2x + 3$.

x	-2	-1	0	1	2	3
y		1	3			

(b) On a grid like this, draw the graph of $y = 2x + 3$.

(c) Use your graph to find
   (i) the value of y when $x = {}^-1.3$
   (ii) the value of x when $y = 5.4$

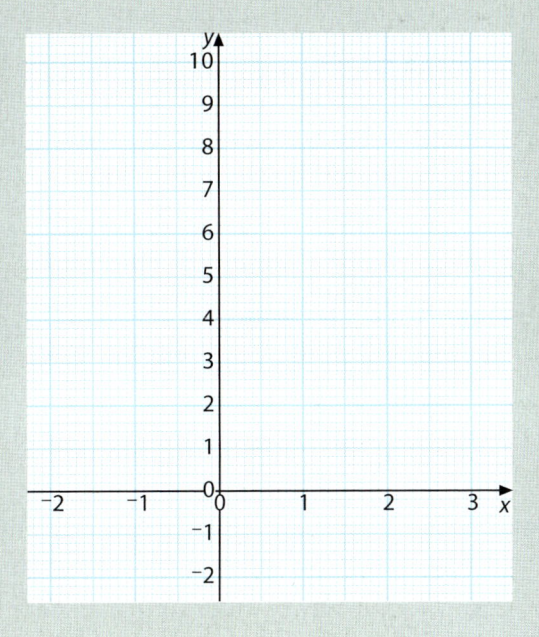

T3 (a) Copy and complete the table of values for $x + y = 6$.

x	-2	0	2	4	6	8
y						-2

(b) On a suitable set of axes, draw the graph of $x + y = 6$ for values of x from -2 to 8.

43 Graphs from rules

44 Working with coordinates

This work will help you use coordinates in all four quadrants.

You will

- complete shapes, describe their symmetry and find their areas
- find the mid-point of a line
- reflect shapes in horizontal and vertical lines
- rotate shapes by multiples of 90°

You need sheet F1–42.

A Shapes on a grid

A1 The diagram shows three points, A, B and C. Copy this diagram.

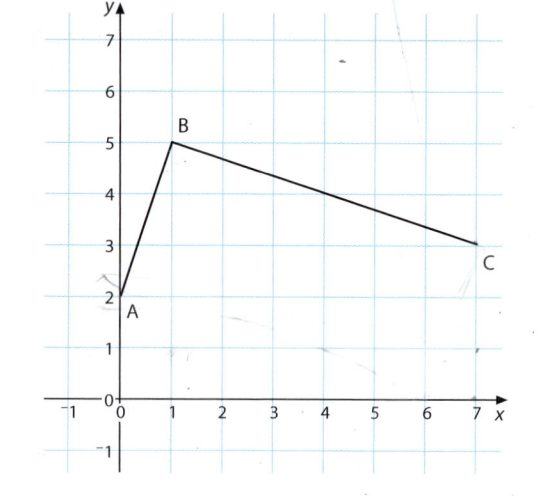

(a) What are the coordinates of A, B and C?

(b) (i) Mark a new point D so that ABCD is a rectangle

(ii) What are the coordinates of D?

(c) (i) Point P has coordinates (1, 7). Mark point P on the diagram.

(ii) Draw a line that goes through P and is parallel to BC.

A2 The diagram shows three points, E, F and G. Copy it on to centimetre squared paper.

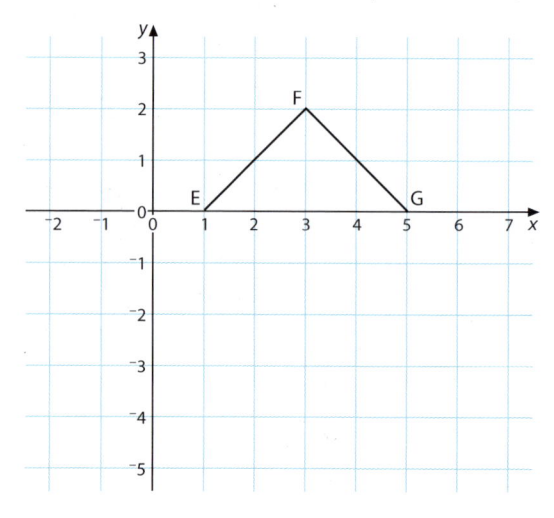

(a) Mark a new point H so that EFGH is a square.

(b) What are the coordinates of H?

(c) Find the area of the square.

(d) Draw in all the lines of symmetry of the square.

(e) What is the order of rotation symmetry of the square?

A3 The diagram shows three points, I, J and K.
Copy this diagram.
- (a) Mark point L so that IJKL is a parallelogram.
- (b) What are the coordinates of L?
- (c) What is the order of rotation symmetry for the parallelogram?
- (d) How many lines of symmetry has the parallelogram?

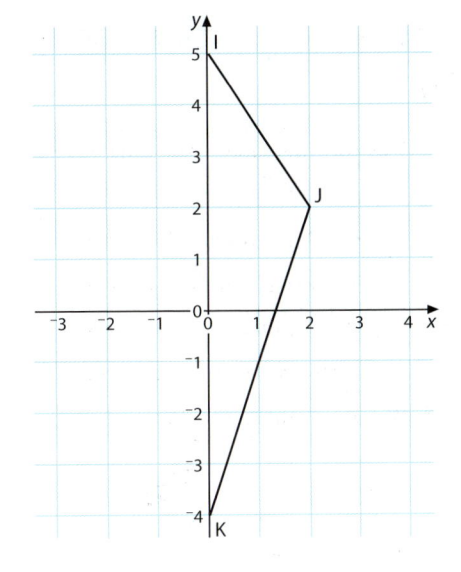

A4 (a) Draw a grid on centimetre squared paper with x- and y-axes going from -4 to 7. Mark points A (1, 4), B (3, 7) and C (5, 4).
- (b) Mark point D so that ABCD is a rhombus.
- (c) What is the area of the rhombus?
- (d) On the same grid, mark points E (3, -2), F (1, -4) and G (-3, -2).
- (e) Mark point H so that EFGH is a kite.
- (f) Draw the line of symmetry for the kite.

A5 MNOPQ is a pentagon.
The y-axis is a line of symmetry of the pentagon.
Three of the points are M (0, 3), N (3, 1), O (2, -2).
- (a) Draw a grid with x- and y-axes going from -4 to 4. Plot points M, N and O.
- (b) Plot P and Q and write down their coordinates.

A6 (a) Draw a grid with x- and y-axes going from -4 to 6. Draw the line with equation $x = 2$.
- (b) ABCDEF is a hexagon.
  Three of the points are A (5, 5), B (6, 1), C (5, -3).
  The line with equation $x = 2$ is a line of symmetry of the hexagon.
  Use your diagram to find the coordinates of D, E and F.
- (c) The hexagon has a horizontal line of symmetry. What is the equation of this line?

B Mid-points

Stuck in the middle a game for two players

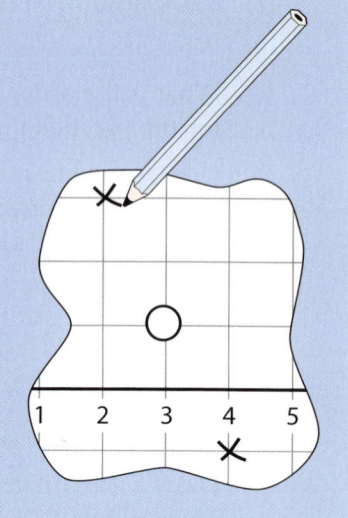

Sheet F1–42 has a game board with a grid and 'targets'.
- The first player says the coordinates of a point on the grid. The second player then places a cross at that point. You cannot change your mind once you have said a point.
- The second player then says a point for the first player to mark with a cross.
If one of the targets is exactly halfway between the new cross and any other marked cross, the second player wins the target. Write your initial in any target you win.
- Players then take turns to give new points until all the targets have been won.
You can win more than one point in any one go.

B1 Write down three different pairs of coordinates that would win the point (6, 5).

B2 Write down three different pairs of coordinates that would win the point (2, ⁻3).

The point that is halfway between points A and B is called the **mid-point** of AB.

Here the mid-point of AB has coordinates $(2, 1\frac{1}{2})$.

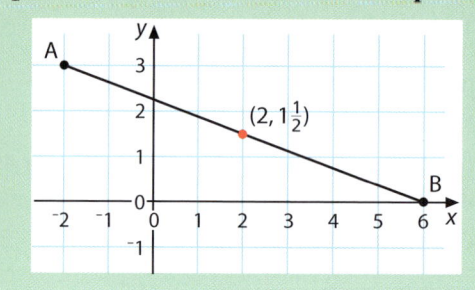

B3 Write down the coordinates of the mid-point of each line below.

(a)

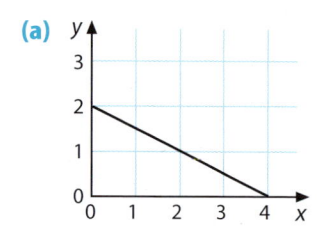

(b)

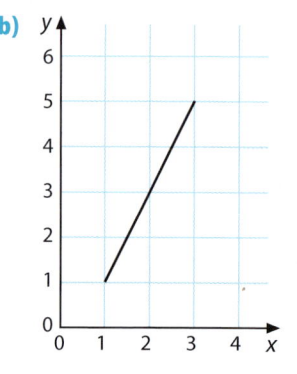

(c)

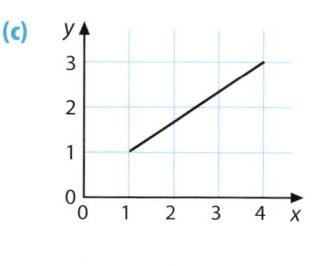

322 44 Working with coordinates

B4 This diagram shows triangle ABC.
What are the coordinates of the mid-point of
(a) AB (b) BC (c) AC

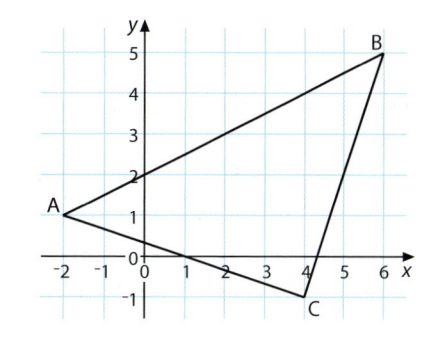

B5 (a) Draw a grid with x- and y-axes going from $^-4$ to 6.
Draw the quadrilateral whose corners are at $(4, 4)$, $(^-2, 4)$, $(^-3, ^-3)$ and $(6, ^-3)$.

(b) What type of quadrilateral is this?

(c) Mark the mid-point of each side of the quadrilateral.
Label each mid-point with its coordinates.

(d) Join the mid-points to make a new quadrilateral.
What type of quadrilateral is the new one?

B6 Draw some quadrilaterals of your own on grids.
Join the mid-points of the sides of each quadrilateral to make a new shape.
What do you find?

C Reflection

This diagram shows two triangles P and Q.

We say that triangle Q is the **image** of triangle P after reflection in the y-axis.

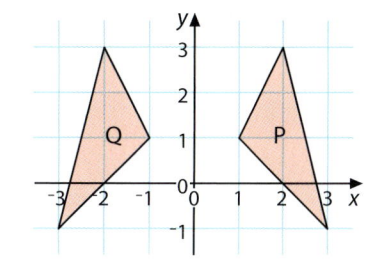

C1 What is the image of the point $(2, 3)$ after reflection in the y-axis?

C2 Copy this diagram.

(a) Reflect shape A in the y-axis.
Label this image B.

(b) Reflect shape A in the x-axis.
Label this image C.

(c) What is the image of the point $(3, ^-1)$ after reflection in the x-axis?

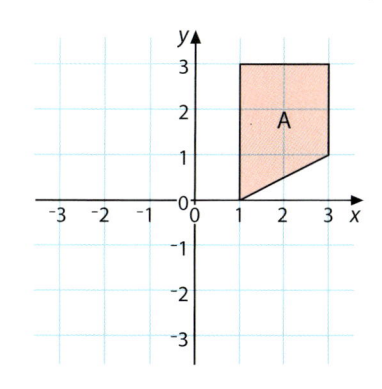

C3 (a) Which shape is the image of P after reflection in the line $y = 1$?

(b) Describe the reflections that take

  (i) shape R to shape S

  (ii) shape R to shape Q

(c) What is the image of the point (4, 2) after reflection in the line $x = 2$?

(d) What is the image of the point (0, ⁻3) after reflection in the line $y = 1$?

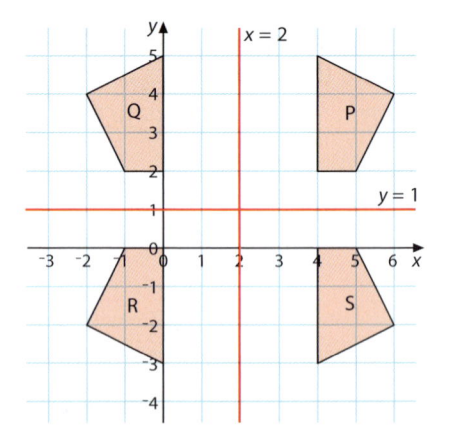

D Rotation

Tracing paper can help to find the image of a shape after a rotation.

Here is how you can use it to rotate a shape through 90° anticlockwise about the point (4, 4).

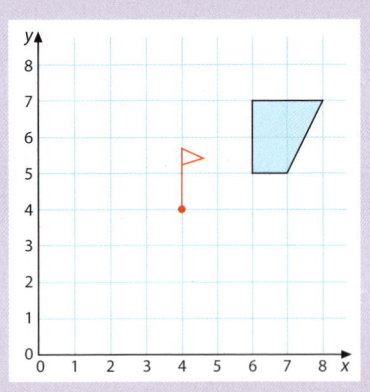

Draw a 'flag' pointing up from the centre of rotation.

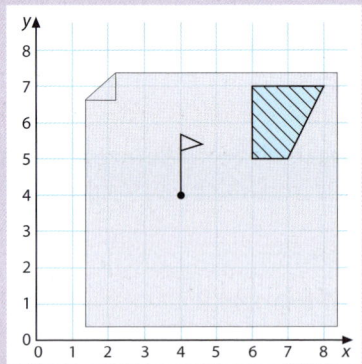

Trace the shape, centre of rotation and flag.

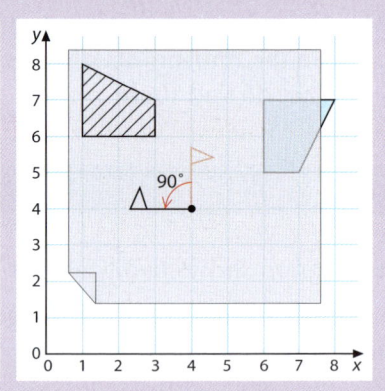

Rotate the shape about (4, 4) until the flag has turned through 90° anticlockwise.

- What is the image of the point (6, 5) after a rotation of 90° anticlockwise about (4, 4)?
- Copy the first diagram.

  Using (4, 4) as the centre of rotation, show the image of the blue shape after

  a rotation of 90° clockwise

  a rotation of 180° clockwise

To describe a rotation fully you need to include the **angle**, the **direction** (clockwise or anticlockwise) and the **centre of rotation**.

D1 Copy this diagram.
  (a) (i) Rotate shape A 90° anticlockwise with (5, 4) as the centre of rotation. Label this image B.
      (ii) What is the image of the point (8, 5) after this rotation?
  (b) Rotate shape A 90° clockwise with (5, 4) as the centre of rotation. Label this image C.
  (c) Describe **fully** the rotation that takes shape B to shape C.

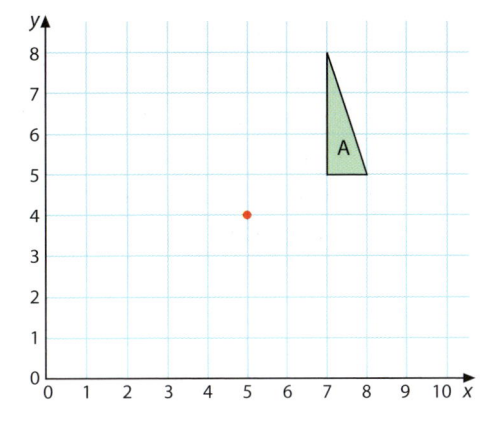

Another name for a rotation of 180° is a half turn.

Another name for a rotation of 90° is a quarter turn.

D2 (a) Draw a grid on centimetre squared paper with x- and y-axes going from ⁻6 to 6. Mark and join the points P (3, 1), Q (3, 4), R (4, 4) and S (5, 1).
  (b) Show the image of the shape PQRS after a quarter turn anticlockwise about (0, 0).
  (c) Show the image of the shape PQRS after a quarter turn clockwise about (1, ⁻1).
  (d) Mark the mid-point of the line RS.
      Show the image of the shape PQRS after a half turn about this mid-point.

D3 (a) Which shape is the image of K after a rotation of 90° anticlockwise about (0, 0)?
  (b) Describe **fully** the rotations that take
      (i) shape M to shape K
      (ii) shape M to shape L

*__D4__ Describe the rotation that takes shape N to shape K.

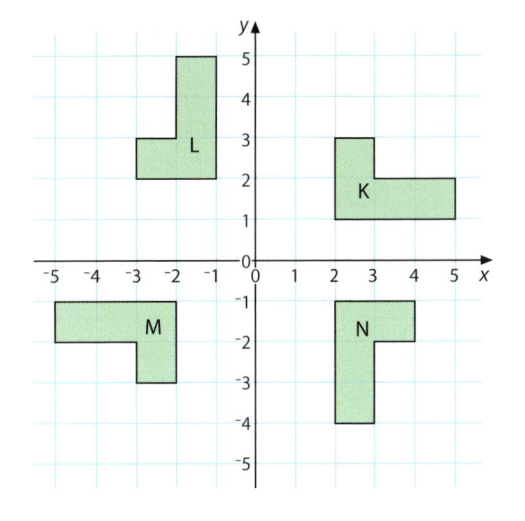

44 Working with coordinates 325

Test yourself

T1

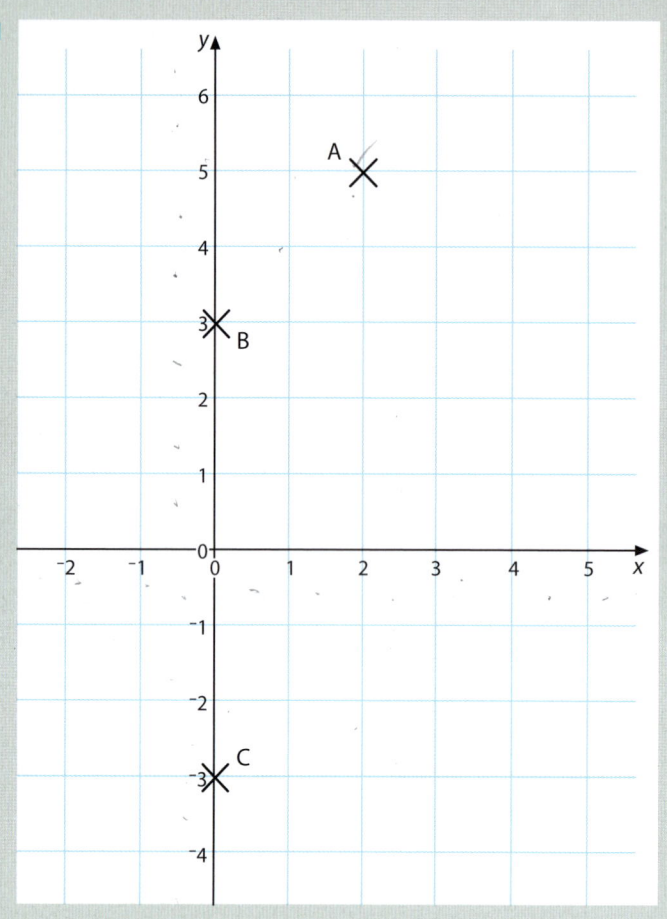

(a) Write down the coordinates of
   (i) C
   (ii) the mid-point of AB

(b) ABCD is a parallelogram.
    Copy the diagram on squared paper, mark the point D and write down its coordinates.

(c) What is the order of rotational symmetry of the parallelogram?

(d) Work out the area of the parallelogram.

OCR

T2

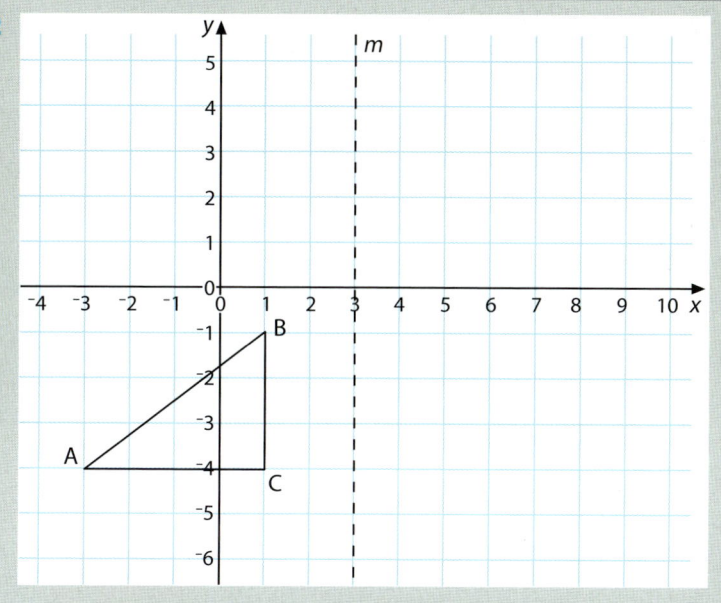

(a) Write down the coordinates of A.
(b) Copy the diagram and draw the reflection of triangle ABC in the mirror line *m*.
(c) Write down the new coordinates of A after reflection in the mirror line *m*.   OCR

T3 Triangle A is drawn on the grid below.
Copy the diagram.

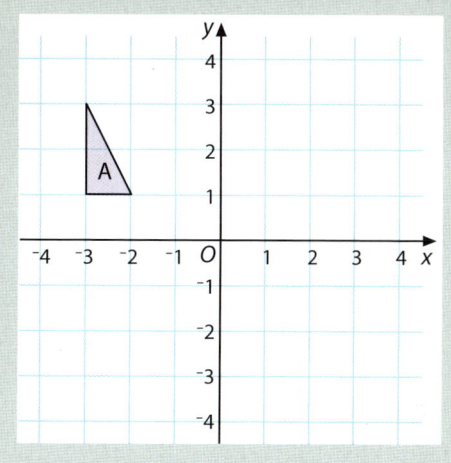

(a) Reflect triangle A in the *x*-axis.
Label the triangle B.

(b) Rotate triangle A 90° clockwise about the origin *O*.
Label the triangle C.   AQA

45 Trial and improvement

You should be able to decide when one decimal is larger or smaller than another.

This work will help you solve problems by trial and improvement.

A Searching for whole numbers

Natasha and Pete are looking for a cube number between 500 and 600.

5 × 5 × 5 = 125, which is too small.

10 × 10 × 10 = 1000, which is too big.

Use your calculator to search for
- a cube number between 500 and 600
- a cube number between 300 and 400
- the cube root of 6859

Consecutive numbers are whole numbers that are next to each other, such as 9, 10 and 11.
- Search for three consecutive numbers that multiply together to give 4896.

23 and 25 are a pair of consecutive **odd** numbers.
- Search for two consecutive odd numbers that multiply together to give 1599.

A1 (a) What is the first cube number that is larger than 3000?
(b) Find all the cube numbers between 1000 and 2000.

A2 Find the cube root of 9261.

A3 Find a pair of consecutive numbers that multiply together to make
(a) 342   (b) 1722   (c) 650   (d) 7656

A4 (a) Find three consecutive numbers that multiply together to make 2184.
(b) Find three consecutive numbers that multiply together to make 85140.

A5 (a) Find two consecutive even numbers that multiply together to make 3248.
(b) Find two consecutive odd numbers that multiply together to make 9999.

A6 Two whole numbers differ by 3 and multiply to give 2548.
Find the numbers.

B Searching for decimals

The method of solving a problem by trying out some values that get closer and closer to the solution is called **trial and improvement**.

It is useful to keep a record of your trials.

Example

Two numbers differ by 0.5 and multiply to make 333.
One number is a whole number.
Find the numbers.

First number	Second number	Multiply together	Result too small	too big
10	10.5	105	✓	
20	20.5	410		✓
15	15.5	232.5	✓	
17.5	18	315	✓	
18	18.5	333	Exactly right!	

10 is too small. 20 is too big. So try a number in between.

You can set up a spreadsheet to solve a problem like this.

- Two decimals differ by 2 and multiply together to make 42.56.
  Use trial and improvement to find the numbers.
  Show your trials in a table like the one above.

Use trial and improvement to solve each of these problems.

B1 Two numbers differ by 0.4 and multiply to make 231.
One number is a whole number.
Find the numbers.

B2 Two numbers differ by 3 and multiply to make 13.75.
Find the numbers.

B3 Two numbers differ by 0.1 and multiply to make 39.06.
Find the numbers.

B4 Two numbers add up to 10 and multiply to make 17.71.
Find the numbers.

B5 Find the cube root of 24.389.

B6 Solve these equations.

(a) $x^3 = 1.331$ (b) $x^3 = 42.875$ (c) $x^3 = 778.688$

*B7 Solve $n^4 = 1384.5841$.

C Searching for approximate values

The area of a rectangle is 94 cm².
The length of the rectangle is 2 cm more than the width.

Find the width correct to one decimal place.

Width	Width + 2 (length)	Area (target 94 cm²)	Result too small	too large
10	12	120		✓
8	10	80	✓	
9	11	99		✓
8.5	10.5	89.25	✓	
8.7	10.7	93.09	✓	

- Carry on to find the width correct to one decimal place.

C1 A rectangle has an area of 40 cm².
Its length is 1 cm more than its width.

Copy and complete this table to find the width correct to one decimal place.

Width	Width + 1 (length)	Area (target 40 cm²)	Result too small	too large
4	5	20	✓	
5				

C2 A rectangle has an area of 650 cm².
Its length is 4 times its width.

Copy and complete this table to find the width correct to one decimal place.

Width	Width × 4 (length)	Area (target 650 cm²)	Result too small	too big
7	28	196	✓	

330 45 Trial and improvement

C3 A cube has a volume of 400 cm³.

Copy and complete this table to find
the length of an edge correct to one decimal place.

Length of edge	Volume (target 4000 cm³)	Result too small	too large
10	1000		✓

C4 A cube has a volume of 4 m³.

Use trial and improvement to find the length of an edge correct to one decimal place.

Test yourself

T1 Find a pair of consecutive numbers that multiply together to make 552.

T2 Two numbers differ by 5 and multiply to make 2646.
What are the numbers?

T3 Solve this number puzzle using trial and improvement.

> I think of a number.
> I divide it by 2.5 then multiply the result by itself.
> The answer is 900.
> What number am I thinking of?

The first two trials have been done for you.
Copy and complete the table.

Show **all** your working.

Trial	Working	Too small	Too large
30	30 ÷ 2.5 = 12 12 × 12 = 144	✓	
90	90 ÷ 2.5 = 36 36 × 36 = 1296		✓

OCR

T4 A cube has a volume of 75 cm³.
Use trial and improvement to find the length of one side to one decimal place.
Show all your trials.

45 Trial and improvement 331

46 Constructions

This work will help you draw accurate diagrams and take measurements from them.

You need a pair of compasses and an angle measurer.

A Drawing a triangle using lengths

To draw a triangle with these lengths … (5.5 cm, 3.2 cm, 6 cm)

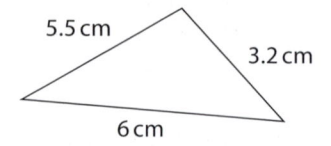

Draw the longest side (6 cm) with a ruler.

Draw part of a circle with radius 5.5 cm from the left-hand end.

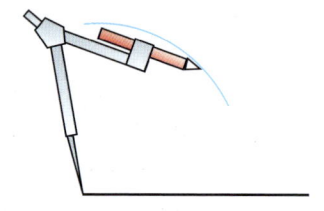

Do the same with a circle radius 3.2 cm from the other end.

Draw a line from each end to where the two part-circles cross.

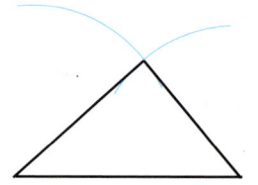

Triangle puzzle

These are sketches of five triangles.
Do accurate drawings of the triangles on paper or card.
Can you fit the pieces together to make a square?

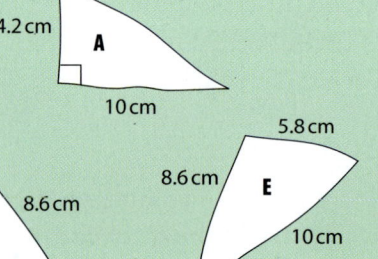

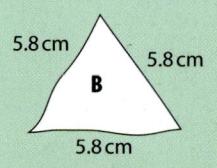

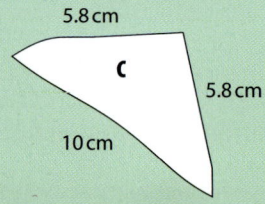

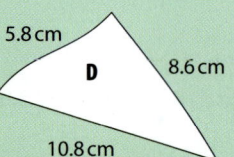

- A: 4.2 cm, 10 cm (right angle)
- B: 5.8 cm, 5.8 cm, 5.8 cm
- C: 5.8 cm, 5.8 cm, 10 cm
- D: 5.8 cm, 8.6 cm, 10.8 cm
- E: 5.8 cm, 8.6 cm, 10 cm

- What special types of triangle are A, B and C?
- Why can you not draw a triangle with side lengths 10.4 cm, 3.7 cm and 5.3 cm?

A1 (a) Draw a triangle with corners A, B and C so that AB = 13 cm, BC = 12 cm and CA = 5 cm.

(b) What type of angle is ACB?

(c) Calculate the area of the triangle.

A2 (a) In the middle of a piece of paper draw a line DE that is 7 cm long. Complete the triangle DEF, with DF = 6 cm and EF = 5 cm.

(b) Measure and write down the angle F of the triangle.

(c) Using DE as the base, draw another triangle with its third vertex G on the opposite side of the line DE, and with DG = 5 cm and EG = 6 cm.

(d) What type of quadrilateral is DFEG?

A3 (a) Make an accurate drawing of the sketch.

(b) On your drawing, measure the size of the angle marked $x°$.

5.4 cm

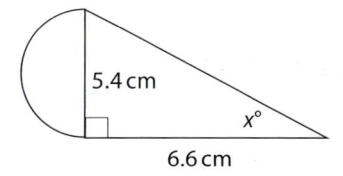

6.6 cm

$x°$

Edexcel

A4 (a) In the middle of a piece of paper draw a line PQ that is 5 cm long. Complete the triangle PQR, with QR = 5 cm and RP = 7 cm.

(b) Using RP as the base, draw another triangle where RS = PS = 8 cm and point S is on the opposite side of line RP to Q.

(c) What type of quadrilateral have you drawn?

An impossible shape

This is a well-known 'impossible' object.
The drawing looks real but the object cannot be made.

Here is how to draw one.

First draw an equilateral triangle with sides 11 cm long.

Mark points on the sides, 1 cm and 2 cm from each corner.

1 cm

Join the points to make this diagram.

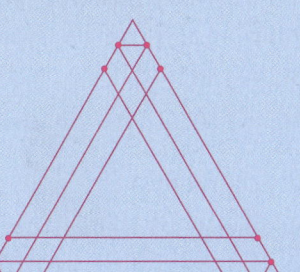

Make these lines thicker or go over them in ink.

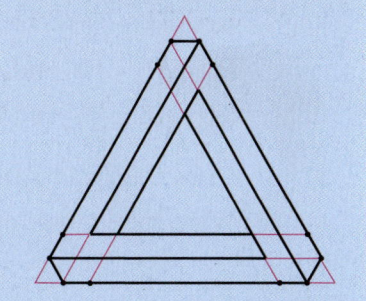

Now shade the drawing to give it a solid appearance.

46 Constructions

B Drawing a triangle using angles

A triangle can also be drawn using a side and the angle at each end.
To draw a triangle ABC where AB = 8 cm and CAB = 40° and ABC = 77°,

Draw a line 8 cm long. Mark angle 40° at A. 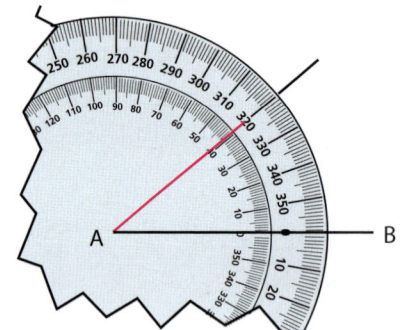 Mark angle 77° at B. Complete the triangle.

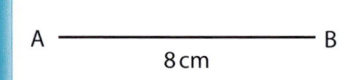

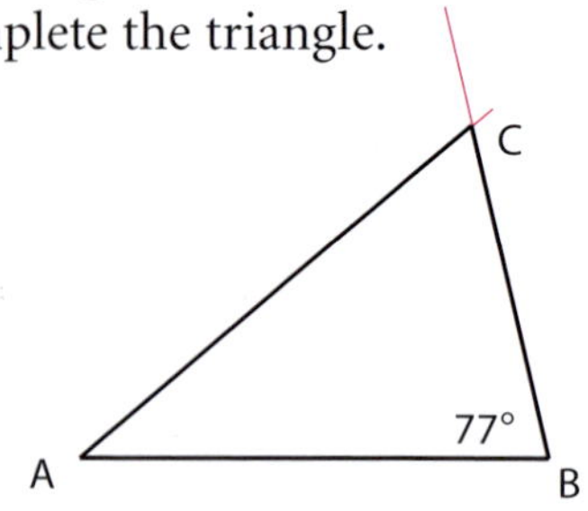

- Draw this triangle accurately.
- What is the angle BCA?
- What is the perpendicular height from line AB to point C?

Does everyone get the same results?

B1 Draw these triangles accurately.

(a) Triangle with A = 57°, B = 35°, AB = 8 cm
(b) Triangle with A = 110°, B = 38°, AB = 6.5 cm
(c) Triangle with A = 76°, B = 55°, AB = 7.5 cm

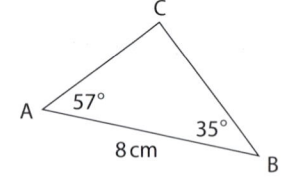

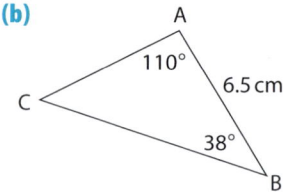

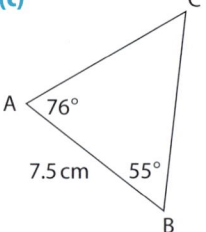

For each triangle measure length BC and angle BCA.
Check your results against other people's.

B2 (a) Try to draw a triangle where AB = 8 cm, angle CAB = 55° and angle ABC = 135°. What happens in this case? Explain why this happens.

(b) With length AB equal to 8 cm, say whether each of these pairs of angles can be used to draw a triangle.

(i) CAB = 50° and ABC = 130°
(ii) CAB = 45° and ABC = 140°
(iii) CAB = 30° and ABC = 120°
(iv) CAB = 125° and ABC = 60°

B3 (a) Draw this quadrilateral accurately.
(b) What special type of quadrilateral is this?

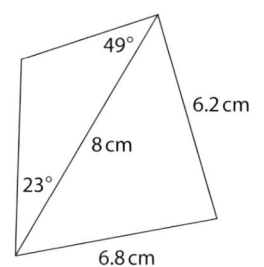

Quadrilateral with angles 49° and 23°, sides 8 cm, 6.2 cm, 6.8 cm.

C Drawing a triangle using two sides and an angle

T
- Make accurate copies of these two triangles.

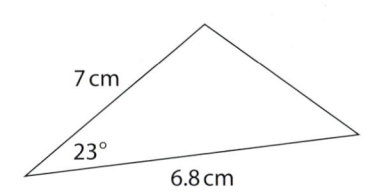

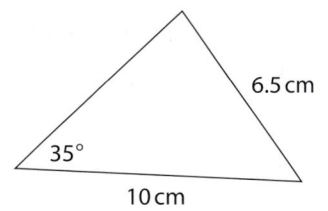

  7 cm, 23°, 6.8 cm

  6.5 cm, 35°, 10 cm

- Measure the remaining side and angles in each case. Does everyone get the same result?
- What is different about the information given in the two cases above?

C1 (a) Make accurate drawings of these triangles.

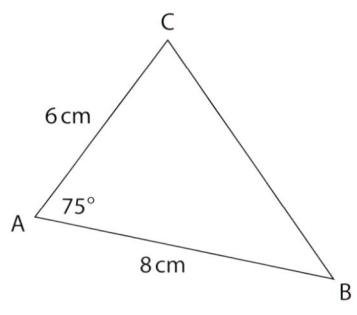

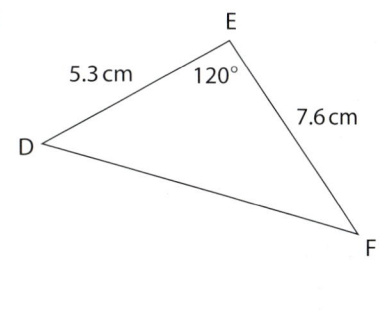

(i) Triangle ABC: AC = 6 cm, angle A = 75°, AB = 8 cm

(ii) Triangle DEF: DE = 5.3 cm, angle E = 120°, EF = 7.6 cm

(b) Measure the missing sides and angles and write them on your drawings. Would everyone who used these instructions draw exactly the same triangles as you?

C2 Draw two different triangles that have the measurements shown in this sketch.

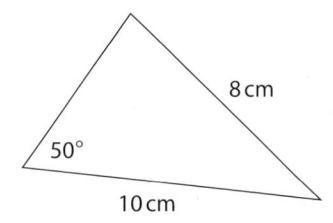

8 cm, 50°, 10 cm

C3 (a) Make an accurate drawing of this right-angled triangle.

(b) Is there more than one right-angled triangle with these measurements?

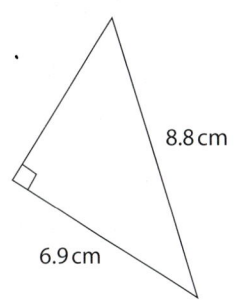

8.8 cm, 6.9 cm

46 Constructions

D Scale drawings

D1 A surveyor needs to draw an accurate plan of this awkwardly shaped field.
A scale where 1 cm represents 10 m is to be used.

(a) What lengths will these distances be on the plan?

(i) AB (ii) BC

(b) Draw an accurate scale drawing of this field on a sheet of plain paper.

D2 (a) Using a scale of 1 cm to 1 m draw an accurate scale drawing of this side view of a building.

(b) The local council says that new buildings in the area cannot be more than 8 m tall.
Does this building meet this regulation?

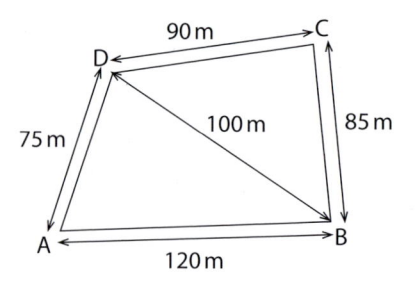

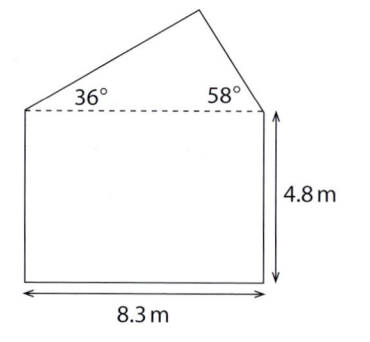

Test yourself

T1 (a) Make an accurate drawing of the triangle shown here.

(b) On your drawing, measure the size of the angle marked *p*.

(c) What type of angle is *p*?

(d) Measure the length of the third side of your triangle.

(e) Work out the area of the triangle. State the units of your answer.

T2 (a) Make an accurate drawing of this triangle.

(b) Measure side BC and write down its length.

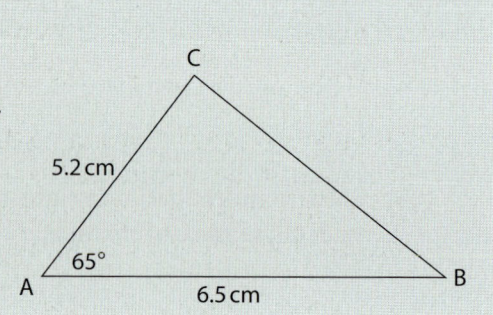

Review 6

You need an angle measurer for question 5.

1. For the rule $y = 2x - 4$ …
   (a) What is y when $x = 3$?
   (b) Copy and complete this table.

x	-1	0	1	2	3	4	5
y		-4					

   (c) On axes like the ones on the right, plot the points from your table. Join the points with a line.
   (d) From the graph, what is y when x is 3.5?
   (e) What is the value of x when y is -1?
   (f) On your axes, draw and label the lines $y = -2$ and $x = 3$.

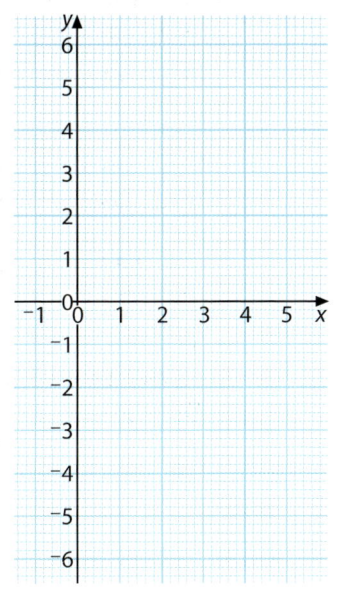

2. A cube has a volume of 80 cm³.
   Use a table like this one to find the length of an edge correct to one decimal place.

Length of an edge	Volume	Result too small	too large
6	216		✓

3. Draw a grid with both x and y going from -3 to 3.
   (a) On your grid, plot and join the points A $(-1, 3)$, B $(2, 3)$, C $(3, -2)$ and D $(-3, -2)$.
   (b) What kind of quadrilateral is ABCD?
   (c) What are the coordinates of the mid-point of AD?
   (d) Mark the mid-points of each side of ABCD.
       Join these mid-points to form a new quadrilateral.
   (e) What type of quadrilateral is the new one?

4. Darren left home at 8:30 a.m. to drive to a meeting.
   He arrived at the meeting at 10:00 a.m.
   He had travelled a distance of 75 miles.
   Calculate the average speed for his journey.

5. (a) Make an accurate drawing of the triangle shown in this sketch.
   (b) Measure and write down the length BC.

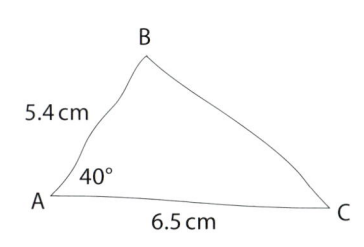

   AB = 5.4 cm, angle A = 40°, AC = 6.5 cm

Index

3-D object
    isometric drawing of 73
    net of 77–78
    plan and elevations for 74–76, 78
    reflection of 79–80
    reflection symmetry of 79–80

adding and subtracting
    decimals without calculator 82
    fractions 22–23
    integers without calculator 82
    negative numbers 110–111, 256–257
angle
    calculating for pie chart 274–275
    of rotation 325
    on pie chart, relating to fraction 270–272
    sum in a triangle 43–46
    sum on line, round point 42–44, 46
    vertically opposite 43–44, 46
area
    of triangle 140–141
    of composite shape 142–143
    of parallelogram 105–108
    to represent product of algebraic terms 284–285
arrow diagram
    forming and reversing to solve equation 32–35, 70–71
    to represent successive operations 29–32
average speed 304–305, 310

bar chart 50, 156–157
    dual 158
    grouped 94–96
bearing 218–219
brackets
    in subtracted term 268–269
    multiplying out in expression 265, 267–269
    to factorise expression 266–267

centre of rotation 325
comparison of data sets 92–93, 96–97
compass directions 212–216
composite shape, area of 142–143

construction using ruler, compasses and angle measurer 332–336
conversion graph 26–28
coordinates in four quadrants 16, 320–325
correlation 189–190
cross-section 78
cube and cube root 197–199, 261
cuboid
    surface area 180–181
    volume 175–179
currency conversion 251–252
decimal
    adding and subtracting without calculator 82
    comparing with another decimal 36–37
    dividing by integer without calculator 86
    multiplying and dividing by powers of 10 41
    multiplying by decimal without calculator 223–225
    multiplying by integer without calculator 84
    reading from graduated scale 26–28, 36–37
    relating to fraction 102–104, 145
    relating to percentage 101, 103–104, 145
    rounding 38–40
diagonal 14, 47
distance, calculating from speed and time 309–310
distance–time graph 306–308
dividing
    decimal by integer without calculator 86
    expression by number 264
    fraction by integer 289–291
    integers without calculator 85, 237–238
    with negative number 259–260
dot plot 50
dual bar chart 158

elevation of 3-D object 74–76, 78
equation
    decimal, negative and fractional solutions 234
    forming from context 234–235, 296–300
    solving by balancing 228–234
    solving by reverse arrow diagram 32–35, 70–71
    to represent 'I think of a number' puzzle 34–35
equilateral triangle 13, 46, 333

equivalent expression 265
equivalent fractions 18–20
estimate
    of answer by rounding 221–222, 225–227
    of length by visual comparison with known length 114–115
exchange rate 251–252
experiment 49–52
expression
    dividing by a number 264
    equivalent 265
    factorising 266–267
    forming linear from context 296–300
    multiplying out brackets 265, 267–269
    simplifying 119–120, 122–123, 254–255, 284–285
    square and cube terms 281–282
    substituting into 63, 119, 121, 253, 280–283

factor 54–57
factorising expression 266–267
factors, prime 59–60
flow diagram
    forming and reversing to solve equation 32–35, 70–71
    to represent successive operations 29–32
formula, linear
    forming from context 64–69, 296–300
    table and graph from 293–295
four-figure grid reference 212–213, 216–217
fraction
    adding and subtracting 22–23
    dividing by integer 289–291
    division to convert to a decimal 102
    equivalent 18–20
    multiplying by fraction 291
    multiplying by whole number 23–24
    of a number 18, 270, 287–289
    relating to angle on pie chart 270–272
    relating to decimal 102–104, 145
    relating to percentage 100–104, 145, 270, 272
    simplifying 19–20
    to express one number as proportion of another 21–22, 270
    to represent probability 132–133
frequency table and bar chart 50, 156–157
    grouped 94–96

graph
    conversion 26–28
    distance–time 306–308
    linear 293–295, 312–316
    of continuous quantity changing over time 126–130
    of implicit linear equation 317–318
    of $x = a$, $y = b$ 316–317
    time series 159–160
grid reference 212–213, 216–217
grouped frequency table and bar chart 94–96

highest common factor 56–57, 59
hypothesis, for statistical survey 200

imperial measures, approximating to metric 206–210
implicit linear equation, graph of 317–318
index notation 198
index number 161
isometric drawing 73
isosceles triangle 13
    angles in 45–46

kite 47, 321

leading question 202
line graph for time series 159–160
line of best fit 191–194
line of symmetry 10, 12–16
linear function as table, graph 312–316
lowest common multiple 56–57, 60

map, interpreting 212–219
mean 51, 97–98
    from ungrouped frequency distribution 98
median 51, 91–93, 98
metric measures 114–115
    approximating to imperial 206–210
    converting between 116–118
mid-point of line 322–323
mirror image of 3-D object 79–80
mixed number 20–21
modal group 94–96
mode 51, 98
multiple 53, 55–57

multiplying
    brackets in expression 265, 267–269
    decimal by decimal without calculator 223–225
    decimal by integer without calculator 84
    decimal by powers of 10 41
    fraction by fraction 291
    fraction by whole number 23–24
    integers without calculator 83, 236–237
    negative number by negative number 257–259
    negative number by positive number 112, 257–259

negative number
    adding and subtracting 110–111, 256–257
    dividing by positive or negative number 259–260
    multiplying by negative number 257–259
    multiplying by positive number 112, 257–259
    ordering 109
negative square and cube root 261
net of solid 77–78

order of rotation symmetry 11–16, 320–321
ordering
    decimals 36–37
    negative numbers 109
outcomes in probability
    listing 134–136
    on a grid 136–137

parallelogram 16, 47, 321
    area 105–108
percentage
    of quantity, mentally 146–147, 270
    of quantity, with a calculator 148, 270
    relating to decimal 101, 103–104, 145
    relating to fraction 100–104, 145, 270, 272
    to express one number as proportion of another
        149–151, 276–279
perpendicular lines 47
pictogram 156
pie chart 270–279
    calculating angle from data 274–275
pilot survey 202
plan of 3-D object 74–76, 78
plane of symmetry 79–80
points of the compass 212–216
polygon 14–15, 321
    regular 13, 15

price comparison
    by unit cost 168–169
    where one item is a multiple of the other 166
primary data 200
prime factors 59–60
prime number 58
prism 78
probability
    from equally likely outcomes 132–137
    listing outcomes 134–136
    outcomes on a grid 136–137
problem, choice of calculator operation for 248–252
product of terms, simplifying 284–285

questionnaire 201–202

range 51, 91–93, 97
ratio
    to describe mixture 170–172
    writing in simplest form 173
recipe, scaling of 164–165
rectangle 13, 47, 320
reflection symmetry
    in 2D 10, 12–16, 320–321
    in 3D 79–80
reflection
    of 2-D object 323–324
    of 3-D object 79–80
remainder, interpretation of 85, 238
rhombus 13, 16, 47, 321
rotation symmetry in 2D 11–16, 320–321
rotation of 2-D object 324–325
rounding
    answer to given accuracy 226–227
    decimal to one significant figure 222
    to estimate answer 221–222, 225–227
    to nearest whole number 38
    to one decimal place 39
    to two or more decimal places 40
    whole number to one significant figure 221–222
rule, from spatial pattern 64–69

sample for survey 203
scale drawing, map 212–219, 336
scale, graduated
    reading and estimating integer value from 25–26
    reading decimal value from 26–28, 36–37

341

scaling of recipe 164–165
scatter diagram 186–194
secondary data 200
sequence 242–246
    from spatial pattern 245–246
simplifying
    expression 119–120, 122–123, 254–255, 284–285
    fraction 19–20
    product of terms 284–285
Soma cube 73–74
speed 304–310
square (shape) 13, 47, 320
square and cube terms in expression 281–282
square and square root 195–196, 198–199, 261
statistical survey 200–205
stem-and-leaf table 89–93
substitution into expression 63, 119, 121, 253, 280–283
surface area of cuboid 180–181
symmetry
    reflection in 2D 10, 12–16, 320–321
    reflection in 3D 79–80
    rotation in 2D 11–16, 320–321
temperature change 109
time series graph 159–160

time, from speed and distance 309–310
trapezium 13, 47
travel graph 306–308
trial and improvement 328–331
triangle
    angle sum 43–46
    area 140–141
    drawing from given lengths, angles 332–336
    equilateral 13, 46, 333
    isosceles 13
    isosceles, angles in 45–46
two-way table 153–155
    with grouped data 155

unit cost 168–169
unitary method 167
    to interpret angle on pie chart as quantity 272–274

views of 3-D object 74–76, 78
volume 73
    of cuboid 175–179
    of solid made from cuboids 181–182
    units 176, 179